ELIZABETH'S FRENCH WARS

ENGLISH INTERVENTION IN THE FRENCH WARS OF RELIGION 1562–1598

Apeuille

Harcelle

Bouteille

of Arques,

R SEstiene

E

F   S

P

P   T

G   Martineglise

Z

Y

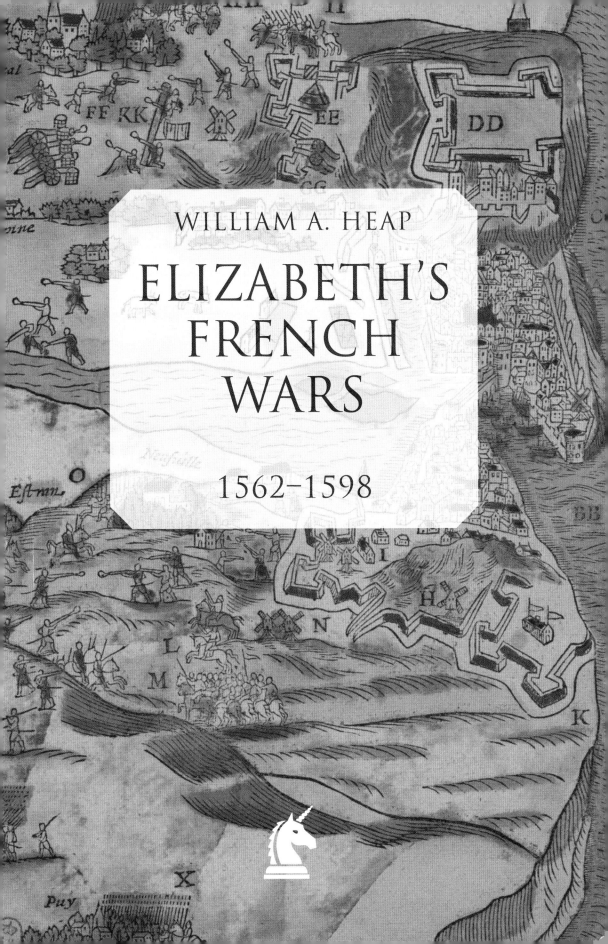

WILLIAM A. HEAP

ELIZABETH'S FRENCH WARS

1562–1598

CONTENTS

CONTENTS

ESSEX & WILLIAMS (1591

WARWICK (1562

ENGLISH CHANNEL

NORRIS (1591–94)

Morlaix

Vire

NO

Guingamp

Châtelaudren

Crozon

Kerhamon

Lamballe

La Dorée

BRITTANY

Corlay

St-Méen-le-Grand

Châtillon

Châteaubourg

Quimper

Montj

La Guerche

Crac

ANJOU

HOUGHTON (1593)

(1569, 1573)

Blaye (La Gironde)

La Rochelle

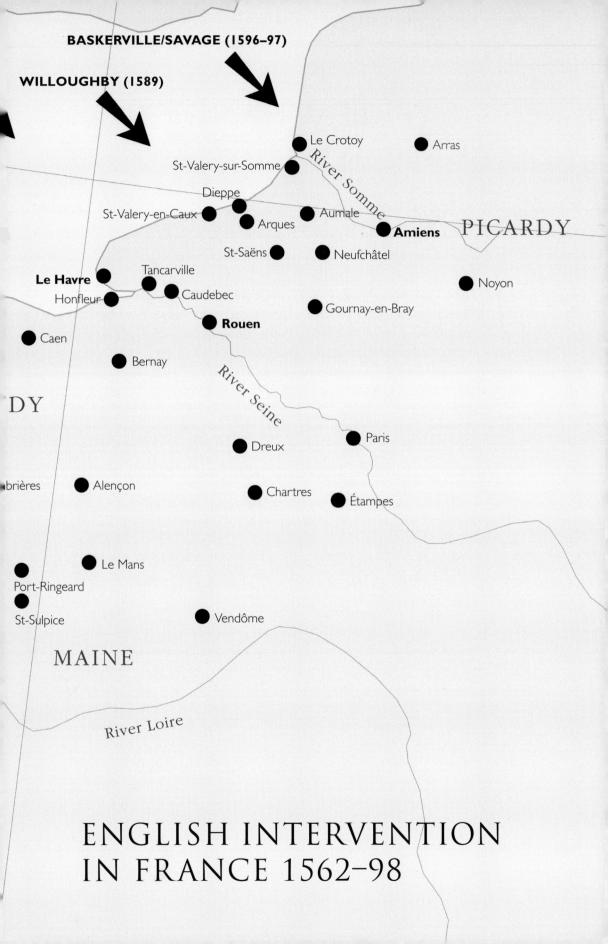

BASKERVILLE/SAVAGE (1596–97)

WILLOUGHBY (1589)

Le Crotoy

Arras

St-Valery-sur-Somme

River Somme

Dieppe

St-Valery-en-Caux

Aumale

PICARDY

Arques

Amiens

St-Saëns

Neufchâtel

Le Havre

Tancarville

Noyon

Honfleur

Caudebec

Gournay-en-Bray

Rouen

Caen

Bernay

River Seine

Dreux

Paris

brières

Alençon

Chartres

Étampes

Le Mans

Port-Ringeard

St-Sulpice

Vendôme

MAINE

River Loire

ENGLISH INTERVENTION IN FRANCE 1562–98

DY

PREFACE AND ACKNOWLEDGEMENTS

*D*URING MY UNDERGRADUATE STUDIES IN History, I remember always avoiding the French Wars of Religion; they all seemed far too complicated. There is therefore some irony in the fact that I should have returned to examine them in detail. I also remember Professor David Loades telling us that an understanding of the French language would double the number of available sources. He certainly was not wrong!

I first became interested in the English role in the wars during research for my *Maîtrise* at the Sorbonne in Paris in 1998 when I came across maps and plans of fortifications in France in English archives. I also became curious as to why English soldiers were depicted in an engraving by Claude Chastillon at the siege of Amiens in 1597.

I would first like to thank Professor Jean Bérenger at the Sorbonne who redirected me towards sixteenth-century military history. I am grateful to Professor Olivier Chaline for his supervision of my *Diplôme d'Études Approfondies* as well as for his advice and guidance throughout my period of research at the Sorbonne. I am indeed extremely privileged to have had the opportunity to study in Paris.

I am indebted to a long list of people who have kindly assisted me during my research. I extend my thanks to: A. Cassandra Albinson, Assistant Curator of Paintings and Sculpture, Yale Center for British Art; Dr Kate Bethune, Assistant Curator, Furniture, Textiles & Fashion Department at the Victoria & Albert Museum; Mr Ray Biggs, Access Manager, Grimsthorpe Castle, Lincolnshire; Captain J.E. Borer, Assistant Secretary, The Institution of Royal Engineers; Sue Chan of the National Library of Australia; Dr Jane Cunningham of the Courtauld Photographic Survey; Hilary Davidson, Curator, Fashion & Decorative Arts, Museum of London; Danièle Véron-Denise, Conservateur en chef, Château de Fontainebleau; Dr Kate Harris, Curator, Longleat House; Nigel Hill, Honorary Secretary, the Friends of St George's Chapel, Windsor Castle; Paul Johnson of the photographic service at the National Archives, Kew; Christine Jordan of the National Art Slide Library at De Montfort University, Leicester; Eva-Lena Karlsson, Curator, Nationalmuseum, Stockholm; Elizabeth King, research assistant at the Royal Academy Library. I thank Professor Erkki Kouri of the University of Helsinki for sending me a copy of his article; *maître d'armes* Florence Le Guy who introduced me to Henri de Sainct Didier, author of *Traicte de l'Espee Seule* (Paris, 1573); Louise Martin, archivist of the Grosvenor Estate; Louise McCall, Curator, Astley Hall, Chorley, Lancashire; Tom McCulloch, Archivist at Oxford University Press; Anne Newport, Librarian, National Art Library; Eva Nygårds, Curator, Konstmuseum, Göteborg; Lisa Olrichs, Rights & Images Officer at the National Portrait Gallery; Suzanne Mohr-Rydqvist, Nationalmuseum, Stockholm; Dr Annette Schlagenhauff, Associate Curator for Research, Indianapolis Museum of Art; Sarah Whale, archive assistant at Hatfield House; Robin Harcourt Williams, librarian and archivist to Lord Salisbury; Professor Barry Windeatt of Emmanuel College, Cambridge.

I would like to thank the publisher, Ian Strathcarron, for having enough faith to take this project on board. I extend my thanks and appreciation to the editor, Elisabeth Ingles, whose expertise has been invaluable in the production of this book, together with Lucy Duckworth at Unicorn. Isobel Gillan deserves a special thanks for her excellent work on its design. Thanks must also go to my mother, Patricia, for her striking depiction of Elizabeth I on the front cover, as well as to my sister, Laura, for her help with the graphics. I am also grateful to the Society for Army Historical Research for their contribution in the form of a generous research grant.

I would like to thank the following who have allowed me to reproduce documents and images:

Her Majesty Queen Elizabeth II
Lord Bath
Lord Salisbury
The Bodleian Libraries, University of Oxford
The British Library
The British Museum
The Photographic Survey, Courtauld Institute of Art
Emmanuel College, Cambridge
The National Archives, Kew

The National Portrait Gallery, London
The Victoria & Albert Museum, London
The Walker Art Gallery, Liverpool

Bibliothèque de l'Arsenal, Paris
Bibliothèque Nationale de France
Bibliothèque Sainte-Geneviève, Paris
Musée des Beaux-Arts, Chartres
Musée du Louvre, Paris

CHRONOLOGY OF TREATIES[1]

1559	Cateau-Cambrésis (2/3 April)	1572	Blois (19 April)
1560	Berwick (27 February [signed 10 May])	1584	Magdeburg (15 December) (secret treaty)
	Edinburgh (6 July)	1591	Greenwich (25 June)
1562	Hampton Court (20 September)	1596	Greenwich (24 May)
1563	Amboise (19 March)	1596	The Hague (16 May)
1564	Troyes (11 April)	1598	Vervins (2 May)
1570	Peace of St-Germain (8 August) (secret clause)	1603	Hampton Court (16 July)

CHRONOLOGY OF ENGLISH ACTIONS IN FRANCE

First Civil War (March/April 1562–March 1563)

1562	Defence and capitulation of Rouen	(October)	defeat
	Capture of Tancarville	(8 December)	victory
1563	Capture of Vire		v.
	Capture of Caen	(2 March)	v.
	Capture of Honfleur	(March)	v.
	Capture of Bernay	(March)	v.
	Defence and surrender of Le Havre	(28 July)	d.

Second Civil War (September 1567–March 1568)

Third Civil War (August 1568–August 1570)

Fourth Civil War (October 1572–July 1573)
Relief of La Rochelle

Fifth Civil War (Spring 1574–May 1576)

Sixth Civil War (December 1576–September 1577)
Île de Ré

Seventh Civil War (November 1579–November 1580)

Eighth Civil War (April 1585–March 1598)

1589	Abortive siege of Paris		d.
	Capture of Vendôme	(19 November)	v.
	Capture of Le Mans	(2 December)	v.
	Capture of Alençon	(14 December)	v.

1590	Capture of Honfleur	(14 January)	v.
1591	Capture of Aumale	(April)	v.
	Siege and capture of Guingamp	(13–23 May)	v.
	Battle of St-Saëns	(20 May)	v.
	Capture of Corlay	(7 June)	v.
	Châtelaudren	(8 June)	
	Battle of Kerhamon	(11 June)	
	Siege of Lamballe	(4–11 July)	d.
	Capture of Noyon	(19 August)	v.
	Battle of St-Méen-le-Grand	(28/29 August)	
	Capture of Châtillon (-en-Vendelais) castle	(3/13 September)	v.
	Capture of Gournay-en-Bray	(26 September)	v.
	Siege and capture of de Goué castle, La Dorée	(17 November)	v.
	Abortive siege of Rouen	(11 November 1591–21 April 1592)	d. [v.]
1592	Bures-en-Bray	(February)	v.
	Yvetot/Caudebec	(20/24 April)	
	Battle of Craon	(21/24 May)	d.
	Assault on Le Crotoy		d.
	Defence of Ambrières-les-Vallées	(1 October)	d.
1593	Capture of St-Valery-sur-Somme		v.
	Capture of St-Valery-en-Caux	(March)	v.
	Siege of La Guerche	(12 April)	v.
	St-Sulpice	(April)	v.
	Capture of Montjean castle	(April)	v.
	Battle of Port-Ringeard	(3 May)	v.
	Siege of Blaye	(April)	d.
	Capture of Bernay	(May)	v.
	Siege and capture of Dreux	(May–June)	v.
1594	Siege and capture of Morlaix	(September)	v.
	Capture of Quimper	(25 September/5 October)	v.
	Siege and capture of Fort Crozon	(c.1 October–7 November)	v.
1597	Assault on Arras	(16 March)	d.
	Capture of Amiens	(19 September)	v.

Elizabeth I (*The Pelican Portrait*), *c.*1572–76, by Nicholas Hilliard (1547–1619)
Walker Gallery, Liverpool, WAG2994

INTRODUCTION

THE SOUVENIR OF HISTORY

*I*N 1562, THE WARS OF Religion broke out in France between the opposing Protestants, known as 'Huguenots', and Catholics. The wars were at the same time a conflict between opposing religions and power blocks: the Huguenots headed by Louis de Bourbon, prince de Condé, and *amiral* Gaspard de Coligny, against the Catholics under François de Lorraine, duc de Guise.

Martin Luther's ninety-five theses in 1517 are regarded as being the start of the religious Reformation that would sweep through much of northern Europe. By the 1520s, Lutheranism had spread throughout France. One Frenchman in particular, John Calvin, played a key part in the advancement of Protestantism in France in the 1540s. Further impetus was provided by Théodore de Bèze from his base across the border in Geneva. While many noblemen across France chose to adopt Protestantism, particularly in the south-west and the ports of Normandy, many did not. Catholicism remained particularly deep-rooted throughout the period in Brittany, Lorraine and Paris.

The challenge to Catholicism coincided with, and was in some ways linked to, a challenge to Latin. Indeed, French was replacing Latin as the *lingua franca.* The new religion was appealing to many Frenchmen, for they could now follow church services that were more adapted to their own language. The same new religion, however, was also a challenge to French royal authority, as the French king at the start of the civil wars, Charles IX, chose to remain Catholic. This was in some ways surprising as, according to the English ambassador, Sir Henry Norris, neither he nor his mother, Catherine de' Medici, understood Latin.

An attempt had been made at reconciliation with the Colloquy of Poissy in 1561. The group of moderates known as the *moyenneurs* aimed at bringing the Huguenots back under the control of the Catholic Church in return for certain concessions. The result of Poissy, however, was a drawing up of battle lines that served to deepen divisions.

This was in contrast to England where Henry VIII had embraced Protestantism and imposed it as the national religion. The subsequent 'land grab' and new wealth acquired from the assets of the old Church strengthened central royal authority here. It meant that, in England at least, the Tudors would be strong enough to deal with any dissenting 'remainers'. One such challenge came in the form of the 'Pilgrimage of Grace' in 1536. Edward VI similarly faced the Prayer Book Rebellion in 1549. By the end of his reign, royal coffers were feeling the strain of war. The Crown was able to sustain the brief return to Catholicism under Queen Mary. Had central authority been weaker and if Mary's reign had endured, England might well have been thrown into the turmoil that now faced France. Instead, the accession of Elizabeth I and the confirmation of the break with Rome would release fresh optimism and a new golden age. Indeed, England would flourish culturally, economically and militarily. This was thanks, at least in part, to a new partnership with France made possible by Elizabeth's relative moderation in terms of religion. As she stated, 'I would not open windows into men's souls.'

There were no fewer than eight wars in France between 1562 and 1598. The young queen of England, who had acceded in 1558, intervened in these wars. The sword of intervention was double-edged: benevolent and exploitative.

The aim of this study is to establish the scale and importance of English intervention during the wars. I attempt to answer a number of questions. Why did Elizabeth I intervene? How did she intervene? Finally, what were the consequences of this intervention? I examine how the 'natural' enemy became an ally and how relations between Elizabeth and the three French kings (Charles IX, Henri III, the last of the Valois, and Henri IV, first of the Bourbon dynasty) were frequently at the heart of grand strategy.

England became the 'arsenal' of first Huguenot then Royalist France. I measure, for the first time, the scale of provision in *matériel de guerre*. I also examine the role of economic and monetary questions and how England effectively kick-started and perpetuated the wars. For many, military intervention was necessary as a way of protecting the continuation of English trade with Europe.

English intervention began in Normandy in 1562 and ended in Picardy in 1597. This period witnessed the sending of five English armies to France, and English intervention proved to be key. Three phases of intervention may be identified, some direct, others indirect, which influenced the character, events and outcome of the wars. During the

Amiral Gaspard de Coligny by François Clouet (*c*.1515–1572)
Bibliothèque Nationale de France, Rés. Fol-NA-22 (6)-BTE

period 1560–63, Elizabeth sought to aid the Huguenots in the power struggle with the duc de Guise while recovering England's lost French territories and ending French interference in Scotland. The reconciliation between Huguenots and Catholics temporarily brought them together against England in 1563. A *rapprochement* followed between England and France, leading to the creation of a defensive alliance in the treaty of Blois of 1572 against an increasingly hostile Spain. Meanwhile, Elizabeth duplicitously continued to support the Huguenots and armies of German mercenaries in the French civil wars from the late 1560s through to the late 1580s. The final period of intervention saw her supporting Henri IV of France as he sought to pacify French Catholics (*Ligueurs*) and eject the Spanish from his country. Conveniently, this also became a method of keeping the war with Spain far from English shores. The signing of the peace treaty between France and Spain at Vervins in 1598 ended the civil wars and thus English intervention.

In this survey I place the emphasis on military history. The fighting in France played an important role in the development of the English armed forces, on both land and sea. It is for this reason that an in-depth study is needed on the subject. The result is a history that is full of detail, as it is often the small detail that makes all the difference in war. I have concentrated my work on the primary and secondary sources of both England and France. My research reveals the real strategy and tactics of Henri IV, allowing a re-evaluation of this military leader. Visual sources, some of which are reproduced here, hold a prominent place in this study.

English intervention in the wars has tended to be ignored, for a variety of reasons. Historians have had a tendency to concentrate on major battles rather than sieges and skirmishes. These formed the core of English efforts. In 1978, John Hale wrote that military activity during the period 1556 to 1572 'was not on a scale, nor had lasting enough results to have encouraged its investigation in depth'.[2] Meanwhile, English military history of this period has aroused much less interest than maritime history. The conflict with Spain at sea, featuring Raleigh, Drake and the Armada, has been at the heart of this. The personal life of Elizabeth has also, quite naturally, diverted the efforts of many historians and cineastes alike away from military issues.

The study of English intervention in France has generally been neglected in favour of the role of the English in the wars of independence in the Netherlands. This tendency was first established by historians such as John Motley in his four-volume *History of the United Netherlands*

(London, 1860–67) and *The Rise of the Dutch Republic* (London, 1889) in three volumes. *The Fighting Veres* (London, 1888) by Clements Markham supported the trend. The story was explained to children, and thus to future generations of historians, in *By Pyke and Dyke: A Tale of the Rise of the Dutch Republic* (London, 1890) and *By England's Aid or The Freedom of the Netherlands (1585–1604)* (London, 1891), historical novels by George Henty (1832–1902). This last book, illustrated by Alfred Pearse, also mentions (in chapter XVIII) the role of English volunteers at the battle of Ivry and at the siege of Paris in 1589. David Trim's thesis *Fighting 'Jacob's Warres'. English and Welsh Mercenaries in the European Wars of Religion France and the Netherlands, 1562–1610,* University of London PhD (2001), is almost exclusively a study of the role of English mercenaries in the Netherlands. Meanwhile, the Dutch themselves remember English intervention because it helped them to gain their independence. There is even a statue of Sir Philip Sidney at Zutphen in the Netherlands (erected in 1913).

By 1591, however, more English soldiers were serving in France than in the Netherlands. Robert Devereux, Earl of Essex, considered that France was 'at thys daye the theater and stage wheron the greatest actions are acted'.[3] The military commander Sir Roger Williams believed that all the English soldiers based in the Low Countries, excepting Flushing and Brill, should be moved to France. The civil wars were far more than an internal affair. France became no less than the battleground of Europe.

The efforts of Elizabeth in France have often faced criticism by historians. The authority on the history of the British Army, John Fortescue, described English intervention in his *A History of the British Army* (1899–1930, vol.1, p.156) as a series of 'minuscule and insignificant operations'. Alfred Rowse denounced the campaign of Le Havre as 'a pitiful story of inexperience and incompetence, of courage and of futile suffering'.[4] Albert Pollard states quite definitely that 'the intervention of England in the first war of religion was perhaps the greatest blunder of the reign'.[5] Lawrence Stone describes the campaign of the Earl of Essex as a 'Greek tragedy'.[6] More recently, Henri Zuber wrote on intervention in Normandy, 'this expedition resulted in disaster while an army sent to Brittany (1591–92) was destroyed by the Ligueurs'.[7] Christopher Haigh also wrote in a similar vein, criticising the expeditions to France without mentioning such successes as the sieges of Crozon and Amiens.

Elizabeth herself gave the French ambassador, Hurault de Maisse, the impression that she did not hold her army in high esteem. 'She said … that they were but thieves and ought to hang, and other words between her teeth which I did not well understand.'[8]

This study draws positive conclusions from English intervention. In the course of my research, I have been frequently surprised at the scale and importance of English involvement in the wars – an involvement that has generally been underestimated in previous studies. In order to fully understand the role of the English, it is necessary to retrace the study of Elizabethan foreign policy from the beginning.

Distinct links are apparent between the study of the subject and the evolution of Anglo-French relations. The English historian William Camden criticised certain French historians of his own era. In their accounts of the role of the English, he said that they 'have beene ignorant or dissembled them'.[9] This tendency has cascaded down through generations of historians. One exception was the anglophile Voltaire in his *Henriade* (1728). Though this work is of more literary than historical interest, it shows Elizabeth as the saviour of Henri IV. It is towards her that Henri turns out of necessity. Voltaire compares an England *libre* and with *lois florissantes* ('flourishing laws') to the *malheurs de la France* ('misfortunes of France'). He also recognises the novelty of the Anglo-French alliance:

> *I know that between them and us an immortal hatred*
> *Allows us to rarely march united.*[10]

Even French artists have conspired to paint their own view of the wars. At the Galerie des Batailles in the château of Versailles and in other historic paintings of the seventeenth and eighteenth centuries, the *Angloys* were kept out of the picture. Following the Napoleonic period, Art became a simple tool to support the restoration of the Bourbons. The incumbents of the monarchy were in search of heroes from the Royalist past. They found one in the form of Henri IV. The English soldiers are there but we cannot see them. All mention of this foreign intervention in France was ignored, perhaps to avoid comparisons with Louis XVI. Similarly, a glance through the catalogues of Lucotte and Mignot, the Parisian makers of lead soldiers, shows that Elizabethan soldiers were never produced. Little French schoolchildren were thus obliged to place French hallebardiers against French musketeers in a very civil war.

English artists of the nineteenth century such as Ernest Crofts (1847–1911) and Andrew Carrick Gow (1848–1920) were mainly interested, even obsessed, by their own civil war. Even the very close ties between the circle of painters known as the St John's Wood Clique in London and the historian James Froude have not left any commentary on the battles in France. Diplomatic affairs and the massacres at least attracted a handful of artists. The francophile Richard Parkes Bonington (1802–1828) painted *Henri III and the English Ambassador* in 1827 (Wallace Collection). The St Bartholomew's Massacre in 1572 inspired *The British [sic] Embassy in Paris on the Day of the Massacre of St Bartholomew* by Philip Calderon. This work was painted during a stay at Hampton Court in the summer of 1862, and was exhibited at the salon of 1863 at the Royal Academy in London. Calderon regarded it as his best painting to date. William Frederick Yeames (1835–1918) contrasts the colourful garb of the French with the English court dressed in mourning in *Queen Elizabeth receiving the French Ambassadors after the news of the Massacre of St Bartholomew* (exhibited R.A. 1866). The massacre also attracted the attention of John Everett Millais (1829–1896) in his *A Huguenot, on St Bartholomew's Day, Refusing to Shield Himself from Danger by Wearing the Roman Catholic Badge* (1851–52) (Makins Collection). His second work on the same theme appeared in 1886, entitled *St Bartholomew's Day* (Private Collection). This theme likewise featured prominently in the 1916 American film *Intolerance* by David Griffith (1875–1948).

Important work was undertaken on Anglo-French relations during the second half of the nineteenth century. Several well-known historians threw their efforts into the subject. The pioneering work of Lucien-Anatole Prévost-Paradol in *Elisabeth et Henri IV 1595–1598* of 1855 was a study based around the embassy of Hurault de Maisse in England.

The tercentenary of the recapture of Le Havre initiated the publication of a number of documents by Victor Toussaint in *Pièces historiques relatives au siège du Havre* (Le Havre, 1862). This useful work was limited to only 110 copies.

James Froude has left a monument to the study of Elizabethan foreign policy in the form of his *History of England from the fall of Wolsey to the defeat of the Spanish Armada* (published between 1862 and 1870 in twelve volumes). This narrates the events of Le Havre during the first war. The only regret is that the work covers only the period up to 1588, missing a decade of English intervention in France.

The importance of English intervention was recognised and underlined by the historian Kervyn de Lettenhove during the 1870s. His six volumes of *Les Huguenots et les Gueux* (Bruges, 1883–85) contain some useful information on Elizabeth. Meanwhile, it is a Frenchman,

Hector de la Ferrière (1811–1896), who made this subject his speciality. His works, *La Normandie à l'Étranger... XVIe–XVIIe siècles* (Paris, 1873) and *Le XVIe siècle et les Valois d'après les documents inédits du British Museum et du Record Office* (Paris, 1879), were influential. His research also led to the publication of *Les Projets de Mariage de la Reine Elisabeth* (Paris, 1882). La Ferrière continued with an article entitled *La Paix de Troyes avec l'Angleterre* published in the *Revue des Questions Historiques* in 1883. The four volumes of *l'Ambassade de France en Angleterre sous Henri IV* (1886–95) by Pierre Laffleur de Kermaingant further added to the body of knowledge. Kermaingant continued with a lecture to the general assembly of the Société de l'Histoire de Normandie (9 July 1891) entitled *Le siège de Rouen par Henri IV et ses préliminaires d'après les documents anglais (1591–1592).* Another eminent historian, Joseph-Étienne Alphonse, baron de Ruble, provided an essential *point de départ* for the study of Elizabethan foreign policy with *Le Traité de Cateau-Cambrésis* (Paris, 1889).

There were also a number of 'dead-end' works. The study by René-Adelstan Guesdon, marquis de Beauchesne, in 1900, *Les Anglais au Bas-Maine pendant les guerres de Religion*, which appeared in the *Revue Historique et Archéologique du Maine* (XLVIII), is one such example. Despite the quality and the novelty of his research, Beauchesne failed to influence other historians and his article has been forgotten almost completely. One reason is perhaps the obscurity of the journal in which it was published.

A vacuum was filled by John Black with *Elizabeth & Henri IV. Being a short study in Anglo-French relations, 1589–1603*, published in Oxford in 1914. Written on the eve of the First World War, the book gave historical backing for the supporters of the *Entente cordiale* between England and France. Elizabethan England also attracted significant interest in Germany before 1914 (and especially prior to the *Entente cordiale*). There does not appear, however, to have been any attempt to relate to Elizabeth's alliances with German princes.

Progress was made in the 1920s thanks to the work of Franklin Weaver. He grouped the sources of the study of Anglo-French diplomacy into a single list in *Anglo-French Diplomatic Relations, 1558–1603* in *Bulletin of the Institute of Historical Research* (1926–29; vols IV–VII).

Another two decades passed before the publication of any important study. Conyers Read used the *Calendars of State Papers* to write on the aid given to the Huguenots during the first war in his *Mr Secretary Cecil and Queen Elizabeth* (New York, 1955). Richard Wernham took over as the authority on the subject at the beginning of the 1980s. His work, *The Making of Elizabethan Foreign Policy 1558–1603* (Berkeley, 1980), though quite short, nevertheless provides a good introduction. He gives France a high value in the formula of English foreign policy. *After the Armada: Elizabethan England and the struggle for Western Europe 1588–1595* (Oxford, 1984) stops in 1595 instead of at the treaty of Vervins in 1598. The reader remains, therefore, ignorant of England's intervention in Picardy and, especially, of its participation at the siege of Amiens. The monumental work of Wernham is recognised and augmented by Paul Hammer in his chapter, *The Crucible of War: English Foreign Policy, 1589–1603* in *Tudor England and its Neighbours*, edited by Susan Doran and Glenn Richardson (Basingstoke, 2005). Other notable works by Susan Doran include *Elizabeth I and Foreign Policy 1558–1603* (London, 2000) and *Monarchy and Matrimony: The courtships of Elizabeth I* (London, 1996).

During the 1970s, the 'Protestant League' was covered by Simon Adams, *The Protestant cause: religious alliance with the west European Calvinist communities as a political issue in England, 1585–1630* (Oxford University PhD, 1973) followed by the Finnish historian Erkki Kouri in *England and the attempts to form a Protestant Alliance in the late 1560s* (Helsinki, 1981). This theme was revisited by David Trim in *Seeking a Protestant Alliance and Liberty of Conscience on the Continent, 1558–1585* in *Tudor England and its Neighbours* (2005). More recent is the work of David Gehring, *Anglo-German Relations and the Protestant Cause: Elizabethan Foreign Policy and Pan-Protestantism* (London, 2013). The thesis by Christopher Croly, *Religion and English Foreign Policy, 1558–1564* (University of Cambridge PhD, 2000) also looks at the siege of Le Havre through manuscript sources. It examines the positive effects of the campaign. On the theme of religion, Erkki Kouri may again be cited, this time with *For True Faith or National Interest? Queen Elizabeth I and the Protestant Powers*, in *Politics and Society in Reformation Europe* (London, 1987), as well as Susan Doran, *Elizabeth I and Religion, 1558–1603* (London, 1994) and the article by Mack Holt, 'Putting religion back into the Wars of Religion' (*French Historical Studies*, 1993). Nate Probasco looks at the English attitude in *Queen Elizabeth's Reaction to the St Bartholomew's Day Massacre*.[11]

The 400th anniversary of Henri IV's accession to the French throne inspired a number of studies. Of direct relevance are those by Mark Greengrass, *Henri IV et Elisabeth: les dettes d'une amitié*; Bernard Vogler,

Henri IV et les Princes allemands in *Henri IV le roi et la Reconstruction du Royaume* (Pau, 1989), and Henri Zuber, *Les Alliances étrangères (1589–1598)* in the exhibition catalogue of the same title (Paris, 1989). Brian Sandberg sought to extend coverage to incorporate previous reigns when he presented a research paper, *Mercenaries, Politics and Leverage: The Politics of Intervention in the French Religious Wars, 1562–1598* at a conference of the Western Society for French History at Drake University in November 1994.

There has recently been some renewed interest in the international dimension of the French Wars of Religion. An exhibition was recently held at York Minster entitled *England and the French Wars of Religion: 16th century Pamphlets held at the Old Palace* (17 October–21 November 2017). The curator Eric Durot has also taken on the post-doctoral topic *The Outbreak of the French Wars of Religion: A Franco-'British' History (c.1543–c.1572)* with Stuart Carroll at the University of York. This was supported by a conference, *Transnational Approaches to the French Wars of Religion* (6–7 July 2018).

On military matters, the works of Charles Cruickshank remain authoritative: his thesis *The organisation and administration of the Elizabethan foreign military expeditions 1585–1603* (Oxford University PhD, 1940), as well as the second edition of *Elizabeth's Army* (Oxford, 1966). These are complemented by the more recent studies by Mark Fissel, *English Warfare, 1511–1642* (London, 2001) and Paul Hammer, *Elizabeth's Wars* (Basingstoke, 2003). Neil Younger's *War and Politics in the Elizabethan Counties* (Manchester, 2012) examines the war effort against Spain (1585–1603). Two works have covered English intervention in some depth: first, *The Rouen Campaign 1590–92* (Oxford, 1973) by Howell Lloyd, and, more recently, a biography of a military leader, *Sir John Norreys and the Elizabethan Military World* (Exeter, 1997) by John Nolan. The life of Peregrine Bertie, Lord Willoughby, was chronicled by Georgina Bertie in *Five Generations of a Loyal House* (London, 1845). His campaign of 1589 drew the attention of Wallace MacCaffrey in *Elizabeth I: War and Politics 1588–1603* (Princeton, 1992). Mention must also be made of the article in *The Historical Journal* by Wallace MacCaffrey: *The Newhaven Expedition, 1562–1563*,[12] although this article concentrates on the political rather than military history of the siege. Several of the Englishmen who fought in the wars have recently been researched for the *Oxford Dictionary of National Biography*: in particular, the articles by Paul Hammer and David Trim may be cited.

The war at sea is covered in *Histoire de la Marine Française* (Paris, 1923) by Charles de La Roncière. This work remains useful in combination with Michel Vergé-Franceschi's *Chronique Maritime de la France d'Ancien Régime* (Paris, 1998), and *The Tudor Navy* (Aldershot, 1992) and *The Making of the Elizabethan Navy 1540–1590* (Woodbridge, 2009), both by David Loades. The article by Tom Glasgow in *The Mariner's Mirror* (1968, LIV), 'The Navy in the Le Havre expedition, 1562–1564', describes the English Navy during the occupation of Le Havre.

TABLE OF KEY EVENTS

Year	Monarchs		French Civil Wars	Key Events	
1558		Henri II		Death of Henri II	
1559		François II			
1560				Conspiracy of Amboise; Siege of Leith	
1561		Charles IX		Colloquy of Poissy	
1562			First Civil War	Massacre of Wassy	
1563				Peace of Amboise	
1564	Elizabeth I				
1565				Capture of Fort Caroline, Florida	
1566					
1567			Second Civil War		
1568				Dutch Revolt	
1569			Third Civil War		
1570				Peace of St Germain	
1571					
1572			Fourth Civil War	St Bartholomew's Day Massacre	
1573					
1574					
1575		Henri III	Fifth Civil War		
1576					
1577			Sixth Civil War	Drake's Voyage of Circumnavigation	
1578					
1579			Seventh Civil War		
1580					
1581				Anglo-French Expedition to the Azores	
1582					
1583					
1584				Protestant League formed	
1585				Catholic Ligue formed	
1586					
1587				Execution of Mary, Queen of Scots	
1588				Spanish Armada	
1589				Assassination of Henri III	
1590		Henri IV	Eighth Civil War		
1591					
1592					
1593				Conversion of Henri IV	
1594					
1595					
1596					
1597					
1598				French (undeclared) bankruptcy; Edict of Nantes	
1599					
1600					
1601					
1602					
1603					
1604					
1605					
1606					
1607					
1608					
1609					
1610				Assassination of Henri IV	

Main English Actions in France	English-funded Campaigns	Treaties
		Cateau-Cambrésis
		Berwick & Edinburgh
Normandy Campaign Siege of Le Havre	Oldenburg	Hampton Court
		Treaty of Troyes
	Zweibrücken	
		Blois
Relief of La Rochelle		
	Casimir	
	Casimir	
		Secret Treaty of Magdeburg
		Joinville
	Casimir	
	Casimir & Von Dohna	
Paris & Maine Campaign	Anhalt	
Normandy & Brittany Campaigns		Greenwich
Gironde Campaign		
Siege of Fort Crozon		
Picardy Campaign		Greenwich
Siege of Amiens		
		Vervins
		Treaty of Hampton Court
		Somerset House Conference

CHAPTER ONE

REASONS FOR INTERVENTION

SEMPER EADEM[13]: ENGLISH INTERVENTION IN FRANCE SINCE 1468

There was nothing new in the action of either going to war with or invading France. Intervention by Elizabeth was only a logical succession in a long history with origins well rooted in the past. It is a history of alliances and wars punctuated by short-lived peace treaties and marriages, which were also sometimes short-lived.

The 'Hundred Years War' ended with the English defeats of Formigny (1450) and Castillon (1453). Following these setbacks, only the town of Calais and its hinterland remained in English hands (as well as the Channel Islands, which had been declared neutral by a papal bull in 1481). Although England was blighted by internal problems and a civil war (the Wars of the Roses between the houses of York and Lancaster, 1455–85), the idea of a reconquest of France never fully disappeared. The war continued, interrupted by truces. In 1468, Edward IV undertook to send 3,000 men to Brittany in case of an attack by France. Friendship was renewed on 25 July 1474, at the same time as an accord with Charles, duc de Bourgogne. By this, the Bourguignons undertook to help the English reconquer their lost lands in France. In return, the king pledged to grant them large portions of territory such as Champagne, Eu, Langres, Picquigny (together with other towns on the Somme) and Tournai. Edward's army landed in France as agreed but the Bourguignon allies were not ready. The treaty of Picquigny (also known as the treaty of Amiens) between Louis XI and Edward of 29 August 1475 brought an end to the war. By this treaty, Louis agreed to pay 50,000 *écus* per year, to be paid in two tranches (at Easter and on St Michael's Day) via the Medici bank. The truce was prolonged in 1479 for one hundred years. Despite this truce, the menace of English

Allégorie de la Victoire en l'honneur de Charles IX, 1564 (detail, see page 45)

intervention in France remained omnipresent. In 1484, a commission was given to John Grey for the raising of 1,000 archers to serve in Brittany. (The truce with Brittany was extended until 1492.)

Meanwhile, it was the French king, Charles VIII, who now played his hand by placing French mercenaries at the disposal of Henry Tudor. Their participation at the battle of Bosworth in 1485 helped Henry gain victory over Richard III and bring the Wars of the Roses to an end. With the accession of the Tudor dynasty, the three lions of England continued to be quartered with the fleur-de-lys of France. This was a symbol of continuity of power, but it was also a symbol of continuity of policy. France remained very much on the agenda.

The new king, Henry VII, prolonged the treaty with France until 1490. It was a non-official army that was sent to Brittany in 1488. Edward Woodville, Lord Scales (governor of the Isle of Wight), landed at St-Malo in May with 400 men. This small force joined the Bretons to defend the duchy against the French. The army (including 1,300 Bretons wearing the cross of St George) were defeated at the battle of St-Aubin du Cormier. Following this defeat, duc François II was forced to sign the treaty of Sablé. Meanwhile, the city of Rennes was managing to hold out. Anne, duchesse de Bretagne (1477–1514), and her guardian, Jean IV, seigneur de Rieux (1447–1518), made urgent calls to Henry VII. By the treaty of Redon on 10 February 1489, Anne agreed to give aid if ever England reclaimed her lost territories in France. She also agreed to give up two fortified strongholds together with artillery and munitions. Henry undertook to send 6,000 men (at Anne's expense of course). An army did indeed land, headed by Robert, Lord Willoughby de Broke (c.1452–1502), but the French forces avoided battle.

The marriage between Anne and Charles VIII in 1491 put an end to the Anglo-Breton alliance and English projects in Brittany. It was therefore without Breton support that Henry VII laid siege to the port of Boulogne in 1492. Lacking any significant military victory in battle, Henry at least managed to make a profit of 745,000 ducats (equivalent then to c.£130,000[14]). Charles paid this sum in return for the withdrawal of the English army. The two kings found an effective method of maintaining the peace. By their own accord, violation of the treaty would allow Pope Alexander VI to excommunicate them both.

It was for Henry's son to restart the war. Henry VIII wished to extend English presence in France in emulation of the victories of Henry V. He joined the Holy League in 1511 with Spain and Venice against France. Henry sent Thomas Grey, marquess of Dorset, to aid Ferdinand II of Aragon in the invasion of Guyenne (Aquitaine) in 1512. He captured Tournai in 1513 with the aid of Emperor Maximilian I. Henry won a victory at the 'battle of the Spurs' (also known as the battle of Guinegatte or Bomy). The war witnessed a number of actions at sea. Sir Edward Howard left the Isle of Wight with twenty-two warships and 3,285 men. He arrived with his fleet off Brest, where there was an encounter between the *Belle Cordelière* and the *Regent*. French galleys riposted, supported by Scottish ships, in a descent upon Brighton on the south coast of England in April 1514. A peace treaty ended the war in 1514. This was followed by the treaty of London in 1518.

A *rapprochement* between the two countries appeared possible when the two kings met at the Field of Cloth of Gold (*le Camp de Drap d'Or*) in the Pas de Calais in 1520.[15] Meanwhile, the two sides were once again at war only two years later. Once again, the French Channel ports found themselves in the front line. The English landed at Cherbourg and Morlaix and the suburbs of Tréport were pillaged. Henry also sent an army under Charles Brandon, Duke of Suffolk (*c.*1484–1545) to march on Paris. Affairs were concluded by a peace treaty, in August 1525.

A period of détente followed. Cardinal Wolsey (*c.*1475–1530) negotiated the terms of the treaties of Westminster (30 April) and of Amiens (18 August 1527). In 1532 we see another treaty, this time at Calais. By this treaty, Henry VIII and François I agreed to put a fleet to sea with 1,500 men against the Ottomans.

During the 1530s, the foreign policy of Henry VIII was governed largely by his divorce from Catherine of Aragon. In 1534 he proclaimed himself supreme head of the Church of England. The dissolution of the monasteries by Henry led to his excommunication by Pope Paul III and the crisis of 1539. In December 1538 the ambassador Sir Philip Hoby, returning from the Imperial Court in Toledo, advised the king 'first, to withdraw the King's council more secret together, and to avoid spiritual men.… More, to establish his ports and to fortify them.… And his Grace to refuse so much costs in buildings, which would be well employed on fortifying havens and ports.'[16]

Fears of invasion by François I and Emperor Charles V pushed Henry to fortify the coast of England. The money and even the materials taken from the Catholic Church were re-invested in new fortresses known as the 'Device Forts' such as those at Deal and Hurst. The threat did not last long. Henry forged a new alliance with Charles. English ships were once again busy attacking the coast of Normandy, including Cherbourg, in 1543. Boulogne was captured and held by the English: the taking of Boulogne was seen as a major success. What is more, Henry had succeeded where his father had previously failed. Landrecies was besieged by an Anglo-Imperial force in the same year.[17]

Once Charles V concluded a separate peace with François I, however (by the treaty of Crépy), Henry found himself alone to defend Boulogne. The French were now free to launch a counter-attack. A French fleet arrived off Portsmouth in 1545. The two fleets managed to lose their two largest vessels (the *Carraquon Philippe* and the *Mary Rose*) by accident. Lacking supplies and with his crews falling sick, *amiral* Annebaut withdrew his fleet to French waters. It was therefore left to the English to take the offensive. Le Tréport was burnt by John Dudley, Viscount Lisle, on 2 September 1545. The treaty of Ardres concluded in 1546 stipulated that Henry could retain Boulogne until 1554. The port would then be handed back in return for a payment of two million *écus*.

The war continued during the reign of Edward VI under Edward Seymour, the Protector Somerset (*c*.1500–1552). Without the support of the emperor, the English were forced to fight a defensive war. This time, the French sought to gain from rebellions in England. Henri II knew about the desperate financial situation in England by the end of September 1549. He was also aware of the religious troubles that had broken out in Cornwall. A French spy in Boulogne wrote:

> *His Majesty the king of England sees that he has no money and the people do not want to pay the taxes which he has imposed on the whole kingdom…. His Majesty … owes a large sum of money to the town of Antwerp which he has taken at interest and it is said that the king owes merchants two hundred thousand pounds sterling.*[18]

Sark in the Channel Islands was occupied by the French in the same year. French success continued with the capture of the forts of Cap Gris Nez ('Blackness'), Slackness and Ambleteuse. These had been constructed to consolidate and extend the English Pale around Calais. The wars were costly to the English. The only recompense was the 400,000 *écus* given for Boulogne in 1550.

THE MARIAN EXILES

During the reign of the Catholic queen Mary Tudor (1553–58), a number of English Protestants (the Marian exiles) opted to take refuge in France. It was here that they became more acquainted with the Huguenots. Lord

Charles Howard of Effingham was living with François de Vendôme, vidame de Chartres, in France by 1552. Henry Killigrew found refuge in his retinue by October 1554. Other exiles included Christopher Ashton, Robert Cornwall, John Dalton, Henry Dudley, Edward (who married a Huguenot in 1556) and Francis Horsey, Roger Reynolds, Francis Russell and Andrew and Nicholas Tremayne.

Some exiles aimed to incite a popular uprising to depose Mary, especially after the announcement of her marriage to Philip II of Spain. There were attempts to gain support from the French king, Henri II. It was said that he had lent a ship, the *Sacrette*, to the Killigrews to aid their privateering activities in the Channel. They also later acquired the *Falcon* via Gaspard de Coligny and La Meilleraye, the governor of Dieppe. According to Richard Uvedale, Sir Henry Dudley solicited aid to take Portsmouth in 1556. It was the Huguenot Jean Ribaut who transported Thomas Stafford to Scarborough on the east coast of England in April 1557. The perception of the complicity of Henri in the capture of Scarborough Castle helped to push the English into supporting Philip in his war against France in June 1557. Captain Thomas Crayer had been employed to raise English mercenaries for him. Some of the exiles such as Killigrew fought at the battle of St-Quentin in August. An army of 7,000 Englishmen under William Herbert, earl of Pembroke, assisted in the capture of the town itself on 27 August, but the loss of Calais and then Guisnes undid all their efforts. Apart from a descent on Le Conquet in Brittany, no further landings in France took place before Mary's death. The treaty of Cateau-Cambrésis in 1559 crowned the French successes of a century.

Although the plots by the exiles came to virtually nothing between 1554 and 1557, their *rapprochement* with the Huguenots formed the basis for intervention in France in 1562. The Marian exiles in effect formed the blueprint for the Huguenots.

EFFORTS TO NEUTRALISE FRANCE AND PREVENT FRENCH INTERVENTION IN SCOTLAND

Scotland proved to be a very useful French ally during the Hundred Years War. French intervention in Scotland was both a recent memory and a current concern. The English were obliged to maintain sizeable forces on the frontier. The towns of Berwick-upon-Tweed and Carlisle absorbed considerable amounts of money. A new citadel had been constructed in Carlisle by the Bohemian engineer Stefan von Haschenperg in the reign of Henry VIII. There was even a project to build a new 'Hadrian's Wall'. England maintained the advantage in holding the town of Berwick. Situated on the north bank of the river Tweed, it served as an English bridgehead in Scotland, facilitating any English invasion. Berwick had been taken and fortified by Edward I in 1296. The town was taken and retaken several times, finally by the English in 1482.

Louis XII of France offered 50,000 *livres* to James IV to re-equip his fleet as well as a squadron of French galleys. In return, James undertook to invade England if Henry VIII set foot in France. While Henry was occupied in France, James invaded England with an army of 30,000 men from the north. The castles of Wark, Norham, Ford and Etal were all taken. The victory of Henry VIII's army and the death of the Scottish king at the battle of Flodden in 1513 saved the situation. Flodden was the template for set-piece battles between the countries for the rest of the sixteenth century. A victory at the battle of Solway Moss followed in 1542. During the 'War of the Rough Wooing', Somerset and his English army, supported by the fleet, won an important victory at the battle of Pinkie (Musselburgh) in 1547.

The victories in battle allowed the English to maintain garrisons in Scotland. This strategy made economic sense. The maintenance of these advanced garrisons in Scotland enabled a reduction in the total number of fortresses on the frontier. By this method, Somerset hoped to keep two or three fortresses instead of five or six.

Nevertheless, the Scottish situation became threatening. Henri II of France envisaged political union between the two countries. The first marriage of James V of Scotland was with Madeleine (d.1537), daughter of François I. His marriage to Marie de Guise (1515–1560) in 1538 tightened the knot. Their daughter, Mary Stuart, married the French king François II. Mary succeeded in provoking Elizabeth's fury by quartering the arms of England with those of France.

French interest in Scotland was highlighted by the production of a detailed chart of the coastline by the French royal cartographer, Nicolas de Nicolai. With French aid, the Scots were able to mobilise their forces once again. The English garrison at Haddington resisted a siege and could have held out but it was reported that in the space of twelve months, 3,500 men died of *flux de ventre* (dysentery) and other diseases.

It was largely thanks to French intervention that the Scots were able to eject the English from their country (except, of course, Berwick) by 1550. Their most important contribution was in their *savoir faire* in the art of artillery and fortification. There were five French gunners, for example, at the castle of Dunbar. A French artillery train under Leone Strozzi was sent to capture St Andrews in 1547. By 1557, there were 3,000 Frenchmen in Scotland. During this war the French constructed fortresses at Aberlady, Eyemouth, Inchkeith and on Inchcolm.

By now, however, Protestantism had taken root in Scotland, thanks in large part to the reformer John Knox. Elizabeth made a treaty with the Scottish Protestants (the Lords of the Congregation), including Châtelleraud, at Berwick in February 1560 with the intention of ousting the French from Scotland. The idea of an alliance based upon religion had been formed some years earlier. We find an entry in the journal of the young Edward VI supporting this dated 12 July 1550: 'It was apointed that under the shadow of preparing for the sea matters there shuld be sent 5000 poundes to the protestauntes to get their good will.' Whether the money was sent to French or Scottish Protestants is not clear, but the significance is that the idea of a Protestant alliance had already taken root. The timing of Edward's journal entry suggests that it could be linked to the Huguenots. The new French Protestant Church in London was founded by Royal Charter some days later, on 24 July.

ELIZABETH AND THE CONSPIRACY OF AMBOISE, 1560

It was not a question of *if* but rather *when* to intervene in France. There are indications that England was being put on a war footing at the start of Elizabeth's reign. We may consider that the level of activity in the naval dockyards by 1559 was not purely defensive. Similarly, Sir Thomas Gresham shipped 100,000 lbs of copper in 1560, hoping to make thirty or forty cannon. In fact, between 1559 and 1562 the Crown spent £139,000 on the purchase of arms on the Continent – an enormous amount considering that a harquebus (a predecessor of the musket) cost only 10 shillings (a musket cost 23 shillings in 1589).

The internal problems of France offered fresh opportunities to the English, a situation that had arisen with the accidental death of Henri II in 1559, mortally wounded in a joust by the Huguenot Gabriel de Montgomery when a splinter from a shattered mace passed through his visor. Montgomery found refuge on Jersey.

François and Charles de Guise had enjoyed considerable influence over Henri II but they now had the opportunity to consolidate their power. The young François II came to the throne at the age of fifteen. The omnipresence of Henri's widow, Catherine de' Medici, appeared to offer some stability. Issuing from Florence, the Medici family remained a major player in European politics. Catherine had to contend with the growing influence of the Guises. The power of the Guise family had increased through marriage and war.

A plot was organised by the Huguenots under the direction of Jean du Barry, sieur de La Renaudie, in March 1560 which became known as the *conjuration d'Amboise*. The conspirators aimed the plot against the Guises who they believed had assumed too much power around the new young king. The plot was discovered and the conspirators executed.

The historian Joseph Kervyn de Lettenhove was convinced that there had been English complicity in the conspiracy. There is indeed strong evidence to support this. Elizabeth sent Edward Tremayne to France to see the Huguenot leaders. Meanwhile, La Renaudie visited England where he was apparently encouraged by her. We know that La Renaudie had funds from 'unknown' sources and that it was perhaps at this moment that he received monetary aid. The French ambassador to Spain, Sébastien de l'Aubespine, the Bishop of Limoges, declared that it was indeed Elizabeth who had provided the rebels with money. One thing certain is that, by 1560, Elizabeth's ambassador to France, Sir Nicholas Throckmorton, had departed on a war of propaganda against the Guises. He suggested to Elizabeth that he should circulate a proclamation via merchants throughout Brittany and Normandy to incite people against them. At the same time, Throckmorton announced the discovery of a plot by the Guises to poison Elizabeth.

To the French, an English invasion appeared imminent. *Amiral* Bouillé warned the governor of Brittany, 'The world is so changed … divison and rivalry so great that … St-Malo could be lost to the English.'[19] Chantonnay, the Spanish ambassador in France, likewise reported to King Philip II, 'They have great fear that the English will land troops in Brittany or Normandy where they will be welcomed by the inhabitants.'[20]

Following the failure of the conspiracy, Throckmorton was instructed by Elizabeth to deny any allegations of English complicity. It was perhaps in an effort to choose a better moment for their intervention that Throckmorton sent a copy of the book by the astrologer Michel de Nostre-Dame (known as Nostradamus) to Elizabeth's Secretary of State, Sir William Cecil, in October.

The duc de Guise came out of the conspiracy of Amboise with his position strengthened. He was named *Conservateur de la patrie*, a French equivalent of Lord Protector. Nevertheless, there were some positive consequences for Elizabeth. First, France's internal problems meant that Guise was obliged to suspend his projects in Scotland. The Franco-Scottish alliance also showed little sign of healing. The French began to take precautions by reducing the number of Scotsmen who had access to the king. Writing later, in 1584–85, Richard Cook remarked that 'These archers of the garde were sometyme all Scottishmen but for certayne suspitions of treason moved at Amboyse the[y were] retrenched to the number of a hundred, so that at this daye there be but a hundred Scottishmen that be archers of the Kinge's garde, the rest be all Frenchmen.' The Protestants also took further steps to protect themselves. In Normandy, Coligny withdrew the captaincies of Honfleur and Le Havre from the Catholic *vice-amiral* La Meilleraye.

French intervention in the war in Scotland was one of the first worries of the reign for Elizabeth but it was also the scene for one of her first successes. A French force, including Henri Clentin, sieur D'Oysel, Jacques de La Brosse and Sebastien de Luxembourg, vicomte de Martigues, was besieged by an allied force of English and Scottish Protestants at Leith. The siege was conducted by William, Lord Grey de Wilton. He had led a spirited defence of Guînes in the English Pale following the fall of Calais in 1558. The siege of Leith was notable for the failure of an English assault on 7 May. The English naval blockade under William Winter, however, proved conclusive. One report stated that the garrison were reduced to a daily ration of only 16 oz of bread and a salmon shared by six men per week. The garrison surrendered shortly after the death of Marie de Guise, who had sought refuge in Edinburgh Castle. By the articles signed on 5 July, the French were to withdraw after first having razed the fortifications. The treaty of Edinburgh on 16 July brought about the withdrawal of French forces from Scotland, save for 120 Frenchmen divided between Dunbar and Inchkeith who would remain in Scottish rather than French service. Diplomatic intervention by Sir Nicholas Throckmorton and the *Connétable*, Anne de Montmorency, also succeeded in persuading the French not to use English devices in their heraldry.

The fragile peace was maintained, though punctuated with invasion scares. In November, Throckmorton warned the queen of rumours of an enterprise against the Channel Islands. He also informed her that Johann Philipp, Wild und Rheingraf, Graf von Salm (usually referred to as simply 'the Rhinegrave' in England), was visiting German princes. The shipping of 800 cattle from Auvergne and Brittany to Normandy, together with the expectation of eight galleys from Marseilles arriving in *ponant* (i.e. the Bay of Biscay and the English Channel), would have confirmed their fears of military preparations. These fears were in turn erased by the sudden death of François II at Orléans on 5 December 1560. The succession of the new king, Charles IX (aged ten), put the French monarchy in a fragile position.

In January 1561 Francis Russell, the Earl of Bedford, was sent to forge ties with the Huguenots. He established a relationship with *amiral* Coligny. England had maintained allies in France until the end of the Hundred Years War. The old Bourguignon alliance disappeared once the reunification of the country was complete. By the treaty of Arras in 1482, Burgundy was re attached to the French royal domain. The failed Breton alliance was replaced by a new alliance with the French Protestants. An alliance with the Huguenots could prove beneficial. An alliance strengthened by the bonds of religion could also prove to be long-lasting. English intervention in a religious war overseas was also a method of galvanising Protestantism at home.

There were, however, some doubts about whether troops should be sent to France. Some Englishmen did not want to send money to the Huguenots. The Privy Council were divided on the subject, as Sir William Cecil wrote, 'these varieties of th'affaires in France, which have so turned both ourselves and our counsell here into so many shapes from time to time'. There were likewise some Huguenots such as Morvilliers, the governor of Boulogne, who were against English involvement. The attitude of Elizabeth herself towards these co-religionists was later expressed in a letter to Mary, Queen of Scots, when she wrote, 'a name till late unknown to me, now too familiar – too often heard – the name of *Huguenots*'.

INTERVENTION IN THE FIRST CIVIL WAR

Attempts at reconciliation between the Huguenots and Catholics in France ended in stalemate with the colloquy of Poissy. The English authorities did not have long to wait for a new crisis. The situation that presented itself in 1562 offered a chance. The appearance of Protestantism in the Guise heartland in the east of France proved intolerable. What is more, in Wassy, the new religion set up a place of worship within the town and close to the Catholic church of Notre-Dame. It was here that the scene was set for the massacre of Huguenots during a sermon on 1 March. The reluctance of François, duc de Guise, to restrain his soldiers resulted in between twenty-five and fifty dead as well as 150 wounded. The ensuing conflict would be both long and bitter.

King Charles IX c.1561, by François Clouet (*c*.1515–1572). Royal Collection,
RCIN 420931 Royal Collection © Her Majesty Queen Elizabeth II

It was Elizabeth who gave her name to English foreign policy. The
longevity of her reign assured continuity in policy. Her reign straddled
those of as many as eight popes, five kings of France and two kings of
Spain. Her reign and policies became synonymous with the career of Sir
William Cecil. Created Lord Burghley in 1572, he was succeeded by his
son, Sir Robert Cecil, in 1598.

Elizabeth's first line of defence, as well as the key to intervention, was
her ambassadors. Throckmorton was a central figure in Elizabeth's early
foreign policy and a chief architect of military intervention in France. He

Sir William Cecil, Lord Burghley,
by unknown Anglo-Netherlandish artist (Arnold Bronckhorst?).
© National Portrait Gallery, London, NPG 2184

wrote to Sir William Cecil in March 1562, 'Spend your money now, and never in England was money better spent than this will be. Use the time while you have it.' Originally, he wanted to send volunteers. In May 1562 he wrote to Cecil to express his wishes: 'I could wisshe that some suche as desyre to adventure and see the world were lett slipp, loking through your fingers, to passe furthwith to Depe [Dieppe] or to Havre de Grace [Le Havre] or bothe either to serve as foetmen or light horsemen.'[21] Then, the following month, we find the governor of Dieppe (a Huguenot) wanting to recruit English soldiers for his garrison.

Meanwhile, as Albert Pollard rightly comments, 'the temptations were almost irresistible'. On 12 July 1562 Throckmorton wrote telling Cecil that if the queen wanted to send money to the prince de Condé, then Le Havre would be the best guarantee. In the month of August, Condé invited the English to land in France under terms. He requested 6,000 English troops. Le Havre and Dieppe would be handed over as guarantees for the loan of 140,000 *écus* (£42,000). Condé also requested a further 20,000 *écus* (£6,000) if Elizabeth could not send men to Rouen.

The authorities could draw encouragement from history. It was not in the distant past that English soldiers had taken and then held Boulogne against considerable forces. Cecil had himself served at Boulogne and knew what to expect. As he later wrote to the English ambassador, Sir Henry Unton, 'by myne oune experience I knew at Bullein [Boulogne]'.[22]

Meanwhile, some English commanders doubted whether they could hold Le Havre under siege. The loss of Calais after only one week was proof that a difficult task awaited them. The English had spent enormous sums on the fortifications of Calais – fortifications that failed. More recently, soldiers such as Cuthbert Vaughan had also seen how the modern fortifications at Leith had been able to resist an English bombardment and assault. Control of the sea would also enable them to relieve a besieged force at will.

English intervention was sealed by the treaty of Hampton Court on 20 September 1562. Several representatives of the Huguenots came to London, including Jean de Ferrières (the vidame de Chartres), Jean de La Fin, seigneur de Beauvoir-La Nocle, François de Beauvais, seigneur de Briquemault, and Robert de la Haye. Let us listen to Elizabeth in an order of 24 September, 1562:

> *The Queen's Majesty, upon divers great and necessary causes tending to the honour of God, the preservation of her realm and subjects, and*

lastly for saving to the crown of England in good season that which of late times being evicted from it ought to be restored....

Wherefore her majesty letteth all her subjects assembled either at Portsmouth or at Rye to understand that this her intent is not to make war or use any hostility against the French King or any of his faithful subjects (with whom she chargeth all her subjects to keep good peace), but only to preserve the next ports and towns in Normandy by defensible manner from the usurpation of such as, being the first authors of all these troubles in France, have manifestly advanced themselves in force out of the compass of the authority of the French King her majesty's good brother, and intend nothing more than, by getting into their power the ports next to this realm, to prosecute their former unjust and violent purposes against the same....[23]

'That which of late times being evicted from it ought to be restored' is certainly a reference to Calais. At the heart of Elizabeth's initial policy was the issue of Calais, lost by her sister Mary in 1558. Calais remained a weapon in Elizabeth's diplomatic arsenal until the peace of Vervins in 1598. Despite the clause of the treaty of Cateau-Cambrésis by which France would either leave Calais after eight years or pay a forfeit of 500,000 *écus*, it is doubtful that the French had any intention of surrendering the town to the English. William Camden informs us that the new occupants had taken leases on properties for a period of fifty years and that others had been granted land in perpetuity. At the end of 1560, Throckmorton was informed that Jacques Bourdin, the French *secrétaire d'État*, had construction projects on the 700 acres of land in his possession. One other investor had already spent 3,000 *couronnes* (£900) on constructions outside Calais.

Another proclamation, in French, of 27 September aimed to reassure the people of Normandy that the English aim was for 'the deliverance from the violence of the said house of Guise'.[24] Elizabeth also spoke about the preservation of their liberty of conscience.

By inviting English relief and handing Le Havre to the English, Huguenot leaders risked reprisals such as the confiscation of their land and property. Elizabeth was able to reassure them on this point by offering them either pensions or land in England. They were right to be worried. Charles IX wrote directly to Elizabeth to ask for the handing over of the rebels to the French ambassador, Paul de Foix: 'we have found out the truth that there are today in England a large number of our subjects

Sir Nicholas Throckmorton (1515-1571), by unknown Anglo-Netherlandish artist
(Arnold Bronckhorst?). National Portrait Gallery, London, NPG 3800 (displayed at
Montacute House, Somerset), © National Portrait Gallery, London
The portrait of Throckmorton may be attributable to Arnold Bronckhorst
(fl.1565–1586). Both the composition and style are similar to the portrait of Sir
William Cecil (NPG 2184). Comparison may be made with the portrait of Sir
Henry Sidney (1573) at Petworth House attributed to Bronckhorst. Records show
that Bronckhorst was paid for a painting of Sidney in 1565/6.

declared seditious and rebels by order of our court of the *Parlement* of Paris'.[25] Jean de Ferriéres, the vidame de Chartres, was one of the names on the list.

Paul de Foix was aware of preparations but he was told that the soldiers were merely volunteers and therefore not under the authority of the queen. De Foix was informed of the movements of the English privateer Sir Henry Strangeways and that he had between 300 and 400 men. He also knew that he was on board a ship named the *Phoenix*. He therefore searched to find the truth. Meanwhile, Elizabeth fell ill with smallpox in October. The queen's illness was useful in that it provided a shield against the French ambassador, as she could not receive him.

The English force was placed under Ambrose Dudley, Earl of Warwick. It appeared that they would be able to hold and consolidate their control of Normandy and the mouth of the Seine. The unexpected occurred, however, with the reconciliation between Huguenots and Royalist Catholics, facilitated by the death of the duc de Guise in February. The Edict of Amboise was signed on 19 March by which the Huguenot party agreed to peace in return for certain rights of worship. For the time being, Elizabeth would be without an ally in France. Strategically, this meant that it would be more difficult to extend, and thus consolidate, the zone of occupation in French territory.

Charles IX undertook to retake Le Havre *par amour ou par force* ('by love or by force'). On 3 July 1563 Elizabeth notified her ambassador Sir Thomas Smith that she was ready to surrender Le Havre in return for the payment of loans and the return of Calais after three years. Meanwhile,

A scene from Homer's *Iliad* depicting Ulysses chiding Thersites (1563/64), attributed to Niccolò dell'Abbate (1509/12–1571). British Museum, London, 1860,06.16.81, © The Trustees of the British Museum
The fifty-eight frescoes of the Galerie Ulysse were unfortunately destroyed in 1739. Two surviving preliminary drawings may provide some further indication of the composition in addition to the engravings made by Theodoor van Thulden (1606–1669) in the 1630s. One depicts Ulysses (the Latin name of Odysseus), King of Ithaca, chiding Thersites. Thersites clearly represents the Huguenots and probably Gaspard de Coligny or Condé. The English ambassador may have seen the painting based on another drawing by Niccolò dell'Abbate, Dame conduisant un chevalier en armure devant une cité assiégée *('Lady leading a knight before a besieged city'), the knight being Charles IX. A knight and woman in the background depict the abduction of Helen (Musée du Louvre, Inv. 20746).*

diplomacy was overtaken by military events. Faced by the plague and an effective siege battery, the defence of Le Havre faltered.

Meanwhile, many Huguenots remained in England. The Bishop of London, Edmund Grindal, wrote to Cecil in the hope of helping the refugees: 'I praye you amonge your weightie affaires (as you maye) remember to give to my Lord Mayor, and soe other godly honeste persons, order for the poor afflicted Frenshe, exiled for religion, that they be not taken prizoners (as they now are at London), by virtue of your late proclamation'.[26]

THE TREATY OF TROYES AND THE *RAPPROCHEMENT* WITH FRANCE

There was little wish to continue the war following the recapture of Le Havre by the French. John Somers was sent to Paris to negotiate a truce. He met Sébastien de L'Aubespine, Bishop of Limoges, and Nicholas de Neufville de Villeroy at the hôtel Villeroy on 9 December 1563.[27] Peace negotiations and the signing of the treaty were to be held at Troyes in Champagne in 1564. The visit to Troyes was included in the itinerary of the royal tour of the kingdom. The royal party stayed there despite reports of the plague in the city. Catherine saw these as a ruse by the townsfolk to get them to move on. The city was certainly not chosen by chance: it had been the scene of the signing of the humiliating treaty imposed by Henry V of England in 1420. The Royalist party also wanted to make full use of the allegory of the siege of Troy from Homer's *Iliad*. At the château de Fontainebleau a new painting was commissioned, depicting the retaking of Le Havre. The English ambassador saw this in 1567. The fresco was made by Niccolò dell'Abbate after drawings by Francesco Primaticcio (known as le Primatice) in the Galerie Ulysse.

Meanwhile, the Huguenots produced their own fresco, which has survived in the Tour de la Ligue at the Château de Tanlay in Burgundy. This depicts Elizabeth in the top left corner. The leaders of the opposing factions are depicted as mythological figures. Coligny, for example, is portrayed as Neptune. The château was a centre of Protestant resistance until the Colignys were forced to leave during the third civil war in 1569.

Jean de Ferrières and Condé were both present in Troyes. On the French side, the commission included Jean de Morvillier and Jacques Bourdin, sieur de Villaines. The English were represented by Sir Thomas Smith and Sir Nicholas Throckmorton, assisted by John Somers. By the treaty, ratified by Elizabeth at Richmond, the French undertook to pay

Allégorie de la Victoire en l'honneur de Charles IX, 1564, by Niccolò
dell'Abbate (1509/12–1571). Musée du Louvre, Paris, Inv. 5880r. Photo © RMN-
Grand Palais (Musée du Louvre)/Michèle Bellot
It appears that Niccolò dell'Abbate was called upon for his services at Troyes.
This drawing in the Cabinet des Dessins of the Louvre corresponds with written
accounts of the celebrations given during the presence of the king. The scene
was held before the town hall at Troyes. There was a chariot 'mounted on four
wheels with some engines that made it turn all ways without any horses'.[28]
The lady on the chariot was the daughter of the mayor, who presented a laurel
wreath and a gold ring to the king.

120,000 *couronnes* (£36,000) for the hostages in England. The French
king ratified the treaty at Bar-le-Duc on 1 May. A medallion was struck to
commemorate the treaty. Produced by Steven van Herwyck after a design
by Charles Utenhove, the medallion shows a portrait of Elizabeth on the
obverse side and *Faith* seated by a fountain on the reverse (London,
National Portrait Gallery).

Following this success, it was decided that the moment had come
to declare the majority of Charles IX. This was held in the *Parlement*

of Rouen. Here, Michel de L'Hôpital delivered his speech in which he declared that Elizabeth had lost not only Le Havre but also all claims on Calais. As Charles IX later wrote to his ambassador in London, La Motte Fénelon, 'God, by his grace, had separated and bordered these two kingdoms with the sea for [their] well-being'.[29]

Needless to say, there was little ceremony in England except for a *Te Deum* sung at St Paul's Cathedral, London, on 23 April. Elizabeth wrote to Charles at the end of December 1564:

> *Friendship which appears to have already taken such good root in your heart that it will not easily be broken.... We have already started to plant in our heart the same plant of true friendship.... What we hope is that with the aid of God these two plants will be long-lasting ... and shall produce such fruit.... Our Kingdoms, country and people will also receive great profit.*[30]

Further intentions of friendship were declared by Pierre de Ronsard as he celebrated peace with a dedication to Elizabeth in his *Elegies, Mascarades et Bergerie* (1565).

THE 'INTER-WAR' PERIOD

The years 1562–64 had seen direct intervention by both land and marine forces in France. During the second civil war, 1567–68, the English mainly took the role of spectators. This was the role taken by the English ambassador, Sir Henry Norris, and his son John as they took up positions to view (and sketch) the battle of St-Denis. Sir Henry was charged with the role of mediator between the Huguenots and the Royalists to end the war in 1568. The peace of Longjumeau, signed on 23 March, lasted until the month of August. It was described as a *meschante petite paix* ('a short, cruel peace') by François de La Noue.

Elizabeth maintained a similar position during the third war (1568–70), using only her money to pay the mercenaries. In 1569, the English felt that Coligny was stronger than the king, even after the defeat at Jarnac (Bassac) on 13 March and the death of Condé. English intervention therefore became less urgent, though the Huguenots met with a fresh defeat at Moncontour on 3 October that year. Elizabeth pursued a policy of 'war by procuration' between 1569 and 1587.

During the second and third civil wars (September 1567–March 1568 and August 1568–August 1570) English intervention was less pronounced.

The French chronicler Claude Haton remarked how English relief no longer came as freely as during the first war. 'The Huguenots try to draw the support of English men … but none wish to put to sea for them, remembering the poor recompense that they had during the first troubles … with all the loss of their goods and lives.'[31]

Elizabeth herself hesitated before supporting the rebels yet again. According to Henri de La Popelinière, Gabriel de Montgomery was given a poor reception in England. Jules de Belleville, seigneur de Languillier, a gentleman from Poitou, was also sent to England in search of relief. Similarly, in 1569, certain English lords objected to offering any financial support to the Huguenots. William Camden's view, however, was that this was merely a method of countering Cecil's influence on Elizabeth. Nevertheless, Elizabeth still sought to maintain links with them. Thomas Wilkes was sent to France and made agent to the Huguenot army. A number of Huguenots found refuge in England. Odet de Coligny, Cardinal Châtillon, settled in England in 1568 and remained until his death at Canterbury in 1571. Sir William Cecil had given him a good report:

> *The Cardinal Chastillon sheweth himself so quiet a person, and all his languages so faithfull a servant to the King his master, as he meriteth great commendations; he medleth in nothing here, but wholly occupied in exercise of his religion; he continually lamenteth, that grave counsellours persuading peace are not of more power and credit in the court.*[32]

Diplomats such as Bertrand de Salignac de La Motte Fénelon worked to maintain the peace but Elizabeth remained wary of the Guise faction and French intervention in Scotland. In January 1570, it was reported that six ships and 3,000 harquebusiers were preparing to invade England. The aim was to raise the Catholic provinces in the north. We know that the purchase of two ships, the *Levrier* and the *Hirondelle*, was planned and that Charles IX wanted to send these to Scotland filled with munitions. Fears of invasion were made worse by the excommunication of Elizabeth by Pope Pius V. Admiral Clinton was ordered 'to sink at once, and without question, any French vessels he might find carrying troops to Scotland'.

In time, however, the Scottish problem was replaced by the Irish problem, the energy once consumed by the wars against Scotland now transferred to Ireland. Sir Francis Walsingham had learned that soldiers under the command of the Protestant governor of Morlaix in Brittany, La Roche, had left France to fight in Ireland. It was to the house of Lorraine that the Irish rebel Shane O'Neill later turned to ask for aid. Other French eyes also looked towards Ireland. François de Noailles wrote:

> *There is, behind England, a Peru. It is the kingdom of Ireland, one of the best countries in the world. And I wish to be stripped of nobility if sieur Strozzi and Captain [Dominique de] Gourges cannot subdue this kingdom with 7,000 or 8,000 French harquebusiers, 800 or 1,000 horse and six pieces of artillery in less than a year. Well ruled and managed, it will have a greater revenue than England in less than twenty years after its subjugation.*[33]

A crossroads in Elizabeth's foreign policy was reached by the beginning of the 1570s. There was a choice to make: should England pursue an alliance with France or Spain? Sir Francis Walsingham favoured an alliance with France for both religious and strategic reasons: 'that though France could not yield like Profit that Flanders did, yet might it yield some Profit with less Hazard and more Safety… That the Entrance into the League with France, would not only be an Advancement of the Gospel [i.e. Protestantism] there, but elsewhere'.

Elizabeth was also keen to protect France if it was to England's advantage, as she stated, 'whensoever the last day of the Kingdome of France commeth, it will undoubtedly be the Eeve of the destruction of England'.[34]

Catherine de' Medici was keen to see Elizabeth declare openly against Spain. French schemes of expansion in Florida had already brought France and Spain into conflict there. Seen as a threat to the Spanish treasure fleet, the French garrison at Fort Caroline was put to the sword in 1565.

Anglo-French friendship was at last sealed with the treaty of Blois in April 1572. Charles IX swore to uphold the treaty in a ceremony near the Louvre at the church of St-Germain l'Auxerrois in the presence of Edward Fiennes de Clinton. The treaty had gone ahead despite Spanish and Guise attempts to prevent an alliance between the two countries. It is clear that the signing of the treaty strengthened Elizabeth's position. By the defensive treaty, the signatories each undertook to furnish men and ships if the other was invaded. Very clearly now, both England and France had become worried about the threat of Spain.

INSTRUMENTS OF PERSUASION

Despite all, the young Anglo-French alliance held firm. This was a considerable achievement, but how was it accomplished? The multiple personal relationships played a key part. One example is that of the influential francophile courtier Sir Philip Sidney. He maintained friendships with Hubert Languet, agent of Christian I, Elector of Saxony, and the Huguenot diplomat Philippe Du Plessis Mornay. He accompanied the Earl of Lincoln's embassy in 1572. During this embassy, Sidney was named *Gentilhomme Ordinaire de la Chambre* by Charles IX with *honneurs, autoritez, gages, droictz, hostellages, proffictz et esmolumens accoustumez et qui y appartiennent* ('honours, authorities, pledges, rights, lodgings, profits and the usual emoluments that belonged to him').[35] He was also named as guardian to Mornay's daughter, Élisabeth, who had been born in England on 1 June 1578. One not insignificant victory was achieved when Elizabeth agreed to be named as godmother or *comere* to Marie-Isabelle, daughter of Charles IX. She offered a font of gold and sent William Somerset, 3rd Earl of Worcester, to France to attend her baptism. Unfortunately, Elizabeth's goddaughter died young (on 2 April 1578), but this episode was real evidence of the improvement in relations between the two countries. Marie-Isabelle was not Elizabeth's only French godchild. The queen also became godmother to children of Jean Ferrières, Guillaume de L'Aubespine, sieur de Châteauneuf, Christophe de Harlay, comte de Beaumont, and Henri de la Tour d'Auvergne, duc de Bouillon.

In the same way that foreign policy became an instrument of marriage for Henry VIII, marriage now became an instrument of Elizabeth's foreign policy. The Anglo-French alliance was fortified by the French 'obsession' with marrying Elizabeth. Charles IX, Henri, duc d'Anjou, and his brother François-Hercule, duc d'Alençon, were all interested parties (or, rather, parties put forward by Catherine). Even Henri de Navarre was suggested. It should be noted that in reference to 'the Alençon/Anjou marriage', there are two possibilities: Henri, duc d'Orléans (1551–1589), became duc d'Anjou in 1566; his brother François-Hercule (1554–1584), until then duc d'Anjou, became duc d'Alençon. Anjou became King Henri III in 1574. To further complicate matters, Alençon became Anjou once again in 1576.

There was a long-standing custom of marriage (and courtships) between the two countries. We may cite Mathilde de Boulogne and Stephen in 1125 and Aliénor d'Aquitaine and Henry II in 1152, as well as King John and Isabelle d'Angoulême in 1200. Henry III married another Aliénor (this time de Provence) in 1236. Marguerite, daughter of Philippe III, was the second wife of Edward I. His son, Edward II, married Isabelle, daughter of Philippe IV of France. Richard II took Isabelle, daughter of Charles VI, as his second wife in 1396. By the treaty of Troyes in 1420,

Henry V 'won' Catherine, the other daughter of Charles VI. Following Henry's death in 1422, she married a Welshman, Owen Tudor, grandfather of the future Henry VII. Henry VI married Marguerite d'Anjou in 1445.

By and large there were no marriages between the two royal houses in the Tudor epoch. Henry VII suggested marriage between Anne de Bretagne and the Duke of Buckingham. Mary, daughter of Henry VII, married the widower Louis XII in 1514 but she herself was widowed the year after. By the treaty of Amiens in 1527, Mary, daughter of Henry VIII, would marry Henri, duc d'Orléans (the future Henri II). This proposal, however, remained only a project in 1541 following negotiations. Henry VIII looked for a marriage with Marie, duchesse de Longueville (the future Marie de Lorraine). Henry's track record appears to have caused this idea to be axed. A marriage between Edward VI and Élisabeth, daughter of Henri II, was agreed in 1551 but the death of Edward two years later put an end to this plan.

Behind the declarations of love lay a political agenda. The offer made by Charles IX for Elizabeth's hand has since been described as *simple courtoisie* but an alliance with England was desirable for the French Crown. One of the initiators of the marriage had apparently been the prince de Condé. He asked Sir Thomas Smith, 'Why does your sovereign not marry the very Christian king [Charles IX]? He has more inclination to the Gospel [Protestantism] than one thinks and union between the two crowns would be a devastating blow for papism.'[36]

The project found backing in England from Robert Dudley, Earl of Leicester. Marriage with Elizabeth would have simultaneously calmed the Huguenots and avoided a civil war, while maintaining the status quo of power in Europe against Spain. Nevertheless, the marriage proved elusive. Elizabeth told Michel de Castelnau, sent to England to negotiate the arrangements, that her suitor was *trop grand et trop petit* ('too large and too small'). Probably to push home this point, the Garter offered to Charles IX by Elizabeth was too large for his leg!

The question of a French marriage returned, perhaps thanks to the persistence of Catherine de' Medici. Astrologers were consulted in 1570 on a match between Elizabeth and Henri, duc d'Anjou, but the idea ended in stalemate by July 1571. This time, religious differences proved too great. Elizabeth may well not have wanted to marry, using the negotiations merely to further the *rapprochement* with France. Further, too many people remembered the unhappy marriage between Mary and Philip II of Spain. They also saw the menace which such a marriage posed to Protestantism.

The preferred suitor was François-Hercule, duc d'Alençon, despite the fact that Elizabeth was put off by the traces of smallpox on his face. He was considered to be a moderate in terms of religion. Looks were important. Elizabeth had previously sent Sir Thomas Randolph on a mission to France to check the true resemblance of Alençon to his portrait – a full-length one had been offered to her in March 1572 (National Gallery of Art, Washington DC). Nicholas Hilliard, who had sailed for France in August 1576, also produced a miniature of him.

Meanwhile, the publication of the *Gaping Gulf* (London, 1579) by John Stubbe did little to help Elizabeth win over public opinion. In this book, Stubbe set out his opposition to the French marriage. He started by retracing the origins of the conflict between the two countries. In this way it was very similar to *Discours de l'origine du different d'entre les Français et Anglois...* (Paris, 1563) by Nicolas Natey de la Fontaine. It is very possible that Stubbe had 'high-level backing' but he was also simply expressing the general consensus when he wrote 'if they went up to the knuckles in French blood, they will up to the elbows in English blood'. The menace posed in Stubbe's book was taken seriously. The authorities took a number of measures. A royal proclamation denounced the book in September 1579. Attempts were made to hide the visit of Alençon, and for good reason. The discontent that his visit provoked is illustrated in the letters of the Spanish ambassador, Bernardino de Mendoza. Sir Philip Sidney had more than a few words to say on the subject in his letter to the queen:

> *He French, and desiring to make France great, Your Majesty*
> *English, and desiring nothing less than that France should not grow*
> *great.... As for this man, as long as he is but Monsieur in might,*
> *and a Papist in profession, he neither can, nor will greatly shield*
> *you. And if he grow to be King, his defence will be like Ajax's shield,*
> *which rather weigh'd them down, than defended those that bare it.*[37]

The intended marriage contract demonstrates the preoccupations of the Council. It was stipulated that the king would not be allowed to take munitions of war out of the country nor to engage England in a foreign war, two very clear references to regrets from the reign of Mary. It was for this last reason that Elizabeth could not consent to marriage while Alençon was engaged in a war in the Low Countries.[38] Eventually the French marriage failed to materialise, even though rings had been exchanged on 22 November 1581. Once more, the obstacle of religion proved too great a hurdle. An air of regret is apparent in the verse written by Elizabeth on the departure of *Monsieur* ('My very dear Frog') in 1582.

I grieve and dare not show my discontent;
I love, and yet am forced to seem to hate;
I do, yet dare not say I ever meant;
I seem stark mute, but inwardly do prate.
I am, and not; I freeze and yet am burned,
Since from myself another self I turned....

Some gentler passion slide into my mind,
For I am soft, and made of melting snow;
Or be more cruel, Love, and so be kind.
Let me or float or sink, be high or low;
Or let me live with some more sweet content,
Or die, and so forget what love e'er meant.

Elizabeth Regina[39]

Elizabeth's heart was ultimately commanded by common sense and duty. As she declared to Sir Edward Stafford, ambassador to France 1579–80 and 1583–89:

Shall it be ever found true that Queen Elizabeth hath solemnised
the perpetuall harm of England under the glorious title of marriage
with Francis, heir of France? No, no it shall never be.... We willingly
will not repose our whole trust so far in the French nation, as we
will give them in pawn all our fortune, and afterward stand at their
discretion.[40]

She continued to use marriage as a tool of diplomacy. She looked to create ties between Catherine, sister of Henri de Navarre, and the Scottish King James VI (the future James I of England).

The other useful tool of diplomacy was the conferring of orders. The English Crown offered the Order of the Garter while France offered the Ordre de St Michel. Charles IX, Henri III and Henri IV each received the Order of the Garter, which was founded by Edward III in 1348 'dedicated … to noble persons markable for extraordinary valour and command in martial affairs'.[41] According to legend, the device *Honi soit qui mal y pense* ('May he be shamed who thinks badly of it') was attributed following a feast to celebrate the taking of Calais in 1347. The other inscription, *Dieu et mon droit* ('God is my right'), are the words of Richard I before his victory at the battle of Gisors in 1198. It is therefore curious how the Order became an aid in Anglo-French relations. Henri III was received into the Order by Elizabeth 'that shee might binde unto her the French king in the stronger band of amity'.

The French order of St-Michel could not be conferred on women, thus excluding Elizabeth. Charles IX therefore gave 'two roomes of his ordre'[42] in return for his Garter. For the first, Sir Robert Dudley, Earl of Leicester, was named and Elizabeth gave her accord. Johann Philipp, the Rhinegrave, who had fought against the English at Le Havre in 1562–63, now came to England to confer this in November 1564. For the second, Elizabeth made her own choice. As with the question of marriage, she again took her time. She was still deferring her decision one year later. It was not until 1566 that a decision was finally made to grant the honour to Thomas Howard, Duke of Norfolk.

THE CRISES OF THE 1570S

The coming together of leading Huguenots and Catholics in Paris to celebrate the marriage of Henri de Navarre and Marguerite de Valois (la Reine Margot) on 18 August 1572 provided the opportunity for reconciliation. Indeed, this appears to have been Catherine's intention. The religious tensions in France were exacerbated by the rising taxes which, some believed, were being used to pay the Huguenots. The Huguenot leader, Coligny, was assassinated, as were other leaders in turn. The selective assassinations, however, degenerated into a general massacre, during which some Englishmen, including Sir Philip Sidney, found refuge with Sir Francis Walsingham. The massacre of Huguenots in Paris on St Bartholomew's Day (24 August) placed Anglo-French relations under enormous pressure.

The French ambassador, La Motte Fénelon, found himself in a difficult position at court. Edwin Sandys, the Bishop of London, was also worried about his own clergy:

> *The preachers appoynted for the crosse in this vacation are but yonge men, unskilfull in matters politicall, yet so carried with zeale, that they will enter into them and poure forthe their opinions. If the league standeth firme betwixte her Majestie and the Frenche King, (as I suppose it dothe,) they maye perhappes, being not directed, utter speache to the breache therof; howe that will be lyked of I dowte.*[43]

There was a fresh wave of Huguenot refugees in the wake of the massacre, including Jean Ferrières, the vidame de Chartres.

A SCOTTISH PROBLEM

The question of Mary, Queen of Scots, complicated matters yet further. She had fled to England following her defeat at Langside on 2 May 1568 at the hands of Scottish Protestants led by the regent Charles Stewart, Earl of Moray, and Sir William Kirkcaldy of Grange. The presence of a Catholic queen in England provoked alarm because she was also a legitimate pretender to the throne. Her grandmother was Margaret Tudor, daughter of the first Tudor king, Henry VII. Mary effectively became the prisoner of Elizabeth in the custody of George Talbot, Earl of Shrewsbury, and then Sir Amias Paulet. Among her 'lodgings' were Tutbury castle, Chatsworth and Chartley Hall. Charles Neville, Earl of Westmoreland, and Thomas Percy, Earl of Northumberland, led a rebellion in 1569 supporting Mary's claim to the throne in the hope of reinstating Catholicism in England. This became known as the 'Rising of the North'. The Earl of Warwick was despatched to counter the rebellion. Mary's defeat in Scotland and the disintegration of English support meant that she was now destined to become no more than a tragic sideshow. Referred to as the 'bosom serpent' by Walsingham, Mary also had allies in France. Her own maternal family, the Guises, had done all that they could to prevent the Anglo-French alliance, as they saw nothing worse for her position. As will be shown, however, even a united France, lacking a sizeable fleet, would have been powerless to intervene in England. The state of the country's finances would have made the construction of a new fleet impossible. France would have had to ally with an increasingly hostile Spain to mount an invasion. There was therefore no real or immediate threat except a possible attempt on Elizabeth's life.

In 1571, Edinburgh Castle was being held by Mary's supporters under Sir William Kirkcaldy of Grange, her former enemy, in defiance of the regent, Matthew Stuart, Earl of Lennox, and the young King James VI. The fact that Kirkcaldy was a Protestant demonstrates a blurring of the lines of allegiance. The treaty of Blois, the following year, relieved English worries over Scotland. England and France agreed not to interfere in the affairs of that country. Elizabeth did, however, reserve the right to intervene against the Scots who were supporting English rebels, such as those implicated in the Rising of the North. Charles IX even gave a helping hand as he now sent an ambassador to Scotland to try to convince Mary's party to submit to the new regent, James Douglas, the Earl of Morton. The eruption of violence in Paris in August 1572 was a fresh opportunity for Elizabeth. The fact that France was by now fully occupied with affairs at home effectively gave her a free hand in Scotland: 'Now, the French being thoroughly occupied, is the best tyme to do that enterprise which is to be done',[44] wrote Sir Thomas Smith on 12 February. An English force was sent from Berwick with artillery to support the siege in Edinburgh. The surrender of the castle on 26 May effectively ended the 'Scottish problem', although Mary was not executed for another fifteen years.

Over time, the initial reaction of shock and horror at the massacre of Huguenots in France gave way to the need to preserve the Anglo-French alliance. The attempts against La Rochelle did not help. The Huguenot stronghold was besieged by the Royalists under Henri, duc d'Anjou, in November 1572. English relief, including the supply of gunpowder, helped to maintain the town's defence until the siege was raised in June the following year.

BATTLEFIELD FRANCE

Despite the fact that the French were now official allies, Elizabeth was determined to maintain France as the battlefield of the Reformation.

'It is shown by experience that nothing hath hitherto so much stayed the two great Kings of France and Spain from offending this realm as their own domestic troubles.' This statement by Burghley mirrors English foreign policy of the period. The idea of Elizabeth taking advantage of troubles in France is repeated frequently. In 1576, Walsingham wrote to Sir Henry Sidney, 'Here at home, we live in security as we were wont, grounding our quietness upon other's harms.' This view was shared on the other side of the Channel. The French chronicler Jean Nagerel wrote how 'The Queen of England … sought to put sulphur on the fire, nourish our lamentable quarrels and the people from obedience to their prince, and in the way of her predecessors, come to benefit from our ruin.'[45]

Michel de Castelnau warned Henri III in 1584 of a Protestant alliance:

If they join together, principally by sea on the defensive, and for the offensive, if their league continues with the Protestants of Germany and the Huguenots of your kingdom, they will have men and money to set the fire alight and make war all over as a means to keeping it away from their lands.[46]

It may be said that English intervention both exacerbated and prolonged the internal problems of France. For England, a civil war in France was advantageous. The French would be less willing and also less capable of interfering in affairs in Scotland. Elizabeth wished to prevent the resurgence of an all-powerful France allied with Spain. One way to do this was to foster Franco-Spanish rivalry.

No sooner had the fourth civil war ended (in July 1573) than the fifth began (spring 1574–May 1576), followed by the sixth (December 1576–September 1577) and seventh (November 1579–November 1580). The intermittent peace treaties granted the Huguenots more *places de sûreté* (places of safety). These were concentrated in the south-west of the country, south of the Loire. The places of safety or refuge had first been accorded by the edict of St-Germain in August 1570. They included towns such as La Rochelle, Cognac, Périgueux, Montpellier and Aigues-Mortes.

During this time François, duc d'Alençon, had opposed the siege of La Rochelle. He now became a figurehead for the *Malcontents*. This faction formed in opposition to royal absolutism. The leaders came from both Catholic (Henry Montmorency-Damville and Guillaume de Montmorency-Thoré) and Huguenot sides (Henri, prince de Condé, and Henri de Navarre). Henri de Navarre and Monsieur (François, duc d'Alençon) were imprisoned at the Château de Vincennes east of Paris in 1574. They would remain here until the death of Charles IX later that year. Thomas Wilkes was sent by Elizabeth in an effort to secure their release. The death of Charles helped to repair the harm caused by his alleged complicity in the massacre in Paris. In a strange twist of fate, like the previous signatory of the treaty of Troyes, Henry V, Charles also died at Vincennes. The treaty of Anglo-French mutual defence was ratified by Henri III in February 1575.

There followed a chain of events which pushed England further away from Spain. The origins of the conflict with Spain may be traced back to the reign of Mary Tudor and the refusal of Philip II to help England regain Calais. The circumnavigation of the globe by Francis Drake in 1577 was seen as a direct challenge to Spanish hegemony in the New World. The Spanish expedition to Smerwick in Ireland in 1580 served to strengthen the need for an Anglo-French partnership. Negotiations to renew the offensive-defensive alliance between France and England recommenced in 1581. The fact that Drake was dubbed by a Frenchman, Pierre Clausse, seigneur de Marchaumont, on his return further nurtured the alliance. Because of it, the French had the confidence to follow a more aggressive policy against Spain, culminating in an expedition to the Azores. This would be sent in support of António, Prior of Cato, a claimant to the Portuguese throne. It has been stated that António had secured support from Catherine de' Medici in return for the promise to cede the colony of Brazil and that the secret destination of the fleet was Brazil itself. Significantly, Elizabeth accorded the support of four English ships under William Hawkins.

In the same year as Drake's circumnavigation, there were still certain men who doubted the French alliance. Sir Nicholas Bacon considered that France remained the enemy. Some continued to hold this opinion even after Spanish retaliation. The pro-Catholic William Parry attempted to influence Lord Burghley when he wrote expressing his supposed concerns in 1582:

> Many are of opinion that it is a matter of less difficulty for us to confirm the auncient league with Burgundy, then to contynue our intelligence with France, with whom for five hundred yeres I do not finde that we have had any long peace. And out of doubt I am, that we have very mighty enemyes in France to our quietnes.[47]

Meanwhile, events in the Low Countries sparked reactions from Elizabeth. French intervention here created serious concerns. The year 1566 saw the start of a revolt by the *Gueux* (Calvinists) in the Netherlands. The revolt turned into a war against the Spanish rulers. A war of independence for a free Netherlands was in the interest of both England and France. A Spain occupied would mean a Spain that was also less dangerous. Gaspard de Coligny saw another advantage in that the conflict in France could perhaps be transferred to the Low Countries. Coligny met Sir Henry Middlemore and Sir Arthur Champernowne in Paris in June 1572. In their meeting he insisted on the need for intervention in the Low Countries against the Spanish. In the words of the historian Richard Wernham, 'The aim, put quite simply, was to get the Spanish army out of the Netherlands without letting the French in.'[48]

1578–79 saw the start of a project against the Spanish in the Low Countries by François, duc d'Anjou. He was invited by the States-General to become the head of the Seventeen Provinces in 1581. Anjou arrived in the same year, followed by an army, the raising of which had been made possible thanks to loans from Elizabeth. This was to coincide with the French naval expedition to the Azores raised by Catherine de' Medici. Anjou, however, resolved to increase his power by using his French army to capture towns by force. He attempted to take Antwerp by surprise but his force was routed in the 'French Fury' on 17 January 1583. Anjou left the Low Countries in the same year. It was in 1584 that decisive steps were taken. Elizabeth openly declared for the United Provinces by the treaty of Nonsuch. From 1585, English soldiers were garrisoned in the towns of Bergen-op-Zoom, Brill, Flushing and Ostend. The Earl of Leicester was sent in 1586.

ELIZABETH AND HENRI DE NAVARRE

The death of François, duc d'Anjou, in 1584 once more altered the political spectrum, placing an air of doubt around the Anglo-French alliance. Elizabeth was still unsure of the true colours of Henri III. She took precautions by sending Sir Arthur Champernowne to see Henri de Navarre. She promised aid to Henri if the king took the wrong side. Links were later maintained with Henri via Anthony Bacon, who took up residence in Montauban in south-west France in the mid-1580s.

An important step was the signing of the secret treaty of Magdeburg between Elizabeth, the king of Navarre and the German princes on 15 December 1584. Meanwhile, only two weeks later, the Catholics formed their own league. On 31 December the Catholic princes signed the treaty of Joinville with Philip II of Spain. The manifesto of this new Catholic *Ligue* was proclaimed at Péronne on 31 March 1585. The *Ligue* would support their own claimant to the French throne in the form of Charles X (Cardinal Charles de Bourbon). Elizabeth wanted to prevent an alliance between Spain and France. Henri de Navarre was seen as being the key in any future conflict with Spain. Walsingham declared, 'How greatly it importeth her Majestie to have the King of Navarr upheld.... There is no waye so apt to stopp the Spanish expeditions agaynst this realme.'[49]

The French ambassador, Guillaume de L'Aubespine, intervened in an attempt to prevent the execution of Mary, Queen of Scots. According to William Camden, L'Aubespine was himself implicated in a plot to assassinate Elizabeth following a confession made by Trappy, his secretary. At last, Mary's incessant intrigues (both perceived and real) led to her execution at Fotheringhay on 8 February 1587. In France, line after line of anti-English propaganda was written. Mary was seen as a victim of 'Jezebel', *bastarde incestueuse et vilaine publique* ('incestuous bastard and public villain').

Elizabeth would have at least felt reassured by a letter from her ambassador, Sir Edward Stafford. Stafford gave her his opinion of Henri

III, that he was good for England and that he wanted peace. Sir Thomas Bodley was sent on a mission alone to France in 1588 for a meeting with Henri. English diplomatic efforts succeeded in forcing a wedge between the Catholic *Ligue* and Henri but it was not until 1588 that he threw in his lot with the Protestants following *la journée des Barricades* (12 May). Stafford sent William Lilly to report on this to Elizabeth. Henri had violated the privilege of Paris by sending in foreign (Swiss) troops. Henri, duc de Guise, led a popular uprising to take control of the city. Barrels (*barriques*) were used to 'barricade' the streets. The French king was subsequently forced to flee the capital. Henri de Guise was assassinated at Blois in December 1589.

A divided France also suited Philip II perfectly, as he was keen for the French not to interfere in his planned invasion of England. Philip attempted to invade England in 1588 with an Armada of 138 ships, 7,000 sailors and 17,000 soldiers. A Spanish army waited in the Low Countries for transportation. In fact, many of Henri's subjects soon showed their support for the Spanish. The French garrison of Calais intervened following the capture of a Spanish ship by English sailors. Men of the *Margaret and John* of London had taken a Spanish ship washed up on the coast. They were forced to give up their prize under fire from French artillery, which pierced their hull twice. At 'Newhaven' French artillery supported a Spaniard in a duel between two ships. Reports were also received that Frenchmen had cut the cables of six English merchantmen on the Seine. Many feared that the French would choose to support the Armada. Walsingham was informed that French ports had provided the Spanish ships with provisions, including corn. Beaten back by English ships, fireships and storms, the remains of the Armada returned to Spain, with the loss of around 60 ships and 10,000 to 15,000 men. The defeat of the Armada in 1588 was not only a victory for Elizabeth but also the Protestants of France and the Netherlands. The victory gave the English fresh military confidence.

The reconciliation between Henri III and Henri de Navarre was muted by the assassination of the former during the siege of Paris in 1589 by the Catholic Jacques Clément. So ended 300 years of Valois rule. Soon after, Philippe-Emmanuel de Lorraine, duc de Mercœur (1558–1602), *Ligueur* and governor of Brittany, offered to make the coasts of Brittany available to Philip II for a second Armada against England. This Spanish intervention caused alarm in England. Sir John Puckering declared in his speech at the opening of Parliament in 1592 that Brittany was seen as 'a Country of more facility to offend us than the Low Countries'.[50] The fact that several French ports sided with the *Ligue* was also a cause for concern. Lord Burghley declared that he preferred to have the friendship of Rouen and Le Havre than four of the best towns of the Spanish Netherlands.

Elizabeth mobilised the 'hands, purses and prayers' of her country in the struggle with the *Ligue*. She was reminded of the need for an aggressive strategy by Sir Walter Raleigh when he said, 'I hope also that you will remember it is the Queen's honour and safety to assail and not defend.' A prayer written later for English soldiers is revealing:

> *That which armeth us, is neither desire of enlarging our owne borders, nor thirst of blood, nor ravine of spoyle, but onely our owne just defence, onely to breake the power of our enemies, and to turne away the battell from our owne gates. For that if we sit still, and suffer them to gather strength, they will suddenly make a breach upon us, and destroy the mother with her children.*[51]

Nostradamus made an interesting prediction referring to *siècle I 93* (the year 1593):

> *Lion & cockerel; not too allied,*
> *In place of fear, one will aid another.*[52]

Does the cock represent France and the lion England? The cockerel was already recognised as a symbol of France. Of course, this is a matter of interpretation. Whether we accept it or not, these two lines are a good description of the Anglo-French alliance of the 1590s.

The parlous state in which the as yet uncrowned Henri IV found himself in 1589 was summarised in a *mémoire* made by Beauvoir-La Nocle. He remarked that Henri was in a better position before his accession, given that being on the defensive cost less. Now that he had an army, he would have to find ways to maintain it. The problem was that trade had ceased almost entirely and Henri was obliged to sell his own lands in return for cash. It was Beauvoir too who declared that Elizabeth was *le vray medicin de nos misères* ('the real remedy for our misery').[53]

From now on, the real pressure would be on Henri IV. He could not fight on all fronts simultaneously. The geography of France was in itself a challenge: the sheer size of the country was a significant problem. It was difficult to control the country's interior at the same time as defending the extensive coast and frontiers. In short, Henri had too much to defend and too much to attack. Furthermore, compared with the European average,

France had a large population, standing at around 13,700,000 in 1600 (in 1560 the total was 16,200,000). The population of England was, by comparison, minuscule. It stood at 2,980,000 in 1561, rising to 4,100,000 in 1601. A large population in a united country could be an advantage in times of foreign war but it was a handicap in a civil war. Given these two factors, it is not surprising that Henri took nine years to subjugate the whole of his country.

The strategy which he undertook in 1589–92 involved securing the territory between the Somme and the Seine. This would allow English forces to intervene directly via the port of Dieppe as well as the two estuaries. The area included lands which were a source of revenue for the Guises, and the taking of such lands would have served to weaken their power and to fill royal coffers. Later, as the war progressed, we see an effort to prevent the loss of Brittany. Here, the prince de Dombes (Henri de Bourbon-Vendôme, governor of Brittany) knew that he would not be able to rely on the king for reinforcements. Alone with 700 men in Brittany and facing a force of 4,400 Hispano-*Ligueurs*, Dombes appealed directly to Elizabeth for aid in November 1590.

The Royalists attempted to justify the presence of foreign Protestant forces in France in *Advis d'un François à la Noblesse Catholique de France*. According to their propaganda, published in Tours in 1590, 'The English and Germans are paid by us and interfere in our affairs … as little as we please, having no other retreat in this kingdom as the *marechaux de camp* give them in our armies. In a word, we use them not them us.'[54]

A new treaty was concluded between England and France at Greenwich on 16 May 1596. A treaty with the United Provinces signed at The Hague followed on 31 October, the 'Triple Alliance'. The Anglo-French alliance was revitalised with the presentation of the Order of the Garter to Henri IV. Henri had been elected to the Order in 1590, though he had to wait until 1596 for the ceremony. Elizabeth gave the reason that 'she had hesitated because of the uncertainty of his residence during these wars'.[55] It is most likely that his religious conversion was also a cause for the delay. William Dethick, the Garter King of Arms, was sent (paid 10 shillings per day as well as a 'reward' of 10 shillings) with the Earl of Shrewsbury and Sir Anthony Mildmay to invest Henri in September 1596. The journey of the diplomats to France took as much as a week, because of wind and sea conditions. They landed at Dieppe and were entertained by the governor, Aymar de Chatte. Following a few days of hunting, the party continued and were met by Guillaume de Hautemer who accompanied them to stay at the château de Clères, north of Rouen. Accommodation for the English in Rouen was provided by an Italian merchant named 'Cenamil'. Henri made a grand entry into the town. The ceremony itself was held on 10 October in St-Ouen Church in Rouen. The Fuggers and the court painter William Segar provide us with colourful descriptions. A sort of guide was offered to Henri IV, written by the Garter King of Arms, entitled *Statuts de L'Ordre de la Jarretière*. The book (now in the Bibliothèque de l'Arsenal in Paris) was bound in blue velvet and decorated with fleurs-de-lys and gold braid. Inside were nineteen folios of text in French. Two pages carried the arms of Henri quartered with those of England and France. According to one source, Henri did not have a high regard for the Order, despite all the pomp and ceremony. Nevertheless, he is known to have celebrated St George's Day at least once. One occasion was at the church of St-Pierre, Nantes, in 1598.

Following the ceremony, six heralds dressed in white proclaimed across Paris: 'Both sovereigns bind themselves to the defence of their realms and thrones and promise each other everlasting protection and assistance. All those who would cause these Powers detriment or offence are threatened by them with war and destruction of their lands and subjects.'[56]

THE MONETARY STATE OF FRANCE

The political will was directed by France's monetary situation. The historian John Black identified the precarious financial state as being at the heart of the problem and added that 'French statesmen lost all hold on the international situation'. The French Crown had fallen into a vicious circle. Part of the responsibility can be traced back to the reign of Henri II. The collapse of the bank established in Lyons by Henri left the French Crown with a debt of 25,000,000 *livres*. One consequence was the loss of credit with European bankers. The situation was exacerbated by declining revenue. The rebellion of La Rochelle, for example, deprived the French Crown of much-needed revenue from the salt tax.

Charles IX had sought a loan from Elizabeth but this does not seem to have materialised. In 1569, Sir Henry Killigrew informed Sir William Cecil that Charles was obliged to send a jewel with a value of 300,000 crowns to Venice as security on a loan for 100,000 (*livres?*). Elizabeth would have been reassured and even encouraged by a letter that she received in September of the following year from Sir Henry Norris, her

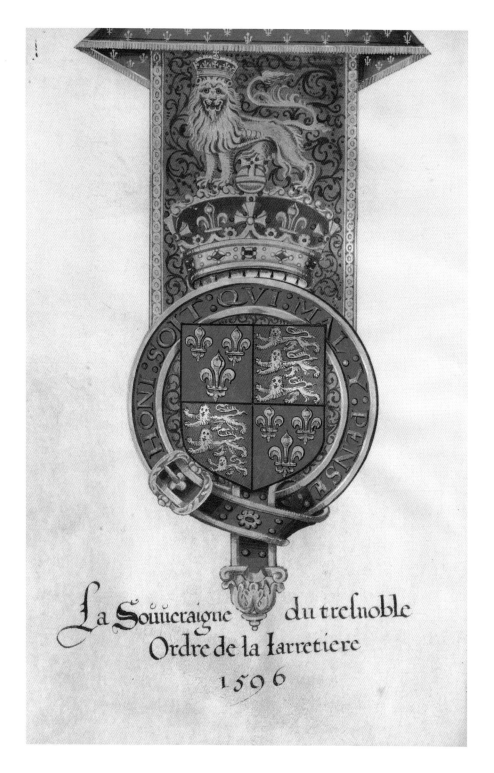

Book of the Order of the Garter presented to Henri IV, 1596, by William Dethick
(c.1542–1612). Bibliothèque de l'Arsenal, Paris, MS 2307

ambassador in Paris. She was informed by this letter of Charles's massive debts. These were so considerable (37,000,000 *livres*) that a sudden attack against England would have been out of the question. In 1574, there was a shortfall of 16,000,000 *livres* in the royal coffers before the start of the fifth war. Catherine hoped to obtain loans in Italy, in Venice and Florence, as well as Lyons, but without success.

By 1577, the debts had risen to 100,000,000 *francs*, according to Sir Amias Paulet. We also know that Henri III was looking for a loan of 1,200,000 crowns in 1584. At the end of his reign, the public debt stood at an unbelievable 245,000,000 *livres* (£24,500,000). The financial position remained critical at the accession of Henri IV. During the 1590s it was said that there were more *doublons* in France than native *escus de soleil*.

THE PROTECTION OF COMMERCE

At the heart of the new *rapprochement* was the protection of commerce. In the short term, the capture of Calais in 1558 was actually an economic blow to both countries. By protecting commerce, both governments could assure customs duties. With the disruption of trade caused by war, the ordinary revenue from the customs (known as the *Pipe*) would of course fall. The quest to re-establish a *staple* in continental Europe mobilised and maximised Elizabeth's efforts. The *staple* was the concentration of exports of English wool in a single place, which facilitated the collection of taxes. Catherine de' Medici was also enthusiastic about the question of commerce between the countries. 'Free trade' had been established, in theory, by the treaty of Troyes in 1564. Catherine was ready to see the re-establishment of the English *staple* in France (previously situated in Calais). The *staple* was administered by the *Merchant Staplers*. Catherine uses the word *fondicq* in her letter of 28 May 1572. She saw the advantages of this system for both countries. A clause for the establishment of a *magasin, etape, hanse ou fondic de draps & laines d'Angleterre, ou autres marchandises* ('warehouse, storehouse, guild or staple of cloth and wool from England, or other goods') was included in the treaty of Blois. Charles IX was particularly worried, following the massacre of Protestants in Rouen, that English merchants would leave.

Another important trade route was the river passage on the Garonne to Bordeaux. There was a long tradition of English merchant vessels making the voyage to transport wine. Despite the risks, the wine trade continued with England during the wars. In the first war, for example, the wine merchant

John White travelled to Bordeaux disguised as a Flemish merchant. He succeeded in transporting 200 barrels of wine to Middelburg in two vessels from Hamburg using false papers. Sir Edward Horsey received a patent to grant licences to sell wine in 1570. A new grant was given to Sir Walter Raleigh following Horsey's death in 1583. Prégent de la Fin, the vidame de Chartres, also sought to make a profit from the wine trade. He sought permission to import 600 barrels of French wine tax-free to England in August 1593. The tax on wine was an important source of revenue for the English government, with a value of five shillings per tonne.

A certain level of commerce with the *Ligue* was tolerated. Henri IV permitted Caen and Dieppe to trade with *Ligueur* towns in Normandy and Picardy, allowing the sale of their goods in return for cash to fill their own coffers. He also wanted to collect revenues from the sale of salt from Brouage. He complained to his English allies, who had become used to stopping his merchantmen.

THE FRENCH ARMY IN CRISIS

The promise of English aid against Spain was regarded as being crucial in the face of the crisis in the French army. This period of crisis lasted more than two decades, from around 1573 to 1597. In the mid-sixteenth century, the French army could be regarded as one of the best in Europe. Henri II's conflict with Imperial forces (including the English) nourished its efficiency. The army's reputation was founded largely on the indigenous cavalry and artillery supported by foreign mercenaries.

By the end of June 1563 the crisis had become serious for the forces besieging Le Havre. Charles de Cossé, maréchal de Brissac, wrote incessantly to his brother about the lack of money to pay his soldiers. The Rhinegrave sent four letters to Catherine in the space of five days (on 3, 5, 6 and 7 June), warning her of unrest in the army. In his letter of 6 June, he told her:

> *Madam, each day I do not see any progress for my relief either in men or equipment. Even the French … are leaving, not having any money to live.… Mine are likewise malcontent to live on borrowing. I am weakened daily and our neighbours are being reinforced.*[57]

The Rhinegrave also took the opportunity to renew his request for compensation to cover his own personal costs. He asked for a donation of land and the confirmation of his rights. On 3 June he wrote to Catherine, 'everything is dear … the soldier cannot live off air [alone].… Where there is hunger and necessity he becomes disordered.'[58] The twenty-three companies of French foot were three to four and a half months behind in their pay. Charles was obliged to ask for 100,000 *écus* (£333,333 6s 4d) from the city of Paris. On 18 June, Brissac wrote to Catherine explaining that without money and provisions, the soldiers and pioneers were on the verge of deserting. As the historian James Wood has shown, the French Crown struggled to maintain an army in the field for longer than two or three months through its own means.

The French forces fighting in harmony during the first war showed what they were capable of. Fresh divisions, however, led to a decline that would last more than two decades. The reason was quite simply battle fatigue; too many campaigns and too many losses combined with a chronic lack of money. Failure before La Rochelle in 1573 blunted the army's cutting edge.

A good barometer of the French army of the sixteenth century is the state of the artillery. It was the real 'jewel in the crown'; an arm forged during the Hundred Years War and improved in the struggle with the Habsburgs. James Wood identifies a decline of the royal artillery under the tensions of the wars. The situation had become acute by May 1573. The decline may also be linked to the resignation of Jean d'Estrées as *Grand Maître de l'Artillerie* (Master of the Ordnance) on 1 August 1569.

English gunners were in demand in France. Boulogne requested that some be sent in 1590. In 1591, Henri IV asked for as many as twenty English gunners to be sent to Normandy. Two years later, in 1593, a request was made for more English gunners as it was noted that the French took little care of their pieces, causing damage to them. According to Ottywell Smith, one English cannon lent to the French was damaged by the gunners, who placed too much powder in the piece and did not give it time to cool.

The French cavalry, most of whom were raised by the nobility at their own charge, could not be counted on to remain in the field for long. Coligny said of his own volunteers, 'they talk only of returning home when things do not turn out as they wish'.[59] Later, Henri IV admitted to Sir Roger Williams that 'he could not absolutelye comand his Nobilitie and dispose of them as he would, for that they served withoute Paie upon their own Expenses, and therefore would retourne at their pleasure to their Houses'.[60]

The English horse could not compete with the French in terms of numbers but they were appreciated for their quality. Describing a company of English horse under Champernowne, who saw action in 1569, the historian Antoine Varillas comments, 'The English were truly so well mounted that the horses of their riders neither ceded for their size nor for the vigour of those of the French men-at-arms.'[61]

Meanwhile, the real crisis was in the quality of the infantry. Throughout the sixteenth century, the French Crown preferred to recruit mercenaries as infantry so that they frequently formed fifty per cent of forces. The reason was that French infantry was *fort médiocre* ('very mediocre'). In the eyes of François de La Noue, the nobility had not been attracted to joining the infantry. He called for the formation of three *légions*, each made up of 2,000 men, in Picardy, Champagne and Burgundy as a way of enticing more noblemen to join. In 1564, noblemen generally took charge of thirty lancers. These included, for example, Morvilliers at Boulogne, the Rhinegrave at Vitry-le-François and Vielleville at Metz. This was in contrast to England where infantry raised for service in France and the Netherlands attracted gentlemen. The high population of France was not in itself a guarantee of the quality of recruits. Writing in 1597, Francis Bacon in his *Essays* considered that 'the middle people of England make good soldiers, which the peasants of France do not'. It is also Francis Bacon who informs us of the view held by Henry VII. He declared to Parliament, 'France hath much people and few soldiers. They have no stable bands of foot. Some good horse they have, but those are forces which are least fit for a defensive war.'

Sir John Norris was himself disappointed by the French soldiers sent to support him in Brittany. He described them as 'the worst that ever I sawe, as themselves wyll confesse'.[62] Not only was the quality lacking but also the quantity. Norris pointed out the need for more men to garrison towns. He did not know where these could be found. He reported that Brest was full of peasants and that there was a distinct shortage of harquebusiers, apart from those of Jean de Beaumanoir, marquis de Lavardin.

The foot companies (of all kinds) were not always maintained at full strength. The situation in Picardy in 1597 may be cited as an example. Here, according to William Lilly, the companies were 'reduced almost to fifties'.[63] Lilly also observed that there were brave men in the French ranks but that they were 'most boys and worth nothing. Of these their garrisons are stuffed full.'[64] During the siege of Amiens, the Spanish spoke of the 'base and unworthie French and how when they come, wee make accompt wee have nothing to doe that day, but play at Cardes, or sleepe upon our Rampart'.[65]

One consequence of the state of the French infantry was an augmented dependence on foreign soldiers. This over-dependence on such mercenaries was an inherent weakness. Swiss, Germans and Italians all served in the royal army. Italian mercenaries (*condottieri*) such as Martina, Carresecchi, Tortorelli and Orsini had led their soldiers to France since the first war.

Though the royal army frequently had enough horsemen, they were often lacking in pikemen. The pike was an essential weapon in forcing the breach of fortifications. Even though most Swiss soldiers carried pikes (nine out of ten in 1567), very few wore corslets (breastplates). Only one in ten of the men of the twenty Swiss companies wore a corslet in 1567. The men attacking the breach of a stronghold were at a clear disadvantage. The English pikemen, made braver by a little more protection, were therefore an important asset. Furthermore, by the end of the sixteenth century, the hardness of Greenwich armour was equal to that of Augsburg, giving a hardness of nearly 400 kg:mm². Soldiers such as Nicolas Harlay de Sancy, the then colonel of the Swiss in French service, even called for the replacement of the Swiss by Englishmen. In his own words, 'I have suggested employing English instead of Swiss for a long time as much to facilitate filling the companies as for they will serve on all occasions which the Swiss do not do.'[66] Bouillon held the same opinion. One reason why Sancy and Bouillon wanted to replace their Swiss with English was for economy. They believed that they could have 1,500 Englishmen for the same price as 1,000 Swiss.

In the same way, the horsemen were essential in an open war or on the field of battle but they were less useful in siege warfare against trenches. The duc de Bouillon did not like to dismount his cavaliers to fight against infantry in the trenches. This was a contrast to Brissac who had used *dragons* (dragoons), mounted infantry, back in 1554. Then, faced with a lack of horsemen, he was obliged to mount infantry. The effort to raise the siege of Cambrai in 1595 is an example. Henri IV had enough horsemen but he was lacking in infantry. The few Swiss he had would not serve for lack of pay.

'ALL AT SEA'

In 1585, the French ambassador Michel de Castelnau declared that Elizabeth was 'the Queen and Goddess of the sea'.[67] The importance of the English fleet becomes clear upon examination of the state of the French fleet during this period. The French fleet that appeared off Portsmouth in 1545 was made up of more than 200 vessels but, according to the historian Jan Glete, following the treaty of Cateau-Cambrésis in 1559, 'France would disappear as a naval power until the 1620s'. French maritime power was fragmented and proved difficult to harness under the Crown. French ports still maintained the old tradition of operating their maritime affairs independent of central government.

The decline was predetermined by the central problem: the lack of money. The empire of the ship-owner Jean Ango collapsed owing to the *pénurie* of the royal treasury. Ango had been a key figure in the campaign against England in 1545.

The incapacity of the French fleet to take the offensive or to mount a counter-invasion of England would have been one reason why Catherine did not wish to continue the war after the fall of Le Havre. It was therefore unlikely that Henri Valois, then duc d'Orléans, would gain the English throne by force as in Jean Passerat's *Chant d'Allegresse…* of 1564:

> *That Charles one day, having conquered them in war,*
> *To his brother will give the sceptre of England.*
> *Oh God what joy he will have in his old age*
> *When the Mother shall see her two children Kings?*[68]

The royal fleet also showed its weakness during the sieges of La Rochelle. Even though a squadron of galleys had been sent from the Mediterranean under Filipo Strozzi and Antoine Escalin des Aymards, they were unable to prevent relief from reaching the town. The defeat of the French fleet of sixty ships sent to the Azores in 1582 by the Spanish was yet another failure for the policy of French expansion. The battle of Ponta Delgada took place on 26 July 1582, when among the losses was Strozzi.

Henri IV's lack of money would have similarly prevented any aggressive policy at sea. Henri did attempt to reverse the situation by imposing a tax on maritime transport aimed at paying for a fleet.

The French fleet also had an inherent weakness. It was essentially made up of two fleets which were rarely combined, those of *levant* (based in the Mediterranean) and *ponant* (on the Atlantic seaboard and in the English Channel). The sending of galleys from the Mediterranean to fight in the Channel took time. This was also a risky manoeuvre for the galleys, which were ill-suited to the waters of the Bay of Biscay and the Atlantic. During the first war, the order was given for Gaspard de

Pontevès, seigneur de Carcès, to take the galleys from the Mediterranean. The situation was aggravated during the conflict with the *Ligue* when Carcès became one of its leaders. Even though Toulon remained loyal to the Crown, the main port, Marseilles, went over to the *Ligue*. The king's galleys were therefore obliged to remain in *levant*. Henri's weakness at sea led him to do the unimaginable and pursue an alliance with the Ottomans. Even though he solicited and won the support of a Turkish squadron, his own galleys were required as a counter to the *Ligue*. Meanwhile, the English ambassador at Constantinople, Edward Barton, attempted to prevent the Ottomans from putting to sea. He also offered to mediate a peace between them and the emperor. His actions frustrated the French, leaving the ambassador in France, Thomas Edmondes, with some explaining to do. Some Englishmen doubted his wisdom. There was a real concern that peace in the east would allow the Spanish to turn their German mercenaries against England. The château d'If, which guarded the approaches to Marseilles, was taken in April 1597 but returned to Henri only the following year.

Recent French expeditions overseas had ended in failure. Sailors were still alive who remembered the landings on the Isle of Wight in 1545. More recent were the memories of the disaster that awaited the French fleet en route for Scotland in which vessels were either wrecked by bad weather or captured.

The weakness of the fleet was apparent as early as 1562–63 when the French Crown was unable to cut communications between England and the ports of Normandy. Operations would have no doubt been aggravated by the taking of so many vessels by the English at Le Havre. In May 1563, sailors were sent from England to return with fifteen French ships. One of the vessels, the galley *Eleanor*, was given as security by the Huguenots. The *Eleanor* was based at Portsmouth and reconstructed in 1584. Evidently, the weakening of French maritime forces strengthened those of England. By the end of June 1563, Captain John Bryan had taken as many as twenty-three Breton and Norman vessels. Captains Appelyard and Jones took four and six vessels respectively. The Huguenots also played their part. The historian Raphael Holinshed informs us that by 6 February 1563 François Clerk had captured eighteen vessels. The value of these was estimated at £50,000.

The French royal fleet lacked large warships. Charles IX maintained a permanent royal fleet of only fifteen galleys, holding the opinion that this number was sufficient to defend the coast. The size of vessels in the

French fleet had perhaps also been limited by diplomatic pressure. A survey of the size of merchantmen at La Rochelle in 1563–64 indicates that French ships were also on average much smaller than others in Northern Europe. The dissolution of the Franco-Scottish alliance similarly deprived the French fleet of any support from Scottish ships, as had been the case in 1514.

As in the army, there was also a lack of gunners in the French navy. Aymar de Chatte, the governor of Dieppe, wrote to the Earl of Essex requesting English gunners to serve in French vessels in 1598.

The problem was exacerbated further by a lack of leadership and by what the historian Michel Vergé-Franceschi describes as *que confusion* in the *Amirautés*. In 1589, the admiral of the French navy was Antoine de Brichanteau, marquis de Nangis, who was not at all interested in maritime affairs.

The critical position of the French navy was confirmed during negotiations when Henri IV offered both men and vessels to aid England. Cecil retorted, pointing out that he had no ships: 'Your vessels? But you sell the skin of the bear [before having killed it]. I know well that the king hasn't any.'[69]

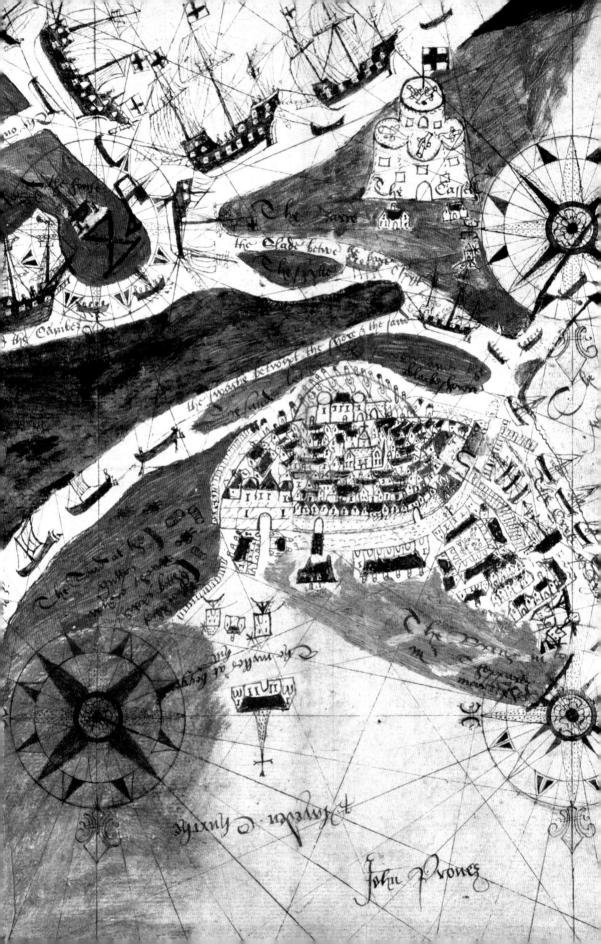

The Castell

The Barre

the Slade betwe the bare clyff

the fyffe

the swarthe betwyxt the shore & the same

blacke heron

The Cavibez

The land at

John Crones

Haven. Nuxthe

CHAPTER TWO

METHODS OF INTERVENTION

ELIZABETH AND THE ALLIANCE OF THE 'FIVE FINGERS': THE 'PROTESTANT LEAGUE'

*E*ngland was not the only Protestant country to intervene in the wars in France. Others also made alliances to counter the Catholic threat. Initially this was informal, as the Protestant parties did not wish to provoke the formation of a Catholic counter-league. Writing in 1573, the Venetian ambassador, Sigismondo Di Cavalli, described the alliance between La Rochelle, England and the German princes, 'The understanding between these heretics is like a solid mass which only moves by a common consent'.[70] The alliance culminated with the Concordat of Magdeburg on 15 December 1584. England, France, Holland, Denmark and Scotland formed an alliance known as the 'Five Fingers'.

Sir William Cecil had originally envisaged paying German princes to send men to fight in France in July 1562. Efforts to involve the German princes are apparent from the level of English diplomatic activity. Sir Henry Knollys visited them in the autumn of 1562. Their number did not facilitate the task. The count palatine, the landgrave of Hesse at Kassel (by procuration), the dukes of Saxony, Zweibrücken (Wolfgang of Bavaria, d.1569) and Württemberg, followed by the king of Bohemia, were all on the list. Knollys also visited the emperor at Frankfurt. Diplomatic activity was again intense in 1569 (this time Sir Henry Killigrew), in 1577 and then in the mid-1580s. German diplomats visited England in 1585. The English ambassadors saw several German princes in 1593 and again in 1598.

The German princes had been quick to follow England's example in 1562. Christoph, count of Oldenburg, for example, offered to serve with 4,000 horse and 8,000 infantry. Cecil described Oldenburg as a 'notable,

Rye Harbour, Sussex (map produced between 1572 and, possibly, 1595), by John Prowse (detail). The National Archives (TNA), MPF 1/212

grave and puissant Captayn, and fully bent to hazard his life in the cause of religion'.[71] One of the most ardent supporters of the Protestant cause was Johann Casimir, Count Palatine of Simmern. As he wrote to Elizabeth in 1569, 'It is to be feared lest, if a proper medicine is not applied in time, this disease may spread to other members.'[72] Casimir, yet another suitor to Elizabeth, made his name as a mercenary leader and was elected to the Order of the Garter.

Besides the religious cohesion, Elizabeth also found common ground politically with the German princes. They too feared the unification of the Low Countries with France. It was with their complicity that Elizabeth found a way to continue to intervene in France. The employment of *Reiter* (German mercenary soldiers) to invade France from the east would enable Elizabeth to continue to support the Huguenots and keep any French enemies, potential or real, busy at home. The diplomat Thomas Wilkes concluded a secret treaty with Johann Casimir on 11 April 1575. By this treaty, Elizabeth would support the conduct of an army of between 15,000 and 16,000 men going into France. Like Elizabeth, Casimir also saw the civil wars as an opportunity. It did not take much to draw him into the war except the promise of riches. He also sought payments from the French themselves. He was interested in regaining authority over Metz, Toul and Verdun (the *Trois Évêchés* lost as recently as 1552). All this escaped him, but he received assurances of compensation in 1576 including the duchy of Étampes, the *seigneurie* of Château-Thierry, jewellery, precious stones as well as 12,000 *écus* in gold as pension and 700,000 *écus* in silver to pay his army. Henri de Navarre made his own agreement with Johann Casimir in 1577. Later, as king, Henri dealt directly with Casimir. As with Elizabeth, he was never enthusiastic about presiding over the dismemberment of his country. When Casimir offered money to Henri in return for land, he was again refused.

The death of the duc d'Anjou in 1584 pushed Elizabeth to strengthen her links with other Protestant countries. The treaty of Magdeburg was important. It was kept secret to avoid Imperial and Catholic reactions. As Sir Horatio Palavicino later remarked, the German princes did not like to put things in writing.[73] It is probable that Thomas Bodley was sent to Magdeburg. In May 1585 we find him on a visit to the duke of Brunswick.

Elizabeth also wished to establish an alliance with the Protestant powers of the north: Denmark and Sweden. Erik XIV of Sweden was another suitor to Elizabeth: he had proposed to her while she was still a princess. Between 1563 and 1570, Denmark was too occupied in the Seven Years War against Sweden to think about aiding the Huguenots. Once the war was over,

Frederick II of Denmark was free to participate in the general struggle. By 1569, Danish soldiers were looking for employment under Elizabeth. A certain Captain Clerk wrote to Cecil in the hope of finding work for 1,500 Scottish harquebusiers currently in the service of the Danish king. In 1571, Frederick II sent a letter to Elizabeth recommending Captain Jerome Minsinger. In 1585, shortly after the treaty of Magdeburg, Peregrine Bertie, Lord Willoughby, was sent to visit Frederick. One of his missions was to obtain aid for Henri de Navarre. Even though Frederick was Protestant, like Elizabeth he did not wish to aid rebels. For him, it was the duty of subjects to follow their prince. He believed that it was for God to protect the Huguenots and, at worst, they could always leave their native land. Meanwhile, Willoughby had success in negotiations with the Danish king. He agreed to the possibility of molesting Franco-Spanish vessels in the Oresund. It was said that Frederick had promised aid to Elizabeth of the order of 20,000 men and sixty vessels if war broke out with Spain. In 1586 he offered 2,000 horse for English service commanded by his own son. Furthermore, he contributed 100,000 *Thaler* to help pay for Casimir's army. The fact that Frederick visited England in person was a sign of the goodwill between him and Elizabeth. This willingness was still apparent in the 1590s when Denmark accommodated the fitting of a ship for Henri IV.

SUBSIDIES AND FINANCE

'You know that money is the principal nerve of war', as the comte de Montgomery wrote to the Earl of Leicester in 1563.[74] Elizabeth, we are often told, was frugal. Dozens of examples may be cited that support this point of view. However, economising in certain sectors allowed her to spend considerable sums in others. Her enterprises in France were not exercises in frugality. It is even tempting to say that Elizabeth was generous.

English money kick-started the wars of religion in France, money lent to the Huguenots by Elizabeth and English merchants. According to François de La Noue, the amount was as high as 150,000 *écus* (£45,000). We know that 50,000 *écus* (£15,000) were delivered to Coligny at Caen in the month of March 1563. It is also known that the first payment to the Germans (in June 1563) stood at 133,333 *écus* (£40,000).

The capacity to give generous subsidies to the German princes was in part made possible by a surplus in the treasury. In 1569, the surplus stood at £33,153, £140,298 in 1572 and in 1584 an impressive £298,954: in 1574, Elizabeth had become free of debt for the first time.

The history of Elizabethan monetary aid to France and the German princes is complex.[75] It took the form of loans and subsidies. A clear understanding is obscured by the number of secret clauses in treaties, for example the secret clause of Charles IX in the Peace of St-Germain in 1570. By this he was to give over two million *livres* to the Huguenots, to be used to pay for the support given by England and the German princes.

The largest single subsidy (£60,000) was made in 1569. The prince de Condé had sent the sieur de Cavaignes to England in 1568 to raise money from Elizabeth. This money was needed to pay the army, of 6,000 horse and 30 ensigns of foot, in all some 14,000 mercenaries, offered for service by Wolfgang of Bavaria, duke of Zweibrücken. During the 1570s and 1580s, the main recipient was Johann Casimir. In 1587, for example, Elizabeth found 100,000 *écus* to pay for an army to be raised under him. Later, in 1590, she lent 33,333 crowns (£10,000) to raise soldiers in Germany under Christian, duke of Anhalt.

The amount of money was important, but even large sums were worthless if they were not delivered to the army on time. The Elizabethan subsidies were essential in paying the *Eintrittgeld* (or *Anritgelt*) to German soldiers before the start of campaigns. It was a kind of incentive. Without this payment, numbers would have fallen short of required levels.

ELIZABETHAN SUBSIDIES TO GERMAN PRINCES (1562–93)

1562	Amount unknown	Count of Oldenburg
1563 (June)	133,333 *écus* (£40,000)	
1569	200,000 crowns (£60,000)	Wolfgang of Bavaria, duke of Zweibrücken
1575	50,000 crowns (£15,000)	Johann Casimir
1577	Amount unknown	Johann Casimir
1586–87	£30,937	Johann Casimir
1587	£8,000	Johann Casimir
1587	£30,468	Baron Fabien Von Dohna
1589–93	£10,000	Christian I, prince of Anhalt

Elizabeth also started to lend directly to the French Crown by the 1580s. In 1581, for example, she lent 100,000 *écus d'or sol* (£30,000) to François, duc d'Anjou, followed by the same amount the following year.

It was not the first time that the English had given money to the French. Between 1527 and 1529, £112,437 11s (including £49,148 in silver) was given to François I for his war in Italy.

For each loan, it was normal for the Crown to add interest of five per cent if the loan was to be repaid in months and ten per cent in a year. The obligation of 30 October 1589, for example, stipulated the payment of interest of £750 on the loan of £15,000.

English monetary aid proved essential to the Huguenots and Royalists. At Arques, at the moment of battle, Henri IV's Swiss pikemen changed sides because of a lack of pay. In the same year, Henri had to use cloth to a value of 10,000 crowns to pay a Swiss regiment. In October 1590, the *Reiter* started to mutiny, again for lack of pay. The following month, Henri was obliged to sell part of his ancestral lands. In Normandy alone, 300,000 *écus* were raised from the sale of Crown lands. Henri hoped to find new revenues from the sale of new hereditary titles, allowing him to pay his Swiss soldiers.

The non-payment of troops could prove catastrophic if there was also little booty, as at the siege of Rouen where, 'in the absence of the king, the soldiers, having not been paid, spread into the villages and abandoned their posts and all their duties'.[76] This came at precisely the moment of the approach of the duke of Parma (Alessandro Farnese, 1545–1592, governor of the Spanish Netherlands) with his relief force. According to Sir Philip Sidney, there was a greater reliance on booty in the French army than in England. He said that the soldiers 'as are used to serve without pay, so as they may have shew of spoil'.[77]

Henri IV's lack of cash came at a critical moment during the siege of Amiens. On 8 July 1597 he wrote to his minister of finance, Maximilien de Béthune, marquis de Rosnay (later duc de Sully), telling him that his men did not want to fight and asking for 4,000 *écus* for the artillery: 'today five gunners have already left and the other officers do not want to serve without money'.[78] He wrote again only five days later asking for 4,000 or 5,000 *écus* to allow him to continue the trenches nearer to Amiens: 'if our soldiers have no money they will never hold the trenches and I will be poorly served'.[79] The discontent of Henri's men came to a head on 26 September, the day following the capture of the town. Fires erupted within the king's camp at the Madeleine, and 'great thefts were made by the soldiers themselves of the finances of His Majesty'.[80]

Paying for an army for more than two months was difficult, even impossible, for the French Crown. Around 90 per cent of the army's costs were spent on wages. Henri IV even told the English ambassador that he needed money more than men. Sir Thomas Coningsby remarked upon this lack of money in Henri's regiments before Rouen:

> *This daie we sawe marche into the kampe twoe of the king's regiments of lawnce knights, where more pore people did I never see nor worse armed and attired … they growe dyscontented for wante of money, and yt is for assured that if her majestie be not a meane to detayne them they wilbe gone before we shall see the end of this service.*[81]

The English army in Normandy had the support of a government that was financially stable. Elizabeth benefited from certain reforms made during Mary's reign. This financial stability was mirrored in the state of the army and navy. The money was used to strengthen the fleet and the soldiers now generally had the luxury of knowing they would be paid on time. It was Elizabethan financial strategy that made English intervention possible, in 1562 as well as in subsequent campaigns. This was a combination of solid and opportunist policy based on traditional methods of revenue. The ordinary revenue included the payment of rents and the customs duties. The 'Fifteenth' and the 'Tenth' were a tax on each city, borough and town. In time of war, Elizabeth expected Parliament to authorise a subsidy. The subsidy voted by the Parliament of 1563, as well as two Fifteenths and Tenths and the subsidy of the clergy, brought in £249,722. In 1589, a double subsidy was requested and granted. The Parliament of 1593 granted three subsidies. These were payable in tranches: the last tranche of the subsidy of 1589 was due on 12 February 1593, that of 1593 in February 1597.

Elizabeth supplemented her ordinary revenue with the regular sale of land. Thus, for example, Sir Martin Frobisher purchased the manor of Whitwood near Castleford in Yorkshire for £948 17s 3½d. In the space of twelve months (between November 1589 and November 1590) Elizabeth amassed £126,000 from such sales. Other forms of revenue included forced loans and profits from the recoinage. (The recoinage of 1560–61 brought in a profit of around £45,000.)[82]

Further funding for the campaigns came from the counties. Those counties not called upon to provide men could be required to pay for the clothing of others. Cambridgeshire had to provide £31 5s for clothing twenty-five men destined for service in Picardy in 1597. Cambridgeshire, like other counties, was divided into 'hundreds'. In certain regions in the north of England, the county was divided into 'wapentakes', literally 'weapon takes', denoting their military origins. Each hundred in Cambridgeshire had to contribute the following:

Staploe	48s	Armingford	£3
Staine	39s	Longstowe	55s
Flendish	39s	Wetherley	57s
Radfield	39s	Thriplow	58s
Cheveley	22s	Papworth	45s
Chilford	44s	Northstow	45s
Whittlesford	39s	Chesterton	45s
Total:	**£13 10s**	**Total:**	**£18 5s**

The constables of the shire were ordered to deliver money at the Griffin Inn in Newmarket by 9 a.m. on 9 August 1597.

Elizabeth's financial readiness for the war in 1562 perhaps gives some indication of the early intention of intervention. Preparations for intervention in France were already well advanced by August 1562. In April that year, Sir Thomas Gresham had borrowed £38,558 on the Continent. This was not an enormous amount but it was enough to assist with preparations for war. According to Frederick Dietz, at the moment of the departure of English forces for Le Havre, most (or all) the foreign loans had been paid.[83] The loans taken at Antwerp stood at £306,113 by April 1562 and almost £500,000 by 1564. The annual interest on the Antwerp loan was fixed at 30,000 *écus*. The government had already paid all the debts from the first war by 1566. Elizabeth's reputation among European bankers was well founded. Her credit on the Continent was an important element in assuring the functioning of the war machine. Philip of Spain, despite the enormous potential wealth of his empire, would have been slightly envious of her.

A project was devised whereby the City of London would borrow money on the Continent. By this project, £100,000 would be borrowed at 5 per cent and then lent at a higher rate. The other aim was to deprive the enemy of money: 'That the same money beynge in the realme is therby withdrawen from the possebylyte of them havinge it that myght use it to the hurt of England'.[84] The City merchants were also ready to loan money to Elizabeth and the French. They paid for the flotilla of merchant vessels accompanying Sir Martin Frobisher to the siege of Crozon in 1594. The services of the Merchant Adventurers and the Staplers were also employed.

Meanwhile, opportunities also presented themselves from time to time, the taking of the duke of Alva's ships carrying money in 1568, for instance. Despite infuriating the Spanish, this effectively gave the government a free loan. Part of this money may well have been used to pay the subsidy for the prince of Orange and the duke of Zweibrücken the following year. The consequence of this action, however, closed off direct English access to Antwerp.

Elizabeth's monetary aid was channelled to the Huguenots through the German states. By the Treaty of Hampton Court in 1562, 100,000 *écus* (£30,000) was payable at either Frankfurt or Strasbourg. Of the £20,000 paid to the Huguenots in 1569, £7,469 was delivered via the Merchant Adventurers at Hamburg and the rest at London. The subsidy of 1575 (50,000 crowns) to Johann Casimir was payable at Cologne. Frankfurt was used again in 1590.

Plain cash was also delivered directly from England itself. On one occasion (1589), £9,000 in silver was placed in ninety bags, with £2,000 made up of *angels, pistolets* and *francs*. In 1581, four horses were used to transport money to the duc d'Anjou. When the count of Oldenburg offered his services during the first war, he stipulated that he wanted to be paid in English money. In 1568, the French *livre* had a value of 2s 2d,[85] giving around ten *livres* to each pound sterling.

La Rochelle paid for much of the English aid in salt. William Cecil records that the town shipped salt valued at £1,534 13s 3d in 1567. Wool from the region of Poitou was also used in lieu of cash. The town even melted down church bells to pay for provisions sent by Elizabeth. Cecil records that 41,628 cwt of bell metal, valued at £470 2s 7d, was shipped from La Rochelle in 1567. Jewels were similarly used as security for the £20,000 that she lent to Henri de Navarre and Condé. In the State Papers, we find a receipt given to her for 'a large necklace where there are twelve large diamonds, that of the middle in point, the eleven *en table* at the end of the said necklace, with three large pear-shaped pearls and twelve couplets of gold, each garnished with eight pearls … plus a ring … a large ruby and a large pear-shaped pearl which hangs at the end'.[86] The same pearl is perhaps visible in the *Pelican Portrait* by Nicholas Hilliard of around 1572–76. A pear-shaped pearl is also apparent on the effigy of the queen at Westminster Abbey. Henri IV had also later planned to use the 55.23 carat Grand Sancy diamond as security before it went missing. In 1569, Claude Haton mentions a lady in his memoirs, the *veuve* de Mouy, who had been sent as security to England for the Huguenot loans!

During the peace negotiations of the first war, the Huguenots stipulated, astonishingly, that the king would pay for the English and German soldiers sent to France: 'Item, the king was held to pay the reiters and foreigners, both German as well as English, money that the said prince and those of the cause was held to pay them and to send them to their countries with rations for them and their horses.'[87] Meanwhile, English persistence in holding Le Havre appears to have allowed Charles to renege on his part of the contract.

Finance could also come 'from source' in France. It is clear that Elizabeth hoped that intervention would be self-financing. This had previously been the case in English Calais, where a special tax on wool was levied to pay for works on the town's fortifications. In 1562, the Huguenots of Rouen set out the value of the revenue of Normandy for Elizabeth: the archbishopric of Rouen, 50,000 *livres* (£5,000); the abbey of St-Ouen, 10,000 *livres*; and those of Fécamp, 40,000 *livres* and the *gabelles salines* (salt tax) 50,000 *écus*. It was intended that the English naval squadron in the Gironde were to be paid directly by Bordeaux. A tax on goods carried by merchant vessels would cover the cost of their protection. It was also intended to take half the profits from the capture of Morlaix. In Brittany, Norris expected payments to come from taxes: 4 *couronnes* (£1 1s) on a *pipe* (477 litres) of wine and 3 *couronnes* (18 shillings) from rates on each chimney. Norris was also interested by the revenues of Paimpol. In particular, Elizabeth hoped to cream off the revenues from Rouen in 1591.

In the hope of procuring continued aid (including more men), Henri IV had to offer a carrot. He agreed to grant Elizabeth the revenue from Rouen, the richest city in the country, as well as Le Havre: 'The King obliges himself and his heirs, the most surely as can be done, that the said king shall accord to Her Majesty, her heirs and successors, in writing sealed with the great seal of France, before the landing in Normandy of the said troops, that Her Majesty and her commissioners shall receive … all the profit from all sorts of *tailles*, taxes, customs and rights which come from within and around the town of Rouen and Havre de Grace.'[88] There was an important clause, however, in that the towns would first have to be captured: 'Item, it must be understood that Her Majesty and her commissioners shall commence to receive the said commodities in the said town of Rouen or Havre de Grace as early as the one or other shall be reduced in obedience to the King.'[89]

Ottywell Smith estimated that the annual revenue of Rouen stood at £100,000 (1,000,000 *livres*). It was seen as the equivalent of a third of the total revenue of France. Many Parisian merchants had relocated to Rouen, thus augmenting the wealth of the town. In 1589, Smith suggested that the merchants of Devonshire, Lancashire, London, Yorkshire and Wales should lend money to Elizabeth to lay siege to Rouen. Smith himself came from Rochdale (where he was constable in 1566), a centre for cloth production in Lancashire. Elizabeth would have been content to see Rouen besieged in 1591 simply to assure the sale of English cloth in this town.

To better understand the scale of costs and the sums both lent and borrowed, it is necessary to make some comparisons. Just two years of war in France under Henry VIII cost almost £400,000. During Mary's reign in 1558, the Crown estimated that £153,500 would be spent on the war in only six months. This was divided as follows: £70,000 for wages and fortifications in the north (Berwick and the Scottish frontier), £72,500 on the fleet, including wages and provisions, £5,000 on the defence of the south coast and £6,000 on artillery, arms and armour. To give another example, between 1558 and 1570 the sum of £128,648 5s 9d was spent on the fortifications of Berwick.

ENGLAND: THE ARSENAL OF FRANCE

'Beyond the Rhine … that is where the seeds are sown that make the bread but the flour is found in England,' wrote Castelnau on 15 May 1577.[90] During this period, England profited from the wars to become a major exporter of cannon, cannonballs and gunpowder. Clothing and other provisions were also sent in great quantities. Supplies from England became vital to the war efforts of the Huguenots and then the French king. By 1572, Elizabeth was obliged under treaty to furnish France with *matériel de guerre* if France was invaded: 'Harquebuses, morions, gunpowder, sulphur, saltpetre & other similar things useful to beat back the enemy.'[91] The armaments 'industry' was sufficiently developed to be exportable in reasonable quantity. The centre of armour production in England was Greenwich. Cannon manufacture had expanded in the Sussex Weald during the reign of Henry VIII. The English gun founders provided a range of artillery in different sizes, for example cannons, demi-cannons, culverins, sakers, minions, falcons, falconets.

In the war with Sweden (1563–70) Denmark preferred to import iron cannon from England, as they were the only such items that could be delivered with speed. Speed was of the essence for the Huguenots and later for the French Royalists.

For the Huguenots, the acquisition of new pieces of artillery would not have been simple. Many of the foundries in France in the second half of the sixteenth century were in Lorraine. The extensive work carried out by Arthur Kennard shows that out of nine founders working in France during this period, at least four were based in Catholic Nancy. Furthermore, one of the others, Bartolomeo Campi de Pésaro, left France in 1568. Even though the names of some founders would have escaped this list (many cannon were subsequently melted down for recasting, which thus effaced the founder's name) it is apparent that Catholic Lorraine was an important centre of production. Further capacity would have been provided by the cluster of foundries between Langres and St-Dizier. A royal foundry had been established at Paroy-sur-Saulx by 1564, while the duc de Guise had his own at Charmes-en-L'Angle on the Blaiseron by 1576. It is probable that Protestant bell-foundries turned their art to producing cannon, as these were very similar professions. One probable direct consequence was the increase in coal exports from Newcastle to France. Coal was more efficient than coke in metallurgy and the production of arms, armour and artillery. For the period 1593–94 coal exports from Newcastle reached 9,889 tons.

Artillery trains of the period required extensive logistic support. In this respect, the royal armies held a clear advantage as the central hub was the Arsenal in Paris. The administration was moved from the Louvre to the Arsenal near the Bastille following the royal edict of December 1572. The pieces required care and attention. Once cracked, the cannon would have to be recast to avoid disaster. On the accession of Henri IV, the union of Paris with the *Ligue* effectively ended royal control of the Arsenal. This, and the sacking of the Arsenal by the local populace, left Henri even more dependent on English support. In short, the Huguenots and then the king came to depend on England to assure the momentum of war.

The scale of the supply of arms and munitions passing through French ports is apparent from the mosaic of records in the (non-exhaustive) table below. The records show that French ports frequently acted independently from central control. Governors such as René de Rieux, seigneur de Sourdéac in Brest, and Raymond Roger de Bernet in Boulogne ordered *matériel* directly from England.

On 7 February 1593 a request was made by René de Montbourcher, seigneur du Bordage in Brittany, who feared an attack by the duc de Mercœur. His 'shopping list' demonstrates that England was able to provide a full set of defensive kit: six pieces of artillery (to defend his castle), 2,000 cannonballs, 3,000 lbs of powder, twelve harquebuses, twelve muskets, fifty pikes and twenty-four halberds. A later record (10 August 1593) shows Bordage being allowed to purchase five pieces of artillery and 1,200 iron cannonballs.

Protestant La Rochelle received considerable supplies. Pieces of artillery were delivered to the port around the end of 1568, including, in December, six cannons, 3,000 lbs of powder and cannonballs. During the siege of 1573, 22 kegs of powder were delivered just at the moment that the defenders' reserves had run out. It was perhaps an English cannonball fired with English powder that killed Claude de Lorraine, duc d'Aumale, while he was aiming a cannon at the siege. The delivery of munitions continued afterwards. At the beginning of the eighth war, we find a licence for the export of powder to the port. Later, in 1592, the town received imports of 45.5 tons of artillery via the port of Meeching (Newhaven) in Sussex. This was the equivalent of at least 20 culverins.

The armies of the king required munitions on a much larger scale. One consignment in 1589 included 150 harquebuses, forty muskets, 300 lbs of powder, forty corslets, fifty halberds and 100 pikes. In the same year, 20 lasts (*c*.45,900 lbs) of powder with a value of £2,000 and 3,000 cannonballs (at a price of £383 17s) were sent to Henri. In June 1590 a further 50,000 lbs of powder crossed the Channel. The following year came a request for 40,000 lbs of powder. Later, in July 1597, during the siege of Amiens, La Motte was permitted to purchase 50,000 lbs of powder, 5,000 cannonballs, 600 pikes and six iron sakers; 4,000 or 5,000 cannonballs were deemed necessary for a campaign.

England also helped to supply French ships. In January 1590 the governor of St-Malo, Robert Maçon, seigneur de la Fontaine, sought a licence for the export of twenty-eight or thirty iron pieces of artillery for a 400-ton vessel under construction in Danzig. The pieces were to be sent to Denmark where the ship would be ready. Similarly, on 6 April 1591, permission was given for the shipping of twenty iron pieces to Denmark for a vessel ordered by Henri IV. This particular order included twelve demi-culverins and eight sakers. A further request was made directly by Henri to Elizabeth on 24 May 1592. He requested 'thirty or forty iron cannons' for his ships in Normandy. As may be seen, Elizabeth's refusal to send men to France in 1595 did not prevent the continued sending of arms and munitions.

Artillery and munitions could also be lent. Having been disappointed by Henri at Rouen, the English authorities demanded the return of everything that they had lent the French for the siege.

Year	Destination	Artillery	Arms	Armour	Gunpowder	Match	Ammunition
1568	La Rochelle	6 cannon			3,000 lbs		
1573	La Rochelle				22 kegs		
1589	Henri IV		150 harquebuses, 40 muskets, 50 halberds, 100 pikes	40 corslets	20 lasts & 300 lbs [46,200 lbs]		3,000 cannonballs
1590	St-Malo	28 or 30 iron pieces					
1590	Boulogne	4 falcons			10,000 lbs, 2 or 3 barrels of tar	2,000	3,000 [lbs?] lead for harquebus shot[92]
1590	Henri IV				50,000 lbs		
1591	Henri IV	20 iron pieces (12 demi-culverins, 8 sakers)					
1591	Henri IV				40,000 lbs		
1592	Boulogne				2 lasts		
1592	La Rochelle	45.5 tons					
[1592]	Brest		25 harquebuses, 12 muskets, 12 partisans	6 corslets	1,000 lbs	500 lbs	1,000 1½ lb cannonballs (for *falcons*)
1592	Henri IV (Normandy)	30–40 iron pieces					
1592	Caen		Copper to cast: 2 culverins, 4 sakers, 6 minions, 6 falcons				
1593	Brittany (request)	Up to 6 pieces	12 harquebuses, 12 muskets, 50 pikes, 24 halberds		3,000 lbs		2,000 cannon balls
1593	Brittany (permission)	5 pieces					1,200 iron cannonballs
1593	Normandy		Bronze culverin				
1595	La Rochelle	7 tons					
1595	Cherbourg	3 tons					
1595	Brest		100 pikes	50 sets of armour			
1597	Henri IV	6 iron sakers	600 pikes		50,000 lbs		5,000 cannon balls

England possessed natural resources for the manufacture of cannon: copper and tin. A bronze cannon was made using 90 per cent copper and 10 per cent tin. By the end of the 1560s, the price of a quintal (112 lbs or 50.8 kg) of copper was 65 shillings (£3 5s). The cost of copper for a single culverin therefore stood at £193.[93] The other English export that was vital for a modern army was lead, which was difficult to obtain elsewhere in Europe. Sources of lead in England included the Peak District of Derbyshire, the Mendip Hills in Somerset and around Richmond in Yorkshire. Lead, which melts at only 327.5°C, was the ideal material for making musket balls. In 1594, Ottywell Smith gained the monopoly for the export of lead to Normandy and Picardy for a period of seven years. This allowed him to sell lead at high prices or like *dorr* (i.e. gold).

The provision of powder was likewise essential to the effort in France. A lack of powder had prevented the capture of Avranches in Normandy by Henri de Montpensier, prince des Dombes, seigneur de Châtellerault (1573–1608), in 1590. The purchasing of powder in England held economic advantages as it was much less expensive than in France itself. The manufacture of gunpowder required supplies of alum, charcoal, potassium nitrate and sulphur. At least some of the alum exported to France may well have been used in the manufacture of gunpowder.

What was the importance of this powder in practical terms? According to William Bourne, 40 lbs of powder were required to fire a single shot of cannon, 18 lbs of powder to fire a culverin and 6.5 lbs for a falconet.[94] (Bourne also states that a 'last' weighed 2,400 lbs but contained 2,112 lbs of powder.) After 1588, the pound weight increased from 6,750 to 7,000 grains. Estimates varied due to the differences in sizes of artillery, though forms of standardisation had already been introduced. In 1591, the 'official' measure of powder for a cannon, today found in the State Papers, stood at 27 lbs. This estimate is particularly relevant as it appears to be linked to Essex's campaign in Normandy. It stated that a last of powder would provide eighty-five shots, therefore placing the amount of powder in each last at 2,295 lbs.

Based on this estimate, the four amounts of powder sold to Henri IV cited above (186,200 lbs) were enough to fire just short of 6,900 shots from a cannon and far more for a smaller piece. Some of this powder would have been taken by the harquebusiers and musketeers. According to one 1591 estimate, a company consumed 640 lbs of powder per year. Based on a company strength of 135 men, that translates as around 4¾ lbs per man. The exact level of powder would have depended on its quality and wastage due to humidity.

The domestic supply of cannonballs could not be assured in France. During the siege of Chartres in 1591, the *Ligueurs* set fire to the forges used for making the besiegers' cannonballs. They took back with them not only the munitions that they found but also the foundry workers.

The discovery of graphite at Borrowdale in the Lake District in the north of England facilitated the manufacture of cannonballs (or 'gunstones'). According to legend, graphite had been discovered by shepherds who had used it to mark their sheep. Later, graphite was used by artists and the first pencils appeared in the 1560s. It was found to be easy to work with and therefore ideal for making moulds. The graphite moulds speeded up and improved cannonball production. The size of the balls in relation to the barrel of the cannon was crucial. Balls of correct size were essential for accurate, effective fire. A ball placed correctly in the barrel required less powder. Production was aided further by the increased development of the metallurgy industry in the Sussex Weald.

England was not the only provider of *matériel*. As we have already seen, at least one vessel was ordered from Danzig. Cannonballs also came from as far away as Sweden.

England was an important provider of clothing, shoes and leather goods to the French armies throughout the period. On 8 February 1569 Odet de Châtillon sought the right to export shoes and leather for Condé's army, requesting 200 skin *buffles* and *buffelins*. A *buffelin* or *buffletin* ('buff coat' in English) protected the soldier against sword cuts. In September 1589, a London merchant named Eloye Echard (Orchard) was authorised to transport 300 sets of clothing, each consisting of a cassock, doublet, breeches and stockings, as well as 200 pairs of boots and 1,000 pairs of shoes. During the siege of Paris by Henri IV in 1590 Beauvoir-La Nocle, the French ambassador, obtained the right to export 3,000 skins, 1,200 pairs of shoes and 240 pairs of boots tax-free. Similarly, the king's Swiss were also clothed by the English. Several times, the merchants of London and Ottywell Smith sent shipments of clothing. In 1597, Henri IV wrote directly to the queen informing her of the need for 'up to 6,000 outfits composed of shoes and mandyllons [a coarse cloak] for our men of war'.[95] Consequently, on 17 December, David Chamberlain was authorised to export free of tax 6,000 outfits (mandyllon, breeches and stockings).

The French also looked to England to supply horses. Henry VIII had established studs following losses of horses in the Wars of the Roses. Hampton Court (Surrey), Eltham (Kent), Tutbury (Staffordshire) and

Malmesbury (Wiltshire) were all chosen as sites. Horse breeding was regulated during Elizabeth's reign. In 1580, each man holding a park of more than one square mile was required to keep two mares. Those with four miles had to keep four mares. The authorities also regulated the height (scantling) of horses. There was an apparent lack of horses in Royalist France. Henri IV was at one point unable to find a horse for the English ambassador Stafford. Henri and De Sancy asked the Earl of Essex for help in finding horses for his stables. Henri wanted twenty geldings and De Sancy wanted the same number of hackneys. At Dieppe, we find the import of all the horseman's accoutrements, including bridles and stirrups. As many as 1,600 horseshoes were shipped from England to supply Henri's army in 1589, together with 70,000 nails. On the eve of the battle of Arques, Henri's army included around 1,000 horse. Meanwhile, the Guises had established their own stud at Éclaron near St-Dizier.

Other English exports included candles. Candles weighing altogether 14,000 lbs were ordered for the army in 1589. The following year Gourdan, the governor of Calais, was granted a warrant for their export. On 22 June 1592 Favet of the Dieppe garrison was authorised to transport 50 tonnes of wood from Southampton.

As well as the manufacture and export of *matériel*, there was also an important trade in the re-export of goods. For example, large quantities of saltpetre were imported from Pomerania before being re-exported to France. This was one way of avoiding duty. Le Fort, for example, sought permission to take goods from German states and the Netherlands to France via England. In this way, he had to pay only half the customs duty.

France was also important to England as a supplier of *matériel*. In the space of a single month (June 1596) 27,200 ells[96] of canvas from Normandy were imported through the port of London alone. The canvas would have found its way back to France in different forms. Much of the canvas would have surely been destined for use on Elizabethan warships. Indeed, it appears that France was the near-exclusive source of sailcloth for the Royal Navy. The canvas was also used in the manufacture of doublets, tents and cartridges for artillery. The gunner William Bourne also advised on using canvas to camouflage artillery emplacements in fortresses.

Of course, arms and clothing alone would not have been enough to maintain an army in the field. During the siege of La Rochelle, the English looked to supply the town with victuals. A vessel with a cargo of biscuits was intercepted by the royal fleet. In February 1589, six vessels were sent to Dover to transport grain to France. In September 1589 the French army in Normandy was 'in some distresse of vyctuell'.[97] Four Huguenots were required to transport provisions from Rye to Dieppe, including:

boar	32	
pork	200 stone	(1271.20 kg)
powdered beef	200 stone	
flour	40 barrels & 40 quarters	
wheat	40 quarters	(508.48 kg)
oats	110 quarters	(1,398.32 kg)
barley	50 quarters	(635.60 kg)
cheese	2,000 weight	(908 kg)
butter	50 barrels & 40 firkins	(+ 40.86 litres)
biscuit	30,000	
beer	90 barrels & 10 tonnes	

The men were also allowed to transport as much as 500 quarters (6,356 kg) of wheat from Norfolk.

In 1592, the counties of Kent and Sussex found a solution to their surplus of grain by exporting their harvest to the French army. The surplus had previously forced a collapse in prices. The project also facilitated the provision of English armies in Normandy and Brittany. A list is to be found in the State Papers detailing a request by Sourdéac at Brest for: 4,000 lbs of butter, 2,000 lbs of tallow, twelve cowhides, 100 tons of wheat and 30 barrels of beef as well as 50 *coustez* of lard. Wheat was subsequently transported to Brest by the merchant Jean de Gast in the same year.

Apart from legal exports, there was also an illicit trade in goods. For this reason, it would be difficult to establish a comprehensive list of all exports to France. Reports from English agents in French ports give us some indication of the scale of this trade.[98] This commerce was born out of the ravages of war. Entire regions of the country had been emptied of cattle, sheep and horses. The lack of these animals at home in turn increased demand for leather, wool and tallow from England. Walter Orme informed Sir Robert Cecil in 1594 that 'forbidden' goods with a value of £10,000 had been transported from Rye. Orme summed up the situation: 'some water will pass by the mill that the miller sees not'.[99]

The other side of the war effort involved preventing supplies from reaching the enemy. A proposal was put forward to stop the export of Newcastle coal to France. The total interdiction of commerce with the enemy was not an easy task. At least one English Catholic travelled to Dieppe in an attempt to buy iron artillery. In 1591, Thomas Cely, a sea captain, in a letter to the Lord Treasurer, the Lord Admiral, wrote how the enemy had had too many pieces over the last fifteen years. The *Ligueur* town of Avranches in Normandy, for example, had managed to procure six cannons from England via St-Malo. In 1591, it was thought that as many as 100 pieces had reached the Spanish port of San Sebastian, having been shipped via La Rochelle. Sir Thomas Fettiplace later brought this issue before Parliament (in 1601). Similarly, Aymar de Chatte's lieutenant in Dieppe complained that English gunpowder had been shipped to *Ligueurs* at Rouen and Le Havre. This complaint was well founded, as the English courier, Wells, reported the shipment of powder to Le Havre in beer barrels. These two ports also received imports of English leather. A royal proclamation was made in 1591 prohibiting traffic with rebels of the French king.

> *And now her majesty, finding that this popular rebellion against the said King is fed and maintained in sundry port towns of France, and specially in Normandy and Brittany, where the people live by bringing to them foreign merchandise, and by vent of their own, and by receiving of succors of victuals and munitions of war from foreign countries without which the rebels in their ports could neither continue their rebellion nor yet relieve their fellow rebels within the land…*[100]

Sir Horatio Palavicino noted how an English barque delivered materials for the fortifications of Calais held by the Spanish in 1597.

INTELLIGENCE

Elizabeth's first ambassador in France, Sir Nicholas Throckmorton, found that the Guises held too much power and that his task of information-gathering would be difficult. He consequently asked to be recalled, but without success. Throckmorton's arrest when he was twenty-four miles from Orléans deprived Elizabeth of an important liaison with Condé and his army.

Sir Francis Walsingham kept as many as fifty-three agents and eighteen spies in foreign courts. The most productive agents were William Lilly and Ottywell Smith. Both were well informed. William Lilly, brother of John Lilly the playwright, was a talented man. He offers us a penetrating analysis of both men and events. One reason for this is that Lilly was accepted in Catholic circles, where he was still believed to be a Papist. Lilly worked as secretary to the ambassador Sir Edward Stafford, and was sent by him to give an account of the *journée des Barricades* in 1588 to Elizabeth. Lilly was also called upon by Henri III to inform Elizabeth of the assassination attempt against him. He became *chargé d'affaires* following Stafford's departure in April 1589. He was still in this post in 1591. Lilly fought at the battle of Ivry in March 1590. He maintained links with another ambassador, Sir Henry Unton. He knew Unton while he was still a student at Oxford. Hoping to return to England, Lilly made contact with Unton in 1595. He accompanied the English army in Picardy in 1596–97. During this time, he remained in contact with his patron the Earl of Essex. Lilly knew France and the French very well. Edward Reynolds, secretary to the Earl of Essex, remarked that he was 'too much infected with some of their humours; and yet I take him to be faithful and honest to my lord'.

Thanks to Walsingham's network, the government remained forewarned against plots and invasion. The French churches in England were also important sources of intelligence. The church ministers themselves became informers, denouncing Frenchmen who did not attend church services. One minister of the French Church in London was Robert le Maçon, known as La Fontaine, who lived in Blackfriars. He acted as agent to Henri IV and would later play an important part in negotiations leading to the treaty of Greenwich in 1596.

Only shortly before the massacres of 1572, Sir Francis Walsingham had written to Lord Burghley to inform him, 'Suche of the religion here, as before did sleepe in securitie, begin now to awake and to see their danger.'[101]

Walsingham played an important part in establishing links during his time in Paris. His contacts included La Noue, Hubert Languet and Du Plessis-Mornay. During the 1580s he employed the services of the Calvinist François de Civille. Jean Bodin, author of *La République* (Paris, 1576), visited England in 1581. It was Bodin who warned Walsingham of a Catholic plot against England. The ambassadors remained alert even in times of peace. We know that in 1583 Sir Edward Stafford sent out spies along the coasts of Brittany and Normandy. Stafford even used his own wife as a spy. She gathered intelligence from other ladies at court:

> *There are four women ... Madame Villeroy, Retz [wife of Albert de Gondi du Perron, maréchal de Retz, 1522–1602], princess of Condé and Nevers, that have all the news, and most secretest devices of the Court; for there is never a one of these ... that hath not either a lover, an honourer, or a private friend, of the secretest Council ... that will almost hide nothing from them.*[102]

One result of this was that, by 1584, Lord Burghley was able to annotate his copy of *Theatrum orbis terrarum* (1570) with detailed intelligence of French ports. This included notes on the names of governors and garrisons of ports such as Blaye, Nantes and La Rochelle. He noted, for example, that Blaye was held by two companies reduced to fifty men each.

The number of letters written varied depending on events. One ambassador, Sir Thomas Edmondes, was reprimanded because he wrote too often! 'I could wishe yowe, not to send so often letters with so small advertisementes but to reserve the writing of your letters to matters of moment and necessarye to be knowen.'[103]

A Scotsman, John 'Lislye', was also providing information directly from France. He appears to have served at the very heart of the Ligue. A certain 'Lyill' served the duc de Guise[104] for a period of fifteen years, followed by the duc de Mayenne.[105] He became *intendant* to Mayenne in February 1596. We find a 'Lisle' in the service of the duc de Mercœur in 1598. In December 1590, the authorities had sought specific information from him including 'what number of men of war be kept in Rouen, and who hath the commandment of them as generals and captains?'[106]

Much of the cost of this intelligence-gathering was paid for by the Crown; however, there were exceptions. Elizabeth was unwilling to pay for certain expenses incurred by Sir Anthony Mildmay in 1599. As Sir Robert Cecil explained to Sir Henry Neville, 'all things being now quiet' and that there was 'much to be learned without great payments'.[107]

The embassy of Sir Henry Unton of August 1591 to June 1592 was constantly on the move. With the port of Dieppe as the start and the end and staying within the limits of the Somme and the Seine, the embassy travelled as far as Noyon and Compiègne in the east. During this time, Unton covered more than 750 miles (*c*.1,200 km) following Henri IV. He maintained contact with his own court via Dieppe. Once in the field, instructions would be sent to the ambassador in the form of a 'packet'. One of these packets is clearly illustrated in the portrait of Sir Anthony Mildmay in 1596.[108]

The letters were frequently written in code. This practice was a guard against the copying of letters. One code fell into enemy hands when Throckmorton was arrested. Sir Henry Unton feared the loss of his letters following the lifting of the siege of Rouen. He took the precaution of writing in code and sending at least one courier disguised as a peasant. Sixteenth-century codes were quite basic. That of Unton was made by simple substitution:[109]

a	b	c	d	e	f	g	h	i	k	l	m	n	o	p	q	r	s	st	t	v	w	x	y	z
1	3	4	7	8	9	5	6	a	b	c	h	i	k	d	e	f	l	m	n	&	b	c	q	w

Sir Anthony Mildmay, Ambassador to France, 1596, by unknown artist.
Emmanuel College, Cambridge, ECP19, © The Master and Fellows of Emmanuel
College, Cambridge

Unton simply assigned different names to important people. Elizabeth was called 'Emanuel', Henri IV 'Vespasian' and Philip II 'Bersa'. Unton was known as 'Adamus' and the Earl of Essex as 'Cyrus'. Place names were also replaced. Among others, England became '100' and France '200'. Brittany became 'Worcester' and Normandy 'Lecester'. In an effort to confuse the enemy even further, Unton's letters were mixed with insignificant numerals: ii, iiii, vi, viii, xii, xiiii and xv.

The mail was directed by the Master of the Posts. During Elizabeth's reign, this office was held by the Stanhope family: Sir John Stanhope held the post for life and was succeeded by his son. The royal post between London and Paris frequently passed through Dieppe and Rye. Thomas Randolph, the Controller of her Majesty's Posts, ordered Rye to keep three post-horses for this purpose. The payment for this service would be 20d per day as well as a rate of 2d per mile for each horse ridden, and 4d to the guide.

Official couriers were used as well as trusted personal servants. Couriers included the Frenchmen Nicolas England and Anthony Guérin. Nicolas England operated on the route from France from 1559 to 1562, carrying dispatches for Sir Nicholas Throckmorton. Stephen Davis worked on the England to France route during the same period as well as Henry Middlemore from 1560 to 1564. Francis Barlow, William Cathorne, Cawode, Henry Crampe, Rogers, Edward Tureur and Charles Wilson served Sir Thomas Smith during his embassy. Barlow was paid £36 13s 4d for carrying letters between England and Smith during Charles IX's tour of France in 1564. The warrant refers to carrying letters to and from the ambassador at Bar-le-Duc and Lyons. At the same time, letters from Sir Nicholas Throckmorton were confided to John Barnaby who was paid £22 for his services. Being a courier in a foreign country did present risks, as the Italian Baptista de Favori discovered in 1563. He was hanged at Rouen for carrying intelligence to England. Other couriers in the 1560s included Sawle, John Somers, John Spritewell, Tirrell (John or Henry), Nicholas and Richard Tremayne.

The time taken to send a letter varied considerably. News of the taking of the Spanish fort at Crozon, for example, on 7 November 1594 reached Sir Thomas Edmondes around 13 November. Lord Burghley, meanwhile, had to wait until the 17th of the month, ten days after the event.

No grand strategy would have been possible without a sound knowledge of the geography of England and its position in relation to the Continent. Cartography therefore had an important role to play.

There were a number of professional cartographers such as Christopher Saxton and Laurence Nowell as well as soldiers who produced their own campaign maps. The engineer Edmund Yorke provided detailed depictions of the sieges of the Normandy campaigns in 1591–92.

There were two great collections of maps in England during this period: those of Elizabeth and Sir William Cecil. Cecil sought to expand his collection by purchasing maps from the Continent. He thanked the ambassador, Sir Henry Norris, for sending him a map of Paris in 1566 and other maps of France two years later. Elizabeth and Cecil had the usual maps available in printed editions. The thirty-four maps of English counties drawn by Christopher Saxton between 1574 and 1578 would have been a useful tool in the recruitment and movement of forces. *The Mercator Atlas of Europe* by Gerhard Mercator (1512–1594) reproduced the map of Picardy by Nicolas de Nicolai.[110] *A Survey or Topographical Description of France with a new Map from the French* translated by John Eliot became available around 1592. Meanwhile, 'made-to-measure' maps were particularly useful. It is said that William Cecil always carried one particular map with him, the *General description of England and Ireland* by Laurence Nowell.[111] It is likely that Cecil carried this plan with him during the first war. Another map produced during the same period (1563) is that of Jersey.[112] A map of the western coast of Europe,[113] meanwhile, provided Elizabeth and Cecil with a panoramic view for their strategy.

It must be asked whether faults on the maps could have caused errors in strategy. It is probable that the maps gave Elizabeth and Cecil a false impression of access up the Seine towards Rouen.[114] The available maps do not show the meanders or the steep banks of the river. The bends could easily hide dangers and artillery could fire on approaching vessels. The maps show us a river which is wide, offering easy access to Rouen. One consequence was that the sending of relief proved more difficult than expected. It is possible that Elizabeth also lacked a detailed map of Brittany until the one produced by Radulphus Treswell in 1594.[115] Such a map would have allowed her to watch her men advance towards the interior of France.

(*overleaf*) Map of Brittany, 1594, by Radulphus Treswell. British Library, Cotton MS Augustus I.ii.58. © The British Library Board

Bretanie
1594

A Scale of Leagues

part of Britaigne from Sir John Norris
1594

Despite Cecil's efforts, there were still a number of 'blind spots' in English intelligence. In 1591, Cecil complained to his ambassador in France, Sir Henry Unton:

> Whan you wryt of Journeys and Removes from Places to Places, I, beyng desyrous to consider therof, do view the best particular Charts of Normandy and Pycardy, but I cannot fynd sondry of the Towns or Castells named by you in your Voyadge, and therfore I pray you bestow but in a Shete of Paper the Situation of such Places as are not expressed in the Charts and yet mentioned in your Letters.[116]

Maps also allowed the English to take the fight beyond the old world. The French colonies in America now became targets. Thomas Stukeley devised a project to strike against French colonists in Florida. Mention must be made of one advocate of overseas expansion in particular, Richard Hakluyt.[117] He served as chaplain to the ambassador in Paris, Sir Edward Stafford, between 1583 and 1588. Part of his mission was to gather information on French and Spanish voyages in America. In Paris he met the royal cosmographer André Thevet, who lent him a manuscript by René Goulaine de Laudonnière, *L'Histoire notable de la Floride*. This was published by Hakluyt in London in 1586.

THE COMMANDERS

It was said of Elizabeth, 'She was not a warrior but she knew how to produce warriors.'[118] The commanders and captains were normally selected by the Privy Council. The commanders could also nominate captains for the Council's approval. For example, Sir John Norris nominated Edward Spring in 1591. In theory, the selection of captains was based upon merit. Certain men saw action in the two services, on land and at sea. One captain before Amiens in 1597, Arthur Chichester, from Pilton in Devon, had previously served as captain on the *Larke* against the Spanish Armada of 1588.

There was an element of competition between captains to participate in the campaigns. Many appointments came through personal ties. This willingness among the gentry was combined with an obligation of service.

The role (or at least the image) of the English commanders under Elizabeth had changed considerably since the reign of her father, Henry VIII. Henry had been inspired by Henry V. He took an active role in the military life of his country. He led armies to France, fought at the battle of the 'Spurs', and was ready to defend Portsmouth against the French fleet in 1545. As the supreme commander of forces, he took all the credit for victories. Henry's presence on the field of battle would have made a difference. In terms of motivation, the soldiers would have been pushed by the presence of their sovereign. After his death, neither the young Edward VI nor Mary filled the vacuum. Of course, Elizabeth was never present. She could not encourage the garrison of Le Havre to defend at all costs, just as she could not lead a cavalry charge at Rouen or an assault on the fort at Crozon. The notion of her presence before the army at Tilbury ready to meet the invincible Armada is firmly implanted in history. With their queen at home, the commanders assumed greater authority in the field.

French armies encountered similar experiences through the centuries. French kings had not always had a lot of luck. Jean II was captured at Poitiers in 1356 and François I was doing quite well until his capture at Pavia in 1525. Henri II appeared before Boulogne in 1550, hoping to make an impression. His death in a tournament did not help the prestige of kings. It was for the French *maréchaux* to take the glory in their place: Bertrand Du Guesclin (and also Jeanne d'Arc) during the Hundred Years War and later Montmorency and Guise.[119] During the first war in France, Charles IX was in much the same position as Edward VI. Still too young, he was not allowed by his mother to get too close to the trenches before Rouen and Le Havre. As the soldier and author Piere de Bourdeille, seigneur de Brantôme, informs us, *la reyne le tenoit tousjours de court* (in other words, the queen always kept him on a short lead).[120] Catherine's importance is captured in the painting *Troilo Orsini coming to the aid of Catherine de' Medicis* by Anastasio Fontebuoni, depicting events in 1569. Even though Catherine was herself present at the sieges, it is not certain whether she was a good leader of men. The same is perhaps also true of Henri III. Thus the appearance of Henri IV served to fill a long-standing vacuum.

Some of the commanders, such as Lord Willoughby and Sir John Norris, gained iconic status at home. The ballad *The Brave Lord Willoughby*, to music by John Dowland, did much to augment their reputation in popular culture. This would in turn have earned them the confidence of their men.

In Holland, the English were 'partners', with considerable authority being granted to the Earl of Leicester. In Ireland, the English operated without any allies except for loyal Irishmen. In France, except at Le Havre, they played a supporting role. The powers of the English generals were therefore limited.

As Elizabeth could not be present on campaign, all instructions for her commanders had to be written before their departure. Ambrose

Dudley received 'ordinary' instructions as well as 'special' ones, the latter kept secret from the Huguenots. The instructions issued to Sir Thomas Baskerville reflect the experience accrued by the time of his expedition in 1596.[121] The queen gave written authority to Baskerville's successor, Sir Arthur Savage, to 'invade, burn, spoil, destroy, and do all manner of other hostile acts upon the enemies of our good brother the French King'.[122]

On occasions, the commanders simply chose to ignore Elizabeth's orders altogether. Willoughby left England with his army, despite having received the order to stay. Norris also ignored his recall from Brittany. Sir Roger Williams 'forgot' his duty by marching his men to the suburbs of Paris and to Noyon. As for the Earl of Essex, Elizabeth was not always kept informed: 'Where he is, or what he doth, or what he is to do, we are ignorant.'[123]

One ideal candidate to lead the men to France would have been William, Lord Grey de Wilton. With his death in 1562, the army lost one of its most experienced commanders.

Ambrose Dudley, Earl of Warwick *(c.1530–1590)*

Dudley was chosen to lead the first campaign in Normandy in 1562. It appears that he was selected by Elizabeth in place of his brother, Robert. Warwick was named *locumtenentem et capitaneum principalem et generalem ducemque primarium et gubernatorem* ('lieutenant and principal captain and primary leader, general and governor'). In some ways, he was following in the footsteps of his father, John Dudley (1504– 1553), who had served as governor of Boulogne during its occupation. Warwick had military experience, having assisted in the subjugation of the revolt of the Duke of Norfolk[124] in 1549. He had experience of siege warfare, having been present at the taking of St-Quentin in France in 1557. There are differing points of view from his contemporaries. Sir John Hayward wrote that he was 'a man more noble in birth then any other abilitie'.[125] Raphael Holinshed was somewhat kinder, calling him 'a right hardie and valiant capteine'.[126]

Ambrose Dudley, Earl of Warwick, by unknown artist. © and reproduced by permission of the Marquess of Bath, Longleat House, Warminster, Wiltshire
In this portrait, the gift given to Warwick by Elizabeth may be seen. He mentions this in a letter to his brother during the siege of Le Havre: 'I ... have ye quenes token she sent abowt my neck'.[127] The gift encouraged Warwick who wrote, 'my thincks I shuld do wonders'.[128]

Edward Fiennes de Clinton *(1512–1585)*[129]

Clinton, born in Scrivelsby in Lincolnshire, had also already seen action in France. He had held the post of governor of Boulogne[130] and, following the loss of Calais, he led an attack against Brittany with 250 ships. In 1564 his title was 'great admiral of England, Ireland and Wales and of the dominions and islands of the same, of the town of Calais and of the marches of the same, of Normandy, Gascony and Aquitaine and captain general of the fleet and seas of the said kingdoms of England and Ireland'.[131] He was present at the marriage of Princess Marguerite to Henri de Navarre in August 1572, days before the St Bartholomew's Day Massacre.

Peregrine Bertie, Lord Willoughby *(1555–1601)*[132]

Willoughby spent a significant amount of time serving on diplomatic missions. He accompanied the duc d'Anjou to Antwerp in 1582 following his stay in England. As mentioned previously, he was later sent to the Danish court. He served under the Earl of Leicester in the Low Countries and was named as governor of Bergen-op-Zoom. He took part in the capture of Axel in 1586. Willoughby took charge of the army following Leicester's departure. He led the expeditionary force to Normandy in 1589, and was present at the siege of Paris in the same year. It is probable that he would have led further campaigns to France were it not for ill-health.

Willoughby was the patron of the composer William Byrd, whose work *In Fields Abroad* perhaps makes direct reference to Willoughby's campaign in France.

Sir Roger Williams *(1539/40–1595)*

Williams, who was born in Penrhos, Monmouthshire, was present at the battle of St-Quentin in 1557. He is often more closely associated with the campaigns in the Low Countries. Like other commanders, he also performed diplomatic functions. He came to distrust the French, 'I durst not truste the most of them further than I see them.'[133]

Williams did not enjoy good relations with Norris but he made his mark in 1589 when he played a role in achieving victory at the battle of Arques. Seeing Henri's army break up, he cried, *Noblesse française, retournez; voulez-vous fuir, votre roi étant en terre?* ('French noblemen come back [!] do you wish to flee [with] your king lying on the ground?').[134]

*Peregrine Bertie, Lord Willoughby, c.*1589, by Isaac Oliver (1558–1617).
Victoria & Albert Museum, London, P.5-1947
The white sash in this portrait, worn by forces loyal to Henri IV,
indicates that it was painted during his campaign in France.

Williams accompanied Willoughby during the siege of Paris. He also had
knowledge of the art of fortification. It was thanks to his experience that
he was able to write on this subject in *A Briefe Discourse of Warre.*[135]

Williams sought to lead his own campaign to France. He managed
to keep his own companies in Normandy despite orders to join Norris
in Brittany. He was also able to conduct operations semi-independently
from the Earl of Essex. Williams never married but we know that he kept
a mistress during the campaigning in France.

Robert Devereux, Earl of Essex *(1565–1601)*

A favourite of the queen, Essex, originally from Herefordshire, was not from the same mould as puritan commanders such as Willoughby. He clearly amused himself on campaigns as if he were still at court. Essex was recently dubbed a 'glorified juvenile delinquent' by John Nolan,[136] but he was well liked by his captains and he established good relations with the French. One reason for his popularity was perhaps his generosity. During the siege of Rouen he awarded as many as twenty-six knighthoods in the field. It is certain that Essex had energy, as Sir Thomas Coningsby said of him: 'such a body hath he made of yron, supporting travaile and passioned in all extremyties, that the following of him did tyre our bodies, that are made of flesh and boane'.[137]

Essex and his retinue certainly impressed Pierre Palma-Cayet:

> *As for the person of the said Earl of Essex and those of his suite, nothing can be seen more magnificent, because, entering Compiègne, he had before him six pages mounted on large horses, dressed in orange* [Devereux tangerine] *velvet all embroidered in gold. He had a velvet orange cassock all covered in stones. The saddle, the bridle and the rest of the horse's harness were dressed the same. His clothing and the ornament of his horse alone were worth more than 60,000 écus. He had twelve tall footmen and six trumpets who sounded before him.*[138]

John Clapham said that he was 'more stiff in his own opinions than was thought convenient for a man of his employment, that had ofttimes the chief commandment and direction of mighty armies'.[139]

During the Normandy campaign, Essex was reproached for a charge which he ordered against a larger force of horsemen. Fortunately, the 'enemy' that he found were allied French Royalists! One of the duties given to ambassador Sir Henry Unton was to keep an eye on Essex, 'givinge him understandinge from tyme to tyme, what judgement is had of his actions, approving to him such as are good, and such as you shall knowe or heare to be commended; and informing him of such thinges as you shall understand to be contrary, givinge him good advice to reforme the same'.[140] A similar duty also fell on Essex's deputy at Rouen, Sir Thomas Leighton.

Robert Devereux, Earl of Essex, c.1591, attributed to Nicholas Hilliard (1547–1619). National Portrait Gallery, London, NPG 6241, © National Portrait Gallery, London

Sir John Norris *(c.1547/50–1597)*[141]

Norris, born at Yattendon Castle in Berkshire, was arguably the most capable of all the commanders. He had already served in France under Coligny during the second war. We find him in France again between 1569 and 1570 during the third war. He had been a key figure in the preparations to repel the Armada. He was named Lord Marshal of the army assembled at Tilbury.

Sir John Norris, attributed to Sir William Segar (*c.*1564–1633).
Private Collection (original unlocated; reported stolen). Photographic Survey,
© Courtauld Institute of Art, London

Sir Thomas Baskerville *(d.1597)*

Baskerville's early life was spent in Herefordshire where he became the JP from around 1569 to 1585. He had gained experience in the Low Countries, having fought at Sluys in 1587. He was knighted in 1588 by Peregrine Bertie, Lord Willoughby. Baskerville was also a member of the Privy Council and MP for Carmarthen Boroughs from 1593. He had long experience of combat in France, having already participated in three different campaigns. He served during Peregrine Bertie's campaign in Normandy in 1589 in the role of Sergeant Major and he was captain of 180 men. Later, under Essex, he took part in the siege of Rouen. Baskerville was left in charge of the army at Dieppe when Essex went to visit the French king. He later served as sergeant-major at the siege of Crozon (where he was wounded) in 1594 under Sir John Norris. In 1595 he was at Panama. Baskerville returned to France, this time to Picardy. His wife, Mary, despite being 'great with child', also went to France.

Sir Arthur Savage *(fl. 1597)*

Savage succeeded Baskerville at the siege of Amiens. Savage had previously seen action in the Low Countries, at Flushing, before taking part in the Portugal expedition. The band of men under Savage was one of ten companies retained for service in Brittany in March 1591. We find him in the Low Countries in May 1592, participating in the siege and capture of Deventer. In November 1592 his men were at Flushing. Savage participated in the expedition to Cadiz in 1596 at the head of a company of 200 foot. It was here that he was knighted by the Earl of Essex. In 1596, he was captain of a company of men from Sussex.

RECRUITMENT AND ASSEMBLY

The size of the English armies varied. At Le Havre, the garrison reached 6,000 in December 1563. 7,843 men had been sent by June 1563. By comparison, in October 1563, there was a garrison of 1,433 men at Berwick and at Zutphen in 1586 we find as many as 6,696 (more than the number of Dutchmen). Willoughby had as many as 4,000 men under him in Normandy. 4,000 is also the number of men with the Earl of Essex, who preferred an army that was both small and efficient. A force of 5,000 men was planned to serve under Norris in Brittany in 1591, though this was later reduced to 3,000. This comprised twenty companies divided into three regiments: those of Sir John Norris, his brother Sir Henry and Sir Anthony Sherley, commander of horse. The following year, Elizabeth offered 4,000 men and 100 horse supported by seven pieces of artillery.

By the treaty of Blois in 1572, the signatories undertook to provide 6,000 infantry and 500 horse if the other was invaded. They would also have to send eight ships with 1,200 soldiers. In 1581 the secret league included the provision of 6,000 men and vessels with 1,200 men as well as the right to buy munitions freely if invaded. By the treaty of Magdeburg, Elizabeth promised as many as 12,000 men to support the Huguenots. The numbers found in the treaties, however, do not always correspond with reality. Even though the treaty of 1596 stipulated a relief army of 4,000, a secret clause limited intervention to only 2,000. Historians such as Davila state that 4,000 Englishmen were present at the siege of Amiens. The figure of 2,000 is supported by figures in the Acts of the Privy Council.[142]

All subjects between the ages of sixteen and sixty could be called upon to serve with the exception of the clergy, the lords in Parliament (and their servants), the Privy Council and the justices of the peace. Charles Cruickshank points out nuances in these obligations. The Church provided men as a sign of loyalty, while the recusants were forced by their disloyalty.

The more opulent classes and institutions such as the colleges of the universities of Oxford and Cambridge provided soldiers and/or arms and armour. Those with a revenue of between £5 and £10 per year were obliged to equip a man on foot. Those with a revenue of more than £1,000 would have to provide sixteen horse, eighty suits of armour, fifty helmets and twenty harquebuses.[143]

England already possessed something approaching a permanent army during this period. The soldiers in garrisons such as Berwick could be called upon to serve elsewhere; in particular to reinforce expeditions overseas. 300 of the best men at Berwick, for example, were sent to support the garrison of Le Havre in June 1563. The numerous fortresses protecting the coasts, such as Deal, Southsea and Pendennis, were important sources of artificers and gunners necessary in a modern army. These men lived, slept and ate beside their arms day after day. The other professional body, the Yeomen of the Guard (the queen's bodyguard), comprised 146 men at the beginning of the 1560s. Although few in number, they performed the function of a *corps d'élite*, serving as a model for the rest of the army.

The army was divided into regiments with a colonel and then ensigns or companies of between 100 and 200 men. The average size of a company was 135 men. On paper, this number appeared as 150. The captains received 10 per cent of the soldiers' wages ('dead-pays'). The same system was also applied to the navy ('deadshares'). Deadshares disappeared in the navy in 1582 with the introduction of new rates of pay. By this system, pay varied according to the vessel.

It happened that the number of veterans in an army could outnumber the new recruits. This was the case in the 'new' army of Sir John Norris in January 1593, when they made up more than two thirds of the force.

Elizabeth herself estimated that a period of three weeks was required to mobilise an army from the moment that she gave the order. The levy, roll and equipping of the soldiers were conducted by the Lieutenant of the county or, in the counties where this post was vacant, by sheriffs and justices of the peace. In time of war, the justices could also oversee rolls of harness and men. The Lieutenants did not hold their office on a permanent basis but were appointed as and when necessary. One person could be the Lieutenant of more than one county at once. Each Lieutenant also normally had a deputy. A deputy was particularly necessary if his senior was the Lieutenant of more than one county, when the deputies often performed the function of Lieutenant. The analysis of papers relating to this office reveals an efficient administration. The Lieutenant was also responsible for the militia.

A kind of 'fallow field' system was used in the levying of men. This held numerous advantages. It meant that no single county would carry all the burden of recruitment or the departure of many men at any one time. The system similarly softened the consequences of war, as no single county would be left with all the sick and wounded on their return; neither would they have all the deaths to lament.

For the expedition to Le Havre, men were recruited in Essex, Devonshire, Gloucestershire, Norfolk, Suffolk and Wiltshire. For the expedition in Normandy of 1589, Kent, Hampshire, Sussex and London provided men. The army of the Earl of Essex in 1591 was made up of men from twenty-one counties (including London). The fact that the largest levy came from Yorkshire was an exception. For the Brittany campaign under Norris, men were drawn from at least fifteen counties. In the beginning, the army was divided into twenty companies. Men were drawn from thirteen counties for service in Picardy in 1596 (see below). The men raised for service in France from Cheshire, Derbyshire, Lancashire and North Wales in 1596 are not included: they were redirected to fight at Cadiz in Spain.

ORIGIN OF MEN RAISED FOR SERVICE IN FRANCE 1589–97[144]

	Normandy 1589	Normandy 1591	Picardy 1596	Total 1589–97
Bedfordshire	0	50	0	250
Berkshire	0	100	0	480
Buckinghamshire	0	100	0	380
Cambridgeshire	0	50	0	150
Cheshire	0	0	0	0
Cornwall	0	0	0	350
Cumberland	0	0	0	0
Derbyshire	0	0	0	0
Devon	0	0	0	750
Dorset	0	0	100	600
Durham	0	0	0	0
Essex	0	150	150	800
Gloucestershire	0	150	0	500
Hampshire	1,000	100	150	1,400
Herefordshire	0	0	0	0
Hertfordshire	0	0	100	600
Huntingdonshire	0	0	0	150
Kent	1,000	0	150	2,250
Lancashire	0	0	0	0
Leicestershire	0	150	0	150
Lincolnshire	0	300	0	300
London	1,000	300	450	4,420
Middlesex	0	0	100	250
Norfolk	0	150	150	450
Northamptonshire	0	200	0	450
Northumberland	0	0	0	0
Nottinghamshire	0	150	0	150
Oxfordshire	0	100	0	440
Rutland	0	50	0	50
Shropshire	0	0	0	138
Somerset	0	0	150	1,200

	Normandy 1589	Normandy 1591	Picardy 1596	Total 1589–97
Staffordshire	0	0	0	0
Suffolk	0	150	150	450
Surrey	0	50	100	200
Sussex	1,000	0	150	2,060
Warwickshire	0	150	0	150
Westmorland	0	0	0	0
Wiltshire	0	0	100	350
Worcestershire	0	0	0	0
Yorkshire	0	400	0	400
Wales	0	0	0	300
Total:	4,000 (3,600 excluding Dead-pays)	2,850	2,000	20,568

Between 1589 and 1597 the largest levies sent to France (at least on paper) came from London (4,420), Kent (2,250), Sussex (2,060) and Somerset (1,200). One reason was their proximity to France, while Ireland was more often the destination for men from the northern and western counties. Nearly all of the men raised in Welsh counties went on to serve in Ireland. The reasons were both economic and strategic. The transporting of men over longer distances took both more time and money. The total number of men raised for service in France during this period 1589–97 was 20,568, each contributing county finding on average almost 676 men.[145] This figure rises significantly if we add the men also raised during the first war together with sailors and volunteers. The figures should be compared with the levies for service in the Low Countries between 1585 and 1602. Fewer soldiers were sent here (18,180) than to France.[146]

The flexibility of the system allowed the rapid transfer of soldiers from one theatre of war to another. In 1589, for example, men were taken from Arthur Savage's company, ready to serve in the Netherlands, and sent to Normandy. In May 1591, Burnham was instructed to send 2,000 men and 100 horse from the Netherlands to France. Similarly, 2,000 men under Norris in Brittany were to be deployed in Ireland. Ireland was also the destination for 800 men who had participated in the taking of Amiens.

In the levying of pioneers, the English authorities had an easier task than Henri IV. At the critical moment during the siege of Amiens in July 1597 he was unable to find men to continue his siege-works. It must also be remembered that many mines in France were to be found in Lorraine, *pays ligueur.*

The county gaols were also a source of recruits. In 1563, the Privy Council authorised the release of prisoners condemned for acts of piracy in certain counties. Eight pirates were released from prison in Pembroke to serve in the navy. Thomas Fettiplace is another example. He received a pardon for acts committed before 12 May 1563. The famous pirate Sir Henry Strangeways, who had been condemned to death with his eighty men in 1559, was similarly released from the Tower of London. This policy was carried to extremes in 1597 when as many as 700 'vagabonds' were authorised to be sent to reinforce the expedition in Picardy.

At least the Earl of Essex was interested in the quality of his recruits. He wanted his own company of horse to be made up of tall men. Sir John Norris also insisted upon the quality of his recruits. He left a number of men from Somerset at Portsmouth whom he considered too weak to travel to France.

Mercenaries had previously been employed in the English army. During the reign of Edward VI, Italian soldiers served the English in Scotland. Edward paid German and Italian mercenaries during the rebellion in the south-west of England in June 1549.[147] In the reign of Mary, mercenaries were employed such as Gothart de Bochotz. During her war with France Sir William Wallerthum was named as colonel of 3,000 men from Saxony and Estonia ('Eastland') intended for the defence of England. Now, under Elizabeth, mercenaries were employed but they usually only saw service outside the zones where English forces were already operating.

The English armies sent to France were largely made up of infantry. The Earl of Essex had 350 horsemen, of which 250 were lancers. Lancers are clearly depicted in the plan of the siege of Rouen by Edmund Yorke.[148]

THE 'FREEBOOTERS'

Intervention was not confined to purely official means. Many men came to France of their own accord either to serve 'the religion', to gain profit or for glory. English gentlemen were free to participate in the wars as volunteers or 'freebooters'. Edward Berkeley is one example. He served during the second war, including at the battle of St-Denis. After this battle he joined a company of the prince de Condé. Following the death of the prince at Jarnac, he joined Henry Champernowne. William Norris served in the second war in 1567 (with his brother John). George North and Thomas Cotton were serving the following year and then Richard Patrick and Hugh Offley in 1569. In the same year, the young Walter Raleigh joined Henry Champernowne and his hundred horsemen as a volunteer (with Philip Burshide and Francis Berkeley). Henry Hastings, Earl of Huntingdon, proposed the selling of his land to fund his expedition to France (also in 1569). Sir William Russell also probably participated in 1576 as well as Matthew Sutcliffe. Roger Hussey and Edward Stanley fought under Henri de Navarre during the fifth war in 1577. In the same year, we find Christopher Carleill, John Norris and John Zouche involved in the fighting. Zouche, a veteran of the first war, saw action on the Île de Ré. Fulke Greville served as a volunteer in 1587 and was present at the battle of Coutras. The two brothers Sir Charles and Henry Danvers joined the forces of Henri IV following their exile from England. Eighty Englishmen chose to remain in France to serve Henri instead of returning home with the rest of Lord Willoughby's army. Sir John Burgh fought with distinction at the battle of Ivry on 14 March 1590. Henri IV made him a 'knight of the collarde',[149] as well as Sir Lee Brown who was also present. It was also at Ivry that Captain Roger Dudley was killed. The official figures state, very precisely, that there were 498 volunteers by 1592. Among the ranks was Sir William Sackville, son of Lord Buckhurst. He served under François de La Noue. He was present at the siege of Paris, and at Meaux as well as Lagny. He died during an attack on the village of Bures-en-Bray in February 1592. Scotsmen may also be mentioned. It was at the hands of Robert Stuart that Anne de Montmorency was wounded at the battle of St-Denis in 1567. He died some days later from a bullet wound to his spine.

Sir Anthony Mildmay was in France around 1575, during the fifth civil war. He may well have gone to serve as a 'freebooter'. One clue to this is the portrait by Nicholas Hilliard now in the Cleveland Museum of Art.[150] We know that Hilliard was in France from 1576 to 1579, so the portrait probably dates from this period. Mildmay is depicted in *tenue de campagne*, complete with armour. It is interesting to compare this with the later portrait of Mildmay in 1596.

Interestingly, some Englishmen occasionally found themselves fighting for the 'wrong' side, as Francis Vere later admitted. He had joined the duc de Guise.

LONGBOW VERSUS HARQUEBUS

A major change came with the decline of the longbow. During the second half of the sixteenth century, there was a heated debate between those for and against the weapon. A number of treatises were written by both sides. Those in favour included Sir Roger Ascham with his *Toxophilus* (London, 1545) and Sir John Smythe, *Discourses concerning ... the formes and effects of divers sorts of weapons ... and wonderful effects of archers...* (London, 1590). Later, a gentleman named simply 'R.S.' wrote *A briefe treatise, to proove the necessitie and excellence of the use of archerie* (London, 1596). Those against were in favour of firearms. They included Sir Roger Williams, *A Brief Discourse of Warre* (London, 1590), and Sir Humfrey Barwick, *A breefe discourse concerning the force and effect of all manuall weapons of fire, and the disability of the long bowe or archery* (London, 1591).

A matchlock weapon, the 'harquebus' weighed 7–9 lbs and had a barrel length of 39–43 inches. The calibre was around .58. They were often referred to as a 'harquebuse' or a 'hagbuse' during the period, directly from the French word *arquebuse*. Claude Desainlien's dictionary of 1593 gives the translation of *arquebuse* as simply 'hand-gunne'. Henry Barrett, writing in 1562, refers to the soldiers as 'hagbutters'. Later, during the seventeenth century, the term 'harquebusier' was applied to cavalry armed with short 'carbine'-type weapons.

Calivers weighed 10–12 lbs with barrel lengths of around 39–44 inches, calibres from .76 to .80. Desainlien translates this as *arquebuse à croc*. Muskets were more powerful, heavier weapons (typically weighing around 20 lbs) that required forked rests for support when firing. Musket barrel lengths were also longer (45–55 inches). The calibre of .80 to .92 could deliver a lead shot around twice the size of those fired from a harquebus.

English archers suffered two defeats at the end of the Hundred Years War, at Formigny and Castillon, at the hands of French artillery. Despite these failures, the tradition of archery continued in England for another century. The armies of Henry VIII that crossed the Channel still included large numbers of archers. Sir Roger Ascham argued that firearms and the bow should be 'so joined together that the one should be always an aid and help for the other, might so strengthen the realm on all sides, that no kind of enemy, in any kind of weapon, might pass and go beyond us'.[151] Ascham's influence should not be underestimated. He was tutor to Prince

METHODS OF INTERVENTION

Edward and later Princess Elizabeth. He joined the Embassy at the court of Charles V and became Latin Secretary to Queen Mary in 1554.

English archers had played a role in the defence of the Calais 'Pale'. They are depicted in a view of the attack on Guisnes in 1558 by Nicolas de Nicolai. The real decline began during the reign of Elizabeth. At the beginning there were still enormous reserves of longbows and arrows. In 1559, eight fortresses on the Isle of Wight held reserves of 1,040 bows. Furthermore, a bowyer was still employed here. The cost of replacing arrows would have been a concern for the authorities. Already, by 1554, a sheaf of arrows cost 2s 4d, more expensive than a bow (at 2s). Part of the legacy of Henry VIII in 1547 included nearly a million arrows. These would have cost £5,000 to replace.[152] Bowstrings would also need replacing. A gross (twelve dozen) of bowstrings cost 4s 6d in 1593.

During Elizabeth's reign, there were attempts to enforce existing Acts on the practice of archery. Despite these Acts, archery was becoming increasingly a lost art. For Roger Ascham the reason was a lack of teaching. Already in 1545 he was writing, 'many buy bow, because of the Act, but they shoot not; not of evil will, but because they know not how to shoot'.[153] The longbow was also a victim of field enclosure, which prevented archers from training, as John Stow reported in 1598:

> What shoulde I speake of the auncient dayly exercises in the
> long bow by Citizens of this cittie, now almost cleane left of and
> forsaken. I over passe it for by the meane of closing in the common
> groundes, our Archers sor want of roome to shoote abroade, creepe
> into bowling Allies, and ordinary dicing houses nearer home,
> where they have roome enough to hazard their money at unlawfull
> games.[154]

The period of relative peace from 1564 to 1585 contributed to the decline of the longbow (though archers were among the Earl of Leicester's force in the Netherlands in 1585). The longbow continued to see service in the Royal Navy, though by 1575 English ships were carrying four or five times more harquebuses. In 1588, during the Armada, archers were set to play an important role in defending London.

The traditional English longbow had a length of six feet and was made of yew (*Taxus baccata*). Longbow production was a craft and bowyers were employed to stock royal fortresses. According to research on longbows found on board the *Mary Rose* (lost in 1545), they had a draw weight of between 45 and 80 kg. The initial speed of the arrows could

• 115 •

reach 200 km (125 miles) per hour. Arrows reaching a target at 30 m (98 ft) per second could penetrate armour with a thickness of 1.5 mm (1$^1/_{16}$ in.). The longbow did in fact hold a number of advantages over the harquebus. In the hands of an expert, the rate of fire was considerably higher. An English archer could fire ten arrows per minute. The longbow was also less expensive. The rise of the harquebus, however, continued. Soldiers had an incentive to give up the longbow. By 1594, a musketeer could earn 12d per day, 4d more than an archer. Though a harquebus cost more than a bow (10s), ammunition cost less. What is more, a harquebusier could also carry more lead shot than an archer could carry arrows.

The *coup de grâce* finally came on 26 October 1595 when an Order in Council finally obliged men to replace their bows with muskets and calivers.

The decline of the longbow was regrettable. If the numbers of English archers had been maintained, they would surely have proven their worth in France, not only for their efficiency but also their ability to cause fear. French soldiers as well as surgeons feared English arrows as they were also difficult to extract. Surgeons preferred to push them through a wound instead of drawing them out, as they were often barbed. If the surgeon pulled out the arrow, he risked leaving the head behind. A French soldier wounded at Leith in Scotland in 1560 had just this experience. The massed indirect fire of archers would have been useful at the siege of Le Havre. Here, a plunging fire would have fallen on the besiegers behind their gabions. John Smith recounts how at Le Havre archers had forced French skirmishers to withdraw. Ambrose Dudley, however, signalled to Sir William Cecil that he had neither bowstrings nor arrows.

THE RISE OF THE ENGLISH PIKEMAN

The number of pikemen, meanwhile, was on the increase. In 1563, out of 300 soldiers sent to Le Havre from Berwick, 210 were harquebusiers and ninety pikemen. Around 40 per cent of the infantry in the Earl of Essex's army in Normandy were pikemen, while just over 50 per cent carried firearms. This figure is confirmed by the pen and ink sketch of the siege of Gournay-en-Bray by Edmund Yorke in 1591. A small percentage (around 7 per cent) carried halberds. Around the end of the century, we find a levy for France made up of two thirds pikemen and the rest harquebusiers.

The pike had a length of between 18 and 22 feet (between 5.5 and 6.7 m). The pikemen would form a square in defence against cavalry.

(*top and centre*) *English infantry at the siege of Gournay-en Bray,* 1591 (details). The National Archives (TNA), SP 9/200 46 (MPF1/153)

(*bottom*) *Musketeers, pikemen and lancers at the siege of Rouen* (detail). British Library, Cotton MS Augustus I.ii.90. © The British Library Board

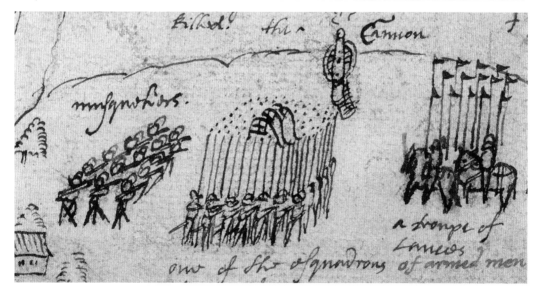

The men in the front rank formed in threes with their pikes crossed. Another pikeman was placed in the second rank between each of these groups of three. A harquebusier was positioned between each pikeman in the second rank, firing over the men in front of him. These men would be supported from behind by ranks of pikemen. Against infantry, the pikemen would form differently. The pikemen would once again form a square but with the harquebusiers either on each corner or all around.[155] The other method would be to mix columns of harquebusiers with pikes. The harquebusiers in column could maintain continuous fire known as 'wading'. By this method, the harquebusier retired in the column to reload his piece. During an encounter against infantry, the pikemen would close ranks. The entire weight of the square would combine to push the enemy back. Henry Barrett recognised the advantage held by infantry on higher ground in such an encounter.

This period also witnessed the rise of the hand grenade, which proved especially useful in siege warfare. According to one account, they were used against the English at Rouen as they attempted to scale the walls: 'The English … came upon us around midnight to scale our walls, but they felt the pips of the grenade … rain on their backs.'[156]

The basic weapon of the soldier, the sword, also came under scrutiny. There was a rivalry between the shortsword and the rapier. According to one source, the English had a tendency to 'cut' while the French would 'thrust'. The French fashion is clearly illustrated in the work of Henri de Sainct-Didier, *Traicte de l'Espee Seule* (Paris, 1573). During the 1570s, over-length rapiers had become fashionable. Sir Martin Frobisher had adopted one of these, perhaps not the best weapon to have at sea, where rigging could inhibit movement. It is probable that he had abandoned this sword by the time of the siege of Crozon in 1594. Elizabeth herself is known to have objected to these swords. A number of proclamations were made restricting the length of English rapiers to a 'yard and a half-quarter'.[157]

The English contingent in Picardy in 1596 appears to have been well equipped for siege warfare. A warrant to pay Sir Henry Lee, Master of the Armoury, for sixty-two musket-proof shields and fifty-nine pistol-proof shields coincides with the moment of preparations. Such shields were something of an anachronism in open battle, though useful in sieges where mobility was less important. They offered protection against enemy fire at close range.

Each company of infantry usually had a captain, lieutenant, ensign, two sergeants, two drummers[158] and a surgeon. A cornet of cavalry had a trumpeter instead of a drummer. The navy, at least during the first war, had drummers and trumpeters on board their warships. They shared the task of sounding commands with the bosun's call. A ship carried more trumpeters if the admiral was also on board. The *Galley Mermaid* carried a drummer and a fife while the Lord Admiral's ship, the *Elizabeth Jonas* (800 tonnes), had as many as five trumpeters. Meanwhile, the *Aid* (250 tonnes) had two trumpeters, a drummer and a fife.

Willoughby's army in 1589 had twelve drummers and six fifes per regiment, giving a total of forty-eight drummers and twenty-four fifes. These drummers, accompanied by those of Henri IV, would have been heard from far away by the Parisians. The English army was recognisable from the distinct sound of its drums: the drummers of the French army beat at a faster rate. Armand de Gontaut, baron de Biron (1562–1602), remarked that the beat of the English drums was slow, to which Sir Roger Williams retorted, 'That may be true but slow as it is, it has traversed your master's country from one end to the other.'[159]

There is a whole series of pieces by the composer William Byrd written to celebrate the exploits of English soldiers.[160] The music scores are particularly interesting because they give us the sounds of the drums and trumpets issuing commands on the field of battle. By comparing this music with earlier pieces such as *La Bataille* (a pavane from around 1542 in *Musicque de joye* published in Lyons), it can be seen that the pace of battles had started to quicken. This was due to a reduction in the amount of armour worn by both foot and horse. The soldiers of Byrd moved with a certain *gaillardise*. In one of his pieces, *The Battle*, we are perhaps witnessing the birth of 'heavy metal' on the virginal muselar. There were signals for each movement including the march, quick march, assault, the alarm and the retreat.

English gunners and artillery were also present. The largest contingent was engaged in the defence of Le Havre. Other small artillery trains followed forces to lay siege to towns and fortresses. Sir John Norris wanted a mobile artillery train of two demi-culverins to accompany his men. He appreciated the value of artillery in defence. There were twenty horse in the campaign train in 1593.

The other professional arm was that of the engineers. The engineer was responsible for the design and construction of fortifications. The main engineers sent to France were Sir Richard Lee, Edmund Yorke and the Italians Giovanni Portinari and Meliorino Ubaldini.[161] Except at Le Havre in 1562–63, the English engineers in France practised offensive fortification, in other words, siege-works. It was in the Netherlands, in Ireland and in England itself where they perfected the art of defensive fortification. In Holland, the lack of natural obstacles, excluding water, rendered the art of fortification more important. The flat terrain allowed the practice of 'perfect' fortification as illustrated in *The Practice of Fortification* (London, 1589, 1594) by Paul Ive. Ive worked at Pendennis, Castle Park, Kinsale, Haulbowline Fort at Cork, and elsewhere. Robert Adams undertook works at Flushing, Ostend and other ports. Edmund Yorke was previously employed on the fortifications at Weybourne Hope in Norfolk in 1588 and then in Ireland at Duncannon, Limerick and Waterford (at the Fort of the Rock). Having been sent to France, Yorke witnessed the siege of Chartres by the French king in 1591. Here he would surely have been employed as an adviser. Part of his legacy of the siege includes his cavalier view ink drawing of the town.[162] At Rouen, where he was also wounded, Yorke was named 'Trencheman of the Field'.

Sir Richard Lee was one of the most experienced engineers in England, having worked on the fortifications on the Scottish frontier, the Isle of Wight and in France. Lee had also served the Duke of Savoy in the Low Countries and, like Ambrose Dudley, was present at the capture of St-Quentin. He worked with a number of Italian engineers including Antonio Ferramolino da Bergamo and Gian Tomaso Scala. Before Le Havre, Lee had been employed as chief engineer at Berwick and at the new fortress at Upnor on the River Medway. He had also participated in the siege of Leith.

Giovanni Portinari, the other engineer, had, according to Holinshed, 'ripe skill, deepe judgement and great experience in matters of fortification'.[163] He had worked on the mines during the siege of Boulogne. He was employed on the new fort at Sandown Bay on the Isle of Wight in 1545 and also worked for the French. He presented one of his projects to Henri II of France: on 'how to make a fortification such as no battery shall be able to prevail against it, though there were 150 cannons continually beating upon it'.[164] Despite being well paid by the king of France for his services in Piedmont, by 1554 Portinari wanted to return to England. He did not want to be sent to Scotland to fight against the English. In April of the same year he wrote to Nicholas Wotton, the English ambassador in Paris, in the hope of finding employment. By 1560, we find him at Berwick.

It is interesting to note that the two engineers Sir Richard Lee and Giovanni Portinari both played an important role in fortifying Berwick-upon-Tweed. A simple comparison of surviving plans of Le Havre and of Berwick reveals certain similarities. Apparently, the engineers applied their experiences in France to their work in England and vice versa.

Another engineer of Italian origin was also employed on the fortifications of Le Havre: Meliorino Ubaldini. He was previously in the service of France but now wished to serve England. He arrived at Le Havre at the beginning of June 1563.

The pioneers executed the work but they could also perform other functions such as keeping guard 'when theie be not over labored in the daie time'.[165] During the siege of Le Havre, it was intended for the pioneers to be armed. Two thousand black bills (halberds) were ordered. England had a natural source of pioneers in the form of the tin and lead miners of the south-west. These miners, however, could not be raised directly by the county Lieutenants or the captains. A special licence was first required from the Privy Council. Miners were also employed in the specialist work of undermining fortifications. These sappers were organised separately from the pioneers. They were also paid more; a miner in Brittany in 1591 could expect a daily wage as high as 1s.

COSTS OF LEVYING AND EQUIPMENT

The system of 'coat and conduct money' (money for clothing and transporting the men) was introduced during the reign of Henry VII. The money was paid up-front by the shire and reimbursed by the Crown. The levying and maintaining of an army entailed considerable expense. A single soldier could be levied, clothed, fed and transported to France for 20s (including the soldier's allocation of conduct money). The actual cost of transporting a man from the port of debarkation to France was 2s.

The payment for the clothing ('coat money') for an expedition was normally made by the Crown. The authorities were open to offers for the provision of clothing. The producers worked from official patterns. Some steps were also taken in the development of uniform. At Le Havre, 600 men from Norfolk and 300 from Suffolk were provided with blue and yellow cloaks. There is also evidence that English soldiers wore uniform at the siege of Rouen in 1591 – dressed in red. Here, a Welsh captain mistook an enemy sentinel as one of his own, as he also wore a red jacket. This was in contrast to clothing worn in Ireland, where steps were taken to 'camouflage' men. Here, in 1584, 'sad green colour' or 'russet' were suggested for the soldiers. Canvas doublets were issued, the price of which remained at 8s 6d through the 1590s (see below). These offered some protection from sword cuts. In 1589, Willoughby provided his men with shoes and stockings at his own expense. Many of the socks (stockings) of the period were produced in the Suffolk town of Kersey. Kersey gave its name to this particular weave of wool, which was in turn adapted by the French as *cariset*.

Cost of clothing per man 1589		Cost of clothing per man 1597	
shirt	3s	shirt & band	3s 2d
canvas doublet	8s 6d	canvas doublet	8s 6d
kersey stockings	16d	stockings	20d
pair of shoes	22d	pair of shoes	20d
cassock	14s 11d	cap	16d
		'ventians' [breeches]	8s
total	£1 9s 7d	'bande'	8d
		total	£1 5s

Two sets of clothing were intended for the army in Picardy in 1597: for summer and for winter.

In theory, the soldiers were furnished with armour by the shire. The Armoury Office also provided corslets and morions. Once in France, armour was often damaged, lost and even sold. Large quantities of armour therefore also had to be purchased on the Continent. The sale of soldiers' clothing and arms was a particular concern. The authorities ordered the marking of arms in an effort to prevent this. The harquebus recovered from the Alderney wreck bears the monogram 'W' on the stock. Further finds must be made to confirm that the monogram is an official mark.

TRAINING

Roger Ascham regarded military training as being vital for any English gentleman 'to ride cumlie to run faire at the tilte or ring to plaie at all weapones: to shote faire in bow, or surelie in gon ... be not onelie cumlie and decent, but also verie necessaries, for a Courtlie Jentleman to use'.[166]

Military training was also a regular feature in the life of the militia man in the defence of his country. Training was, in the first instance, the responsibility of the county. The county would pay men 8d per day, normally for ten days per year. Yeomen from Elizabeth's guard performed an important function in ensuring uniformity of training between units. One Yeoman, Henry Barrett, wrote a training manual in 1562 entitled *A breife booke unto private captaynes leadinge ffootemen, their officiers necessary Instructinge to marche, trayne and imbattell their noumbers as to service ys convenient.*[167]

Frequently, however, many men were sent abroad with very little or even no prior training. It was for this reason that some powder was set aside to train new recruits. Following a request made by Ambrose Dudley at Le Havre in 1562, the Crown issued 2 lbs of powder to each man. Sir Thomas Baskerville found himself in a similar situation at the start of the campaign in Picardy in 1596, describing many of his men as 'raw'. The period of inactivity gave the captains time to train their men. As Sir John Aldrich reported to the Earl of Essex, 'We have had opportunity in this idle time to make our men perfect in martial exercises, which we have not failed to do, and have so bred so good an opinion in them of themselves, that they desire to put in execution and make proof what they have learned.'[168] Meanwhile, he was obliged to expend some of his reserves of powder on musketry drill.

THE JOURNEY TO FRANCE

Crucial to the expeditions to France were the transports and ships of the Royal Navy. The ships were in a constant process of development. The 1,000-tonne *Triumph* (launched in 1562) was the largest English ship since the *Henry Grace a Dieu* of 1514. Her sister ship the *Victory* was almost as large at 800 tonnes.[169] The Admiralty established a plan in 1559 proposing the maintenance of a permanent fleet of twenty-four ships. They expected to reach this target by 1564. Most of their objectives had been reached by 1562, with the construction programme hastened either by the menace of or preparations for war. The intensity of the programme is apparent from the naval account books. At Deptford in 1562, for example, 199 carpenters were employed in the construction of the ships.

There were physical differences between English and French ships. In time of war, the Royal Navy could requisition vessels from the merchant fleet. These vessels were larger than their French counterparts. At La Rochelle in 1563–64, the average size of a French merchantman was 55 tonnes, while those of Northern Europe averaged 170. Back in 1544, when François I sought vessels of more than 300 tonnes for an invasion of England, he was told that there were not even vessels of 200 tonnes in Brittany. This disparity was in part due to the queen's policy of encouraging English merchants to construct larger vessels at their own expense. The *Exchange* of Bristol is one example. For the construction of this 140-tonne vessel, the owner received a recompense of 140 crowns (one crown per tonne).

The requisitioning of merchant vessels could be done at short notice and they could be put into service quickly. At Plymouth in 1591, a pinnace en route for La Rochelle was unloaded, equipped and provisioned in the space of twenty-four hours. It was important for the Crown to know the correct tonnage. Merchant ships were hired and paid for by the tonne. The queen once paid one third too much for one ship.

The Royal Navy had several functions. First, it was a guard against invasion. The queen's ships were used to transport armies and protect other vessels transporting men and supplies. English merchantmen were sometimes unwilling to cross the Channel without escort. English squadrons were frequently stationed to guard the 'narrow seas' throughout the period. Fresh fears of invasion in 1568, for example, led to the maintenance of four ships: *Aid, Antelope, Phoenix and Swallow.* The years 1591–92 saw the stationing of up to 800 sailors in the Channel.

The recruitment of sailors to serve in the navy should also be examined. They were drawn from a number of counties. By 1588, there were around 17,000 sailors in the kingdom. During the first war, there was one instance when 229 sailors were sent from Newport in Wales to Chatham. Other men were drawn from the Forest of Dean. Bargemen working on the Thames were also pressed into the fleet.

The transporting of men between England and France was an art in itself, a real exercise in logistics. Navigating a course to France was a relatively simple task for the sailors. In 1562, the Royal Navy was certainly well equipped with compasses. As many as seventy-two were ordered from a certain Richard Stevens, compass-maker of Tower Hill in London, at a price of 2s 8d a piece. Such a compass may be seen in the portrait of Admiral Clinton.[170]

During the first campaign in Normandy, the transport of the soldiers was often at the mercy of the wind despite the use of complex rigging, sprit-sails, mizzen masts and yards. The voyage to France would have been more difficult than the return voyage. This was due principally to the south-westerly winds. All too often, fleets left port but were prevented from going farther. This was the case on Monday 28 September 1562, when the fleet of seventeen ships sailed out of Portsmouth destined for Le Havre. They were back in port the following day. Looking at the instructions issued to the engineer Sir Richard Lee, it is clear that the authorities knew that the wind was unpredictable: 'Ye shall use all spede to transport yourself to Newhaven in Normandy or the wynd shall not commodiosely serve to carry yow thither; yet if yow may arryve at Depe [Dieppe], yow shall rather so doo than to remayn upon the cost of England.'[171]

The problem persisted at the end of the century. At the beginning of 1592, the French ambassador, Philippe Du Plessis Mornay, was stuck in Dover for three weeks. Similarly, soldiers being transferred from Picardy to Ireland in 1598 found themselves pushed towards the Downs (the sheltered waters off Deal and Walmer in Kent). Despite the capriciousness of the winds, transport by sea was normally faster than on land. The voyage from Plymouth to Morlaix or Roscoff, for example, took 'a night and a day'.[172] According to Catherine de' Medici, only three hours separated the two countries.

The storms that appeared sporadically in the Channel were a nuisance for English vessels. Ships charged to relieve the garrison of Le Havre were dispersed by one such storm as far as the Low Countries. Occasionally, entire vessels were lost, such as the *Greyhound* which sank off Camber near Rye in March 1563. The ship had been forced to return to port in the face of bad weather, and taking the tide at the wrong moment it either hit a sandbank or the rocks of the Black Shore. Another vessel, carrying dispatches from Burghley as well as the army's account books, was lost off Alderney in November 1592.

The main ports of embarkation were Chatham, Dover, Portsmouth, Rye and Southampton. Other ports such as Plymouth and Weymouth were also used. Vessels loaded with soldiers and their arms would have affected the draught of the ships so that only deep-water ports would have been suitable. The authorities encountered such a problem during the preparations for Willoughby's expedition to Normandy in 1589. They contemplated unloading the men from their ships at Arundel, Chichester and Newhaven before sending them to Rye. Here, the twenty feet of water at high tide would have been more than adequate.

The defence of the ports was also an important task. Ships at anchor were vulnerable to attack from fireships. A sudden descent by the enemy could prove fatal. The defences of Portsmouth and the Solent were the most complete. They had already been put to the test during Henry VIII's reign in 1545 when the French fleet landed a force on the Isle of Wight.

Rye was particularly busy with ships and armies passing through the port during this period.[173] The Italian engineer Federigo Giambelli (also written 'Genebelli' or 'Gianibelli') arrived at Rye in March 1593 in an attempt to improve the harbour. The main defence of the port was the Henrician fort at Camber. Camber was typical of the circular artillery fortresses (the Device Forts) on the south coast of England. It was most similar to the fortresses at Deal, Sandown and Walmer in Kent. The port of Chatham was defended by the fortress of Upnor, built in 1559 under the direction of Sir Richard Lee. The construction of this fortress gave the navy an additional secure base. From here, ships could protect London and the east coast as well as being ready to intervene on the Continent. In particular, this base facilitated operations against Calais and the north of France, assuring the seaways if the winds prevented intervention by the fleet from Portsmouth.

The Channel Islands were also important. They played both defensive and strategic roles. During the first war, they were used as a base for ships providing a screen to protect forces in Normandy (guarding against ships from Brittany). The isles further proved their importance during the years of intervention in Brittany. They offered a stepping stone for men, arms and provisions being carried to France. We find, for example, four pieces of artillery being sent from Guernsey to France in 1591. The importance that the authorities attached to the Isles was underlined by the incessant investment in the fortifications. Much of the work involved the conversion of medieval castles into fortresses. The castle of Mont Orgueil (also known as Gorey Castle) had been rendered much stronger during the reign of Edward VI. Work was carried out at Castle Cornet on Guernsey in 1593. New fortifications were added. Elizabeth Castle (Fort Isabella Bellissima) was begun by the engineer Paul Ive in 1594.

All the ports remained secure against attack despite the Catholic plots to burn ships at anchor. Allegedly, ships at Chatham and Dieppe were targets.

Transport was required for the soldiers as well as their horses, carts and baggage. One captain under the Earl of Essex, Robert Carey, took more than five warhorses, a cart with a further five horses, as well as 'one little ambling nag'.[174]

For shipping the army of Sir John Norris to Brittany in 1591, the ship-owners expected to be paid per tonne. Sir John Hawkins, who had prior experience carrying slaves as early as 1562, transported Willoughby's men from London in 1589. He was assisted by Sir Thomas Scott, Lord

Buckhurst and the Earl of Sussex to transport men from Kent, Sussex and Hampshire respectively. Hawkins also directed the transporting of soldiers in his capacity as Treasurer and Comptroller of the navy. A permanent controller of transport was appointed by the Privy Council in 1596. Two years later, two officers were responsible for requisitioning ships. These reforms gave the authorities more control over the movement of men. According to Charles Cruickshank, the soldiers were not a worthwhile cargo and the ships' captains were rarely keen to give assistance.[175]

The number of vessels used to transport the soldiers to France varied according to their tonnage. In 1591, for example, twenty-one vessels were used to transport 3,060 men. For the transport of 700 soldiers of London to St-Valery in Picardy a large ship (the *White Hind*) and four smaller vessels (hoys, single-masted coastal and riverine merchant vessels of around 60 tonnes) were used. For the return of Willoughby's army in 1589, two of the queen's ships were tasked to bring the men back to England. Captain Ward was sent to France with these two vessels with orders to hire merchant ships.

During the first campaign in Normandy, one vessel in particular was used to transport important men between England and France: the *Aid*. Having been launched in the autumn of 1562, she maintained a high status. In the navy accounts we find a payment made to Captain John Basing 'for the mendinge of the Glasse windowes in the cabbon of the same shippe, for the bettar trannsportinge of suche nobell personages as from tyme to tyme he transported from Portesmouth to Newhaven [Le Havre] in Normandie'. Montgomery sailed to Le Havre aboard the *Aid* in December. He was accompanied by Sir Hugh Paulet.[176]

The transports required escorts. In 1592, the *Vanguard, Nonpareil, Tremain, Quittance, Charles* and *Moon* were employed.

Emmanuel van Meteren describes the voyage with Sir John Norris and the army to Brittany:

> *This morning being Sonday, my Lord Generall with Sir Henry Norice Captaine Anthonie Shirley, Maister William Devoreux, & c. tooke Posthorses at London to ride to Southampton where (in taking order for shipping & for divers considerations) his Lordship staid untill Sonday the 25. day.*

(*overleaf*) *Rye Harbour, Sussex* (map produced between 1572 and, possibly, 1595), by John Prowse. The National Archives (TNA), MPF 1/212

Monday the 26. dict. we embarked and fell downe with the shipping to Portesmouth where his Lordship staid that night at Captaine Richard Wingfields house.

Tuesday morning the 27. dict. we set sayle being of us in all 23 ships and other small vessels, and having a scant shifting winde at north and north east, we cast an anchor before Saint Helenes poynt in the Wight.

Wednesday morning about ten of the clocke (being untill then becalmed wee hapned of a small gale of wind blowing N.N.west, wherewith we recovered the Haigue [Cap de la Hague in Normandy].

Thursday about ten of the clocke at night, we anchored before the Castle of Gernsey and my Lord Generall and some other Gentlemen with him lay at the Castle that night.

Friday morning we set saile from thence and about five of the clocke in the evening we put into the road of Jarsey.

Monday my Lord Generall expecting the Companies out of the Low Countries, were this daye arived with Captaine Anthonie Wingfield Sergeant Major of the Campe his Lordship went abord, and lay at anchor in the road all that night.

Tuesday in the morning we loosed from thence, and having a fine winde at North and by West, about eight at night we anchored in the road of Pimpowle [Paimpol] ariving in the road called Lemoys de Guelle [Le Mez de Goëlo] neere Pimpoule [sic].[177]

IN SEARCH OF A BETTER PLACE OF RETREAT

The establishment of a harbour or a place of retreat on the other side of the Channel was a major concern for the English authorities. Only ports that could shelter ships of at least 200 tonnes were expedient. During the first war, Dieppe and Le Havre were designated as bridgeheads. Charles IX also feared the occupation of La Rochelle. During the siege of 1572–73, certain Rochelais wished to surrender the town to Elizabeth but the future Henri III made an arrangement with La Noue to prevent the debarkation of the English in the town. During the second and third Normandy campaigns, English forces mainly used the ports of Caen, Cherbourg and Dieppe, given that Le Havre and Honfleur were held by the *Ligue*.

Lord Willoughby's army was given little opportunity to establish itself in a port, as it was kept on the march. Willoughby, by his own calculations, believed that he had marched at least 400 miles. He compared their efforts to a great biblical exploit, 'Our men having passed the children of Israel's march in the land of Egypt, (having worn themselves, their shoes, and their apparel,) cry out homewards.'[178] Using a modern map to estimate the distances covered, we find that Willoughby was not far out. Around 500 miles (*c*.800 km) were covered in two and a half months. It must be noted that Willoughby was not marching in the middle of summer. Among the prayers of English soldiers in *Certaine Prayers set fourth by Authoritie...* (London, 1597) was a request for God to give them 'feete of flint', such was their importance to an army on the march. The addition of heels to shoes (at least for some) by 1588 would have made marching easier. The men under Sir John Norris, by comparison, covered at least 800 miles (*c*.1,300 km) but this was over a longer period (May 1591–October 1594). The itinerary below sets out the route travelled by Willoughby and his men in October–December 1589.

THE NORMANDY CAMPAIGN, 1589

Date	Town
Oct 11	Dieppe
	Cropus ['Corpue']
13	Vieux-Manoir
14	Bourg Beaudoin
15	Frêne l'Archevêque
16	Dampsmesnil (?) ['Dominique']
17	Vétheuil
18	Morainvilliers via Meulan-en-Yvelines
20	St-Cloud
21	Paris
24	'Morson' via Bourg-la-Reine
26	Lardy
29	Étampes via Etréchy ['Tressye']
30	Outarville

Nov	1	Cormainville
	3	Ozoir-le-Breuil
	4	la Gahandière
	5	[Villeterre]
	6	Vendôme via Selommes
	11	Prunay-Cassereau
	13	Chenillé
	14	Marçon
	16	Challes via la Chartre-sur-le-Loire
	18	Neuville-sur-Sarthe via Champagné
	19	Le Mans
	23	Rouillon
	28	St-Jean-d'Assé
	30	St-Christophe-du-Luat
Dec	1	Sougé-le-Ganelon
	3	near Alençon
	14	La Roche-Mabile via Alençon
	17	Tanville
	19	St-Martin-des-Landes
		Loucé
	21	Montgaroult
	22	fauxbourgs de Falaise ['Melaville']
	23	les Isles-Bardel
	25	['Melaville à Pont St Croye']
	c.31	Dives-sur-Mer

Concern was raised by one English captain in 1592:

I do hear news from Normandy, that our men be also removed from the Pellord [Le Pollet], where they lay by Dieppe, and that they be very weak, and are marched up into the country toward St-Valery; so that if they do not look well unto themselves, they are like to be cut off as the others were in Bretagne; for in that they have no place to retire into for their relief.[179]

Henri looked to secure the centre of his kingdom before pushing towards the exterior. For Elizabeth, on the other hand, it was essential to give priority to the coast. In the same way, if the king occupied the ports of

Le Havre, St-Malo and Morlaix, the *Ligueurs* would not be able to receive aid from Spain. She demanded a greater effort in Brittany given that, 'if the Sea Coast should be abandoned by the Prince, the King could never have convenient Ayde out of England to withstande the Ennemie'.[180]

Elizabeth wanted to avoid heavy losses. She wished to keep her army intact and ready to serve in Ireland or in the defence of England. She let her wishes be known to Henri. 'I … dare promise that our subjects are of such good disposition, and have hearts so valiant that they will … destroy many of your enemies.… I ask … that they will be cherished as those who serve not as mercenaries but with good affection; also that they will not be burdened with too violent danger.'[181] Elizabeth was also keen that they should not go unsupported.

Despite Henri's frequent promises of a place of retreat, nothing ever materialised. Caudebec and Harfleur were proposed in 1591 as well as the Île de Bréhat, in 1593, and later Morlaix and Boulogne. In short, Henri feared the presence of the English in a town of any importance. This attitude was in sharp contrast to the Dutch, who gave the English places of surety as needed. As William Lilly comments, 'we shall come into no towns for garrison, for that they think us too strong'. Lord Burghley complained that the army had been 'more wasted in 2 or 3 yeares in France for lacke of relief and places of retreit then hath bene in any open warre these many yeares paste'.[182]

Despite the fury of Elizabeth, Henri managed to constantly avoid the ceding of a port of any size. In the spring of 1592, Sir John Norris considered an assault against the port of St-Malo. A plan was prepared and he was granted the right to raise 1,000 volunteers at his own expense.

Henri indicated that he was ready to give ports such as Paimpol but the English found that this town lacked adequate defences. Furthermore, Norris was refused entry to the town. According to Emmanuel van Meteren and signed letters, Norris stayed at the Abbaye de Beauport on the coast south-east of Paimpol. Here, the Baie de Poulafret at least offered shelter for the vessels. He was also refused the Île de Bréhat. Henri gave his reasons to Sir Robert Sidney who was in France as special ambassador, telling him that it would be difficult in the eyes of the nobility. The debate over Paimpol and Bréhat continued until the start of a new campaign. A contract was agreed whereby the English would be allocated the port of Morlaix following its capture. The English held that they had been promised Morlaix as a place of retreat for the 'poor tyred soldiers'[183] of Norris. Fearing hostility from the native Bretons, *maréchal* d'Aumont tried to dissuade Henri. D'Aumont made a pact with the people of Morlaix to allow only Catholics to enter the town. The pact was put to the test when English ships arrived to take Norris and his force. They were refused entry to the port, being obliged to disembark at Roscoff. Once more, Henri managed to avoid the question. He maintained that his local officers had disobeyed his orders.

Sir Thomas Lake, writing to Sir Robert Sidney, insisted on the need for a port in return for English aid: 'if we were sure to have some of our old footinge in Pycardy, for a place of retraiet, or in pawne … I think it wilbe moved'.[184]

Elizabeth was worried that her forces would be drawn too far into the interior of the country. For her, the maintaining of an army near the coast was necessary so that they would be ready to defend England and Ireland. According to Sir Robert Cecil, Henri considered 'that her majestie provideth an armie for places more remote, to bring her private utility, and doth therby abandone him to the ennemies violence'.[185]

A clause was included in the secret section of the treaty, agreed on 10 May 1596. The treaty stipulated that the English force should be in garrison at either Boulogne or Montreuil or with the French king's army in Picardy. Even if they were with the king, they were to stay near the coast. It was also decided that if French soldiers were to be sent to aid Elizabeth should England be invaded, they would be allowed to advance only fifty miles inland. The treaty was not carried out to the letter. The men under Sir Thomas Baskerville found themselves divided between the small ports in the estuary of the Somme. This positioning later proved ideal for their participation in the siege of Amiens, but these were not the kind of ports that Elizabeth expected.

During the alarm created by the Spanish siege of Calais, Elizabeth continued to push her demands in return for support. It was decided to use the same rhetoric as with Johann Casimir. When Casimir asked for the return of Metz, Nicolas Harlay de Sancy replied: 'It is better … that the duke of Lorraine takes the place by force than if the king gives it to a foreign prince … for the king is obliged to conserve … the kingdom in its entirety.' This impressed Louis de Revol, Henri IV's foreign minister, as he noted that Elizabeth 'made similar demands':[186] 'if the Spanish take it [Calais], we hope to retake it from them'. Henri saw the problem with handing Calais to the English, 'and instead of one enemy, we will have two'.[187] Henri also commented to Sir Robert Sidney that he preferred 'to be bitten by a lion than a lioness'.[188]

It is certain that Henri feared a repetition of the occupation of Le Havre of 1562. More recently, he will have remembered the lodging of Johann Casimir at Langres with his army 'where he lived like a German waiting for his payment'.[189] His fears were so strong that they influenced his strategy to extremes. Even the 'friendly' towns were concerned about billeting English soldiers. The town of Vitré, for example, would let them stay only in the suburbs. They pleaded to Henri de Montpensier each day to have them sent elsewhere. Inhabitants certainly had grounds to fear the arrival of an English army. The village of Pavilly was damaged by fire after a short stay by English soldiers besieging Rouen. Guillaume Valdory claims that this was done intentionally.[190] At Osemount, a third of the town was lost when the thatched houses caught fire. There was also a fear that their presence would attract the enemy. It could be said that their presence had the opposite effect, except during the first war when the English at Le Havre attracted the entire royal army. Between 1589 and 1597, English forces were rarely on the defensive. It may be noted that they were besieged only once, at Ambrières in 1592.[191]

The lodgings varied according to the place. Local inns along the routes taken by the levied men would certainly have profited from the wars. The Mermaid Inn at Rye, which remains open today, would doubtless have been one of these.

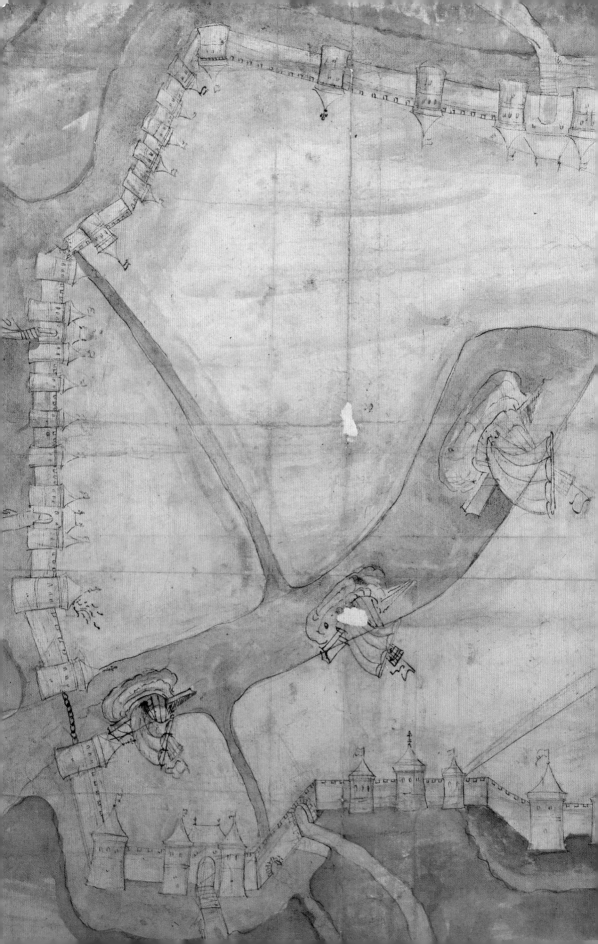

CHAPTER THREE

OPERATIONS

ROUEN AND LE HAVRE, 1562–63

La Crainte s'envola avecques le
Danger Duquel nous menaçoit le
Pariure estranger. Qui asoit esperer
Que nôtre Seine prise Obeiroit au
Lois de l'Angloise Tamise

'Fear flies with danger with
which the wagering foreigner did
us threaten. Who had hoped that
with our Seine taken would obey
the laws of the English Thames.'

On 8 September 1562, the governors of Rouen (Jean du Bosc, sieur de Mentreville, Vincent du Gruchot, sieur de Soquence, and Noël Coton, sieur de Berthonville) wrote to Cecil saying that they were ready to recognise Elizabeth as their *maîtresse*, 'who will defend us … her natural subjects, as we had been in the past'.[193] Preparations were made across Normandy to receive the English. At Dieppe, two French captains were imprisoned for objecting to an English garrison. At Caen, all resistance to English landings was declared illegal.

On 7 October, Jean de la Fin, sieur de Beavoir La Nocle, lieutenant of Le Havre, informed Catherine de' Medici of the arrival of 4,000 English at Le Havre and 4,000 at Dieppe, 'for the glory of God and the deliverance of the minority of the king'.[194] The plan for surrendering Le Havre had been finalised in August, prior to the treaty of Hampton Court. The plan would be for Sir Adrian Poynings to first take possession of the port.

Claude de Lorraine, duc d'Aumale, had already tried, unsuccessfully, to take Rouen before the arrival of the main body of the royal army. He was joined later by Jean d'Estrées, *Grand Maître de l'Artillerie*. The besiegers of Rouen did not believe that the town could hold out for long. The fact that Rouen was so dominated by the surrounding countryside was an

Plan of the fortifications of La Rochelle, c.1562–69 (detail).
The National Archives (TNA), MPF 1/118

inherent weakness. The key to the town was the Colline Ste-Catherine: 'From the said Mont Sainte Katherine all the streets of Rouen may be seen and discovered.'[195]

The Catholic forces, conducted by the Italian engineer Bartolomeo Campi de Pésaro, attempted to block the Seine between Le Havre and Rouen. At Caudebec they filled large boats with sand and stones linked with ropes and chains. An English relief force attempted to break through the barrier on 9 October. The English privateer Henry Strangeways was mortally wounded in this encounter. The exploits of Strangeways are recounted in the ballad by William Birch, *A new ballade of the worthy service of late doen by Maister Strangwiye in Fraunce, and of his death.*[196] His ship, the rowbarge *Brigandine*, which had a crew of seventy, was lost to the French, together with the *Flower de Luce*. A barque belonging to John Awger carrying supplies was sunk by gunfire at Caudebec. Awger himself was taken prisoner. Two other vessels were forced to withdraw. Meanwhile, most of the soldiers managed to force a passage to Rouen. According to the Venetian ambassador, as many as four English companies (between 400 and 550 men) entered the town.

François de La Noue provides us with one of his rare references to English forces: 'There were inside with count Montgomery 700 or 800 soldiers of old bands and English companies commanded by Sir Kilgré [Sir Henry Killigrew] who all did marvellous work.'[197] Relief came at just the right moment to support the defenders against the assault of 13 October. A Huguenot writing during the siege felt exasperated by the fact that the merchants had not yet delivered the arms that he was awaiting. The Earl of Warwick was made aware that 'to a sleeping fox, no pray happenyth'.[198] The English defenders of Rouen would have been reminded of the historic links between England and Rouen. Its cathedral was, after all, the resting place of the heart of Richard I, the Lionheart.[199]

The Italian engineer Stefano da Urbino assisted French Royalist forces during the siege. A battery of seventeen royal cannon were trained on the fort on Ste-Catherine. The Swiss and German mercenaries were held in reserve during the French assault. The fort fell on 5 October. Meanwhile, some 3,000 pioneers advanced three trenches against Rouen's western defences. Rouen itself finally fell after eight assaults. The city endured pillaging which lasted twenty-four hours. François de Guise ordered *nulle mercy des Anglois, anciens ennemis de la France* ('no mercy to the English, ancient enemies of France'). Gabriel de Montgomery fled on a galley which had previously been used to transport Mary Stuart to Scotland.

In November 1562, reinforcements were planned for Le Havre: 600 soldiers from Essex and 500 from Devon, bringing the garrison up to 4,535, excluding the pioneers. A further 229 pioneers and fifty Scottish horsemen were also sent.[200] On 14 December, Cecil wrote with confidence to Sir Thomas Smith now that they had 6,000 men to defend the town.

Following the capture of Rouen, English forces were not content simply to defend Le Havre. Together with their Huguenot allies, they participated in the capture of several other towns. Vire was taken by assault. According to Michel de Castelnau, English pioneers had assisted in the capture of the town. The success came with the loss of an English captain, 'respected in matters of siege-works'.[201]

The château of Tancarville, east of Le Havre on the north bank of the Seine, also fell to the English. Here:

The Double Rose with certaine other botes and French shallops, passed foorth of the haven Edward Dudleie, and capteine John Ward being aboord in the said Double Rose, with diverse other Englishmen and Frenchmen, to the number of a hundred good soldiors, who sailing downe the river landed beside Tankerville, and laie close all that night to the wood. And in the morning about nine of the clocke monsieur Bimar, enseignebearer to the counte Montgomerie, with six or seaven Frenchmen unarmed went to the castell gate, and there fell in talke with monsieur Dimenée, who was capteine of that fortresse, having with him about ten soldiors that were appointed to remaine with him upon the gard of the same castell. Whilest they were thus in talke, the Englishmen and other Frenchmen comming foorth of the wood that was there at hand, reared up their ladders, which they had brought with them for that purpose, at the breach which was made the summer before by the duke Daumale; and entring by the same, came downe into the base court. Which thing when the French soldiors that kept talke with them within at the castell gate perceived, they began to laugh. The capteine of the castell therwith turning his face, and beholding as good as thrée score armed men within the castell at his backe, he suddenlie said Ha, je suis vostre, I am yours sirs, and so yéelded with his ten soldiors. And in this sort was the castell taken, and the capteine brought prisoner to Newhaven.[202]

A force of 300 English was placed in garrison at Tancarville. The Seine offered a route for retreat by boat in the event of a siege. Despite the loss of Rouen, the Huguenots remained confident and gave promises to hand over other towns such as Abbeville. Then, in March, the town of Bernay to the south was taken. At sea, the English had little trouble in keeping the 'narrow seas' open, assuring two-way traffic hampered only by the wind. The Huguenots were therefore able to continue their trade with England.

Meanwhile, the situation was becoming less favourable north of Le Havre, where the Royalists were tightening the noose. The first target was Dieppe, where the duc de Guise hoped to *desnicher les Angloys* ('unnest the English'). Communications had been cut between Dieppe and Le Havre by mid-January. The Rhinegrave took his force of *Reiter* and horse through the area of Caux, 'which cannot be abandoned without putting the country at the mercy of the English'.[203] He had his ten companies of foot together with some French and three cornets of *pistolliers* 'to confront the English' (*pour faire teste aux Anglois*). The presence of the Rhinegrave's force restricted the free movement of the English around Le Havre. Brantôme writes, 'he held them blockaded, pressed and constrained, not allowing the English to spread out at their ease on land' (*il tint bloqué et serré et constrainct, ne se pouvant l'Anglois estendre à son ayse sur terre*).[204]

With the arrival of winter and the cold, Warwick realised that his garrison was not quite so well prepared. He asked the Council to send 2,000 mattresses because of the number of men falling ill. He also remarked upon how there was a lack of wood all around Le Havre and that they did not have any coal.

Maréchal Brissac held that Le Havre was a *place fortifiee a la moderne* ('a place fortified in the most modern way').[205] François I had employed Antonio da Castello on the fortifications in 1540. They had been improved in the early 1550s during the reign of Henri II. An Italian named Jean Thomas (perhaps Gian Tomaso Scala) was employed on the works. The historian Jean Nagerel thought that Le Havre was strong, being 'impregnable for being in marshland, not commanded by hills, [and] as well walled'.[206]

Warwick and Sir Richard Lee inspected the fortifications upon their arrival. Warwick informed the queen that although the situation of the town was good, he found that its strength had been exaggerated. Lee had received his instructions in October:

> *Your principall purpoose shall be to goo to Newhaven but if ye shall*
> *be constrayned to land at Depe; ye shall consider the state of that*
> *towne, and of the forts at both ends of that towne, and conferr*

Johann Philipp, Wild und Rheingraf, Graf von Salm (the Rhinegrave)
(1520–1566), by François Clouet. British Museum, London, 1910-2-12-68.
© The Trustees of the British Museum

*therin with such principall English captayn as hath chardg there,
and shew to hym your opinion of the strength or weaknes therof,
and gyve advise for the amendment of any default there to the best
of your knowledg, and use as much spede as yow can to depart
from thence to Newhaven.*

*At your comming to Newhaven, ye shall conferr with sir
Adrian Poynings, or any other of the capitanes at your plesure;
and therupon view and consider the strength and weaknes of that
towne in fortification and theruppon shall shew your opinion to sir
Adrian Poynings and the comptroller there, what were mete and
necessary to be doone; and move them furthwith to procede with
spede to the reformation or fortification of that which ye shall judg
mete. And as soone as ye have so considered and devised; we will,
that ye shall certefy as or our counsell, and abyde onely till yow
may receave answer, which shall be sent to you without deelaye
and thereuppon yow may retorn hyther ageyne. In your devise you
shall have regard, that our charges grow not grete therby; but that
the garrison may voluntarely furder the same with their labor.*[207]

It was not the best time of year to be building fortifications. The
earthworks were susceptible to being washed away by the rain. The
engineer Giovanni Portinari arrived at Le Havre on 31 November aboard
the queen's ship the *Hare*, and wrote two reports concerning the state
of the town's defences. The first, made during his first visit, described
the fortifications and gave his advice on defensive measures to be taken
and on the number of men needed to defend the town. The second
report was made in January 1563. Much of his advice was based upon
common sense – he recognised the importance of maps and plans of the
terrain. Portinari's original report was written in Italian, with an English
translation. From it we glean further details of the town's defences.
He confirms, for example, the use of 'two chaynes whiche shotte the
mouth of the haven'[208] to prevent enemy ships from entering the port,
as depicted in a plan now at Hatfield House (see pp.144–145). Portinari
recognised the threat of 'disease & plague whiche entreth emongst thy
men & distroyeth them without stroke of sworde'.[209] He recommended
that 'the whole towne must be kept cleane & swete & order must be
taken that all the filth be conveyed to the rampieres & mingled with the
earth so that it be incorporate therwith & so troden that the rampiere
be made sodde & hard', and called upon soldiers to 'digge in the earth

pittes & holes wherin they shall burie all their ordure & not cast it in the streetes as they dayly accustome wherby both the whole towne is anoyed & the sicknes engendred'.[210] Portinari also recognised the risk from rotting animal carcasses and called for orders

> to all bouchers & suche as kill beastes as also to our souldiors (who open & bowelle beastes in their houses & leave the [pancreas] eyther in the courtes or cast them out into the streates, the whiche engendre stinke & corrupte the ayre) that they shall carie them to the sea side & there eyther burie them under grounde or cast them into the sea. The whiche order being observed the sicknesse shall neyther so soone be engendred nor take suche force as it dooth with the towne.[211]

Portinari warned of attacks from the sea. He advised searching all vessels before they were allowed to enter the port. He identified the 'weakenesse & imperfection of the fortification' at the harbour mouth. To remedy these faults, he called for the construction of a ditch in front of the gate. He also advised the construction of a building to shelter men from the rain, and called for the maintaining of 100 men to guard night and day the St-André bastion, the *boulevard* de Granges, the Granges bastion, the *boulevard* Royal and the bastion Royal. These bastions had been constructed to cover the main walls with artillery and harquebus flanking fire.

By mid-February 1563, as much as 40,000 crowns (£12,000) had been spent upon improving the defences. In an attempt to make economies, the authorities cut back the number of pioneers to be sent. In March, Warwick insisted that he needed 2,000 more. Nevertheless, the works continued and even accelerated. By the end of May 1563 a titanic effort was under way to improve the fortifications. As many as 5,000 baskets were sent for moving earth by hand. These reinvigorated efforts came at the same moment as the naming of Portinari as surveyor of the works at Le Havre, but there was still a need for more pioneers. On 11 April, there were 734 at roll, including those who had previously been sent to Caen. Many of these were to die or return to England, leaving only around 600 by the middle of May. The pioneers at Le Havre were under the direct command of William Pelham, who had previously been employed in the same role at the siege of Leith in 1560. Pelham had been sent to aid Coligny at the siege of Caen before returning to assist at Le Havre. Unfortunately, Portinari was not respected by the pioneers, who proved unwilling to follow his orders. There were only sixty fit pioneers remaining by the

(overleaf) Plan of Le Havre, 1563. Hatfield House, CPM II/45

Le cap decaux

La chaussée doringouuille

de la ville iusques à la môtagne y a neuf cents pas

grange

La porte doringouuille

huuer

La porte de la mer

Le haure

The hilles along the Seine

pont

Le basard de la ville

La porte de Heure

Le basard
de la ville

grange
Roy

harfart

W T

huflen

a Seine à Rouen

second week of July. 2,000 were hastily found in Devon and Cornwall, but they were to leave England only on 20 July.

The church belfry was transformed into a cavilier (artillery platform). A new construction, Fort Warwick, guarded the approaches to the town from the east.[212] The decision to construct an artillery platform on the quay to provide enfilading fire along the shore was made only on 29 June. The seaboard fortifications were vulnerable 'as the English, being confident in this depth of sea, had neglected to fortify this wall which was very weak'.[213] Vieilleville remarked that the moat by Ste-Adresse had been damaged by the sea. The besiegers looked to try to empty the water from the moat.

THE ARMAMENT OF LE HAVRE, 1562

cannon	19
culverin	15
demi-culverin	31 (2 iron)
saker	2
falcon	29 (6 iron)
falconet	8
espringale	14 (iron)
fowlers	4
mortar	3
Total	**125**

A list survives detailing the artillery pieces at Le Havre in October 1562. The Huguenots had agreed to hand an inventory of all pieces of artillery and powder to Poynings within twenty-four hours of his arrival. Other light pieces included thirty-five harquebuses *à croque*. The shipping of 1,000 harquebuses and 500 *curryars* (calivers) was also planned. Total firepower was impressive when compared with that of Calais in 1547.

The English garrison could not afford to lower its guard, as the Rhinegrave demonstrated in January 1563:

> *a soldyar apparyled lyke a paysant with a basket with capons &*
> *chykyns therin ... came unto the gate and wold have entred. They*
> *of the ward loked in his basket and some of them feling him abowte*
> *the bodye & sleves of his cote ... fonde [a] very lode many blanke*
> *papers ... nothing to be sene apon them to ther sight.*[214]

The guards asked what such a simple man of the country was doing with so much paper. He was taken before Warwick, who held the papers before the fire. Only then did words appear. The letters were addressed to certain French captains in the town, who were called upon to assassinate Warwick and take the keys to open the gates. Here, the Rhinegrave would have lain in wait with his men. According to Harry King, those named in the letters were taken for execution, including *capitaine* Blondeville.

The château of Tancarville surrendered to the Rhinegrave following an eight-day siege. The garrison (now reduced to 100 men: seventy English and thirty French) exited with baggage and departed by boat. Elsewhere, the campaign saw new successes. Caen fell on 2 March and Montgomery remained here as lieutenant. 300 Englishmen under captains Tuttie and Fisher participated in the capture of Honfleur. The port capitulated after six salvoes from the artillery. The garrison left the town with only their swords and daggers.

The position of the defenders changed suddenly, however, with the death of the duc de Guise on 24 February when he was shot with a pistol (though Coligny was already looking to make peace by early February 1563). This event was followed by the declaration of the peace of Amboise on 19 March between the Huguenots and the Royalists. This meant that either Elizabeth would have to surrender Le Havre or face the now united Huguenot and Royalist forces.

It was the fear of conspiracy that led to the expulsion of the inhabitants of Le Havre. Portinari had already made the recommendation to 'drive out of the towne the most part or all the inhabitants, or at the least wise suche as are judged unfaithfull or doubtfull' back in January. The expulsion was carried out in stages. First, 'all strangers, forreners and French souldiers' would have to leave the town by 23 March.[215] A proclamation was made on 16 May whereby all the French (men, women and children alike) were to leave before six o'clock the following day. Only those in 'essential' occupations were excepted: apothecaries, bakers, blacksmiths, butchers, carpenters, locksmiths, masons and surgeons.

Catherine sent Florimond Robertet, baron d'Alluye (1531–1569), to England to negotiate the restitution of Le Havre. In fact, it was not until the end of April that Catherine accepted that the English should be expelled by force. She ordered *maréchal* Artus de Cossé, seigneur de Gonnor (1512–1582), to cast sixteen new cannon 'of the sort that we may have between thirty and forty good [ones] to make a furious battery'.[216] These pieces were possibly identical in all except scale to two surviving models. (The Musée National de la Renaissance at the Château d'Écouen possess a miniature piece of artillery that bears the arms of Catherine de' Medici. Another piece, bearing the arms of Charles IX, may be found at the Musée du Louvre.)[217] Anne de Montmorency, as *connétable*, would command the besieging army.

Meanwhile, the fortifications across Normandy were repaired and consolidated in readiness for English assaults. Mont St-Michel had to pay for its own repairs to a tower that had been damaged by the sea. 20,000 *livres* were set aside for other towns, including 2,000 to improve the defences of Cherbourg. Fearing a second landing, coastal towns of northern France were put into a state of alert. Bayeux, Cherbourg, Falaise and Granville all had to be strengthened.

Gaspard de Coligny gave his excuses to Catherine de' Medici that he would be unable to attend the siege of Le Havre. Several other Huguenots, including François de Coligny, comte d'Andelot, nevertheless did appear before the town.

In an effort to ensure that his besieging army was well provisioned, Charles granted letters patent allowing merchants to transport and sell supplies at the camp free of tax. The French merchants who chose to deliver their merchandise by sea were taking considerable risks. Several of these vessels were taken by seamen based in Le Havre.

The French resolution to drive the English from Le Havre was repeated by the French Chancellor, Michel de l'Hôpital, before *Parlement* on 17 May: 'if we leave the enterprise of Le Havre, we are in danger of losing the kingdom, as the loss of Le Havre will bring the loss of Normandy'.[218]

Nevertheless, the declaration of war against the English was made only on 10 July. The Rhinegrave led his *Reiter* in an attack on Fort Warwick. According to Marc'Antonio Barbaro, the Venetian ambassador, around 200 men were killed on each side.

Meanwhile, the French besiegers were having their own problems. Previously, in January, the Arsenal in Paris had caught fire, destroying vast quantities of powder. The Huguenots were blamed for the 300 deaths and the destruction of fifty homes. Brissac proposed importing powder from Flanders to ensure the continuation of the siege. The loss of eight French cannon was reported on the Seine at Vernon. This was out of a total of forty being transported in this way. They were not, apparently, recovered. Charles IX later recalled how a battery of thirty pieces was assembled.

Despite their efforts, they still had not amassed enough men before Le Havre. The *maître de camp*, Antoine du Plessis, sieur de Richelieu, wrote to Brissac on 17 June informing him that he had between 2,200 and 2,300 men. This was appreciated by Catherine, who now wrote to the Rhinegrave:

> considering your small forces and that they are as strong in the town as you are outside and that it will be easy for them, being able to be re-inforced by sea, to undertake something against the few men that you have … makes me ask you to try hard not to come to these great skirmishes but to hold some rein until the [arrival of the] Swiss that I am sending you.[219]

Cases of gout among the French commanders did not help matters. During the siege, Brissac himself was *fort malaisé de sa personne, à cause de ses gouttes (comme chacun sçait)* ('really unwell because of his gout, as everyone knows').[220] Brissac also made excuses for a colonel named Charamont, whose attack of gout made his duties difficult to perform.

There was also a concern that France's internal problems would reappear. As Catherine told Jacques de Goyon, comte de Matignon (1525–1597), *maréchal* in 1579, *tenir main que le feu ne se rallume poinct* ('take care that the fire does not re-ignite').[221] Furthermore, the English defence was far from being passive. 'There are often skirmishes in which the English have always done best until now because they brought out no less than 2,000 or 3,000 men and did great damage to the French and their artillery.'[222] This probably explains why the first cannonball to land in the town came as late as 8 June. This was ceremoniously carried before Warwick.

One particular assault by Richelieu on Fort Warwick was met with fierce resistance from the two pieces of artillery defending the gate and *rempars farciz de harquebusiers* ('ramparts full of harquebusiers'). Christophe de Bassompierre was wounded in the leg by a harquebus and taken prisoner. The English nevertheless suffered losses. Captain Nicholas Tremayne was killed by a pistol shot. It was certainly Tremayne who was described by Richelieu in his letter to Catherine de' Medici: 'they have lost many men … and among others have lost one of their captains of cavalry (we have taken his horse which is richly gilded)'.[223]

The garrison continued to carry out sorties such as the one of around midnight on 14 June. Sallies by the English were important for maintaining the garrison's morale; but only if they could inflict losses on the besiegers. In the action of 'spiking', the French artillery could be rendered useless by hammering headless nails into the lanterns (touch-holes). French pioneers could also be driven back as they approached the defences with their earthworks. The defenders, meanwhile, would have to sustain losses, replacing men killed in skirmishes. The garrison received reinforcements by sea on 15 June. According to the Rhinegrave, the men arrived in six ships.

The French had *entière cognoissance* ('complete knowledge') of the fortifications of Le Havre.[224] Furthermore, Bartolomeo Campi de Pésaro arrived to assist with the siege in June.

Brissac used the same tactics as at Ambleteuse in 1549 and which Piero Strozzi and Guise had used at Calais, when efforts were concentrated on the seaboard defences. The English found themselves once more in the same position. Once again they would have to face the French siege artillery. This was to be directed by Antoine d'Estrées, lieutenant and son of Jean d'Estrées, the *maître et capitaine-général de l'artillerie.* The main French assault was to be made against the fortifications between Ste-Adresse and the harbour entrance. The battery against the bastion of Ste-Adresse commenced on 12 July. The same day, it was estimated that as many as 1,200 shots had been fired against the town. The belfry of the church of Notre Dame was hit and the artillery here put out of action.

One of the defensive measures of the English garrison was to mount counter-batteries at sea. The idea is clearly depicted in the plan of the fortifications during the siege.[225] Two vessels at anchor are shown. The mainmasts, foremasts and rigging were removed to accommodate artillery platforms. A galleass is also present, secured to another vessel. The initials 'MVF' (i.e. M.U. *fecit*) enable us to link this plan to Meliorino Ubaldini. The queen wrote to the Earl of Warwick on 16 July, informing him that she had seen Ubaldini's 'cunningly devised' ideas and that the counter-batteries should be put in place.[226]

We know that a galleass named the *Fox* left the port in the afternoon of 14 July with a crew of fifty men on board. Its mission was to bombard the French assembled on the beach. This demonstrates that the garrison still maintained access to the port. During the bombardment, however, an English gunner dropped a linstock into a cask of powder and the *Fox* sank, leaving only fifteen survivors.

Meanwhile, the 4,000 French pioneers were fully occupied with their trenches. Women as well as men worked round the clock. By 5 July, they had established a battery of cannon only 120 paces from the walls. The battery was well equipped with forty cannon and, according to Catherine de' Medici, enough munition to fire 20,000 shots. On 19 July, the trenches had advanced to a distance of at least thirty paces. It was a difficult task. The absence of earth in which to dig the trenches obliged the pioneers to use sacks filled with earth, woolpacks and fascines. All these were combined with wet sand, gathered at low tide. These were not the only materials used in the earthworks, as the surgeon Ambroise Paré informs us:

> As we made the approaches to set down our artillery, the English inside killed some of our soldiers and several pioneers who were gabioning … those who had so many wounds with no hope of recovery were unclothed by their companions who put them, still alive, in the gabions, which served as filling.[227]

Meanwhile, Montmorency, Richelieu and François de Scépeaux, seigneur de Vieilleville (1509–1571), *maréchal* in 1562, were all wounded. After being hit in the shoulder, Richelieu was forced to hand over command of his regiment to Remolles. Montmorency had both hands *esgratignees* ('badly scratched') and was hit in the shoulder. The Frenchmen attacking on the beach had to face not only the direct fire of the defenders but also the showers of pebbles caused by cannonballs falling short or past the mark. The English also suffered losses. William Bodley was wounded during the last stages of the siege, receiving a halberd and a sword in his thigh. Warwick himself was hit by a harquebus shot.

With less than six salvoes from the battery of eight cannon, the defences *fust du tout renversée et comme mise en poudre* ('all was knocked down and turned to powder').[228] The success of the artillery inspired the following verse dedicated to Estrées:

…Par bon consen, moyen & diligence,	'…By good accord, method & diligence,
Faict rendre au Roy, &	Made surrender to the King, &
remettre à son nom	reinstate in his name
Soubs le seul bruit du foudroiant	Under the singular noise of the terrible
canon:	cannon
Tesmoing dernier est le Havre	Last witness is the Havre
de grace,	of Grace [Le Havre]
Lequel avés par le vouloir & grace,	Which had by the wish and grace
Du Dieu puissant, & Dieu victorieux	Of God almighty & God victorious
Osté des mains des Anglois	Ousted from the hands of the envious
envieux,	English,
Anglois malings qui l'avoient usurpé,	Cunning English who had usurped it
Contre tout droict raison & equité…[229]	Against all legal right & equity…'

The Venetian ambassador cast an eye on the siege:

On my arrival here there was a truce for the convention, so I was able conveniently to inspect the outer walls, the trenches, and what had been done thereabouts. The garrison within were in fact reduced to a sorry plight, for the besiegers were about to storm the place, as they had already battered effectually and dismantled a bulwark and several towers of the port, and filled up the whole moat, so that with but a little more work they would have opened the road for themselves securely with the spade.

The besiegers had battered so furiously that I know not what fortress could have withstood them; and they had moreover a battery of forty cannon, so that whereas at first they used only to fire twenty or thirty shots each day, they now discharged more than 120, so that it is almost incredible to conceive the actual force which was poured forth from the batteries; and notwithstanding that the besieged have used their powerful artillery and harquebuses, and killed more than 1,000 of the besiegers, the latter are so confident that they make light of their losses.[230]

Having seen the siege, Barbaro did not want to remain much longer. He wanted to avoid the plague, and he did not much like the idea of sleeping in a tent. Montmorency stayed at the manor of Vitanval.

The scene described by Barbaro is confirmed by Warwick, who now pleaded to Elizabeth, explaining that the defences had been breached in two places. The breach was so wide on the Ste-Adresse side that sixty men could enter in line abreast. He stated that the wall had been completely demolished and that the breach was indefensible.

During this time, the relief force had been making ready. Admiral Clinton was en route with twenty vessels and 3,000 men. Crucially, the weather now played a part. They were detained in the Downs off Deal by the southerly winds.

The situation left Warwick with no alternative but to surrender. The negotiations were followed by the signing of a truce. Ambroise Paré comments, 'The English, seeing that they could not sustain an assault because they were severely struck by illness, and principally the plague, surrendered with baggage.' [231] De Thou describes how the two sides drank to each other's health: 'according to the habits of the English, they presented to our Frenchmen, who had advanced to the enemy positions, silver ewers filled with wine'.[232]

The terms of surrender were signed by Warwick on 28 July. The French entered Le Havre the following day. Once again, history repeated itself. Relief forces had arrived too late to save the English garrisons of both Ambleteuse and Calais. Now, a fleet appeared on 30 July, a single day after the surrender. The English army was free to leave. The *Philip & Mary*, the *Lion*, the *Saker*, two galleys and eight other vessels now assisted in transporting the men back home.

The French moved into Le Havre, 'who had no fear of the plague & were happy to enter, hoping to make good booty'.[233] Meanwhile, the plague continued. The new French governor lost 136 men out of six *enseignes* in the space of two weeks. The inhabitants of Le Havre were unhappy with their new French garrison:

> *despite the plague, the said soldiers have since the surrender ravaged and pillaged all the furniture that remained after the flight of the English…. Not content with this, destroying daily and burning the harbour, wood and shutters of the houses in full view of the burghers who could not prevent them.*[234]

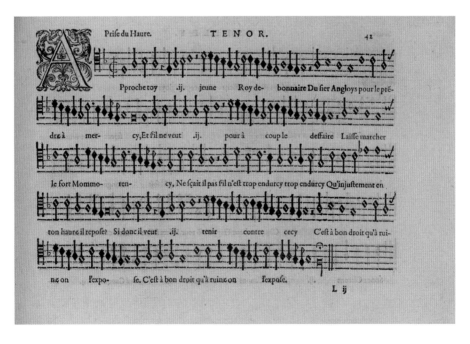

Prise du Havre in *Musique* (Paris, 1570), by Guillaume de Costeley.
Bibliothèque Sainte-Geneviève, Paris, Rés.VM 60
Guillaume de Costeley wrote this piece of music, Approche Toy Jeune Roy Debonnaire, *to celebrate the capture of Le Havre. This was later published with other works in* Musique de Guillaume Costeley, organiste ordinaire et vallet de chambre, du treschrestien et tresinvincible roy de France Charles IX *(Paris, 1570).*

Catherine was congratulated by the Portuguese ambassador, Joâo Pereiia Damtas:

> *For this action, the most Christian King may rightly use the words and speech of Julius Caesar: Veni, Vidi, Vici. And your Majesty those of the prophet Isaiah: Honorem Meum Alteri Non Dabo, all the friends of this Crown and the affectionate servants of your Majesty should rejoice. And myself more than all the rest, being the minister for who I am.*[235]

Corbeyran de Cardaillac Sarlabous, veteran of French campaigns in Scotland, was later appointed the new governor of Le Havre. New defences were added to provide enfilade fire along the beach. These were completed by 1575 as they appear in *Cosmographie Universelle…*, published in Paris by François de Belleforest that year.[236]

THE WAR AT SEA, 1568–98

Apart from Le Havre, English ships were also engaged in operations off La Rochelle and later in the Gironde. The numerous campaigns reveal a fleet that was adept at combined operations.

The relief of La Rochelle

The Protestant stronghold of La Rochelle was threatened by Royalist forces in 1568 and 1573. William Cecil wrote a memo for the sending of aid to the town as early as September 1568. The *lieutenant-général* of the Protestant fleet, Prévost du Chastelier-Portault, left La Rochelle with nine vessels and 900 men in October. He arrived at Plymouth in search of English aid. This was followed by a formal request for aid from Coligny in February 1569. According to La Popelinière, fifty English pioneers were sent to help with the fortification of the town in the same year. This probably explains the presence of a plan of La Rochelle dating from this period in the National Archives.

La Popelinière informs us of a battle off Angoulins near La Rochelle in 1569 between a single English vessel and five French galleys.

> *[Paulin Escalin des Aymards, 1497/98–1578] Le Baron de Garde … chose which Englishman to surround with his galleys. [They] fired shooting right through it. The English set sail … and when they had brought all their pieces to bear on one side, fired them at once at one*

*of the galleys ... then he fired again on the one which was closest in
pursuit, breaking its oars and [hitting] all those who were to the fore.
But no sooner was he out of this when the four others ... rowed at
full speed to grapple and board it, calling for them to surrender. To
this the English only replied with artillery and harquebus fire.*[237]

The English lost around a dozen men in this encounter and their ship
was damaged.

Charles IX knew that Gabriel de Montgomery had been preparing a
fleet since at least the beginning of April 1573. Montgomery had between
fifty and sixty vessels. Some 400 English soldiers were recruited, made
up of pikemen, archers and harquebusiers. Serving under Montgomery
were Captains Nicholas Palmer and Winter. On 27 March, Montgomery
wrote to Essex indicating his desire to leave England for La Rochelle
as soon as possible. The ships sailed from Falmouth and Bristol to take
part in the relief of the port under the flag of St George. The Channel
Islands proved useful to Montgomery as a staging post. Six English ships
succeeded in breaking the blockade to penetrate the harbour. This was
despite *la grande galère* which had been sunk at the harbour entrance by
the besiegers. The arrival of the six ships is confirmed by Walsingham in a
letter to Sir Thomas Smith. Other vessels attempted to make a landing on
Belle-Île but were driven off. According to Henri III, the English lost '35 or
40' men. The failure of French Royalist forces to take the port was partly
due to the provision of English gunpowder.

The Royal Navy also had an important role to play in the blockading
of the ports of the *Ligue*. In 1589, for example, Captain Luke Ward was
sent to the mouth of the Seine with the *Vanguard* to cut communications
with Le Havre and Rouen. This action was repeated during the siege of
Rouen in 1591 when Thomas Grove was given the task of mounting the
blockade. Two pinnaces, the *Charles* and the *Moon*, with eighty men, were
employed on the Seine,[238] together with the *Spy* and the *Gun*. These four
pinnaces (assisted by the Dutch) participated in the daily bombardment
of Rouen. The pinnaces were smaller vessels with keel lengths of around
50 to 60 feet.

(overleaf) Plan of the fortifications of La Rochelle, c.1562–69 The National
Archives (TNA), MPF 1/118. Compare with a view of the siege in 1573:
'Portraict de la Rochelle, & de Forteresses q'les Rebelles y ont faict depuis les
p'miers troubles iusque à p'nt'. 1573. British Museum, London, 1920.0427.25

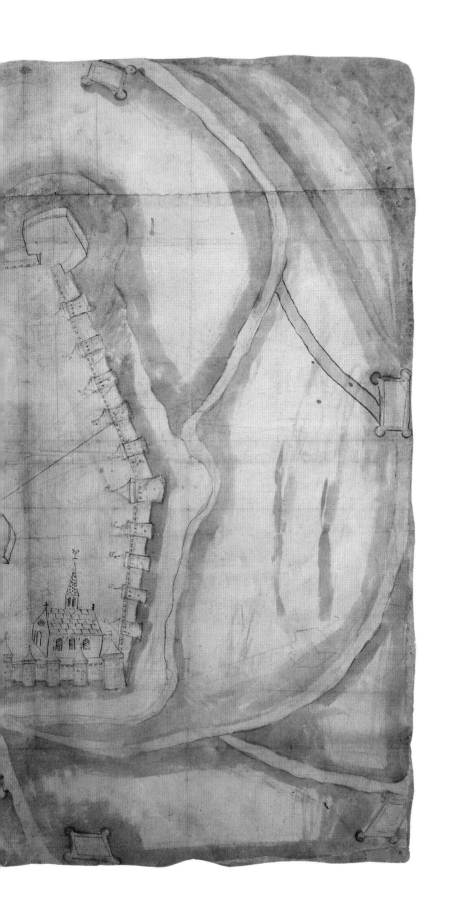

La Gironde

The 'Wine Fleet' was usually escorted by two warships between England and Bordeaux. In January 1594, the 'Bordeaux Fleet' was made up of seventeen ships from London, eight from the North of England and three from elsewhere. The safety of this profitable trade depended on the compliance of the governor of Blaye. From Blaye, traffic in the Gironde was easy to control. The fortifications of Blaye had been strengthened with angled bastions.

In 1589, a flotilla of two French, two English and two Scottish vessels (note that the Scots were also fond of wine) had forced the governor to submit. Beauvoir La Nocle wrote to Burghley on 2 August 1592 requesting the escort to be increased from two to eight or ten warships. At the request of Henri IV, Elizabeth authorised the stationing of a squadron of six warships in the Gironde for an initial period of six months. The following year, Blaye was once again causing problems. This time, Peter Houghton[239] was sent from London. The English squadron of six ships mounted a river blockade of Blaye while Jacques de Goyon, comte de Matignon, conducted operations on land. The siege is clearly depicted in a map in the British Library[240] and is described in a manuscript of the Bibliothèque Nationale in Paris, *Discours du Siège de Blaye.*[241] In April 1593, the English ships were forced to withdraw to the Bec d'Ambès, at the confluence of the Garonne and the Dordogne, on the arrival of the much larger Spanish force of sixteen vessels. There were skirmishes between the English and the Spanish under Pedro de Zubiaur. Two English vessels were lost, including that of Houghton, set ablaze by fireships. A number of English sailors were treated for their burns at a hospital in Bordeaux. The loss cost Houghton £1,500. According to English and French sources, at least two Spanish vessels were lost. Two had reportedly been sunk by Houghton's ship. Matignon finally lifted the siege on 20 July, following the reinforcement of Blaye with men and munitions by six Spanish hoys.

This had perhaps been the most spectacular of all engagements involving English vessels in French waters during the wars. There were no battles such as there had been between *la Belle Cordelière* and the *Regent*, simply because the French lacked larger vessels. The French fleet could also be found lacking in that it had fewer smaller vessels. In 1597, a request was made for six English 'roberges' (rowbarges, a specific type of vessel used in the Tudor navy) to be sent to assist in the capture of Nantes.

The ships of the Royal Navy gained considerable experience during these wars. They found, for example, that galleys were not necessarily the best vessels for coastal waters, at least in the Channel. The galleys were traditionally vessels best suited to the Mediterranean. Their use against an English fleet off Portsmouth in 1545 had led to their adoption by Henry VIII.[242] A French galley had also been captured in the same war. At the beginning of Elizabeth's reign, a Venetian named Augustine Levello was employed to oversee the galleys on a wage of 16d per day.

The main advantage of a galley over ships was that it could operate without the wind. In calm waters, and with little wind, it could advance faster than a ship. By 1545, the English had found a solution to the threat of the galley in the form of the rowbarge. In the 1540s, the French used their galleys in much the same way as modern frigates to operate ahead of the main fleet. Later, the lack of larger vessels raised their status in the fleet.

There were numerous disadvantages. During the Le Havre expedition, the galley was found to be incompatible with conditions in the Seine estuary. Such a vessel, with a draught of eight or nine feet, could not cross the sandbanks. The French, for example, had been able to sail their galley out of Honfleur only at high tide. Small sailing vessels called *fregates* (Claude de Sainliens translates *fregate* or *fragate* as 'pinnase')[243] were found to be more expedient. Their draught of only four feet enabled them to pass through shallow water. The fact that the main armament of a galley (i.e. a cannon, demi-cannon or culverin) was mounted in the prow meant that the whole vessel would have to be pointed in the direction of the enemy. Galleys could not fire broadsides, with heavier pieces. They were vulnerable to attacks from the side as well as astern, where lighter pieces were mounted. Another handicap was the team of oarsmen (*la chiourme*). There were around 250 oarsmen per French galley. In a list of the English fleet of around 1602, the English galleys *La Volatilia* and *La Galeretia* had 216 and 244 oarsmen respectively. The oarsmen in the *chiourme* were effectively non-combatants and placed a heavy burden on supplies. Given that galleys were not built to carry large reserves of rations, they were limited to fighting short campaigns. Similarly, a large crew would also raise costs.

The history of the *Primrose*

The story of one ship, the *Primrose*, is interesting as it is mentioned throughout the wars. The *Primrose* appears in a list of ships of the Royal Navy in 1551. It had a displacement of 300 tonnes and a crew of 200. It was sold to a group of entrepreneurs from London in December 1554.[244] The ship appears in a navy list once more in 1560, having been repossessed. In 1563, during the Le Havre expedition, it was included in the ordinary charges for Portsmouth. There is evidence in the State Papers that the *Primrose* was still a royal ship in 1573. It was lent to Sir Peter Carew, who undertook to either replace or pay for all munitions and material expended during the voyage to La Rochelle. Montgomery himself was on board the *Primrose* at the head of a fleet sent to relieve the port. The story of the *Primrose* (or at least the name) does not end here. It was sold in 1575 to John Thomas, and was due to be sent to the Azores in 1581 in support of the French expedition. The *Primrose* appears on the title page of the book by Humphrey Mote, *The Primrose of London* (1585),[245] in which she was rated as a vessel of 150 tonnes. A *Primrose* of 180 tonnes from London joined Frobisher's squadron sent to Brittany in 1594. Another *Primrose* was on the navy list in 1601, this time of 116 tonnes.

THE MAINE, NORMANDY AND BRITTANY CAMPAIGNS, 1589–94

English military intervention during 1589–94 may be viewed as three separate campaigns under four different commanders: Willoughby (the abortive march on Paris), Williams with Essex (Normandy) and Norris (Brittany/Maine). Norris led two campaigns in Brittany. The force under Sir Roger Williams fought partly independently of the others. Their capacity as leaders apart, the four were victims of Henri de Navarre's strategy. Each force operated with Royalist forces in large-scale *petite guerre* campaigns of sieges and skirmishes.

Willoughby[246]

In 1589, Henri IV faced Catholic forces under Mayenne in Normandy.

Some Englishmen were actively engaged in the defence of Dieppe before the arrival of Willoughby's army. According to an English woodcut, an English gunner participated in the battle of Arques on 21 September 1589, knocking out two enemy guns and killing their master gunner in the process.[247] Aymar de Chatte, the governor of Dieppe, had requested a gunner from England who was 'skilful in fireworks'. The chosen gunner was Edward Webb, who received 20 *couronnes* (£6) per month with free lodging.

On 22 September, according to *Ligue* propaganda, two English ships fell into their hands. The ships were full of armour as well as a pearl-encrusted saddle, reportedly sent as a gift from Elizabeth to Henri. The following day, thirteen English vessels carrying munitions, victuals and clothing arrived in port. Previously, 1,200 Scots had arrived, 'dressed like figures from antiquity, with coats of mail and iron helmets, covered with black cloth like a priest's bonnet'.[248] This image is not far from a drawing of Irish soldiers by Albrecht Dürer done in 1521.[249] François de Ciuille acted as agent in the levying of troops in Scotland.

News of the arrival of the English and Scots may well have forced Mayenne to withdraw. William Camden, on the other hand, writes that the English arrived the day after their withdrawal. Possibly Mayenne could see the English ships on the horizon. Following the battle of Arques and Mayenne's withdrawal, Henri was free to march on Paris.

For the siege of Paris, the English were placed under the command of Biron. They attacked from the east along the south (left) bank of the Seine towards the Latin Quarter, so-called because of the location of the Sorbonne. Here they captured the faubourg St-Marcel. This success, however, was not followed up owing to a lack of artillery support. Now politics came to influence Henri's military strategy. He chose to sound the retreat rather than allow his English contingent to advance too far. He was reluctant to see Paris fall, even partially, into English hands. He will also have been aware that the deployment of foreign troops in the city had previously provoked the *journée des Barricades* ('day of barricades').

Henri showed his unwillingness to use force. He ordered his men into line not only because he preferred an open battle: he did not wish to damage either his capital or relations with his own subjects. As William Camden comments, he 'had no lust to expose it for prey'.[250] In fact, according to Camden, Henri hoped that Paris would soon be under his subjugation. In view of this, he was unwilling to use the full force of a battery against the city. The battery of cannon put in place appears only to have been for show. The fact that the Parisians made fun of the salvoes fired by Henri's artillery seems to support this.

Meanwhile, other towns fell, one after the other. Henri wrote to Elizabeth only one month after the arrival of her men: 'Madam, I have been so virtuously served by your troops and with so many instances of wise conduct and valour of Baron Willeby distinctly seconded also by the other gentlemen your subjects.'[251]

November witnessed the capture of Vendôme, where d'Aumont and the English entered via the *faubourg* St-Georges. The English were at Le Mans by 19 November, where provision was made for the sick and wounded. The city surrendered on 2 December, following the capture of the suburbs. The capture of Alençon followed in the same month. Here, the English had captured a *ravelin*. English soldiers would be confronted by *ravelins* on several occasions in France: they were V-shaped outworks often constructed to protect gateways or bridges. The *ravelin* was an improvement on the medieval barbican, which was semicircular. The town's castle would take longer to subdue, but it finally fell on 14 December. Though certain gentlemen were present, regular English soldiers did not play a part in the capture of Falaise, where the castle was taken by assault on 26 December.

English support enabled Henri to continue his campaign into winter. He captured Honfleur on 14 January 1590 and achieved a second victory over Mayenne at Ivry on 14 March.

Williams and Essex

Sir Roger Williams landed at Dieppe on 10 April 1591. Sixty of his men were placed in garrison at the castle and others were at Le Pollet to the north, which had been fortified to protect the harbour.

All of the 600 men under Williams were employed in the attempt against Aumale in Normandy at the end of the month. They were joined by another 600 under Aymar de Chatte and de Palliseul. Using the cover of a wood, they managed to surprise the town and then set about laying siege to the castle and its garrison of 100 men. In a *tour de force*, Williams grouped his 600 men into a single battalion. The defenders believed that they were only the advance party of a much larger English force and consequently agreed to negotiate terms of surrender.

Two regiments of *Ligueurs* (1,200 men) held the village of 'Cinquessaunce' (St-Saëns)[252] on the Varenne to the north of Rouen. Here they had erected two barricades. The assault on St-Saëns took place on 20 May 1591. The State Papers provide us with an idea of the positions of the English infantry in the line of battle. There were two wings at the fore, each with fifty harquebusiers and twelve halberdiers. The central formation was composed of pikemen *en masse* followed by two wings of harquebusiers behind. Coming to 'push of pike' (*à la pointe*), the two barricades were forced and the English entered the church. This action secured Dieppe and its hinterland and won for Williams a special commendation from Henri. He wrote to Elizabeth, 'Sir Roger Wylemes [sic] shows his valour by the good duty he has done with his troop so that victory may rightly be called yours.'[253]

Following this, Williams found himself involved in operations in the suburbs of Paris and then Noyon. Noyon was not an easy place to invest, thanks to several streams and rivers that ran around the town. Nevertheless, it fell on 19 August 1591.

An attempt against Rouen had been proposed in 1589 but not followed up. When Essex arrived in France, he discovered that Henri had barely considered besieging Rouen – he was occupied with Noyon. Over the Rhine, it was said that he was now planning to march on Rheims. Elizabeth had plenty to say about Henri and his 'preposterous actions', the fact that he divided his forces, the loss of time and his lack of presence before Rouen:

> *We our selfe do well consider howe dangerous it shall be to divide*
> *his Forces, at the leaste so to esloigne himselfe from this Action of*
> *Rouen as, by lacke of his Presence, the Interprise must be more*
> *doubtfull, specially considring he hathe loste such Oportunitie of*
> *Tyme paste since he determined it.*[254]

According to a *Ligueur* captain in Rouen, Guillaume Valdory,[255] Elizabeth had offered a reward to the first gunners to open fire on Rouen.

Having been summoned by Henri, the Earl of Essex left for Noyon, where he arrived with 200 horse shortly after its capture. Thereafter, Essex waited at Pont de l'Arche and sent orders for the rest of his army encamped at Arques to join him. From here, he marched to Pavilly.

Essex received a personal setback on 8 September with the loss of his own brother, Walter Devereux. Leaving Pavilly, his force of 1,000 foot and 300 horse now approached Rouen from the north-west. Essex had given the order to charge to some of his horsemen but had not seen that his brother had also gone forward. Valdory describes the skirmish that took place between the Mont-aux-Malades (today Mont-St-Aignan) and the Porte Cauchoise as seen by the *Ligueurs*. He describes how the English had brought up a culverin that fired three shots. Valdory puts the English losses at between 100 and 120 dead and wounded as opposed to just two dead by Essex. His brother, having advanced too far, was caught in an ambush. 'He fell into an ambuscade and was shott in the face.'[256] This moment was captured on paper by the engineer Edmund Yorke,[257] who clearly shows a volley of shots being fired from behind the

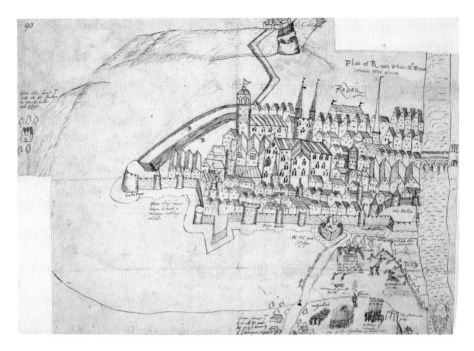

Plan of the siege of Rouen, September 1591, by Edmund Yorke. British Library, Cotton MS Augustus I.ii.90. © The British Library Board. The scene depicts the skirmish before the Porte Cauchoise at Rouen on 8 September 1591

hedges. A church referred to by Essex (possibly St-André-Hors-la-Ville) is also depicted. Devereux's body was placed in a lead coffin before being returned to England.

Before laying siege to Rouen itself, the allies decided first to take Gournay, to the east. The siege of Gournay was justified. By taking the town, Henri IV would be able to block a relief force under Parma. Operating in unison with the English forces were Armand de Gontaut, baron de Biron, his son Charles, and Hacqueville, who oversaw the siege. The arrival of the French before Gournay was expected on 19 September. They were supported by a contingent of 'Swissers' who also had the task of guarding the French artillery. A pen and ink sketch of the siege depicts the arrival of English troops.[258] The plan was drawn by Edmund Yorke and carried back to England by Captain Turner. It shows the town seen from the north. English pikemen and harquebusiers are clearly depicted advancing from the east. The Collégiale St-Hildevert is visible in the centre and the Capucins Convent on the right. The rivers in the sketch are those of the Epte and the Morette. The action at Gournay-en-Bray may best be described as a 'micro-siege'. It had all the elements of a full-scale siege except that everything was in miniature.

English trenches were advanced to the northern walls of the town in George Tuchet, Lord Audley's quarter. Meanwhile, an English battery was established to fire at the walls from the south. Both English and French batteries succeeded in making breaches. 750 Englishmen were committed to give the assault on their breach. This would be in three waves: the first composed of twenty pikemen and twenty musketeers supported by ten halberdiers. The next would be the strongest, with 200 pikemen, 150 musketeers and twenty halberdiers. Finally, these were to be supported by 180 pikemen, 130 musketeers and twenty halberdiers. It appears that Essex himself took part in this assault. He was reproached by the Council for not taking care of himself, 'you did hazard yourself at Gournay by trailing of a pike, to approach the place like a common soldier, a thing not indeed commendable in you, although it was reported by such as pretended to give you great glory for the same'.[259] The English ambassador, Sir Henry Unton, was present.

Robert Carey, Earl of Monmouth, recalled:

> After we had battered the town, and made a breach, in a morning betimes we were ready to give an assault; but the chief commanders of the town, fearing their own weakness, held out a white flag to parley, and upon conference it was agreed, that the commanders and soldiers should in safety pass out of the town, and that the town should be delivered to my Lord for the King's use. All which was performed that morning before twelve of the clock.[260]

Gournay fell on 26 September. It was finally decided to lay siege to Rouen itself in the second week of November. This was far too late. This was normally the moment that armies would settle into winter quarters. The besiegers' trenches risked being flooded at this time of year and fresh earthworks could simply collapse. Luckily, the besiegers benefited from a mild winter in the initial stages but the weather became somewhat harsher. The pioneers were inhibited by heavy rain, deep snow and hard frost. Furthermore, seven pieces of English artillery reached Rouen only by mid-December. (Artillery for Essex's campaign arrived at Dieppe on 22 September 1591 via Guernsey.) Three pieces, together with their English gunners, were diverted by Henri to besiege St-Valery-sur-Somme. The French contingent of siege artillery was commanded by Philibert de La Guiche, who had previously seen action at Ivry.

(overleaf) Plan of the siege of Gournay-en-Bray, 1591, by Edmund Yorke.
The National Archives (TNA), SP 9/200 46 (MPF1/153)

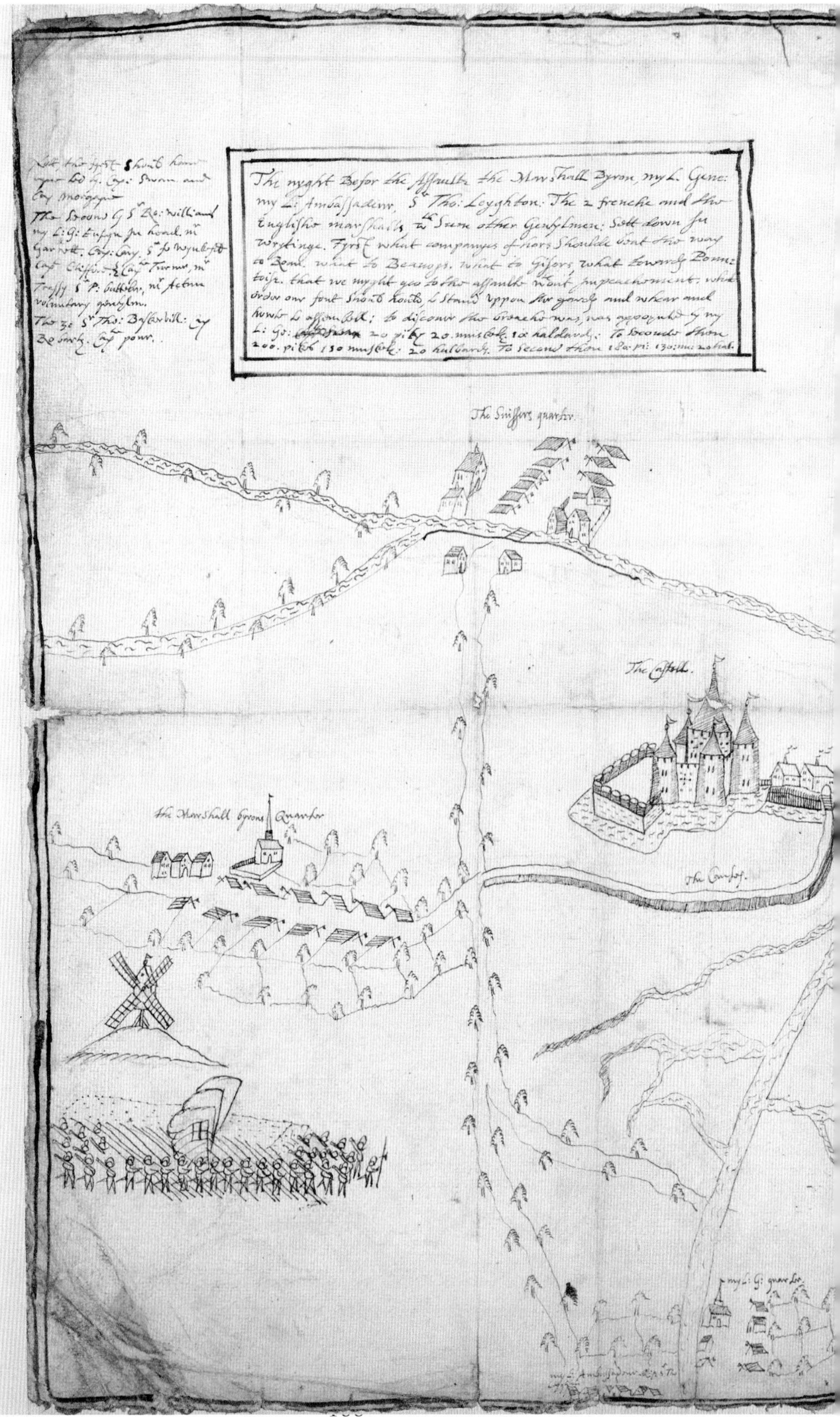

The text in the boxed area (top right):

The nyght befor the assaulte the Marshall Byron my L: Gene:
my L: Ambassadors, S: Tho: Leyghton: The 2 frenche and the
Englishe marshalls to sum other Gentlemen: sett down in
wrytinge. Fyrst what companyes of hors shoulde sent the way
to Roan, what to Beauvps, what to Gysors, what toward Ponn:
toize, that we myght goe to the assaulte w:out impeachment: what
order our fower sward kontes to stand vppon the gards and nekar and
howh to assaulted; to discouer the breaches was, was appoynted by my
L: Go: .... 20 pikes 20 musketts 10 halberds; To seconde them
200: pikes 150 musketts 20 halberds; To second them 180 p: 130: mu: 10 hal:

The Suissers quarter.

The Castell.

the Marshall Byrons quarter

The Camp:

my L: G: quarter.

Stafford Quarter

Eng: for by assault

Tow: Galways w[i]th back, the Enemy from her defaced of the french trench

Galtery for the Eng trenche

Eng: for the assault

Mon: de Boilions quarter

Eng: for the assault

Gorney Towne: taken 26: Sep: 91 Stilo Veter[y].

The English trenche

trench for the assault

The French trench

HER MAJESTYS STATE PAPER OFFICE

Gattery for the french trenche

Swissers for the guard of the ordinance

The hye way to Roane

The trench repared by

The quarter of gandy

The Eng: reproched

my L: Suidy

quarter

3. 153

To besiege Rouen in 1591 would be not be like the siege of 1562. The city's fortifications had been strengthened considerably. A pen and ink drawing of 1610 by Joachim du Viert gives an idea of the strength of one of its bastions at the Porte de Martainville, on the south side.[261] The proof that the defences in 1591 were indeed more advanced than in 1562 is shown by the sophistication of the siege-works that were needed to overcome them. An illustration is the plan of the Colline Ste-Catherine that accompanies *Discours du Siège de la Ville de Rouen* by Guillaume Valdory.[262] The besiegers did far more than just digging trenches. They established a fort with angled bastions, which provided flanking fire. The sophistication of the siege-works is also demonstrated by the project to block the Seine by Edmund Yorke.[263] Sir Thomas Coningsby refers to the plan in an entry in his journal on 16 November 1591:

> *This daie sir Edmund Yorke hath bene upon the ryver to vieue the convenientest place, as well to stopp th'ennemyes passage, as to be accommodated for all necessaries out of base Normandye, and to passe and repasse th'armye on that syde.... Sir Edmund Yorke hath resolved upon a place an English mile distaunte from the towne, and where there are villages on both sydes, and an island in the mydest of the ryver, in all the which there shalbe forts made and peeces of artyllerye planted, and a bridge of boats.*[264]

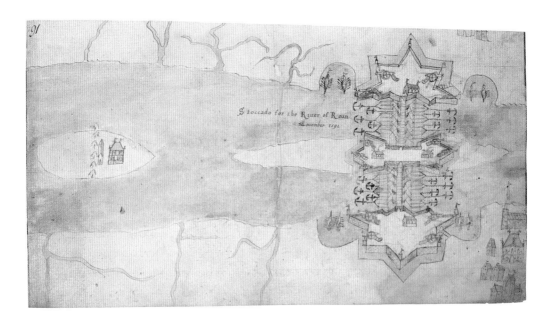

Project for a bridge across the Seine, [16 November] 1591, by Edmund Yorke.
British Library, Cotton MS Augustus I.ii.91. © The British Library Board

The plan involved the construction of fortifications to defend a bridge over the Seine. The bridge had two functions: a crossing point for Royalist forces and a means of preventing relief being sent up the Seine to Rouen. Two pontoon bridges were planned, joined by an island in the middle. These pontoons were held in place using chains and anchors. Yorke would have known of the 'infernal machine' used by Federigo Giambelli to destroy the Spanish bridge during the siege of Antwerp in 1585. He took care to see that the bridge was fortified with a *stoccado* on each side. The *stoccado* protected the bridge from boats attempting to force a passage. They would also protect the bridge from fireships (*brûlots*) or boats filled with explosives drifting from upstream. The English and Spanish bridges had several features in common. Apart from similarities in construction, the bridges were defended by a flotilla of rowbarges. Equipped with a light piece of artillery in the prow, these were both agile and rapid. They would be able to intercept any dangers before they came too close to the bridge.

It was also Giambelli who had worked on the fortifications at Tilbury on the Thames. Here, a boom was constructed using masts and chains secured to boats at anchor. A pontoon bridge was also constructed to link both sides of the Thames. He was later employed at Carisbrooke Castle on the Isle of Wight (from 1597 to 1601). Interestingly, here we find another link with the Carey family, Sir George Carey being the governor. The engineers at Rouen had at least 200 pioneers recruited in London and Middlesex. 400 pioneers had been landed at Dieppe by December. A further fifty miners from Cornwall were to join them.

To some, the Rouen enterprise appeared simple. Elizabeth reassured Christian I, prince of Anhalt, when he was on the verge of abandoning the project (due to non-payment by Henri), telling him that taking Rouen would not be too difficult and that it would not take long. Béthune (later duc de Sully), too, in his *Oeconomies Royales*, found that the city was 'very weak in certain places and consequently very easy to take'.[265]

The main effort was to be made against the Ste-Catherine fort, which also happened to be the strongest point. The fort here had stone bastions with embrasures covering the flanks, as depicted in the drawing by Edmund Yorke.[266] The Colline Ste-Catherine had steep slopes on three sides. On the fourth lay a plateau where the Royalists concentrated their forces. The same side, however, also possessed the best defences. According to Davila, the fort of Ste-Catherine had a ditch with a width of thirty feet and a depth of ten. Even if the besiegers succeeded in taking the first line of defences, they would still have to capture the Abbey of Ste-Catherine and its two bastions.

One thing lacking, however, was more English soldiers. As the English ambassador Sir Henry Unton said, 'The French have no courage to attempt; the landsknechts, until their pay, will not; and the English are so few, poor, and sickly as they cannot effect anything of themselves.'[267] One assault on the fort was condemned to fail from the start, as the ladders proved to be two yards too short!

Among French sources is *Discours Veritable de ce qui s'est fait et passé durant le siege de Rouën* (Paris, 1592), perhaps written by the poet Philippe Desportes, who took part in the defence of Rouen. In this *discours* the author describes the defence against the English assault. Another colourful piece is to be found in *Coq a l'asne fort* (Paris, 1592):

Le muet canonnier se mocque	'The silent gunner makes fun
De vous qui dit à plaine voix,	Of you [as he] shouts,
Qui veut pour six blancs six	"Who wants for six targets six
Anglois,	Englishmen,
Que j'ay du canon attrapez,	That I have got with the cannon?
Et les autres sont decampez	And the others have decamped,"
Car à coups de bonnes rapieres	For with blows of good rapiers
On leur eust taillé des	We've put a spoke in their [English]
croupieres...[268]	wheel...'

Béthune provides an account of a sortie made by 800 men against an English trench: 'after a combat of two hours' duration, where it is said that the English worked miracles, they were at last driven back, leaving more than fifty of them dead and the trench lost for the King'.[269]

English forces regrouped and, in an effort to regain their honour, prepared a counter-attack:

> *The noblemen of England, who had insisted on being at the fore ... were so valiantly assisted by the English musketeers, pikemen and halbardiers that the enemy were stunned by such an impetuous assault ... that they fled towards the fort ... and the trenches were regained in half an hour. In these the English took up positions so strongly ... that not only was it impossible for the enemy to dislodge them but they also prevented them from advancing towards the counterscarps of their ravelins.*[270]

Essex was recalled to England in January 1592. Sir Roger Williams took charge in his place. On the approach of Parma with his relief force, Henri was apparently caught off-balance. He raised the siege on 10 April. Parma would have arrived earlier, but he had been ill with gout in Brussels.

Meanwhile, the Spanish defenders of Steenwijk in the Netherlands, taking heart from this success, sang:

...Roan, ville fidele	'Rouen, town devoted
Au catholicque foy,	To the Catholic faith,
Laquelle est delivre	Which has been saved
Des forces du Biernoys	From the forces of the Béarnais [Henri IV]
Par le bon duc de Parma,	By the good Duke of Parma,
Gouverneur general,	Governor-General,
Qui a acquis gran gloire,	Who has gained great glory,
Et tous ses bons soldats...[271]	And all his good soldiers.'

Steenwijk had been captured by the Spanish in 1581 but was regained by the Dutch in 1592.

Sir Thomas Baskerville criticised Henri in his choice of tactics. The choice of attacking the fort of Ste-Catherine ignored the maxim of war: *ville prise, château rendu* ('town taken, castle surrendered').[272] Even if Ste-Catherine had fallen, it is not certain that Henri would have allowed the bombardment of Rouen itself. The blame for the failure was in part placed upon the shoulders of Biron. As Béthune wrote, 'he did everything out of spite and did not want his town to be taken'.[273] Biron was a useful scapegoat; he was already dead and dishonoured when Béthune finally wrote his memoirs. Parma too was dead. His reputation as a formidable soldier also provided a useful screen over Henri's real intentions.

Henri's attitude towards the capture of Rouen by force is shown by his regular absence from the siege. He did not spend any significant amount of time before the city. Elizabeth had expected him to appear before Rouen with his forces in September. According to Edward Grimston, he was expected there by 23 October. On 20 October, however, he was still at Sedan. He finally arrived in camp over a month later (23 November), but another week passed before he began directing the siege. He was present at Rouen from 3 to 18 December, but left the siege again on 20 January 1592, only to return in March. He put all his energy into skirmishes in the surrounding countryside, at Gournay and Bures-en-Bray. If Henri had been serious about taking the city by force, he would have been present as he later was at the siege of Amiens. Henri's reluctance may in part be explained by his own father's experience at Rouen in the first war. It was during the siege of 1562 that his father, Antoine de Bourbon, was hit by a harquebus shot, and died from the wound a month later.

The English formed the rearguard of the army. Leaving Ste-Catherine around six o'clock in the evening, they withdrew first to St-Aubin to the east of Rouen, on the north bank of the Seine, and then to Quincampoix.

Once Parma had relieved Rouen, Henri found himself in a difficult position. His army, now regrouped, threatened the supply lines to the east. Henri could still feel confident. According to the Bohemian witness Charles de Žerotin, Parma had *cavaliers très-mauvais* ('very poor horsemen').[274] There followed a period of manoeuvring by the two armies, then trench warfare and skirmishes. Henri sought a field battle while Parma did the opposite. Keeping Dieppe to his rear, Henri took his forces north of Rouen to Anglesqueville and then Motteville near Yvetot.

Parma soon found himself at Croisset. Hoping to re-establish communications between Rouen and Le Havre, the *Ligueurs* headed towards Caudebec. Henri, meanwhile, concentrated his army at Valliquerville, west of Yvetot. Caudebec fell to the *Ligueurs* following a brief siege (24–27 April). Mayenne established defensive lines between Yvetot, St-Clair, Auzebosc and Louvetot, north of Caudebec. On 20/30 April the English were engaged in a sharp skirmish near Valliquerville. The combat at Yvetot (28 April) was regarded as a success. Sir Roger Williams and Sir Matthew Morgan were commended by Henri. During this encounter, eight or nine Englishmen were killed and forty-seven wounded. The English were given *la pointe* (the honour of being at the forefront) in the following engagement. Williams still had as many as 1,600 men under him. With these, he succeeded in overwhelming the enemy trenches. Royalist pressure forced the *Ligueurs* to withdraw. Parma and his army fell back on Caudebec on the morning of 12 May. The English pinnace, the *Charles*, was reportedly sunk by artillery fire at Caudebec. The vessels on the Seine gave Parma a *continuelle gresle d'harqbuzades* ('a continuous hail of harquebus shot') and they also threatened his pontoon bridge. Nevertheless, Parma made a successful river crossing with his army on the night of 21 May, assisted by the sunken mast of the *Charles*.

Henri highlighted the need for Elizabeth's continued support when he wrote to the Earl of Essex from Yvetot on 15 May: 'I do not have any way of preventing them … without the aid of the queen, madam my good sister, to whom on this occasion, I again now write for new relief … giving charge to the Sieur de Beauvoir, my ambassador.'[275]

The *Ligueur* success was tempered by the death of Parma at Arras in the same year. The events now left the duc de Mercœur more dependent on Spanish support.

Williams reported to Lord Burghley an attempt against the town of Crotoy in the Somme estuary:

> *Yesternight we passed the River at lowe water with iii. Hundred of ours, one hundred frenche, carrieng with us a few skalling Laders … with some xx. Or thirtie marriners, being arrived two hours before daie harde by Crittoie. By reason of our ill passage through deepe mude and sandes, the fier of our maches were diskovered. Notwithstanding that they were in Armes, we commanded Capten Floode, Lieutenant Bret, Ansigne Heathe to the skale accompanied with three skore Pikes and Thirtie musketeers…. My Lord of Wymes [James Colville, Laird of Wemyss][276] comanded a skottish Capten with some xl. skottishe and frenche to accompanie Floode. Also fortie or fiftie souldiers with the marriners were directed to enter their shipping anckoring under Crittoie. Being attempted with resolucion our ladders were too shorte, all saving one which broke, ells the cowardnes of the defendants was suche that our men woulde a carried the place, for our shott belowe did beate the moste of the defendants from the walls. Having staied there one howre perceaving no meanes to enter we retired our men.*[277]

Williams was still in France in 1593, and took part in the recapture of St-Valery-sur-Somme. At the beginning of April, Williams assembled his 1,600 men before the king and his sister, Catherine de Bourbon. In May 1593 the English marched to assist a French force in the capture of Dreux. This force included English horse. According to Henrico Davila, an English engineer was present at the siege. Here Davila is perhaps referring to Williams himself. The English trenches were dug to approach the left side of the *ravelin* that guarded the *porte de Paris*. An English captain was ordered to take the bastion with thirty men. Williams drove the trenches towards the counterscarp of the castle during the night.

Norris

Rouen was not the only theatre in which English forces were active in France. They were also occupied on the west coast of the country –

Brittany, lower Normandy and Maine. Here they were involved in a war of movement comprising mainly short sieges and skirmishes but which together resulted in campaigns that were long and hard.

In Brittany it became apparent that the English force might require Royalist support, as on 9 April 1591 Norris's force was lacking 2,000 men. Elizabeth was disappointed by Henri's support in Normandy, and it became apparent that she could expect much the same in Brittany. She told him, 'If the coast is lost, from where all your aid comes, how will you keep the rest?'[278]

Henri did not wish to use overwhelming force against Mercœur, the leader of the *Ligue* in Brittany, instead hoping to win him over through peaceful means. Elizabeth warned Henri that she was prepared to withdraw her men if they were abandoned by the governor of Brittany, Henri de Bourbon-Vendôme, prince de Dombes.

The campaign began at Paimpol. Despite the fact that the port was difficult to fortify, it did have a number of advantages. The route south from Paimpol was straight and flat, facilitating the movement of English artillery. Elsewhere, the terrain was undulating. Furthermore, the *bocage* (wooded terrain) of Normandy and Maine was ideal for ambushes. Captains Heron and Jackson led an assault that resulted in the capture of Guingamp on 23 May. The Breton town of Corlay was taken on 7 June.

Mercœur suggested that the two armies should meet in open battle. Dombes replied favourably, leaving the choice of place and time to Mercœur. Mercœur made known that he would be at the most suitable place between Corlay and Guingamp on Thursday at ten o'clock in the morning. At Châtelaudren, Norris stood with his army in face of the enemy for four days. According to William Devereux, Mercœur had a force of 500 horse and 6,000 foot, including 4,000 Spaniards. 300 English under Captains Wingfield and Morton as well as the French under Jacques de Montgomery, seigneur de Corbouzon, the governor of Morlaix, were sent to the fore. They were supported by the English horse under Captain Anthony Sherley and 50 *chevaux-légers* (light horse) under René de Grézille, seigneur de Tremblaye and governor of Moncontour and Paimpol. They swept aside the skirmishers before them. A cannonade was exchanged by the two armies. Not wishing to fight, Mercœur broke off the engagement and his army withdrew on Monday night.

Soon after their arrival, the English force found themselves undertaking a major enterprise with the siege of Lamballe, which occupied a strategic position near the coast. In the sixteenth century the town was still surrounded by impressive fortifications. Its location, however, also made

Norris's task of laying siege somewhat easier, as everything needed could be brought in by sea. Norris joined François de La Noue for the attack, confident that the town would fall, but La Noue received a fatal wound during the siege.[279] English losses included Captain Bainton, Lieutenant Barber and Hugh Paulet.

The campaign proved to be a drain on English forces. By the third week of August, Norris's force was down to 1,200 men. They continued to make an impact. Following the capture of St-Méen by Dombes, Norris sent the English pikemen to bar the route between Mercœur and the town. Mercœur, perhaps over-estimating his adversary, once more avoided battle. Norris had just 700 men remaining at the end of September, forcing the Council to send reinforcements to Normandy from the Netherlands. 300 Englishmen aided Dombes in the capture of the château de Châtillon (Le Plessis Inoguen, Châtillon-en-Vendelais) between Vitré and Fougères in September. The English captain, John Latham, took charge of the garrison at the Château de Goué, La Dorée, which had fallen on 17 November. By the end of 1591, Norris's army was in need of reinforcements and munitions. His brother Sir Henry was sent in January 1592 to request support from Elizabeth.

While Norris was in England, the allies suffered two setbacks. Royalist forces set about laying siege to Craon, defended by Pierre Le Cornu, seigneur du Plessis de Cosmes (d.1612). At Craon, the Royalist commanders neglected to position the army in order of battle, leaving companies to fight in isolation. The English pikemen closed the rear of the army, supported by light horsemen and French skirmishers. These men were used to cover the disorderly French retreat. According to De Thou, *Les Anglois se battirent avec un courage héroïque* ('the English fought with heroic courage').[280] Isolated, they could not hold their position indefinitely. Meanwhile, the fields of unharvested wheat offered at least some refuge for the survivors. The *Ligue* did not miss the opportunity to publish the defeat of Craon. *Discours veritable de la defaite de l'Armee des Princes de Conty, & de Dombes, le 23. May 1592 par Monseigneur le Duc de Mercueur devant la ville de Craon, en Anjou* was printed at Lyons.[281] One estimate put English losses at between 400 and 500 dead and 200 wounded. One consequence of this defeat was the sending of 100 English lancers from the Netherlands to Brittany. The intention was to hold them in reserve to support infantry.

Another setback came in October at Ambrières. Provisions and a new company of men from England had recently arrived at Caen. Concerned about the safety of the men, as well as the soldiers' pay that they were transporting, Anthony Wingfield decided to meet them on the way. Wingfield expected to reach Ambrières by 16 September but they were still at Domfront on the 20th. Wingfield marched his force of 500 men via Ambrières, where they remained for two weeks.[282] He sent a company of men to meet the reinforcements. The *Ligueur* Boisdauphin[283] saw his chance the day the men left. Boisdauphin had enough time to gather a force of 1,500 harquebusiers and 200 horse drawn from local garrisons such as Fougères, Château-Gontier and Laval. With him he had two pieces of artillery.

The English defence was focused on the church of Notre-Dame, a strong stone building on the north bank of the Varenne. Boisdauphin's artillery, however, proved conclusive. The defenders were powerless to hold the barricades that they had thrown up. Even the church was abandoned. Anthony Wingfield managed to mount a last defence in a large house. They held out for two hours until nightfall. Now, with all their powder spent and the buildings on fire, Wingfield sought a truce. He was taken as a prisoner to Laval and was ransomed for 10,000 *couronnes* (£3,000).

If the *bocage* could hide the enemy, it could also provide cover for retreating armies. The hedges would have covered the men heading towards Domfront, offering obstacles to pursuing horse. It was at Domfront that the men were able to regroup with reinforcements from England. Although they were now without their commander and sergeant-major they were still able to muster a force of 500 men.

The combination of recent losses and the cost, as well as Henri and his lack of interest in Brittany, left Lord Burghley considering whether the queen should continue to support Henri in this province.

By February 1593, Norris had around 1,400 well-trained men at his disposal. Minor successes followed, stabilising the situation in Maine. The château of Montjean was taken in April and then La Guerche on 12 April.[284] St-Sulpice, a small village south of Laval, also fell in the same month. On 2 May, the English were once again in combat, this time at a crossing on the Mayenne at Port-Ringeard ('Rhingeard') south of Laval. Their experience overcame men under Boisdauphin. The English lodged at Chammes near Ste-Suzanne on 15 May. Later, we find them at Ballon to the north of Le Mans and at Maigné and Chemiré to the south-west. In a muster made by William Barker at 'Auausy' (probably Ouézy, south-east of Caen in Normandy) on 13 June 1593 there were 205 officers, 1,045 able men and 489 sick (various estimates give different totals). The following force of

2,042 men, including 100 light horse and thirty mounted harquebusiers, mustered at Paimpol in September 1593:

Sir John Norris	239	
Richard Wingfield	81	
Charles Blunt	53	
Thomas Cnoroles [sic]	90	
Marin Wingfield	53	
Alexander Ratlesse	50	
Thomas Williams	53	
Nicholas Bacherind [sic]	95	[this could refer to Nicholas Baskerville]
George Blunt	<u>35</u>	
	749	

Henry Norris	135
Anthony Wingfield	77
Gregory Hinder	67
Richard Green	73
John Protere [sic]	83
Thomas Hardy	71
John Angeli	72
Roger Smith	<u>85</u>
	663

Colonel Charlay [sic]	89
George Morton	64
John Latham	38
William Ashenden	68
Edward Warlock	62
Thomas Raynart	45
Thomas Brell	53
Martin Lister	<u>81</u>
	500

The muster reveals that the companies were each almost entirely well below 135 men.

Following the arrival of English reinforcements under Sir Thomas Baskerville, the Spanish withdrew towards Carhaix in Brittany. With this retreat, the English were free to concentrate on coastal towns. The capture of Morlaix followed in September 1594; Quimper fell after an assault in the evening of 25 September. The climax of the Brittany campaign was the capture of the Spanish fort at Crozon. Today the cape is called the *pointe des Espagnols*. The fort had been built in an effort to control access to the port of Royalist-held Brest, despite Mercœur's opposition to the project. Artillery fire from the fort threatened the passage of vessels from the Goulet de Brest to the port. Spaniards such as the engineer Cristóbal de Rojas favoured an attempt against Brest itself, as Blavet was insufficient for the harbouring of a large fleet.

On 21 June 1594, Sir Walter Raleigh signalled that the new Spanish fortifications at Crozon were complete. They were designed by Rojas, later known as the author of *Teórica y práctica de fortificación* (Madrid, 1598) as well as *Compendio y breve resolución de fortificación conforme a los tiempos presentes* (Madrid, 1613). The fort, called 'Castil León' by the Spanish, had a garrison of around 400 men. It comprised three companies of pikemen under captains Tome de Paredes, Diego de Aler and Pedro Oritz de Galerio. A report of 27 May 1594 shows that Paredes had the largest company of 145 men and de Aler and de Galerio had 109 and seventy-one men respectively. A further seventy-six men were on the sick list.[285]

An idea of the strength of the fortifications remains present on the site today. Although the ramparts have been levelled, the stone curtain wall and the two bastions have survived, with later additions. Though on a smaller scale than the Spanish fort at Blavet, it is clear that *El León* was built to withstand a siege. The construction was similar to that of Blavet where a large part of the Spanish fortifications remains intact. The fort held one advantage over Blavet in that it was in a stronger natural position. All the efforts of construction could thus be concentrated on the southern approaches. The fortress held only six pieces of artillery, much less than the minimum of twenty pieces deemed necessary by Don Juan del Águila.

Norris decided to make an attempt against the fort by 19 September. A formal contract was drawn up limiting the employment of the English troops to the siege before returning back home. Command was given to the aged Jean d'Aumont, comte de Châteauroux (1522–1595), *maréchal de France* from 1571.

Crozon is a good example of combined operations. Eight vessels (or more precisely six ships and two smaller pinnaces) were sent under Sir Martin Frobisher to participate in the siege. The cost of stationing eight ships off Brittany for three months came to £14,173. The squadron included four of the queen's ships: *Vanguard* (of which Frobisher was

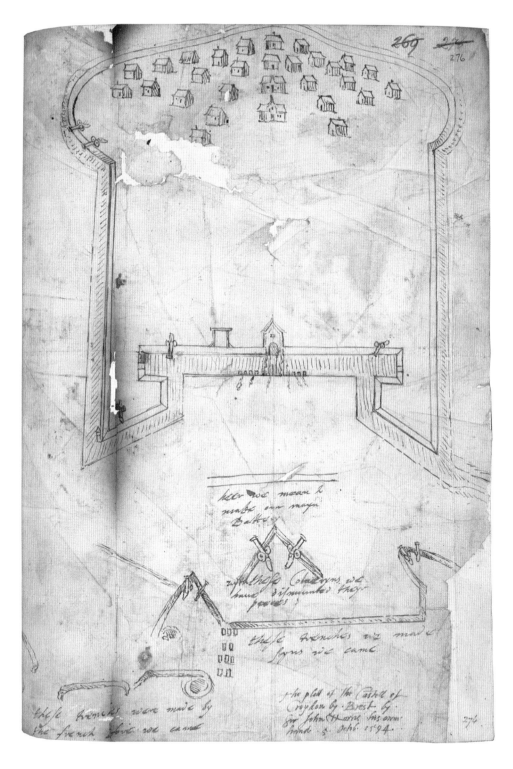

Plan of Fort Crozon, Brittany, 1594, by Sir John Norris. British Library, Cotton MS Caligula E.ix. f.276. © The British Library Board

captain), *Rainbow* (each of 500 tonnes), *Dreadnought* (400 tonnes) and *Quittance* (270 tonnes). The other ships from Frobisher's squadron were the *Crane, Charles, Moon* and the ships of London, *Ascension, Consent, Susan Bonaventure, Cherubim, Minion, Primrose* and *Pinnace.*

Sir John Norris had forty pioneers under his command to execute the siege-works in Brittany. It is not too difficult to imagine the scene in autumn 1594. The path followed by the trench leading to the eastern bastion is still apparent today. The besiegers used barrels filled with earth in place of the usual gabions made from weaving lengths of hazel. Pieces of artillery were taken from ships of the Royal Navy to batter the fort. The besiegers had a battery of fourteen pieces: two cannons, two culverins and two demi-culverins from the Tower of London, two culverins from the *Vanguard,* two demi-cannons from the *Rainbow* as well as two Dutch culverins. Only two pieces were provided by d'Aumont. A sketch made by Norris during the final stages of the siege shows a total of sixteen.[286] The Dutch made a further contribution by transporting 20,000 tons of powder in eight of their vessels.

The battery of fourteen was ready by 23 October. 300 shots fired at the ramparts had little effect so that the battery then concentrated their efforts against the parapets. 800 shots demolished the parapets on the points of the bastions as well as those of the curtain wall. It was the two culverins placed in the centre that proved so effective against the Spanish artillery. Meanwhile, Águila was preparing to relieve the fort. He received a report that the garrison was short of munitions.

D'Aumont fell ill at a critical moment during the siege. He received news that relief was on the way. Norris decided to continue with the siege despite d'Aumont's advice to withdraw. A general assault was launched against bastion 'A' at 11 a.m. following an artillery barrage and the explosion of a mine. The Spanish were desperately lacking munitions by the third assault. At 16.30, the Gascons under Romegou and the English broke through the walls of the fort. Emmanuel van Meteren witnessed a desperate defence by the garrison. He saw how men had been attached to stakes by the breach with only their arms free to ensure that they could not retire. Norris himself was wounded in the final assault to take the fort. The English lost sixty men, in strong contrast to the Spanish. Among the dead was Captain Paredes, who was later accorded a funeral with the honours of war. Only thirteen of the defenders escaped death, three according to d'Aumont, who also noted that seventy or eighty Spaniards drowned: 'Sum of them sowght to escape by swimminge in the Sea, but our mariners made them sinke.'[287] The unwillingness of the English to take prisoners is confirmed by Jean Moreau, who believed that they wanted to avenge their defeat at Craon: 'Those who fell into the hands of the French were humanely held prisoner but the English, sworn enemies of the Spanish, would not forgive anyone and … if they saw some as prisoners of the French … they killed them in their hands.'[288]

Two Spanish prisoners from Crozon, Antonio Henrico de Riveros and Martin d'Assiaigne, were more fortunate in that they were held by Sourdéac, the governor of Brest. He held these to ransom for the sizeable sum of 10,000 *écus* (£3,333 6s 4d). Among the booty from the fort were three standards, which Norris sent to Elizabeth. The successful enterprise, however, did not end on good terms. First, d'Aumont was displeased that he was not offered the standards and that they had been sent back to England. Norris, meanwhile, was displeased at the role played by the French. His complaints confirm the lack of pikemen in French ranks: 'I gave every night 300 men to deffend the french in theyr trenches or els they would have been beaten out every hower, and in truth they were not in all durynge thys seege alone syx or seven hundred weake harghebusyers, tyll toe dayes before the takynge of the fort.'[289]

The consequence was that the English executed their contract to the letter and withdrew from Brittany. According to De Thou, François d'Espinay, seigneur St-Luc (1554–1597), managed to appease Norris. Elizabeth, meanwhile, had other intentions. In her congratulatory letter to Norris, she informed him of her plan to send him with his men to Ireland. The English took up winter quarters at Paimpol, with their last muster taken at the port on 4 February 1595. D'Aumont was mortally wounded at the siege of Coupers the following year.

Even after the destruction of the fort, however, the Spanish threat remained. In July 1595 four Spanish galleys from Brittany raided the Cornish fishing ports of Mousehole, Newlyn and Penzance. Brest was also still threatened. In March 1596, Sourdéac wrote to the Earl of Essex claiming that he had fresh intelligence:

> *I have been assured by two boys … coming from Spain that they have been making great preparations in raising men of war as well as maritime forces for the rebuilding of their fort at Craodon [Crozon] and another on the other point of the harbour mouth opposite…. The loss of this place, falling into the hands of the Spaniard, is no less of consequence to the … kingdom of England as that of France.*[290]

'THRUST UP INTO A MISERABLE CORNER OF FRANCE': THE PICARDY CAMPAIGN, 1596–97

The year 1595 was the year of non-intervention in France; a year of rest for many English veterans except in Ireland where a revolt broke out headed by Hugh O'Neill.

Henri IV's position was in some ways now less precarious. He had previously concluded a treaty with Charles III, duc de Lorraine, on 16 November 1594 at St-Germain-en-Laye. This was ratified by Henri at Fontainebleau in December 1595 and by Charles at Nancy on 12 March 1596. Henri declared war against Spain on 17 January in reprisal against its intervention in France. This was a great risk but it was also a way of uniting the country behind him. There was one other incentive for Henri in that he hoped to acquire continued support from Elizabeth. Meanwhile, St-Luc and the *États* of Brittany appealed directly to the queen for aid. Villeroy was disappointed: 'I cannot tell you how much all France is offended by the coldness of England ... and we are pressed from all parts to reach a new accord.'[291]

Henri had perhaps gained new friends in his abjuration but he destabilised his old alliances. The Huguenots became wary. The Spanish took advantage of the situation in France to act against Henri, who found his frontiers effectively threatened by a simultaneous attack on five fronts. A Spanish army was present in Franche-Comté, threatening Burgundy. In Brittany, after the capture of Crozon, the Spanish remained dangerously present at Blavet.

The precarious state of Royalist interests in Picardy had been reported by the English ambassador, Sir Thomas Edmondes, in March 1595. He observed how an enemy army was free to cross Picardy and that two or three strongholds had been captured near Abbeville. The loss of Abbeville would have enabled the enemy to cross the Somme, threatening Dieppe, Rouen and Paris. It was said quite simply that Henri just did not know what to do in Picardy. Le Câtelet and Doullens fell to the count of Fuentes, and a French force sent to relieve Doullens was beaten by the same commander.

The English were particularly concerned about the safety of Dieppe. Ottywell Smith wanted an English force to be sent to protect trade. The town's governor wanted to maintain 600 English pikemen and musketeers ready to counter any Spanish move to cross the Somme. He wrote directly to the Earl of Essex, 'to help me with your authority and favour towards the Queen to obtain my request ... to soon have the said men of war'.[292]

Fresh appeals also came from Brittany. Montmartin, governor of Vitré, saw no way of freeing the peninsula from the Spaniards other than with Elizabeth's support. When Cambrai was invested, Ottywell Smith was convinced that Henri could relieve the town only with the help of English pikemen. He wrote that if 3,000 men were not sent from England, then all Picardy would be lost. Henri sent Antoine de Loménie on an embassy to procure aid from Elizabeth. This was refused. Étienne Chevalier was also sent, landing in England on 19 August. To make matters worse, Loménie was refused a second audience with the queen.

A French victory at Fontaine Française on 5 June 1595 saved the situation in Burgundy but the Spanish retook all that they had lost in the duchy of Luxembourg. Lacking any English support (and cash), Henri IV was unable to relieve the siege of Cambrai, which finally fell to the Spanish on 9 October.

The events of 1595 would have persuaded Henri that it would be impossible to reconquer his country solely by military means. Further disaster followed with the loss of Calais. Its capture gave the Spanish a useful base for operations against England and the coast of Picardy. From here, they made an attack on lower Boulogne. There were rumours circulating that the English preferred to see Calais in Spanish hands despite the threat that this presented to England.

Lord Willoughby put forward a plan for the convergence of allied armies to defeat Cardinal Albert of Austria (1559–1621, Governor of the Spanish Netherlands from 1598). The plan involved a strike against Ostend by Maurice of Nassau and Sir Francis Vere with a landing by the Earl of Essex with 10,000 men at either Calais or Dunkirk. Willoughby saw the need for a single hammer-blow rather than a series of small-scale expeditions. Indeed, he considered such expeditions to be a waste of time, men and money. Orders were given for the Earl of Essex to take his force to Boulogne, but a new campaign for him in France never materialised – instead he would find fresh glory at Cadiz in Spain. It would be left to Sir Thomas Baskerville to lead a new expedition. Jacques des Réaux, sieur de Fouquerolles, was dispatched to St-Valery-sur-Somme to welcome Sir Thomas and his men and to show 'by all sorts of discussions the contentment that we draw from their coming'.[293]

Sir Thomas's corps of 2,000 men took up winter quarters in three different places at the mouth of the Somme: three companies at St-Valery, five at La Ferté and five more at Le Crotoy. From letters sent by English captains it is apparent that few wanted to be there. Several captains wrote to the Earl of Essex requesting to be taken into his service. Captain Edward Wilton asked Essex to help him procure a transfer to serve under Burgh in Ireland. William Lilly described the area as 'the coldest country of the whole of France'.[294] For Baskerville, St-Valery was quite simply 'miserable'.[295] Life was hardly any better across the water in Le Crotoy: 'we are thrust up into a miserable corner of France, where we understand little and do less, not having the commodity to eat for money'.[296] Captain Wilton had written earlier to Essex:

> *We fight daily against cold, hunger and the infections of the country; everything is exceeding dear with us; we have no wood but that we fetch three leagues off. The plague is grown so familiar to us that to get 6d the soldier feareth not to ransack both the house and the party infected, and we have not yet to my knowledge passed any town or village uninfected. But that which is most strange of all, I have not heard of any soldier amongst us that hath died of the plague, although very few can say that they have not been in the places of contagion.[297]*

The state of the English soldiers became a concern. Baskerville had tried to make his men as comfortable as possible. By November 1596, he had spent £280 on bedding for them. Many had already fallen ill by mid-December. By 29 January the following year as many as 200 men were either ill or too weak to serve. The shortage of wood around St-Valery was a handicap that Baskerville had clearly grasped. He would have been only too pleased to see the start of the campaign season. By mid-February, William Lilly reported that wood had run out and that there were 300 men on the sick list.

The intention had been for the force to hold 'Bulloyn [Boulogne] and Muttrell [Montreuil] and no other where' except if Henri was with them in Picardy.[298] Suddenly, there came fresh news that Amiens had fallen. The sudden capture of the city came as a surprise to many: 'some were at church and most of the citizens were still asleep in the French manner'.[299] According to Baskerville, comte St-Pol did not even have time to put his boots on before his flight to Abbeville. For some, however, the fall of Amiens was less of a surprise. At the end of July 1595 a plot had been discovered: priests and a *bourgeois* had planned to surrender the town to the Spanish after capturing a gateway. Ottywell Smith was convinced that both Abbeville and Amiens would be ready to surrender once Cambrai had fallen. Surprise or not, the loss of Amiens appeared to be a major setback for Henri IV; as he explained to Essex: 'The loss of Amiens has reversed all my designs. I was making preparations to assail my enemy and start by the month of April, but I must go on the defensive.'[300]

Henri had amassed munitions and provisions at Amiens ready for his next campaign. The reserves included many pieces of artillery. According to Sir Anthony Mildmay, there were twenty-six cannons and 40,000 cannonballs as well as a large reserve of powder and provisions. Here the question must be asked: why did Henri place all his artillery in a town that was not defended by the king's own troops? Amiens and Abbeville had both refused to garrison four companies of Scottish soldiers. These same soldiers had prevented the capture of Montreuil in 1595. Was Henri taking too many risks, given that Amiens was now a frontier town? Had he forgotten or did he simply not know about the recent plots? Henri himself had calculated that it took only four days to transport artillery from Rouen to Abbeville by water. Why did he not leave the guns in Rouen until the end of March? At least here they would have been relatively secure. Furthermore, Amiens was too dependent on its medieval fortifications for its defence, though Hieronymo Germanico had been employed there as an engineer in 1553. The curtain walls were long and the bastions were relatively far apart. All that stood between Spanish-held Doullens to the north and the capture of the town was a simple *ravelin*. The town's defences had been surveyed by Jean Errard, the king's engineer, in 1596. Errard had stayed for 'ten or twelve days' to carry out the survey, for which the town had paid him the sum of 100 *écus*. We must conclude that the capture of Amiens was either the consequence of negligence or a well-executed strategy. It is certainly possible that Henri used Amiens (and old pieces of artillery) to bait the Spanish forces. This drew the Spanish deeper into French territory, over-stretching and therefore weakening their lines of communication. Once they were drawn, Henri hoped to defeat a relieving army in open battle. Here we find a strategy often used by him. At Coutras, Arques and Ivry, the king, having chosen the ground, then enticed the enemy to attack him. He was thus able to use natural obstacles together with earthworks to support his outnumbered army. At Coutras, his army benefited from having a river, marsh and woods on its flank. The other advantage was the position of the château of Coutras, which offered a place of retreat for an army beaten in the field. Henri had perhaps hoped to perform the same action at the siege of Rouen, by drawing the duke of Parma into battle. Here, the ground was unfavourable. The ground to the north of

Amiens, though, was ideal for an open battle. Once more, Henri relied upon field fortifications to strengthen his position. Would not also his apparent distress have assured continued support from Elizabeth?

On 2 April, Henri wrote to Elizabeth requesting a further 2,000 men in addition to the 2,000 already in France, stating, 'I am too weak to resist the power of the strengthened enemy.'[301] He reminded her, 'My downfall will bring yours, as the enemy is insatiable.'[302]

1,200 Englishmen joined the French to make a sudden attack against Arras on 16 March. The assault was led by Biron and Épernon with the English under Baskerville. All that barred success was a portcullis that resisted their gunpowder. Baskerville describes the action: 'I never saw any place in greater fear, nor less resistance for the space of two great hours. We lost not above eighty or an hundred men, and some six or seven score hurt. With this we are retired, and here we lie upon the villages between Amiens and Dourlens.'[303]

THE SIEGE OF AMIENS

French Royalist forces undertook to recapture Amiens. The siege-works were conducted by Jean Errard de Bar le Duc, already known for his *La Fortification Démonstrée et Réduicte en Art* (Paris, 1594). Errard was a Protestant engineer who had previously been in the service of the duc de Bouillon. The pioneers had an incentive to work quickly. They were paid 30 *sols* per *toise* (6 ft) of trench. Pierre Matthieu wrote shortly afterwards: 'This siege should be held as one of the greatest and most remarkable of our time … principally with incredible and indescribable earthworks so that neither their great number of artillery nor the depth of their ditches, nor the strength of the place could prevent their approach up to their rampart and ravelin.'[304]

In May, Captain Arthur Chichester wrote to Cecil: 'The King … makes a show to besiege Amiens, but his preparations are small.'[305] The capture of Amiens was vital to Henri's quest for peace and the securing of his crown. He wanted to be sure of success before the final battle. The siege of Amiens would be a show of strength for him.

The aerial photographs taken by Roger Agache provide valuable information on the fortifications constructed during the siege. These photographs reveal that the enormous scale of the earthworks depicted in several plans by Claude Chastillon was in fact a reality.[306] The most detailed plan is held at the British Library.[307] The aerial photographs, combined with different views of the siege from the east, west and north by Chastillon, provide us with a three-dimensional view of the siege.[308]

On their side, the Spanish defenders made their own preparations under Federico Paciotti. The Porte de Noyon was closed and walled up.

The French commanders at the siege included Charles de Gontaut as well as his younger brother Jean. Others such as the ducs de Bouillon (who refused to take part) and Épernon (who arrived too late) were notable by their absence. Several Huguenots chose to remain at home, apprehensive of the *rapprochement* with the Catholics, fearing a *Sainct Barthelemy de campagne* ('St Bartholomew's [massacre] in the country').[309] William Lilly also observed how the Huguenots played little part in the siege. De Saint-Luc was present in his function as *Grand maître de l'artillerie*.

The English corps suffered with the death of their commander, Baskerville, while he was at Picquigny on the Somme to the west of Amiens. All the captains became godfather to his son, Hannibal, as did the Earl of Essex. He was replaced by Sir Arthur Savage, but only after a debate. Both Sir John Aldrich and Captain Henry Power, with his company of men from Hampshire, also wanted to take charge. Henry Power had previously served in France in 1593 with a company of men from Sussex. Elizabeth ordered her men to obey Aldrich until Savage's arrival.

The English contingent were quartered at Camon in June, though they appear to have been moved closer to Henri IV's headquarters at La Madelayne as the siege progressed. They were assigned their own trenches during the siege, covering the quarter near the village of St-Maurice (see figures 'N' and '36' on the British Library map, overleaf).[310]

The English soldiers had facing them not only Spaniards and French *Ligueurs* but also Irishmen and some English Catholics in Sir William Stanley's Irish regiment. Stanley was an English Catholic in the service of Spain. At the end of 1591, it was said that he was earning a pension of 300 crowns per month. Spies had been employed on the Continent to follow his movements. According to a report of 1594, his regiment was made up of only 150 Englishmen and seventy-one Irishmen. By 1597, this had grown in size to 400 men and was placed in garrison under Bastok.

Many of Savage's men who had been sick had recovered by July. Their service at Amiens had a positive effect. They were one element upon which Henri could rely. By the end of July, he was fearing the collapse of his own (unpaid) contingents of French and Swiss troops.

(*overleaf*) *Plan of the siege of Amiens*, 16/26 August 1597. British Library, Cotton MS Augustus I.ii.86. © The British Library Board

Amiens

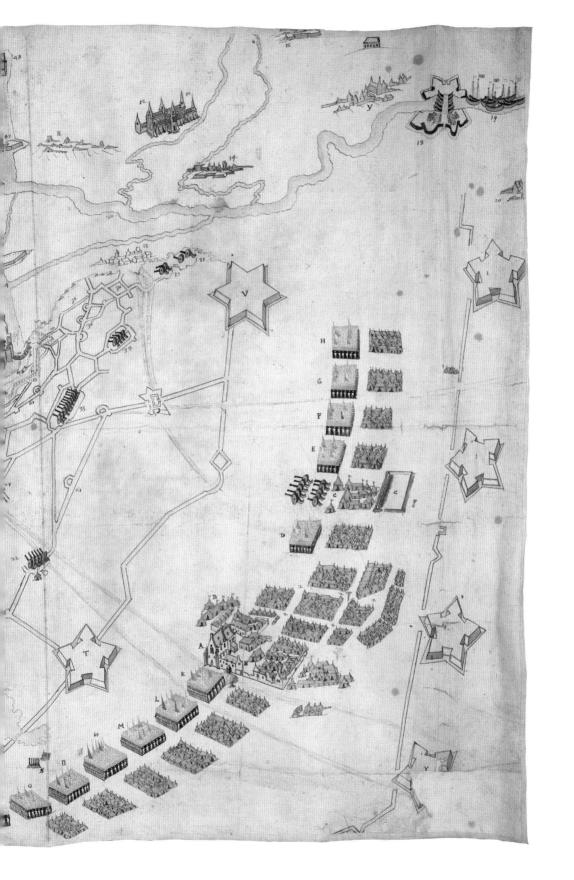

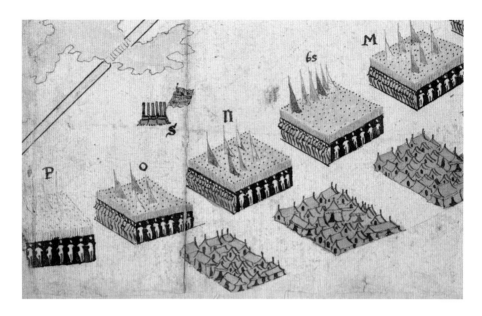

Plan of the siege of Amiens, 16/26 August 1597. British Library,
Cotton MS Augustus I.ii.86. © The British Library Board.
Detail showing English encampment 'N'

The importance of the English force at Amiens is confirmed by personal accounts. Compliments came directly from Henri himself, as Captain Chichester wrote in a letter to Cecil on 6 September: 'The Kinge and his nobles holde a good opinion of us sayinge wee are better to joyne with the enimie then their foote and in placies of daunger the kinge wylbe neare us.' Mere flattery on the part of Henri? Perhaps, but this was also the opinion formed by subsequent historians. The English came to be highly regarded by the 'impartial' Henri Davila: 'The regiment of Swiss and that of the English were more active than all the others because, with the exception of the regiments of Picardy and Navarre, the French infantry was all composed of new levies, who were not up to working nor to camping in the open air.'[311] Obviously the unpleasant *séjour* in the Somme estuary at St-Valery and Le Crotoy had acclimatised the men to life on campaign.

Jacques-Auguste de Thou similarly recognised the good deeds of the English, commenting, 'We would have succumbed under the great numbers if an English regiment had not run to our relief.'[312] De Thou also informs us how on 17 July the English fought off an attack, killing seventy men. The Picardy regiment suffered heavy losses during this encounter. Sir Arthur Savage describes one Spanish sortie that almost succeeded: 'The enemy's purpose was to have cloyed our ordinans and came provided for the same with hammers and great spikes, of which they fayled hardly thereof, for they had wonn the trenches of ye places of batterye, with the losse of muche bloude on our side, and many good men.'[313] This may have been the same encounter referred to by the soldier-historian Agrippa d'Aubigné: *sans la venuë des Anglois, ils alloyent baiser l'artillerie* ('without the coming of the English, they would have spiked the artillery').[314] Finally, the Spanish themselves had complimentary things to say. 'You are tall Souldiers … and we honour you much, not thinking any foote to come neere us in reputation but you, and therefore, when you of the English come downe to the [t]renches wee double our Gard, and looke for blowes.'[315]

While the English were engaged with the siege, Henri was faced with threats of their withdrawal. Antoine de Moret, sieur de Reaux, had already had an audience with Elizabeth on this very subject in June. In fact, Henri had requested 4,000 English troops. Villeroy wrote to Mildmay pleading for the English to be allowed to stay, 'that the Queen leaves the English companies which are very necessary at the siege and that she may care to reinforce them'.[316]

The besiegers had an idea of the serious state of the defenders from an intercepted letter sent from Hernando to Cardinal Albert. He wrote, 'I expect the continuation of the enemy battery from three sides. Human discourse has failed, our hope is in God & in the urgent coming of your highness to give battle.' [317]

The English, however, questioned whether the battery was fierce enough. Once more, we observe Henri's reluctance to use a fierce battery against a town. On 15 August, Savage reported to Cecil:

> *I fynd not any resolution in ye kyng to batter it but to sapp w[hi]ch will be his best course wee ar neare at the foot of the rampier newly entred they have played severall myns uppon us but to smalle purpose saving on Saterday last they slew Capten and a great part of his Company ye cap[tain] him self blown up and yet not found.*[318]

The besiegers were ready to launch an assault by 24 August. The English would assail one side of the *ravelin* and the French the other on the same evening. It was here that sappers had placed 8,000 lbs of powder in four mines. Two of the mines had little effect but the others created two breaches. The French attacked first. After having easily reached the top of the *ravelin*, they were thrown back with heavy losses. At this moment, *maréchal* Biron (who was, according to Henry Power, in 'extreame rage') ordered the English in to the assault. Between 200 and 350 Englishmen took part in this attack. According to Henry Power, the attacking force was split into three groups. They held their positions on the *ravelin* for three-quarters of an hour until finally being driven back. Henrico Davila also described this action: 'The French and the English mounted the assault from the two sides and became masters of the *ravelin*.... Captain [Diego] Durando attacked them with vigour and dislodged them.' The men were then hit by flanking fire from Spanish musketeers under Captain Ignace Ollana.[319] Thirty men were lost including Lieutenant Gorges and, according to Arthur Savage, over eighty men were wounded. Despite their losses, they were not discouraged. Henry Power expected a fresh assault to be made on the same day. Meanwhile, both the French and English continued to advance work on their trenches. It was during these efforts, on 8 September, that St-Luc was killed.

Villeroy visited Sir Arthur Savage each day in early September to press his demands for the English contingent to remain. The real test for the besiegers came with the arrival of a relief army under Cardinal Albert, governor-general of the Spanish Netherlands, and Peter Ernst I von Mansfeld (1517–1604). Henri believed that he had as many as 20,000 men in his army. They marched in good order between their carts with their artillery at the fore. The sheer size of the army forced them to march slowly.

Henri divided his own army into three. One division advanced to form up in order of battle across the plain to the west, leaving others to guard the trenches against any sortie from the town. The third force covered the south bank of the Somme against any attempts to make a crossing. The king formed his army in order of battle in the field before the entrenchments. The two armies faced each other for an hour. During this time, five or six of Henri's heavy pieces gave battery to good effect. Cardinal Albert's artillery replied in kind before he withdrew his army out of range.

Albert remained prudent. The loss of his army would have left the way open to Doullens, Arras and even Brussels. He finally withdrew his army completely from Amiens, 'with neither beat of drum nor sound of trumpet'.[320] The garrison of Amiens realised that they had been left to their own fate and decided to parley the following day. Henri could at last write to Elizabeth:

Madam, God and the joy of your arms which assisted me have
rendered my town of Amiens.… I have sent to good La Fontaine to
present to you with le discours veritable du succés de l'entreprinse
faicte par le cardinal Albert … of which I am sure you will judge as
me, that if he [Cardinal Albert] came as a soldier, he has returned
as a priest. It was the fifteenth that he arrived and only waited
until the sixteenth to return.… I strongly hoped that he would have
wanted to return to decide at one fell swoop all your quarrels and
my own.

Madam, as your prosperity will always be mine, I pray that you
will also be content that I rejoice with you in this victory, the fruit
of which you will always have a part as Your most humble brother
and servant, HENRY.[321]

Henri is referring to a sixteen-page publication entitled *Discours veritable du succez de l'entreprise faicte par le Cardinal Albert d'Austriche pour secourir la ville d'Amiens, les xv. & xvi. du mois de Septembre, 1597* (Paris, 1597), a copy of which is in the British Library.[322]

The rest of the garrison of around 2,500 fit men and 700 or 800 sick and wounded marched out of Amiens. They were allowed to carry their booty with them, such was Henri's desire to regain the town.[323] He allowed Sir William Stanley to leave despite the calls for his arrest.

Arthur Chichester, captain of a company of men from Dorset, had been wounded in the shoulder during the siege. He was knighted by Henri in recognition of his bravery. Henri hoped that the English companies would be maintained in France for use in the continuing struggle in Brittany. De Maisse was sent to perform the difficult task of ensuring this, but he returned empty-handed.

If Henri had used Amiens opportunistically from the start, everything had worked almost perfectly. The Spanish had taken the bait, overstretching their lines of communication. Henri had besieged the enemy. All that was missing was a conclusive victory against Cardinal Albert in open battle. Henri now had a free hand to impose a royal garrison as well as a citadel on Amiens. The citadel would be sited to protect Amiens from the north. Jean Errard's project, now conserved in the British Library, lays out a plan for a pentagonal citadel. Interestingly, it also depicts the position of the old *ravelin* in relation to this.[324]

CHAPTER FOUR

LIFE ABROAD

DISCIPLINE AND RELIGION

*A*t Le Havre, Cuthbert Vaughan, who had previously participated in the siege of Leith in Scotland, saw the need for rules to maintain discipline, 'for otherwyse hyt shalbe in vayne to gyve orders'.[325]

Following complaints from the inhabitants of Le Havre, a number of ordinances were established on 10 November. According to Holinshed, they were proclaimed by the officer-at-arms 'Blewmantell' (Richard Turpin) the following day. Soldiers arriving at Le Havre in 1562 were ordered to treat the French courteously. Certain punishments were draconian. The laws reflect an army in transition between medieval and modern rules. A man could lose his right hand if he drew his sword outside the town. He could also expect to lose his ears and be banished from the town if he paraded for roll at two different places or if he answered the roll call in place of another. Similarly, any captains caught allowing such practices would be cashiered and punished at the discretion of the Lord Lieutenant and the Council.

The Judge Marshal presided over military tribunals while the application of the penalties fell on the Provost Marshal. The sentences were carried out publicly in the market place. There are numerous examples. One soldier was hanged on 25 November after having stolen from a Frenchman, while another received a pardon. A soldier was executed on 6 February after having drawn his sword against another and wounded him. On the same day, another man was condemned to death and two were to lose their hands, but Warwick pardoned them. Two other soldiers chose to run away rather than face punishment for having stolen from their host. During the second Normandy campaign, under Willoughby, a soldier could lose his life for a number of crimes. For traitors, 'death with torments' was prescribed.[326]

*Sir Henry Unton, c.*1596 (detail), by unknown artist. National Portrait Gallery, London, NPG 710, © National Portrait Gallery, London

The English were also inspired by the French in their own punishments. The queen suggested the sending of men to serve in the galley to the Earl of Warwick at Le Havre simply because he could not find enough oarsmen. (The same destiny awaited French prisoners in reprisals for the English taken at Rouen.) There was never, meanwhile, an English equivalent on the scale of the French *chiourme*. A statute was introduced (1597–98) by which 'dangerous rogues' would be sent to the galleys.[327]

One serious problem that the authorities encountered was that of desertion. Two soldiers were hanged for having deserted from the garrison at Le Havre in 1563. The campaigns of Essex and Norris were also hit by this phenomenon. The situation came to the attention of the Privy Council, which ordered that all soldiers or suspicious men arriving in certain ports without passports were to be arrested and imprisoned. Essex held a court martial on 21 October 1591 in which men were sentenced to death for having deserted the army to return home. In 1592, deserters returning to English ports from France were ordered to be arrested. Sometimes officers themselves were complicit in acts of desertion. There were reports that some of them were selling passes.

Elizabeth became concerned over the discipline in the army of Sir John Norris in Brittany and insisted that laws should be written. Military laws set out in the Earl of Leicester's campaign in the Netherlands in 1585 were used as a model.

Henri IV himself sometimes felt obliged to intervene over matters of discipline. At the beginning of 1590, he wrote to Lord Willoughby on the conduct of his soldiers:

> Monsr de Vileby, I have heard from [Pierre de Harcourt] sr de Beuvron that there are some English soldiers staying in his house … where they have committed several breakages and insolences of which I am unhappy.… The said sr de Beuvron is one of my special servants who is presently serving in my army with his company of men at arms.… [I] ask you to give the order that the said soldiers move from the house and parish of the said sr … and that they return and replace the animals and other items that they have taken.[328]

Some soldiers were hardly any better during Essex's campaign. Such acts led to the inclusion of a number of clauses on discipline in the treaty of alliance of 1596. It was stipulated that English forces sent to relieve the French would be subject to the authority of the officers of the king. They could be punished by them but only in the presence of their own officers. By the same treaty, any French soldiers sent to England would likewise be subject to English law.[329] Orders were issued to Sir Thomas Baskerville, instructing him to protect French property:

> *You shall also, considering you are in a straunge countrie, give charge to all the captaines and officers of the bandes severelye to keepe their people in good order without suffring them to quarrell with the Frenche or to spoyle any howses or the persons of the Frenche, or otherwise to comitt any outrage against the Frenche by takinge from them anye of their goodes or victualles without the goodwill or satisfaccion of the owners by payment for the same.*[330]

English soldiers did on occasion prove to be a threat to each other. In a military court held at Arques in October 1591, Lieutenant John Hudson was acquitted of the murder of Captain Thomas Wynchcombe. It was held that he had acted in self-defence. Better known is the duel between Sir William Drury and Sir John Burgh. Drury received a wound to his hand which later turned gangrenous, and he died following amputation.

One method of maintaining discipline was to hold regular church services for the forces. This ensured close ties between faith and the army. Elizabeth wrote prayers in her own hand for her men in Normandy. Soldiers were required to thank God upon their arrival at church or the square at Le Havre. On the night of 14 November 1562, parishioners in England were ordered to pray to God. They were to pray over the next three days for the men who had been sent overseas to fight the duc de Guise.

> *O Most Mighty Lord God … have regard to those her Subjects which be sent over the Seas to the Aid of such as be prosecuted for Profession of thy Holy Name, and to withstand the cruelty of those which be common Enemies.… O Merciful Father, if it be thy Holy Will, make soft and tender the stony Hearts of all those that exalt themselves against thy Truth, and seek to oppress this Crown and Realm of England.*[331]

At Le Havre, captains were required to be present at church with those of their men who were not on guard duty for services on Wednesdays, Fridays and Sundays between nine and ten o'clock. On Sundays they were to return at three o'clock. No one was allowed to leave church during a service. The soldiers were also required to attend prayers at the same times during the week. The English minister at Le Havre was William Whittingham, who received 5s per day for his services. Interestingly,

Whittingham had preached in Geneva and married John Calvin's sister. He became Dean of Durham Cathedral. It is probable that the congregation sang one of his own psalms (Psalm 130), *Lord, to thee I make my moan.*

> *Lord, to thee I make my moan*
> *When dangers me oppress,*
> *I call, I sigh, plain and groan,*
> *Trusting to find release.*
> *Hear now, O Lord, my request,*
> *For it is full dur time;*
> *And let thine ears aye be prest*
> *Unto this prayer mine…*[332]

Soldiers were not allowed to marry without the consent of the Church, at the risk of imprisonment and loss of keep. The penalty for adultery was imprisonment for six days and banishment from the town. Furthermore, no man could keep another woman apart from his own.

Religion was also seen as a way of keeping order. During the first phase of intervention, Sir Nicholas Throckmorton had asked for the sending of clergymen to Le Havre, Dieppe and Rouen to give sermons and to 'retain the people in the fear of God'.[333] By the rules set down by Willoughby, prayers were obligatory before each undertaking. Later, in 1597, eight prayers were printed under the title *Certaine Prayers set foorth by Authoritie, to be used for the prosperous successe of her Majesties Forces and Navy.* Needless to say, the soldiers were to pray to God in the hope that he would give them support against the enemy, 'casting downe their strong holdes in which they doe trust'.[334]

The high wage of a chaplain shows his importance. A chaplain in France in 1589 was paid as much as 20 shillings. The English were not alone in recognising the importance of faith in battle. Prayers were specially written for men in Condé's army in *Prières ordinaires des soldatz de l'armée conduite par Monsieur le prince de Condé: accomodés selon l'occurrence du temps* (Lyons, 1563). These prayers were available both in French and in German for the *Reiter*.

Prior to his expedition to Normandy, Lord Willoughby was instructed not to allow his men to cause offence in matters of religion. They were not allowed to enter churches during services nor show 'insolent conduct'. The Privy Council knew that such actions could seriously damage Henri's tenuous position. This concern was highlighted in the instructions issued to Sir Thomas Baskerville:

and spetiallie you shall see that none of her Majesty's subjectes do
enter disordredly into any church or religious howses or anye wise
to use anye violence to any the monumentes of the sayd churches,
religious howses or religious persons. But you shall take care and
charge for bothe your regimentes that there be usuall prayers made
(as neere as may be) everye daye according to the use of this realme
of England, not doubting but therein you will according to your
duties praye for our Soveraigne Ladie the Queen's Majestie.[335]

Nevertheless, churches did not remain safe from the English during the wars. At least some Catholic churches were attacked by English soldiers. Ornaments and thirteen bells were stolen from churches along the coast north of Le Havre in February 1563. According to Guillaume Valdory, English soldiers set fire to the church at Pavilly, north-west of Rouen. It was alleged that profanities were committed at the church of Notre-Dame at Louviers during the expedition to lay siege to Rouen in 1592: 'horrible impieties were committed there, the holy Sacrament on the altar trampled underfoot, Extreme Unction and the baptismal waters reduced to pure profanity by the English'.[336] Iconoclasm may well have sparked such actions by the English.

Later, d'Aumont alleged that the English had taken bells from churches in Brittany. Norris replied that he had taken more care than other commanders but that it was the custom in war to use churches as strongholds. On the issue of church bells, he blamed the sailors. Norris, meanwhile, did admit that some of his men had pillaged an abbey but that some of these had been imprisoned.

Religion was also an integral component of the instructions set out for ambassadors by Elizabeth and William Cecil. Sir Henry Unton was instructed to hold daily prayers for himself and his entourage, 'wherby you may appeare abroade to be a dutiful subjecte to the lawes of your naturall country'.[337]

PAY

Regular musters were vital in armies. They were held both to keep a check on the number of men and to assure the authorities that pay had been issued to them. Musters and the maintaining of accurate account books had previously been a source of concern at the siege of Leith. In France, the authorities showed a determination to control the accounts. In reality this proved to be a difficult task. In the aftermath of the first campaign in Normandy, certain abnormalities were alleged:

> *dyvers of those that had charge of the Quenes Majesties service at Newehaven alleadge that theyr bookes and accomptes ar spoyled and lost, whereby they can gyve no perfect accompt of theyr doinges, which thing cannot but seme very strange and gyveth theyr Lordships good cause to think the same hath not cume to passe without sume indirect meaning.*[338]

Norris's account book, as previously mentioned, had been lost in the shipwreck off Alderney in 1592. Had this book survived then payments may well have been as well documented as those of Willoughby in 1590. Throughout the period, accounting was a headache for captains. Arthur Savage, before Amiens in 1597, took a particular displeasure in keeping accounts; as he told Cecil, 'I am forced to keep the wecly accounts w[hi]ch ar very troublsome and hurtfulle to me.'[339]

Captains of foot in Picardy in 1596–97 were paid at a daily rate of 2s per every fifty men in their company. This was twice the rate of a lieutenant. A captain of 100 men therefore received 4s and for 200 he would receive 8s. Drummers and fifers were relatively well paid. This reflected their skills, including the expectation that they could speak foreign languages, i.e. French. In Picardy, drummers received 2s per day.

The soldier's wage changed little between 1562 and 1597. The sum of 8d remained his daily rate during this period. Ordinary soldiers were not paid any more for fighting overseas. In 1563, though a gunner at the fortress of Upnor in Kent was paid 12d, at Le Havre he could expect only 9d. Soldiers could expect cash rewards for good conduct. Nicholas Florence received a reward of £20 for his services at Le Havre.

English merchants in France were also useful in times of war. On one occasion the English ambassador, Sir Anthony Mildmay, borrowed as much as £1,242 from the merchants for the men under Sir Arthur Savage before Amiens. It was not difficult to find people willing to transfer English money. Sir Roger Williams, meanwhile, found that the merchants were making too much profit for themselves. His comments reveal the heart of a philanthropist: 'If there be any winnings in it, it were better thousands of poor people won by it than half-a-dozen such merchants should be enriched.'[340]

English soldiers serving in France preferred to be paid in French money, thus allowing them to pay for rations. Meanwhile, those men

CAMPAIGNS OF NORMANDY (1562–63, 1593) & PICARDY (1596–97)

Comparison of daily ordinary wages[343]

	1562–63	1593[344]	1596–97[345]
marshal	£7		
colonel			(40s) (10s + 30s)
second colonel	13s 4d		(20s) (10s + 10s)
treasurer	20s		10s
engineer	13s 4d		
curate	5s		
minister	5s		
comptroller			
provost marshal	5s		
clerk	2s 6d	3s 4d	3s 4d
muster master			6s 8d
captain of foot	4s 6s (150 men)	6s	8s (200 men)
lieutenant	2s 3s (150 men)	4s	4s (200 men)
captain of horse			
master of the ordnance	6s 8d		
master gunner	2s 4d		
master gunner (navy)	1s 3d		
assistant master gunner (mate)	14d		
ensign		18d	2s
sergeant		2s	2s 1s (150 men)
drummer	3s 12d [sic] 12d [sic]	2s	2s
trumpet	2s		
fife	3s 12d [sic]		
surgeon	3s 12d [sic] 12d [sic]	12d [sic]	12d [sic]
quarter-master	10d		
gunner	9d		
horseman	16d		
musketeer		12d [sic] [1594]	
soldier	8d	8d	8d
pioneer	8d[346]		

returning to ports such as Portsmouth found it difficult to use their French money back home. The exchanging of money in France was both difficult and costly. As much as one penny in every shilling was lost in exchange. Given that there were twelve pennies to a shilling, this was no negligible amount considering the thousands of pounds spent. Sir Thomas Sherley suggested that economies could be made by sending the soldiers' pay for exchange at Caen for conveyance at Jersey. This was only one possible solution. Sherley negotiated terms with merchants. The rates of exchange for French *couronnes* at Caen and Dieppe varied from 5s 7d to 5s 11d between 1590 and 1594. The shipping of money was charged at a rate of £10 per £1,000. In Brittany in 1591, John Mole, the treasurer of the army, required a guard of ten men for the pay chest. These men received a daily bonus of 4d. At the siege of Amiens, Henri feared that money for his own men would go missing and entrusted the distribution of the soldiers' pay to Villeroy.

The English claimed that they had little booty. 'The French deal like the Dutch we are first at frays and last at feasts.'[341] During Willoughby's campaign, Henri wrote that the English had had *bon butin* ('good booty') from Vendôme, the suburbs of Paris and Étampes.[342] Sir Roger Williams had more luck at the siege of Bernay. Here the English had taken part in pillaging the town in May 1593.

SUPPLY

The supplying of English armies in France was a significant task for the Commissariat. The main sources of supply were, naturally, England and France, though the Netherlands was also used. The Crown would pay merchants in two tranches: on agreement and on delivery. The first payment provided the merchants with the funds necessary for the purchase of provisions.

An estimate for provisions for a month for the garrison of Le Havre included 615 quarters of wheat, 448 tonnes of beer and 168 cattle. By May 1563, the garrison were consuming at least twenty cattle per day. The garrison made the most of a *vivier* on the old rue Fontaine-de-Viviers in the town to provide them with fish.

At Le Havre, the besiegers cut the natural source of water from Vitanval. The lack of wells and cisterns inside the town forced the garrison to use sea water to do their cooking. During a siege, drinking beer carried less risk than water. At the siege of Rouen in 1591, 'water from the Seine, which flowed into the neighbourhood, being mixed with the tide, was not good to drink and caused incommodities'.[347] The purveyors during the first campaign in Normandy took care to ensure that there was enough beer for the garrison. Barrels were sent to Le Havre from Dover, London, Rye and Weymouth. The capacity of the brewery at Portsmouth was increased to ten tonnes. By 1 October 1562, 300 tonnes of beer had been placed in reserve. Based on the estimate that 300 tonnes of beer were needed to supply 3,000 men for forty days, this amount would have provided each soldier with a daily ration of nearly two and a half litres of beer.[348] To economise on the transport of beer, John Abington sent malt and hops directly to Le Havre to make beer on site. Despite all these efforts, there was a shortage. The men were 'reduced' to drinking wine, to which they were unaccustomed, causing sickness. Besides wine, beer and cider, the garrison of Le Havre could also expect perry.

There appears to have been some demand for English beer in France. The entrepreneur Prégent de La Fin, sieur de Maligny, vidame de Chartres, who wanted to export wine to England, also wanted to export beer to France in even greater quantities. In September 1593 he asked Sir Robert Cecil for help to obtain a licence for the export of as much as one thousand tonnes.

In Brittany and Normandy, there was the local cider (a two-quart[349] pot of cider cost 3d or 3 *sous* in 1591). Cider was among the rations sent by Coligny to Le Havre during the English occupation. In 1591, Henri informed Edmund Yorke that Brittany would not provide the English with drink and that they should take their own supplies. Sir John Norris, meanwhile, stipulated the provision of beer rather than cider for his own men.

The garrison at Le Havre had a diet of powdered bacon, beef, mutton, bacon, biscuit, butter and cheese. There was also dried fish and sugar. The rations were supplemented by foraging and raids on enemy-held territory. Early in the campaign, a detachment of Scotsmen returned with 300 sheep from a single sortie. They had possibly had experience of this on the Anglo-Scots border, where sheep-stealing was common. Warwick, however, did not wish to alienate the local inhabitants and ordered the sheep to be returned. By the end of May 1563 Warwick was becoming concerned over supplies and worried that the garrison was worse fed than the peasants, with rations that were insufficient for active men. He complains of them having to have fish without butter, getting cheese only two or three times per week. They frequently had little meat and no bread, with nothing to drink (i.e. no beer). The lack of sufficient rations was partly through losses. In November, they had lost 200 pigs and eighty cattle, together with quantities of bread and biscuit, to the sea.

A warrant has survived detailing a soldier's daily rations during the second Normandy campaign under Willoughby.[350] It shows that the diet was very similar to that of men serving in the Netherlands. The men could expect the following: biscuit (1 lb), penny loaf (1), beer (1 pottle = 4 pints or 2.27 litres), stockfish (1 quarter = 113.40 g), butter (½ quarter = 28.35 g), cheese (¼ lb = 56.7 g). The provision of rations was at the discretion of captains but by 1593 they had to pay their men 2s 6d per week.

One economic measure was the allocation of two 'fish days' per week (Wednesday and Saturday) by Act of Parliament, as fish was less expensive than meat. There was also another reason. The increased demand for fish would lead to an increase in the number of fishermen, thus providing a larger pool of sailors for the navy. The increase in the size of the navy and the attraction of piracy were such, however, that the coasts soon lacked fishermen. This in turn is reported to have led to shortages of fish by the 1590s.

In each campaign, the English soldier became a forager. For officers and gentlemen this was an opportunity to go hunting. Indeed, the treasurer of war, Sir Thomas Sherley, wrote a book on the subject, published in 1603: *A short discourse of hawking; to the field with high flying long-winged hawks together with the sorting and ordering of spaniels*. During Essex's campaign in Normandy, Sir Thomas Coningsby and other gentlemen took time to go hunting in the park of a château owned by a *Ligueur*. Coningsby describes the countryside: 'We found the villages and howses utterlie abandoned, but yet mylke, syder, freshe water, and bread almoste in everie house readye sett to relieve our soldiers, which the footboyes and groomes broughte to their masters.'[351] This was a contrast to the German *Reiter* who invaded France from the east. They encountered a country that was largely hostile. They would therefore have felt little remorse in ransacking all that lay before them. The capture of *une infinité de bœufs* ('an infinity of cattle')[352] added to Casimir's triumphal entry to Heidelberg as well as depriving the enemy of food.

If the Germans became infamous on land, the English earned their own reputation at sea. Many of the supplies taken to Le Havre during the first war came from captured vessels. This practice, aided by Huguenot sailors, began with the arrival of the garrison. A request was made for the sending of two Breton ships filled with maize from Rye where they were being held. Among the prizes taken by François Le Clerc (known to the English as Francis Clerk) operating out of Le Havre were four ships from Brittany carrying 200 barrels of Gascon wine. A further 100 barrels of wine in a ship from Fécamp were taken by the English ship *Hare*. Occasionally, more exotic cargoes such as oranges would turn up in the holds of captured vessels.

The English and Royalist supply convoys were themselves susceptible to attack by the enemy. One such convoy was attacked while en route to the English camp before Rouen. The main consequence of this was, in the eyes of Sir Thomas Coningsby, the rise in the price of wine. The cost of living in France was a frequent complaint of soldiers and diplomats alike: 'I protest to your lord I have ben forced to paye three shillinges for twoe small loafes of bred not so bigg as penny loafes in England, and three shillinges a horse shoe and foure souls a nayle.'[353] Even the ambassador Sir Thomas Edmondes complained in 1596, 'Living in an army, where the country is so wasted, is very expensive as regards provisions; and shoeing and miscarrying of horses and clothing and sickness of servants eat up much money.'[354]

English armies could expect to pay even more for their provisions if they were attached to the army of the French king. There was a frequent lack of provisions in the French army. During the first campaign to besiege Paris, Buzanval wrote from Lagny to the French ambassador in London describing how the lack of rations was hindering the campaign: 'Everything is ruined around here. It is why there is such disorder in this army; everyone being more in quest of victuals than the conquest of enemies.'[355]

Sir Roger Williams complained of the high prices: 3 or 4 *sous* for a pound of bread, 24 *sous* for a *lot* of wine, a pound of cheese at 12 *sous* and butter at 12 and 15 *sous* per pound. They could obtain 'reasonable flesh' for 5 or 6 *sous* per pound.[356] The table below compares prices in London and Dieppe. The higher prices were set by the purveyors who looked to cover their losses incurred in transit.

COMPARISON OF PRICES IN LONDON AND DIEPPE 1591[357]

	London	Dieppe
beer (barrel)	14s	16s
salted butter (lb)	4½d	5d
cheese (lb)	2½d	3d
beef on the bone (lb)	2½d	3d

French towns themselves could provide rations for limited numbers of English soldiers. In their request for 100 men with two or three gunners, the town of Boulogne offered to supply bread, meat and beer … *if* Elizabeth paid for it.

An essential element in the soldier's diet was his daily ration of bread. Providing bread for an entire army was not an insignificant task. Varying levels of success were achieved. In 1562, nine men were sent to Le Havre to build bread ovens for the new garrison. Five windmills situated on the shore before the town proved invaluable for grinding grain. Later, in Brittany, Sir John Norris had to wait only two days after his arrival for bread to be delivered. This was sent in twenty vessels by Montpensier to the Abbey of Beauport. *Maréchal* d'Aumont promised to provide 4,000 loaves of bread during the siege of Fort Crozon, but, according to Norris, much less was delivered. Norris complained how English wounded sent to Morlaix had to wait fourteen days before receiving any bread. Sir Roger Williams agreed to surrender the port of St-Valery in Picardy in return for the daily provision of 1,600 loaves and 16 hogsheads (864 gallons or 3,992.5 litres) of beer. Williams's bacon, meanwhile, was shipped in directly from Rye. This included six flitches on one occasion.

Officers and gentlemen accustomed to a high standard of living in England also expected more than the average soldier on campaign. Robert Carey, for example, spent £30 per week on victuals. Carey remarks how he lacked nothing. Sir Thomas Coningsby also ate very well: 'We were invyted to monsieur d'O,[358] who intreated us for dayntye chere lyke Lucullus; for we were so farr from want of other meaner thinges, that we did eate muske and amber in tartes.'[359] Following a skirmish before Rouen, he returned to camp to take 'good fyre, and eate capons, plovers, and larkes, and drancke the best wyne we could gett'.[360]

Apart from the normal channels, there was also a two-way illicit trade in provisions. Du Vineau describes, in a direct report to King Philip II of Spain, how an English force under Sir John Norris had procured provisions, gunpowder and cannonballs from the *Ligueur* port of St-Malo. It was therefore a licence given by Philip himself that assisted in the capture of Fort Crozon.[361]

LEISURE

There were moments in the wars when priority was given to feasting and leisure rather than fighting. During the siege of Rouen, Henri held a banquet at Pierrefonds. While they were awaiting the king, gentlemen before Rouen played both tennis and *ballon* (football). 22 October 1591 is an important date in the annals of football. An English team met the French under their captain, the lieutenant-governor of Dieppe. England won the match. English soldiers also showed an interest in the local ladies:

> *This afternoone, to drive awaie idlenes, I wente to a monasterie of nonnes, about a league and a halfe from our quarter, where we so behaved our selves that we receyved very kynd wellcomes, and a banckett of xxtie severall dyshes of preserved fruits.... there was 2 or 3 younger noons, and all gentlewomen of good house, whom I know, if you had sene, you would have pyttyed their loss of tyme; and so, having spente 2 or 3 howres there, retorned home to our strawe bed.*[362]

Ten days later, Coningsby set off once again in search of 'some good and graceful company ... of fayre ladies'. The group had some success; he writes, 'I assure you, the companie was not unpleasing unto my kind harte.'[363]

During the years of aid in the Netherlands, it was not uncommon for English soldiers to marry local girls. There is, however, little evidence for this phenomenon in France. At Le Havre, the English authorities expected that some members of the garrison would get married. A minister and a sexton were appointed to keep a register. Meanwhile, the expulsion of most of the inhabitants together with the death of so many men ended any such projects. One thing is certain: Englishmen in the Netherlands spent more time in garrison. In France, they were rarely in the same place for long.[364]

CASUALTIES

Many Englishmen lost their lives during the French Wars of Religion, most deaths being caused by sickness. At Le Havre, the besieging army's best ally proved to be the plague. According to the calculations of David Stewart, as many as 2,600 men died here of this sickness. The men died faster than they could be buried. Bodies were left to decompose and fester close to living quarters, thus exacerbating the situation. A further 17,404 people died in London between 1 January and 31 December 1563. In addition, 2,732 people died in the suburbs. Blue crosses on white paper were placed on the doors of infected houses. England was not, apparently,

> *This fortress, built by nature for herself,*
> *Against infection, and the hand of war.*[365]

The Channel Islands also suffered heavily from the ravages of the plague. Even the impregnable Castle of Mont Orgueil on Jersey was struck. The court itself chose to avoid London and was still at Windsor in December. Pierre Ronsard refers to the losses in his *Discours des Misères de ce Temps*:

Et tantost les Anglois le viennent secourir,	'And soon after the English came to help them [the people],
Et ne voit ce pendant comme on le faict mourir,	And meanwhile saw not how they died,
Tué de tous costés: telle fievre maline	Killed from all sides: so malign a fever
Ne se pourroit guarir par nulle medecine.[366]	Could not be cured by any medicine.'

The author of *Gaping Gulf...*, John Stubbe, having joined Willoughby to fight in Normandy, died of illness rather than in battle.

The high level of losses sustained by the English in actual combat is perhaps evidence that many were fighting in the front line. At St-Saëns in 1591 casualties came to fourteen dead and twenty-four wounded (including the sergeant and Williams's ensign). Sixty-four men were lost in total at Noyon, including fifteen dead and thirty-eight wounded. As many as three quarters of Willoughby's army died in France and half of the men under Norris and Essex. These losses were difficult for Elizabeth to bear, as she complained to Henri: 'My lord brother. Calling upon our men, after so many dead, mutilated, wounded and ruined, does not seem strange to you...?'[367]

As the historian William Camden comments, 'To thrust forth the English to the slaughter for the benefit of the French, shee in her motherly love of her Subjects utterly refused.'[368]

Sir Martin Frobisher died of wounds received at the siege of Crozon in 1594, despite the reassuring words from d'Aumont to Elizabeth, *ce ne sera rien* ('it won't be anything').[369] He had been hit in the thigh by a shot from a harquebus. Frobisher himself reported,

> *I was shott in with a bullett, at the batterie along St_ _ huckle-bone, so as I was driven to have an insi[sion] made to take out the bullet; so as I am neither [able] to goe nor ride; and the mariners are verie unwilling to goe except I goe with them myself. Yet, [if] I find it come to an extremitie, we will [do] what we are able: if we had vittels, it were easily done, but here is none to be had.*[370]

Although the surgeon managed to pull out the shot itself, the wadding remained in the wound. He died some time after reaching Plymouth. His heart and entrails were placed in the church of St Andrew at Plymouth. His body was taken to the church of St Giles in London, close to his home on Beech Street.

The author Arthur Brooke also met his death during the wars. His poem *Romeus and Juliet* was the inspiration for one of Shakespeare's most famous plays. Unfortunately, Brooke drowned on board the *Greyhound*, en route to Le Havre in March 1563.

Common soldiers were buried near where they fell. At Dieppe in 1591, Catholics refused to bury the English soldiers. It cost the local church 40 *sous* to bury each man.

The number of surgeons in Elizabeth's army compares well with other countries. The English army had one surgeon per company, whereas the Spanish *tercio* had only one physician and surgeon per 2,200 men. According to custom, the surgeons were provided by the Company of Barber-Surgeons of London. In return, its members were exempt from serving in the ranks. At the beginning of the reign, money was deducted from the soldiers' pay to augment that of the surgeons.[371] During the siege of Le Havre in 1562, the Earl of Warwick requested the sending of an apothecary (named Colff) to treat the plague victims.

There were also signs of innovation in the armies. Sir John Norris introduced the concept of a mobile hospital or 'ambulance'. The Privy Council were certainly impressed, as they wrote to Norris, 'A provision you have made of an hospitall, as you call it, for allowaunce unto two principall surgeons, one phisicion, one apothecary and two bloud-letters, we do like very well thereof.'[372]

At Rouen in 1591, men were falling ill in large numbers. By October, 1,700 men had been sent back to England. In Picardy in 1596/97, despite their complaints about the climate, the men appear to have been in good health. At St-Valery in February 1597, fewer than 300 men were ill out of 2,000, a low proportion for a sixteenth-century campaign.

PRISONERS

Some 250 Englishmen were captured at Rouen and Le Havre during the first campaign. Sir Henry Killigrew himself was captured at Rouen, and was released on condition that he would not return to France for the duration of the war. A number of English prisoners held at Caudebec were sent to

Le Havre in January. The Rhinegrave released two Englishmen from the galleys. The Earl of Warwick agreed to free Bassompierre in exchange for his elder brother. The good relations between Warwick, Montmorency and the Rhinegrave facilitated the task. During the siege, Montmorency sent *marcassins* (young wild boar), fruit and other *rafreschissements* to Warwick. The Rhinegrave presented him with a horse and a saddle: 'And as for prisoners who are here, if you please give order to two of your gentlemen to meet tomorrow somewhere between here and your camp. Two of my own will meet them at the time that you appoint, at which I doubt not that we will soon be agreed.'[373] Hugh Paulet (*c.*1510–1573) replied to the Rhinegrave, 'Sir, I have received your letter and when it pleases to meet you tomorrow, because I do not want to cause any impediment to your camp, if you please I will meet you at Vitanval at ten o'clock in the morning.'[374]

It was not unknown for prisoners to be pressed into the French fleet to serve as oarsmen. On 12 June 1563 Henry Killigrew wrote to Sir Thomas Chaloner the elder informing him that fifty Englishmen taken at Rouen escaped from a galley, killing the captain. Some prisoners, however, did not escape, as we later find them writing to Sir Thomas Smith requesting aid. They tell of how they were on the galley of d'Albisse and of their harsh treatment. Despite their pleas, it was reported on 1 April 1565 that there were still twenty-four Englishmen on a galley at Marseilles. The following year, Sir William Cecil was still concerned about 'the relief of the poor Prisoners in the Gallies', as he told the ambassador in France, Sir Henry Norris. Some men remained in *la chiourme* as late as 1568.

The medieval tradition of ransom continued throughout the wars. Robert Baker wrote the following verse while awaiting the payment of his ransom.

> *A prisner therefore I remaine,*
>   *and hence I cannot slip*
> *Till that my ransome be*
>   *agreed upon, and paid,*
> *Which being levied yet so hie,*
>   *no agreement can be made.*
> *And such is lo my chance,*
>   *the meane time to abide*
> *A prisner for ransome in France,*
>   *till God send time and tide.*

From whence this idle rime
to England I doe send:
And thus till I have further time,
this Tragedie I end.[375]

Edward Gorges was captured in 1595. He was travelling to Paris via Calais and Amiens carrying letters from Elizabeth to Henri. Though Gorges was not a wealthy man, 5,000 *couronnes* were demanded for his return. Gorges found his own solution by managing to escape from his captors. At Le Havre, four English hostages were chosen as part of the terms of surrender: Oliver Manners and Captains Pelham, Edward Horsey and Thomas Leighton.

The French prisoners who had been sent to England as hostages for the return of Calais tried to escape with the mariner Jean Ribaut in June 1563.[376] Fears of the plague had led to their removal to houses outside London. The hostages were not closely guarded. News that they had escaped their English 'hosts' appears once more in October. Other French prisoners captured during the first war included soldiers left in Florida by Jean Ribaut in 1562. The outbreak of war left them cut off from France. Having built their own ship in Florida, they sought to return to France. They were intercepted by Thomas Stukeley on their way home and then taken before court.

We know about one French prisoner, a gentleman named De Lestrille, simply because of his complaints during his captivity at Dover. He had been captain of two companies of foot at Calais. His captors had placed both his hands and feet in irons. They did, however, ensure that his wife did not go without money and sent her the sum of £36. The French ambassador, Paul de Foix, demanded his release.

As in many wars, however, atrocities did occur. Warwick complained to the Rhinegrave:

Sir, several times you have written to me to make good war, which
I have always done, but I find that you do otherwise as, the other
day in the last skirmish, after your men had taken five or six of
mine, they took them fifty or sixty paces [and] cruelly killed them
in view of five or six of my captains. If we do the same ... do not
blame me.[377]

THE AMBULANT EMBASSY

Sir Thomas Edmondes, writing in 1596, gives us an idea of the composition of an ambassador's *cortège* (retinue):

> *A horse for himself, another for a servant that writes under him, another for one who goes before with the harbinger to procure lodging and provision and dress his poor diet, another to carry a couple of trunks containing his clothes and bed, another to carry provisions for the kitchen and servants' necessaries and, often, oats. For these horses he requires two grooms.*[378]

Edmondes continued explaining that he had tried to employ footmen but a horse was always needed for one of them.

The sight of several of the embassies would have been quite a spectacle. The *cortège* of Sir Henry Unton was made up of sixteen personal servants. Sixty-two horses were used to transport the coaches. The retinues were sometimes much larger. The Earl of Derby, for example, was accompanied by ninety-eight men in 1585. As many as 240 horses accompanied the Earl of Shrewsbury to France in September 1596. The high price of horseshoes perhaps caused Sir Edward Stafford to take between 700 and 800 with him on his embassy.

The location and quality of the lodgings depended upon circumstances. At one point during the first war, there were two ambassadors in France: Sir Nicholas Throckmorton and Sir Thomas Smith. They were separated; one was sent to the château of St-Germain-en-Laye and the other to Melun. At the same time, the French ambassador in England was detained at Eton College, in the old rooms of Sir Thomas Smith. The ambassador was moved following a disagreement with the Provost. From this moment on, French ambassadors were obliged to find their own lodgings. There were, however, exceptions such as François, duc de Montmorency, who stayed at Somerset House in London in 1572, a practical address as it was situated on the Strand next to the Thames. Michel de Castelnau stayed at Salisbury Court. Huguenot envoys were often well looked after. According to Paul de Foix, Jean Ferrières, the vidame de Chartres and La Haye were hidden in Greenwich Palace. Later, Gaspard de Coligny's brother, Odet de Châtillon, lived comfortably to the south of London at Sheen.

The English ambassadors were free to choose their own accommodation. Besides having his own personal servant, Edmondes had a second simply for helping with the task of finding lodgings. Sir Henry Norris preferred to live in the suburbs away from the 'corrupt ayre of the towne';[379] he had a walled garden with a door leading to fields. His neighbours were the Strozzi family.[380] Catherine de' Medici had visited Norris expressing concerns for his safety; she pushed him to move into the city. Lodgings at the royal palace were given only in special circumstances. Thomas Sackville, Lord Buckhurst, was lodged at the expense of the king in 1571. The Earl of Derby was also accommodated free of charge by Henri III in 1585, but only because he had come to confer the Order of the Garter. Itinerant ambassadors would often find themselves in inns around the country. We find, for example, Sir Robert Cecil staying at the *Escue* on the market square (today's place du Vieux-Marché) in Orléans. Sir Nicholas Throckmorton's son Arthur provides us with the names of other inns used by Englishmen while accompanying Amias Paulet's embassy of 1576, including *La Pomme d'Orée* at Chambéry, *Les Trois Rois* and *L'Ange Noir* at Lyons, and *Le Cygne* on the Place Maubert in Paris.

Among the items to transport was the ambassador's silverware. We know that Sir Henry Norris left silverware weighing 1688½ oz to Walsingham in 1571. An inventory of 1591 signed by John Astley, Master of the Jewel House, lists the items in the service: 'two great platters,… fower demy platters,… 6 lesser platters, eight dishes, nyne demi dishes,… 6 lesser dishes,… one bassin and ewer of silver,… six sawcers…'.[381] The service had been lost by Sir Nicholas Throckmorton when he was arrested near Orléans in 1562.

A portrait of Sir Anthony Mildmay in the Old Library at Emmanuel College, Cambridge, is particularly interesting as it depicts the ambassador on service in his tent in 1596. His armour rests on the ground with a type of wheel-lock caliver used by horsemen.

The itinerary of Sir Henry Unton's embassy of 1591–92 was particularly demanding. In the space of eleven months, he visited at least thirty different locations. Apart from Dieppe and Rouen, he was rarely in the same place for long.

SIR HENRY UNTON'S EMBASSY TO FRANCE, 1591–92

Date			Town
1591	August	3, 15, 23, 30	Dieppe
	September	13	Dieppe
		18	Gaillefontaine
		27	Gournay-en-Bray
	October	1	Formerie
		15, 27	Noyon
	November	6	Hardivillers
		7	Crèvecoeur-le-Grand
		8, 11	Neufchâtel-en-Bray
		18, 19	Rouen
		25	Rouen
	December	4, 9, 19, 20, 25, 29	Rouen
1592	January	6	Gisors
		9	Gournay-en-Bray
		17, 18	Poix-de-Picardie ['Pay']
		26	Neufchâtel-en-Bray
	February	1	Auffay
		3, 8	Buchy
		13, 14	Clères
		20	Boissay
		23	Torcy
		24	Dieppe
		28	Blangy-sous-Poix
	March	3, 5, 10, 15, 17, 19, 20, 21, 23	Dieppe
		29	Dieppe
	April	1	Darnétal
		8	Dieppe
		12	Pont-de-l'Arche (1 league from Pont-de-l'Arche and 2 from Rouen)
		16	Fresnay-le-Lang
		16	Fontaine-le-Bourg
		21, 24, 25, 26	Valliquerville ['Varqueville']
	May	1	Yvetot
		5	Louvetot ['Langtot/Lingtot']
		7	Motteville
		9	Pont St-Pierre
		10, 11	Buhy
		16	Senlis
		24	Compiègne
	June	12	Dieppe
		?	Fère-en-Tardenois

THE PRICE OF SERVING

High personal costs accompanied the post of ambassador. Those less fortunate often refused to accept posts because of the expense. As with men serving in the army, diplomats also found service with the king more expensive. Sir Anthony Mildmay even claimed that he was too indebted to be sent on an embassy. His excuses came to nothing as he was soon sent to France with Gilbert Talbot, Earl of Shrewsbury. The cost of transporting a large embassy across the Channel was not insignificant. In 1571, for example, the transport of Walsingham's entourage with horses and carriages cost £95 50s 7d. Even the wealthy Earl of Northumberland[382] refused one embassy to confer the Order of the Garter on Henri IV, pleading that he was both too deaf and too poor: 'I shall force a King to speak with often repetitions, and to strain his voice above ordinary.'[383] The task of finding someone for this embassy proved particularly difficult. George Carew, Earl of Totnes, declined the position of ambassador to France in around 1586.

Sir Thomas Smith was paid £3 6s 8d per day during his embassy of 1564–66. This was the sum granted to ordinary ambassadors. The amount given also depended on status. The Earl of Worcester, for example, could expect as much as £6 per day during his embassy in 1573. Ambassadors frequently took advantage of their position to procure and advance other sources of revenue. Sir Edward Stafford held the right to export 100,000 cloths per year. He sold the right to export 40,000 pieces to his replacement, Horatio Palavicino, in 1591. The selling of land was another option. Worcester sold land which had an annual income of 100 marks. Less wealthy ambassadors had to find other solutions. Thomas Edmondes, during his embassy of 1593–94, found that the subsistence of 20s per day was insufficient. He was therefore obliged to borrow £2,000 from Ottywell Smith. His situation had improved little the following year; as he wrote again:

> I have inforc'd myself to perform the voyage of Lyons, which, without the help of the alms-deeds of good friends, I had not been able to have done. Yet such hath been the misery thereof, as I have therein spent more than I am worth, and now being arriv'd here, I am forced to seek a new equipage for the journey of Picardy, being unfurnish'd both of horses and money, and all other provisions, whereby I am not presently able to follow the king.[384]

Inflation further aggravated the plight of some ambassadors. The price rises encountered by Sir Thomas Sackville in 1570–71 were in part due to the cold weather. The Seine froze, making the transport of provisions, feed and wood impossible by boat. Price rises also added to the debts of Sir Francis Walsingham. Writing from Boulogne in 1571, he complained to Sir William Cecil about the high charges at the inns in Gravesend, Canterbury and Dover, all staging posts for ambassadors en route between London and France:

> I have not forgot to enform your honour of the great exactions used by the Inn keepers … in the prices of Victualls, whereof besides mine experience, I learned by certain strangers that passed over with me, they are so great as in no Countrie is used the like, where all things bear so unreasonable prices in the market.[385]

During his second embassy of 1581, he wrote directly to the queen asking for money. Sir Edward Stafford also asked to be recalled, complaining of the high cost of living. He was spending between £10 and £12 per day. A large portion of his expenses was going on provisions. He gives us an idea of the high prices in 1590: a sheep 28 or 30s, a chicken 3s and a quart of wine 2s. At this time, a horse cost only 2s 6d. Later, in 1596, Sir Henry Unton was spending as much as £17 per day on his domestic charges. This was at a time when his entourage had been halved and he did not keep more than twenty-five horses. Unton cited the high prices for food and drink sold in camp. He requested limiting his stay to only two months, and reminded Cecil of his situation: a wife and house in London as well as another house with twenty-one servants. It was not infrequent for ambassadors to keep houses in the capital – Sir Anthony Mildmay had a house at Great St Bartholomew's.

In this respect, French diplomats may have had a better deal than their English counterparts. Living in England, we can imagine that they ate quite well if their diets were anything like that of Odet de Châtillon. Among his needs for a single day were two sheep, four capons, twelve chickens, 10 lbs of butter and fifty eggs as well as 2s-worth of bread. All this was drunk with five sextaries (one = six pints) and five pints of wine – a total of thirty-five pints. It must be assumed that Châtillon was not eating alone that day.

THE WELCOME

The welcome (*l'accueil*) given to French diplomats varied according to the political climate. Following the signing of the Treaty of Troyes in 1564, William Cecil took care to organise the reception of Artus de Cossé. He was to be greeted on his arrival at Dover by Sir George Howard and the Sheriff of Kent, as well as by a number of gentlemen. He would stay with the Archbishop of Canterbury before being escorted from Rochester to Greenwich. From here, a journey by barque was planned to take him to court.

Parliament's fears for the queen's safety also created tensions. Fearing her assassination, Mr Grice called for the French ambassador to be received by the Privy Council:

> *Mr Grice hearing it reported (as he shewed) that the French*
> *Embassadour lately arrived, is appointed to have access unto her*
> *Majesty to Morrow at the Court, and fully perswading himself for*
> *his part that the said Embassadour cometh not for any good either*
> *to her Majesty or to the Realm; and knowing that their manner*
> *in such Cases to be attended for the most part with a Company of*
> *Rascals and basest sort of People of their Nation, and all the rabble*
> *of them accustomed to thrust into the presence of the Prince with*
> *their Master, moved, That for the better safety of her Majesties most*
> *Royal Person from peril of any desperate attempt of any of the said*
> *French, it would please those of this House of her Highness Privy*
> *Council to procure that the said Embassador might both be heard*
> *and also receive his answer at the hands of her Majesties Council,*
> *and in no wise to have access unto her Highnesses Person.*[386]

Luxury was very much *de rigueur* during the Anglo-French marriage negotiations. £1,744 was spent on a temporary pavilion at Whitehall. Brantôme describes the extravagance:

> *Monsieur de la Garde made such a superb show of his galleys*
> *and decoration that it is said that it cost him more than twenty*
> *thousand ecus.... Each were dressed in velvet à la matelotte.*
> *The chambers were all carpeted and covered in the same velvet*
> *embroidered a large foot in width with gold and silver. The devise*
> *on this was a gold and silver embroidered palm blown and*
> *shaken by the winds.... The beds, blankets, pillows, chamber seats,*
> *pennants ... all fringed in gold and silver. In short, it was a very*
> *magnificent thing to see.*[387]

Brantôme slept in the stern cabin *en ces beaux licts, où il faisoit très-bon* ('in these beautiful beds, where it was very comfortable').

Ostentation, however, could also provoke ridicule as Albert de Gondi du Perron discovered during his embassy to England in 1573. It was claimed that he had surpassed 'the excess and magnificence of all previous ambassadors' and 'had the insolence to ship from France to England not only all kinds of kitchen utensils including firedogs and larders, all the linen, tapestries and other furniture of the chamber but also that would serve him to drink and eat'.[388]

RISKY BUSINESS

A diplomat's absence away from home in France did carry risks. During the first war, a gentleman from outside Melun found that his house had been ransacked during his stay in England. He discovered that a lot of items had been taken from his house: 'a lot of furniture such as linen, tapestries, crockery, kitchen utensils such as the fire dogs …copper and iron pans and all sorts of pewter'.[389]

English diplomats and their *cortèges* were not free from risk. The ambassadors themselves were in relative safety while under the protection of ships of the Royal Navy until they reached the French coast. Their transports, however, carrying their baggage train, were more open to attack. Part of the Earl of Worcester's train was seized by pirates near Boulogne.

English ambassadors were provided with passports issued in the name of the French king.[390] Even if the English ambassadors were protected, they did not always feel completely safe. Sir Nicholas Throckmorton, for example, saw a situation that was out of control:

> *The daily despites, injuries and threatenings put towards me and*
> *mine by the insolent raging people of this town doth so assure me*
> *of mine own destruction as I am not ashamed to declare unto*
> *Your Majesty that I am afeared and amazed, and by so much the*
> *more as I do see that neither the authority of the King, the Queen*
> *his mother nor other person can be sanctuary either for me or such*
> *as these furious people do malice ... the prince's commandment*
> *is daily despiteously contemned and broken, not forbearing to*
> *kill daily, yet almost hourly both men, women and children,*
> *notwithstanding any edict or defence to the contrary.*[391]

Throckmorton went on to repeat his fears: 'I feare ... I shall fall into more troble & dannger then any body thinketh of or carethe for.'[392] His fears were confirmed when one of his servants was kidnapped and sent to the galleys. Some years later, in 1568, the ambassador Sir Henry Norris himself had to avoid men-at-arms who came to his house. When Sir Edward Stafford was offered a passport in the name of the duc de Guise, he retorted, 'I am under the protection of the law of nations and under the protection of the king to whom you are only subjects and servants.'[393]

Occasionally, diplomats themselves were drawn towards the battle-field. It was not unknown for ambassadors to take part in actual fighting. Thomas Wilkes accompanied the army of Johann Casimir that invaded France in 1575. Sir Henry Unton took part in the fighting at Bures-en-Bray in February 1592, and lost his horse following a pursuit of the enemy. He fought alongside Henri IV in a skirmish to take the village of Yvetot in Normandy in 1592. Here, a Spaniard was captured and another killed by one of his servants. Unton even challenged the duc de Guise to a duel either on foot or on horseback after he had insulted the queen. Ambassadors also found themselves risking their lives in the sieges undertaken by Henri IV: Edward Grimston at Chartres and later Sir Anthony Mildmay before Amiens. This was in contrast to the French diplomats who found themselves in England, far from the troubles of their own country. One ambassador, Jacques Bochetel, seigneur de la Forest, wrote:

As a thick cloud of German Reiter
Rained heavily as if to drown our land
I far from these terrors, lived in England,
Enemy of discord and upheaval.[394]

Diplomats did not escape illness. Sir Peter Mewtas had died at Dieppe in 1562. Sir Thomas Hoby died in Paris on 13 July 1566, leaving the *chargé d'affaires*, Hugh Fitzwilliam, responsible for the embassy. Sir Francis Walsingham was also replaced for a short period in 1571 by Sir Henry Killigrew because of illness. Unton fell ill with jaundice in August 1591. Sir Horatio Palavicino developed gout at Mantes in 1590. Sir Anthony Mildmay was obliged to leave France in 1597 through ill health – or at least this was the official reason. De Maisse, during his embassy in 1597, was told that Mildmay had paid Lord Burghley 5,000 crowns to return home. His remedy was a visit to the baths in England. The following year (2 March), Sir Thomas Wilkes died at Rouen after an illness. The most documented death is that of Sir Henry Unton, who died during his embassy in France in March 1596 at Coucy. He had fallen from his horse in February and became ill. He was treated by the French king's own doctors; his blood was let and he received medication over a twenty-day period. The medical reports describe his suffering. William Paule described the illness and the prescribed medication in a letter to the Earl of Essex.

> His sickness (a malignant hot fever) began with extremity of pain in his head, and about the seventh day his utterance failed him; but this accident was no sooner cured by the careful learned skill of the King's physician (De Lorrayne, doctor of Montepellier), but certain purple spots appeared about his heart, whereupon, with the advice of La Ryviere, the other physician, they gave him Confectio Alcarmas compounded of musk, amber, gold, pearl and unicorn's horn, with pigeons applied to his side, and all other means that art could devise, sufficient to expel the strongest poison and he be not bewitcht withal. These accidents being holpen, which arose of the malignity of his disease, yet his grief increased worse and worse; but the 17th day of his sickness, and the 20th of March, being his last critical day, was worst of all, so that in the accidents of sickness his sickness is cured, and yet he is extremely sick still. This present Monday is the one and twentieth day of his disease, in which space he hath not slept, to their seeming which watch about him his food is only jelly and such nutritive extracted matter, and albeit his body be brought so low that nature seemeth altogether spent, yet his memory and speech serve him perfectly though to little use.[395]

King Henri visited Unton while he was ill in bed on 14/24 March, 'although dissuaded by his own physicians that do attend me, for the danger of contagion'. Henri said 'he had not hitherto feared the harquebuse shot and did not now apprehend the purples'.[396]

Unton on his deathbed is depicted in the painting at the National Portrait Gallery in London.[397] He was buried on 8 July at All Saints' Church in Faringdon, Oxfordshire, where a monument survives today. His funeral was commemorated by the celebrated composer John Dowland in *Sir Henry Umptons Funerall* in *Lachrimae, or Seaven Teares* (London,

1604). A detailed inventory of Unton's personal possessions was drawn up upon his death. This included items which he had taken with him on his embassy, such as his tent, and which were placed in the armoury at Wadley House in Berkshire.

SERO, SED SERIO

CHAPTER FIVE

ELIZABETH AND THE TREATY OF VERVINS

*Elle ne peut oublier le déplaisir
de la paix*

'she cannot forget the displeasure
of the treaty'[398]

*B*Y THE END OF 1596, the willingness for war was beginning to wane in both France and Spain. Pope Clement VIII was equally keen to secure a reconciliation between the two countries. His plans were based upon the simple desire to save Christianity from the Turks. Elizabeth, however, wanted to see the war continue. The Spanish capture of Amiens in 1597 worked in her favour. Henri was obliged to continue the struggle in order to gain a more favourable position at the negotiating table. For the Spanish, the taking of Amiens is best described as a 'town too far'.

Peace came at last with the signing of the Treaty of Vervins. For Philip, this was an opportunity to regroup before renewing the fight. For Henri, Vervins was a way of preserving his kingdom. Elizabeth, though, saw it as an act of treason. The English sought to prevent the French from signing a separate treaty with Spain. Sir Robert Cecil would also pursue the return of Calais. He was sent to France in February 1598, with Dr John Herbert and Sir Thomas Wilkes. According to Nicolas de Neufville, seigneur de Villeroy, Cecil had 250 horsemen with him on his arrival at Dieppe. The entourage included George Carew, Earl of Totnes.

Robert Cecil, 1st Earl of Salisbury, 1602, by unknown artist after
John de Critz the Elder. National Portrait Gallery, London, NPG 107,
© National Portrait Gallery, London

Villeroy[399] visited Cecil on 24 March. He sent an account of their meeting to Pomponne de Bellièvre and Nicolas Brulart de Sillery the following day:

> I believe that he will not tell me his mission, at least not the secret of it, as he will keep it for his Majesty.... He wanted that I find from his language that he had a more peaceful than warlike manner, saying that his sovereign was [because] of her sex ... age and nature more inclined to peace than to arms.[400]

During their meeting on 31 March at Angers, Henri told Cecil that the Spanish had offered him all the terms he requested except the return of Calais. Henri appreciated the issue of Calais. Shortly afterwards he wrote from Nantes, telling his commissioners: 'I do not doubt that they [the English] will be very happy that Calais will be handed back to me.'[401]

There was much speculation, as well as concern, about what position Elizabeth would adopt during the negotiations. Bellièvre and de Sillery wrote to Villeroy, 'If we stop at the advice of the Queen of England ... we will have ten years of war and never any peace.'[402] In almost every letter between the French commissioners and the French court, there is at least one reference to either Elizabeth or Cecil. Their main question was whether the English would participate in the negotiations and whether they would choose peace or war. The French point of view (one of frustration) was summed up in a letter from Henri to his commissioners: 'The English are more fortified than discouraged. How much they held me and several of my servants with language to the contrary.... They ... have for aim to make us swim or drown in the sea of their uncertainty and natural and artificial irresolution to continue to triumph from our calamities and miseries.'[403]

Meanwhile, Philip sought a peace excluding Elizabeth 'because, as we understand, he strongly desires for many reasons for us to conclude this Treaty without her'.[404] Vervins itself was ideally situated for holding the peace negotiations, being equidistant from Brussels and Paris. Similarly, it was also far enough from the coast to give sufficient warning of (and possibly hinder) any English participation. A truce was established over a zone of five leagues around the town.

Henri first tried to pacify Elizabeth: 'I pray you to find good that I pursue this path ... which the necessity of my state and the uncertainty of the willingness of my allies and neighbours have forced me to take, having promised your ambassador to defer the final resolution.'[405] Cecil wrote to Lord Henry Howard, 'The French King hath broken the league and abandoned us.'[406] William Camden highlighted this event in his history by including the extract of a letter from Elizabeth to Henri:

> *If there be any sinne in the world against the holy Ghost, it is*
> *ingratitude. If you get any more reasonable conditions of peace*
> *at the Spaniards hands, you may thanke the English succours for*
> *it. Forsake not an old friend, for a new will not be like him. The*
> *conscience of a League, and the faithfulnesse of contracts, are not*
> *nets to intrap, save onely amongst wicked men. A bundell of rods*
> *bound together is not easily broken. There is not easier meanes to*
> *overthrow us both, then by disjoyning the one from the other.*[407]

The treaty forced the remaining allies, England and the Netherlands, to tighten their own friendship out of necessity. A new treaty was concluded between them on 8 August.

Mildmay lamented to the Earl of Essex during his embassy to France in 1597, 'The times and persons are much changed since your lordship's being there, where there are now daily so many alterations.'[408]

La Boderie was sent to England to 'congratulate' Cecil on his mission to France. The more difficult task of explaining the French desire for peace, however, fell on Hurault de Maisse. De Maisse made it known to Elizabeth that the treaty did not prevent Henri from sending *puissans secours* ('strong relief') to the Dutch in secret. Henri was also prepared, for a limited period, to prohibit the export of grain to Spain. Elizabeth was keen to prevent Spanish aid from reaching Irish rebels. Diplomats who came to France looking for a fresh alliance were disappointed. Béthune informed them that France needed some respite. Elizabeth feared that Spain 'having now the coast of France to their friend' would make a fresh attempt against England.[409] The fears were exacerbated by reports received by the Privy Council in August 1599 that a Spanish fleet was anchored at Le Conquet in Brittany.

The traditional view is that Henri sought a permanent peace before signing the treaty. He brought domestic peace, which would allow him to concentrate on the reconstruction of the kingdom. However, peace at home would also at last allow him to fight overseas. Much of the energy of the reconstruction was invested in the army. This period witnesses a kind of new golden age in French fortifications. Jean Errard de Bar-le-Duc returned to Amiens to construct a citadel, guarding against any future Spanish designs. Henri was perhaps tired of war, but he soon appears to have become tired of peace. Evidence for this quickly appeared in his actions. By 1600 he had returned once more to war, this time with Savoy. Meanwhile, some Frenchmen chose to take part in the ongoing actions in the Netherlands. French soldiers were present at the battle of Nieuport on 2 July 1600. Henri de Coligny, *amiral* of Guyenne, arrived at Ostend with a relief army of 2,000 men. Facing them once more on the Spanish side was Sir William Stanley. Henri also considered the sending of a relief force to assist the English at Ostend in 1602. He offered the support of 6,000 foot and 2,000 horse in a fresh war against Spain.

Later, in 1610, he was making fresh military preparations before his untimely assassination. Henri had spent much of his life under arms, making peaceful life at the French court insupportable. Furthermore, a victorious foreign war, with a country united behind him, would help him to avoid another bloody civil war.

Having won his peace, he wanted Elizabeth to continue the war against Spain. As the historian Laffleur de Kermaingant comments, 'We may be sure that one single thing occupied him, Spain, always Spain, and the fear of seeing Elizabeth and her Council cede to their strong desire to make peace.'[410]

In his speech at the opening of Parliament in 1601, Thomas Egerton, 1st Viscount Brackley, later Baron Ellesmere (*c.*1540–1617), the Lord Keeper, reminds us of the English view of Vervins: 'You see to what effect the Queen's support of the French King's Estate hath brought him; even made him one of the greatest Princes in Europe; but when her Majesties Forces there left him, how again he was fain to ransom a servile Peace at our enemies the Spaniard's hands with dishonourable and servile conditions.'[411]

One year later, there was still bitterness in the air. Christophe de Harlay wrote to Henri advising him 'to give reasons to make her understand that she has sooner won than lost in this peace'.[412]

THE QUESTION OF DEBTS

Diplomacy in the reign of Henri IV post-Vervins was dominated by the question of the repayment of debts. One of the reasons given by Béthune to justify the signing of the peace was that 'I will have more means of … securing money under pretext of paying debts.'[413]

Elizabeth feared that Henri was waiting for her to die before making repayments. The debts of the Huguenots had not been forgotten, either.

Beauvoir-La Nocle informs us that in England if 'we never pay and we do not remember what we borrow, that is called *Vidasmer* or to do the *Vidasme*'.[414]

It may be said that many of the loans were repaid in kind or in the form of rights. The queen would in turn have benefited from receipts from customs duty paid at English ports. Similarly, in 1597, the port of La Rochelle sought an arrangement over the £3,000 that they had borrowed from the City of London. They petitioned the queen, telling her that their removal of a tax on imports of foreign goods benefited English merchants trading at the port.

Forcing Henri to pay was a major task for English ambassadors. In establishing the alliance of 1589, Henri wanted 'the said relief to be at the expense of the provider'.[415] There was already a long list of debts by the time of the embassy of Sir Henry Unton in 1591. This list included, for example, the payment for munitions from September 1589 that had been due in September 1590.

It could be argued that Henri premeditated the failure of the siege of Rouen. An English occupation milking the revenues of the town would not have been in the best interests of the French Crown. As William Camden later wrote, 'for the provident French thought it an unworthy thing to expose that most wealthy City, which they hoped might ere long be reduced under their power, to the pillaging of the English'.[416] Henri would certainly have known the French proverb *Le Roy perd sa rente où il n'y a que prendre* ('The kyng looseth his right, where nothing is to bee had').[417] The peaceful conquest of the richest town in France would have been more advantageous for Henri. During the first siege of Rouen in 1562, 'L'Hospital always insisted that one should not use force and that it was a bad conquest to conquer oneself by arms'.[418] Catherine de' Medici had prevented the duc de Guise from assaulting the town no fewer than three times. The fact that Henri appeared at all before Rouen was simply to satisfy Elizabeth. He had to pretend to be actively engaged at Rouen before sending Du Plessis-Mornay on a mission asking for reinforcements of 5,000 men. Meanwhile, Elizabeth was displeased with Henri and his detours to Noyon, Gournay and St-Valery. This gave Parma time to prepare his relieving army.

Henri needed the revenues from Rouen for himself. According to William Lilly, Henri asked the town for a contribution of 6 million (*couronnes?*) towards war costs and 3 million towards paying his debts at the end of 1596. The issue of Rouen reappeared once the city was back in Henri's hands and peace had been established. Sir Henry Neville wrote to Villeroy in June 1599:

> *Presupposing (which I cannot accord) that the King does not*
> *have the means at present to give contentment in money owing.*
> *How do you excuse the contract of the year 1591 by which the*
> *King undertook to consign into the hands of the Queen … the*
> *reimbursement of several sums here specified: the Gabelles du Sel*
> *[salt tax] and other taxes coming from the towns of Rouen and Le*
> *Havre? You should have at least given her this which is within the*
> *King's power.*[419]

Villeroy gave a Gallic 'shoulder-shrugging' reply by avoiding the question completely. Neville persisted with the same point in his next letter. He tried to negotiate an annual repayment of around 300,000 *couronnes* (£90,000). Despite all Neville's efforts, it was apparent that Henri was willing to give only 20,000 *écus* (£6,000) that year. Diplomacy had its limits, as Sir Robert Cecil commented, 'seeing our sowre or sweet do make them eyther trott or amble, but as they find for their ease'.[420]

There was an agreement in principle that Elizabeth would receive the taxes from Rouen and Le Havre. The proviso, however, was less promising, *si sadite Majesté en pouvoit disposer* ('if His Majesty is able'), the key word being 'if'.[421] Repayments tended to be sporadic, such as the £4,630 that Henri paid following Willoughby's return from Normandy. In 1599, it was calculated that £401,734 16s 6d was still due to the English Crown.

Sir Henry Neville became confused when perusing the trail of unpaid loans left by Henri IV. He was obliged to ask Sir Robert Cecil for explanations. Cecil told Neville that he had found debts of 'good ancient date' but did not think that Henri would pay them quickly. The question of debts was further complicated by the repayment of subsidies by third parties. For example, Henri was to repay the subsidy of £30,937 offered to Casimir in 1586/87 to Elizabeth.

The loans had allowed Henri to maintain his army in the field and continue the wars for nine years. The money that he should have used to repay his debts, however, was used to buy back his country from the *Ligueurs*. It was said that Noyon, for example, cost 50,000 *couronnes* (as well as some abbeys). A city as important as Rouen cost as much as 715,450 *écus* (£214,635). Individual *Ligueurs* submitted to Henri at the offer of titles (and therefore revenue). Claude de La Chastre, baron de la Maisonfort

(1536–1614), joined Henri in return for the office of *maréchal* for both himself and his son. They were also to receive two *gouvernements*. Jean de Monluc was made *maréchal de France* in 1594 and was also promised the hereditary possession of Cambrai. Mayenne received money as well as the *gouvernement* of the Île de France (excluding Paris and St-Denis). His son was given the *gouvernement* of Châlons. The Guise family was also reconciled with cash. Henri paid the debts of the duc de Guise as well as granting him the *gouvernement* of Provence.

Now that the debts had accumulated, Henri found his back against the wall. He found a partial remedy with his abjuration. One recompense was the Pope's accord to Henri's selling of Church land. This, however, could not prevent the (undeclared) bankruptcy of the French Crown in 1598. Henri's predecessors had done little to help – he was in many ways a simple victim of the spending of previous reigns. The lack of money was already apparent by 1559. On the death of Henri II, all building work on the château de Chambord was stopped. Between 1563 and 1586, there were six *aliénations* of Church land followed by a *subvention extraordinaire* in 1588. In 1563, for example, Charles IX gained 100,000 *écus* (£30,000) from the sale of Church property. Though 'the ecclesiastic fowl had been plucked … moderately',[422] Henri was left with a meagre chicken to throw into the pot. Henri himself pleaded that the revenue from Rouen and Le Havre had either been sold or alienated by previous kings. Henri was already taxing Paris to the hilt; it would not be prudent to demand more. Another excuse was the cost of the forthcoming marriage with Marie de' Medici. In fact, Henri owed 1,174,000 *écus* to Ferdinando de' Medici grand duke of Tuscany (1549-1609). The promise of a dowry of 600,000 *écus* alleviated half of this debt.

All these excuses, meanwhile, failed to impress Elizabeth; as she told him, 'Speeches are the leaves. The weight is made of deeds, which are the real fruit of a good tree.'[423]

The French embassy of *maréchal* Charles de Gontaut, baron de Biron, of the same year (1601) was quite diplomatic. All traces of ostentation disappeared as the French opted to wear black. This in turn persuaded their host, Sir Walter Raleigh, to order his own black cloak and leave his coloured clothes at home. Elizabeth's displeasure was manifest in the reception awaiting the embassy. Raleigh found that preparations had not been made and that he 'never saw so great a person so neglected'.[424] He tried his best at hosting the French diplomats, taking them to visit Westminster Abbey and the Bear Garden.

Sir Robert Cecil had previously been optimistic over the repayments. He declared that he would have been pleased to secure a return of ten per cent on Henri's debts. Meanwhile, Henri had very different ideas. He paid only 20,000 *couronnes* (£6,000) in 1599 and 50,000 (£15,000) in 1602. He also intended to pay 200,000 *francs* (£20,000) in 1603. Christophe de Harlay wrote to Villeroy, following his audience with Elizabeth in February 1602:

> *Monsieur, I offered the Queen the one hundred and fifty thousand Pounds. She became a little angry but a lot more modestly ... than I could ever have hoped from [following] such a course. I beseech you to make sure that this money should be carried to Dieppe as soon as possible so that I can place the King in better credit than he is with this princess.*[425]

Charges were also levied for transporting the repayment money to England. An English merchant at Rouen, for example, would have charged more than £100 to deliver 20,000 *couronnes* (£6,000). The payment of 50,000 *couronnes* in 1602 was made in cash. Ralph Winwood stipulated a payment in the coinage *quart d'escuz* (15 *sols tournois*). Henri's minister of finance, Béthune, in a moment of administrative *gaucherie*, determined to pay him only in *dizims*. (A *douzain* had a value of 12 *deniers tournois*.) The problem remained unresolved a month later as Béthune dug his heels in: 'The truth is (and so Monsieur de Villeroy told me), Monsieur de Rhosny hath stood so violentlie in this point that he doth hold it a dishonour now to relent.'[426]

By mid-June, it appeared that Béthune had indeed finally relented. Unfortunately, Winwood was informed by English merchants at Rouen that the *quart d'escuz* would incur losses. They told him that the coins were lacking in weight and that there were also many counterfeits. The irony is that it was the English who had previously produced counterfeits to aid the Huguenots.

An accord was finally negotiated following Elizabeth's death with the signing of the Treaty of Hampton Court in July 1603. By this, a third of France's subsidy to the Dutch would count towards France's repayments to England. The English task of reclaiming the debts was not aided by the mysterious disappearance (or loss) of some of the bonds from the archives. Some payments were subsequently paid by Henri and Louis XIII of £14,322, £45,000 and £15,000 in the years 1603, 1612 and 1613 respectively. The Grand Sancy diamond, now recovered, also found its way to England, as James I took possession of it in 1604.

England was not the only country to lend money to France. Sums were also due to the Swiss cantons in 1598, according to Béthune's figures, as well as to the German princes and the United Provinces. Similarly, the French were not the only country to avoid paying their debts. The English had little satisfaction from the loans of £800,000 made to the Dutch. At least one German house, that of Anhalt-Bernburg, was claiming repayments as late as the reign of Louis XVIII. Then, in 1816, 94,419 *écus* plus interest was demanded from the newly restored French monarchy. Christian I, the prince of Anhalt (1568–1630), had raised 13,100 men in 1591 to serve in France. Only part-payments had been made by the French between 1605 and 1623.

CHAPTER SIX

ENGLISH PERSPECTIVES

*'How much bound are our people to God, that know
not these myseries!'*

(Sir Thomas Coningsby before Rouen, 1591)[427]

THROUGHOUT THE PERIOD OF THE French Wars of Religion, the
English Crown and people showed an increasing interest in events
across the Channel. The sporadic massacres of Huguenots made
front-page news, as it were, in England. French pamphlets giving accounts
of the events were frequently translated into English. The titles themselves
were sometimes altered to reflect the English reaction of shock. News of
the massacre at Wassy, for example, in *Discours au vray et en abbregé
de ce qui est dernierement advenu à Vassy y passant Monseigneur le
Duc de Guise* ('A true discourse and summary of what recently happened
at Wassy with the passing of Monsieur the duc de Guise') became *The
Destruction and sacke cruelly committed by the Duke of Guyse and his
company, in the toune of Vassy.*

Thomas Tymme translated Jean de Serre's *The three partes of
Commentaries, containing the whole and perfect Discourse of the Civill
Warres of Fraunce, under the raignes of Henry the second, Frances the
second, and Charles the ninth. With an addition of the cruel murther
of the Admirall Chastilion, and diver other nobles, committed the 24.
daye of August. Anno 1572. Translated out of Latine into English by
Thomas Timme, Minister* (London, 1574).[428] Other authors translated
existing French histories for use in their own books. John Polemon used
La Popelinière for his entries on the battles of Dreux, St-Denis, Jarnac
(Bassac) and Moncontour in his *All the Famous Battels That Have Bene*

Henri IV at the siege of a town [Possibly depicts the siege of Chartres. Could also
be Amiens], by Gillis van Coninxloo (1544–1607). Detail of plate on page 243.

Fought in Our Age. As Matthias Shaaber points out, just four men were responsible for the publishing of around half of the news from France: Edward Aggas (an important translator), Richard Field, William Wright and John Wolfe.

The thirst for information is apparent in the constant flow of reports from France. Englishmen travelling to France and further afield brought back works to read and translate for their own countrymen. Some wrote their own accounts based on experience at first hand. The common element is an image of desolation. A witness reported from the town of Noyon in 1591, 'the countrie being spoiled about, the bridges broken, all the suburbes of the towne burned, their orchards and gardens utterlie destroyed, their churches beaten downe, the walls rente, the towne within most fylthie, and breifly the countenance and face of all things showing desolation'.[429]

English accounts often substantiated those of Frenchmen. The complicity of children, noticed by Pierre Paschal, was similarly witnessed by the English ambassador, Sir Thomas Smith:

> *They of Paris do still murder one or other for Huguenots, which is*
> *the most cruel and barbarous disorder that ever was seen in any*
> *commonwealth. For it is enough for a boy of 13 or 14 years old*
> *or younger, when he seeth a man in the street, to cry: 'Voilà un*
> *Huguenot' and straight the idle vagabonds and such as go about to*
> *cry things to sell, and crocheteurs set upon him with stones and such*
> *things as they have ready, and then cometh out the handicraftsmen*
> *and idle apprentices and with swords and such other weapons*
> *as they have, every man that may, and then they spoil him of his*
> *clothes and the boys and that canaille trail him down with ropes to*
> *the river, and so casteth him into the water. If he be a town dweller,*
> *after that they have killed him they enter in his house, spoileth and*
> *carieth away all that he hath; and if his wife and children be not*
> *the sooner carried away, they kill them likewise.*[430]

The field of battle could occasionally be less dangerous than the capital. Sir Edmund Yorke was not impressed by the fighting that he observed between Henri IV and Parma in Normandy in 1592: 'Some little skirmishes by French to French, which are as good as a base, but not as a good play at football in England where men's necks, arms, and legs are broken; but here not a man hurt.'[431] Sir Thomas Coningsby witnessed a similar display at Rouen: 'We stood and viewed a skyrmysh betwixte the garrison of the castle of St Katherin's and certaine soldiors of Bellgarde's regymente, where, being above 200 soldiors on eyther syde, and skyrmyshing more then an howre in our sighte, we could not dyscerne any man slaine, and few or none hurte.'[432]

The English impression of Henri IV is also interesting. Sir Anthony Mildmay found that he was easy-going, chatty and very brave but that he was lacking in other virtues. He thought that he was negligent and incapable of concentrating on serious matters for long. Captain Edmond Wilton wrote while he was at Le Crotoy in 1596, 'For the war, many speak strangely touching the person of the King; they say they are without hope to see him ever any more armed in the field, so violent are his affections to his mistress.'[433] William Lilly also mentions her, 'This woman doth him infinite wrong in his reputation, for that she effects great things at his hands, by them Sancy and Villeroy both deceive him, her, and the people.'[434]

Coningsby commented on Henri and his eating habits: 'his dyet is of many meates, and a snatche of every one; dryncketh good wine and lytle water. All the while he talked to one, or one to him in his eare'.[435] Later, 'He made him ready before us, and there brake his faste, where he eate soundly on a pece of powdred beefe, and all his nobles standing about him all armed saving their kaskes [helmets], 3 or 4 playing at prymero [a card game] hard by him while he eate.'[436]

THE BATTLE OF ST-DENIS, 10 NOVEMBER 1567

English reports were not always written – several pictoral representations are of particular interest. One is a cavalier view of the battle of St-Denis in 1567, attributed to William and John Norris.[437] The two brothers were sitting on Montmartre with their father, Sir Henry Norris. He later sent the sketch back to London with his written report. The drawing is interesting in both artistic and historical terms. There is a clear sense of movement with the cavalry charge. The moment of impact, the ensuing mêlée, the retreat and the effect of artillery on the horse are the work of a mature artist.

THE BATTLE OF JARNAC, 13 MARCH 1569

The battle of Jarnac took place during the third civil war. Gaspard de Saulx, sieur de Tavannes, led a Catholic army. Louis de Bourbon, prince de Condé, was killed after surrendering. Sir Henry Norris sent the following report of the battle.

A little before the rencounter, the Admiral defeated near unto Jarnac between 700 and 800 horses, putting to flight Sebastien de Luxemburg, vicomte de] Martigues, Brissac and others and recovered from them the town and castle of Jarnac by composition, which captain La Rivière had taken before. Whereupon, the 11th of this same month the duke of Anjou would have encamped near unto Cognac but seeing the other army ready to rencounter, he returned to Châteauneuf. At the last, having caused to be made two or three bridges upon the river of Charente and been advertised that the Prince would fight with him, he caused at midnight by little and little all his vanguard and the most part of his horsemen to pass over the bridge before the Prince's army was informed thereof, which was the cause that the next day, being the 13th of this month, the Admiral came to assail them and overthrew part of them. But, seeing the strength of the Duke's army coming upon him, he sent forthwith unto the Prince (who had undertaken with seven or eight hundred horsemen to keep the passage of the bridges) that he should retire himself towards him, both to succour him and also that he should not endanger himself among his enemies. And so, by little and little, the said Admiral retired himself near unto a village called Bassac between Châteaunef and Jarnac, where the Prince followed with such a fury and so strangely that he broke the whole vanguard of the Duke but the same being renforced by eight cornets of the reiters, the Prince's men were constrained to retire. As touching the Prince being so hot in the fight as he would not retire himself, his horse was first killed under him and he hurt and taken prisoner by the sieur d'Argence. And it is said that he was killed after he was taken, which was done by Martigues and others who were expressly sent with him for that purpose by the duke of Anjou, and so was his body mangled after he was dead. Stuart the Scottish man was also slain after he was taken and his head carried upon a pike's point about the army. Mons. de Losses was forthwith sent hither to Paris with the news, where he arrived the 18th of this month. It is certain that without the reiters the army of the Duke of Anjou had been wholly defeated, minding nothing else but to fly. But the reiters, being a great company and hard to be broken, pursued somewhat the Prince's men and yet the Admiral and generally all the chiefs except the Prince retired themselves safely and sound to Cognac, where they have in the space of two days assembled all their forces again.[438]

THE SHOOTING OF *AMIRAL* COLIGNY, AUGUST 1572

The following was endorsed simply 'the peteful Frenche Newes':

> *The Admiral tok his jorney home to his owne house, and riding by*
> *the way by a house of Duke de Navers, there was shot of at him a*
> *calvering with three bullets; one of them strok of two of his fingers,*
> *an other stroke him through the wrest of his arme, the third went*
> *through his horse without harme to him; whereupon the Admiral*
> *beseged the house, and not being furnished to win it, left his garison*
> *and departed for anguish home to his house at Paris, and sent word*
> *to the King of the same....*
>
> *The poore Admiral remained in Paris at surgery til Saterday, at two*
> *of the clock in the morning, when they provided him new surgions*
> *that released him of al his paines and miseries, for about that houre,*
> *the Kinges gard for his owne person being called, the old gard, with*
> *a number of the Guisards and al the papistes of Paris came in good*
> *order, and first set sufficient gard at the gates, and then divided*
> *themselves in such order as thei beseged every noblemans house of*
> *any fame, being a protestant....*
>
> *The order of the murdering of the Admiral was in this sort. They*
> *threw him and his secretorie out of his chamber windo into the*
> *streat, and drew him up and downe the streates. Monsieur al the*
> *time of this slaughter rod up and downe so furiously as in one day*
> *he spent three horses, crying 'vengeance, vengeance, to the slaughter,*
> *to the slaughter'.*[439]

THE SIEGE OF LA ROCHELLE, MAY 1573

Extract of a letter from Dr Valentine Dale to the Earl of Sussex, Moret-sur-Loing (near Fontainebleau), 31 May 1573:

> *The town of Rochell is in a maner four square. The west syde lyeth*
> *upon the sea, the south syde lyeth upon salt marshes full of pitts to*
> *make salt, the north syde is overflowen with the tyde at every full water,*
> *and the east syde, which only is accessible, hath at the corner towards*
> *the south, an out bulwark called the bulwark of the porte of the Cogne,*
> *and at the corner towards the north, one other mightie bulwark, St*
> *Angely, which two bulwarks do flank all the curtayne of the east syde.*

Monsieur hath battered the bulwarke St Angely, but holdeth it not himself, and lyeth in the dych at the foot of a breach made into a curtayne of the wall. They of the towne are on the rampart, sometyme at the half pyke. What trenches or fosses be within is not knowne. There are divers gateways and platformes in the towne, that do command the ramparts at the place of the breache.[440]

THE BATTLE OF ARQUES, SEPTEMBER 1589

There are two interesting views of this battle. Curiously, an English inter-pretation may be found at the Bibliothèque Nationale de France,[441] while a French depiction is at the British Library,[442] 'Victoire obtenue par le Roy contre le Duc Maienne a Sainct Estienne le 21 Sept. 1589' (British Library, Cotton MS Augustus I.88). The hand-coloured print shows the participation of English freebooters (L) and the gunner, Edward Webb (GG).

Imprinted in the Blackefriers.

A. The Castle of Arques with his great borough iii. miles from Dieppe.

B. The fort of Arques a Canon shot from the castle of Arques.

C. The great trenches beginning at the corner of the forrest of Arques & continuing neare to S. Estienne by ye river side.

D. The kings Cornet where the king lay the night before the battell, in these trenches.

E. The Cornet of ye Marshal of Byron [the baron de Biron] accompaniyng the king to the assault of the enemy.

F. The companies of the light horsemen of monsieur de Lorges [Montgomery] & Rambures [Charles de Rambures, governor of Doullens] with a part of the Prince of Conti [François de Bourbon-Condé, prince de Conti, 1558–1614] his companie, conducted by monsieur Darmilly which went to spy the lodging of the enemies in Martinglize. [Martin-Église].

G. Martinglize wherin was lodged ye Duke & Chevallier Daumall [Charles de Lorraine, duc d'Aumale] & ye Duke de Nemours [Charles-Emmanuel de Savoie, duc de Nemours, one of the leaders of the *Ligue*] & monsieur Sagonne [Jean Babou, comte de Sagonne, killed at Arques].

H. The fort of Paullet [Polet] against the river of Arques.

I. The Paullet which is one of the suburbes of Dieppe at the bridge foote.

K. The fort of monsieur de Chastillon [Claude Chastillon] against the Sea.

L. Maister Devorar [Devereux] with other English Gentlemen vollontaries going against ye enemy.

M. The Marques Dallegre [Christophe d'Alègre] his companie.

N. The Miles [mills] of Paullet where was made many hoate skirmishes, by monsieur de Chastillon & others, where the kings horse was hurt with a calliver, when he went to spy ye enemies pretence.

O. The enemy coming down the hill to passe the litle river, who was set upon by six horsemen & two footemen among whom was monsieur S. Marke & Sturbe which put them to flight.

P. Our litle trenches begon at S. Estienne [St-Étienne] & continuing to ye litle river.

Q. The kings army in the first fight, who were not above iiii. Cornets of horsemen, who went against twise as many of the enemies & made them retire.

R. S. Estienne where the great fight was, in the which ye king was himselfe, where was slaine on the enemies side 500 & of ours 27.

S. The Launceknightes [*Landsknechte*] that made as though they would yeld to ye king, & after they were sworne to his majestie traitorously tooke our litle trenches, which we requited the same instant by the kings good providence, where he fought both on horsebacke & on foote shewing himself both king captaine & souldier all at one time.

T. The great army of the enemies, who were in number above 25000. men against the kings army, who were not at that time above eight o[r] 9000.

U. A crowne that appeared in the skie over the kings army the day of their fight, which was sene of many persons to the wonder of them all.

W. The camp & artillery of the enemies.

X. The quarter of ye high Allmaine Rutters. [German *Reiter*]

Y. The enemies horsemen.

Z. The enemies footmen.

AA. The towne of Dieppe.

BB. The Haven of Dieppe.

CC. The Castle of Dieppe.

DD. The Citadell of Dieppe.

EE. The mount of Cats [Mont-a-Cats] wherein was made a strong fort, in one day & a night against the enemy.

FF. The enemies six peeces of artillerie, which was discharged within the towne 5. or 6. times killing 4. persons & hurting two ships in ye haven, with no other harme.

GG. Two peeces of artillerie, in the fort of the mount of Cats, which was planted by an English Canonner [the English gunner Edward Webb],[443] who was presented to the king, by my Lord Stafford Ambassadour for her Majestie, who discharged them so skilfully, that there withal he slue ye maister Gunner to the enemy & dismounted two peeces of his ordinaunce.

HH. The enemy in the village of Januall [Janval], upon whom our artillery was discharged without any shot in vaine, they were so thicke in their troupes.

II. The king with his Cornet going to discover ye enemy.

KK. Pallisade neare ye gallowes, where was made many skirmishes on both sides, & the enemy seing he could not prevaile fearing ye kings succours that were coming, raise up his army to his great lose and shame.

(*overleaf*) *The battle of Arques*, 1589, English woodcut broadsheet.
Bibliothèque Nationale de France, GeDD 627 pl.78.
The two platforms as well of the Towne of Dieppe, and the Castle of Arques together with the fortifications and trenches made against the Army of the rebellious Leaguers, by the commaundement of the King, in the moneth of September last past. 1589.

A. The Castle of Arques with his great borough th. miles from Dieppe. B. The fort of Arques a Canon shot fro the castle o. Arques. C. The great trenches beginning at the corner of the forrest of Arques continuing neare to S. Ellene by ÿ riuer side. D. The kings whit Cornet where the king lay the night before the battell, in these trenches. E. The Cornet of ÿ Marshall of Byron accompanying the king to the assault of the enemy. F. The companies of the light horsemen of monsieur de Loiges & Haburée, with a part of the Prince of Conti; h: accompanie, conducted by monsieur Barnilly which went to spy the lodging of the enemies in Martinglize. G. Martinglize wherein was ledged ÿ Duke a Cheuallier Daumall, the Duke de Nemours & monsieur Sagonne. H. The fort of Paullet against the riuer o. Arques. I. The Paullet which is one of the suburbes of Dieppe at the bridge foote. K. The fort of monsieur de Chastillon against the Sea. L. Maister Denozar with other English Gentlemen v lontaries going against ÿ enemy. M. The Marques Vallegre his companie. N. The files of Paullet where was made man up hoate skirmishes, by monsieur d Syadillon & others, where the kings horse was hurt with a calliuer, when he went to spy ÿ

enemies pretence. O. The ene set vpon by six horsemen a two which put them to flight. P. L riuer. Q. The kings army in t who went against twise as man the great fight was, in the whic sco. & of ours :7. S. The Laun & after they were swoine to his quited the same instant by the & on foote shewing himself both nip of the enemies, who were in not at that time aboue eight o army the day of their fight, who The camp faruliery of the ene

passe the litle riuer, who was
monsieur S. Marke & Stu de
Estienne & continuing to y litle
soek iii . Come to horsemen,
retire. R. S. Estiene where
we was saure on the enemies side
web they would yeld re y king,
ir little trenches, which we re-
e he fought both on horsbacke
at one time. T. The great ar-
rst the kings army, who were
ared in the skie ouer the kings
to the wonder esthernall. W.
gh Iduaine Rutters. Y. The

enemies horsme. Z. The enemies comins. II. The towre of Dieppe. BB. The ha-
uē of Dieppe. CC. The Castle of Dieppe. DD. The Citadell of Dieppe. EE. The moūt
of Cats wherein was made a strong fort, in one day & a night against the enemy. FF. The
enemies six peeces of artillerie, which was discharged within the towne 5. or 6. times killing
4. persons & shutting two ships in y hauen, with no other harme. GG. Two peeces at artillerie, in the fort of the mount of Cats, which was plaste by an English Cannonier, who was
presented to the king, by my Lord Stafford Ambassadour for her Maiestie, who discharged
them so skilfully, that there withall he slue y maister Gunner to the enemy & dismounted two
peeces of his ordinance. HH. The enemy in the village of Iannail, vpon whō our artillery
was discharged without any shot in baine, they were so thicke in their troupes. II. The
king with his Cornet going to discouer y enemy. KK. Pallisade neare y gallowes, where
was made many skirmishes on both sides, & the enemy seing he could not preuaile fearing y
kings succours that were comming, raise vp his army to his great lose and shame.
Imprinted in the Blacke friers.

THE BATTLE OF IVRY, 14 MARCH 1590

An anonymous English account sheds new light on this battle in 1590. It becomes apparent that the condition of the terrain played a key part in the result of the battle:

> Our battle was very happy, and more conducted by God's providence than any other natural cause, only the valour of this King who was seven times at the charge ... God who looked on the present right, and forgetteth passed fault of France, gave sentence with us, and withal victory, contrary to all our hopes. For long time the reiters having furiously charged, but ill supported, the lances in like sort did enter with great appearance to overthrow all, but the ground was so ill for them to charge as no leave to make a full career, they were constrained to come against us in a soft gallop. Their horses so enfonced themselves in the earth so as they failed of their hope [and] either rendered to us or were overthrown.... The Marshal Biron stood still with the reiters and some other troops in gross to assure the battle, which did great good, for upon the spavent of the lanciers' charge all ours had run away had [it] not been [for] that assurance.... Sir Lee Broun did wonderfully well, wherefore the King made them 'knights of the cullander'. I was glad that [of] our nation there was some one there to shew the valour of an Englishman.[444]

Once more we see Henri's dexterity in choosing the right terrain to give battle. The forest of Ivry covered his right flank while the heavy ground 'fortified' the front, absorbing the cavalry charge. [445]

THE SIEGE OF CHARTRES, 1591

The plan of the siege of Chartres in 1591 was produced by the young engineer Edmund Yorke, who was also present.[446] It was sent back to England by Edward Grimston from the camp at Dourdan on 24 April. The plan is to be compared with the written accounts of the siege by Agrippa d'Aubigné[447] and Jacques-Auguste de Thou.[448]

Yorke's plan is a useful aid in identifying the siege depicted in a drawing and painting by Gillis van Coninxloo, *Henri IV devant une ville* (Musée des Beaux-Arts de Chartres).[449] The painting depicts details common to both the sieges of Amiens and Chartres. Both had medieval town walls with later additions including *ravelins* to protect gates. The cathedral more closely resembles that of Chartres. The painting shows an assault upon a breach in the town's walls. Jacques-Auguste de Thou may be referring to the interesting device depicted in the painting used to approach the defences. He writes, 'A device invented by Châtillon was placed against the walls with a bridge to counter those who were fighting on the ramparts.'[450] Further evidence is provided by the governor of Chartres, Georges Babou, seigneur de la Beaurdaisiè. He reports how 'The enemy … made wide and deep trenches in the ground the height of a man and covered them with house joists so to enter the moat from underground.' According to him, efforts were concentrated against the fortifications at the Porte des Épars (A. in Yorke's plan) and the Porte Drouaise. At Amiens, it should be noted that the main assault was made against the *ravelin*.

Henri IV at the siege of a town [Possibly depicts the siege of Chartres or Amiens], by Gillis van Coninxloo (1544–1607). Musée des Beaux-Arts, Chartres, Inv. 923. Photo © RMN-Grand Palais/Agence Bulloz

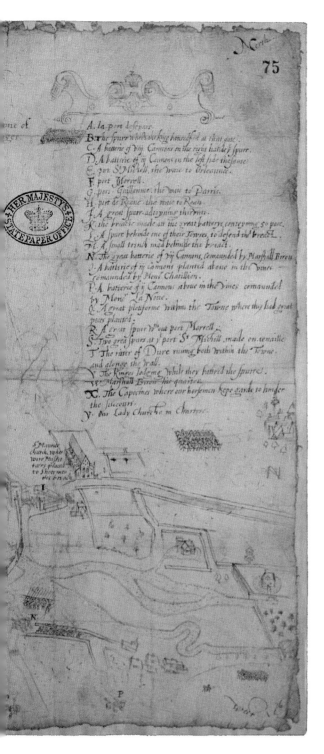

A DISCRIPTION OF THE TOWNE OF CHARTRES AND OF THE KINGES BATTERIES

A.   La port de Separs. [Porte des Épars]

B.   The spurr which the King battred first at that gate.

C.   A batterie of viii Cannons on the right hande ye spurr.

D.   A battereie of iii Cannons on the left side of the same.

E.   port St Michell, the waie to Orleaunce.

F.   port Morrell.

G.   port Guillaume the waie to Parris.

H.   port de Roane the waie to Roan.

I.   A great spurr adjoyning therunto.

K.   the breache made att the great batterye conteyning 50 pace.

L.   A spurr behinde one of their Towres to defend the breach.

M.   A small trench mad behinde the breach.

N.   The great batterie of vii Cannons comaunded by Marshall Biron.

O.   A batterie of iii Cannons planted above in the vines comaunded by Monsr. Chatillion.

P.   A batterie of ii Cannons above in the vines comaunded by Monsr. La Noue.

Q.   A great platteforme within the Towne whre they had great peces planted.

R.   A great spurr wthout port Morrell.

S.   Two great spurs at ye port St Michell made on tenaille.

T.   The river of Dure [Eure] running both within the Towne and alonge the wall.

V.   The Kinges lodging while they battred the spurre.

W.   Marshall Biron his quarter.

X.   The Capocines where our horsemen kepe garde to hinder the succours.

Y.   Our Lady Churche in Chartres. St Maurice church, wher were Musketeers placed to shote into the breach.

Plan of the siege of Chartres, 1591, by Edmund Yorke. The National Archives (TNA), SP 78/24 f.75

THE ATTEMPTED ASSASSINATION OF KING HENRI IV, 1594

Sir Thomas Edmondes to Lord Burghley, 17/27 December 1594:

*The subject of this despatche is to advertise your lordship in hast
(to thend to prevent untrue bruites) of a mischievous attempt made
uppon the kinges person this daie of his arryvall here being gonne to
Madame de lyancortes lodginge, and as he was thither followed by
all men, so amongst others by a young fellowe of this Towne of the
age of 19 yeares, the sonne of a draper dwelling in the Pallace whose
education hath ben amonge the Jesuittes who ... approched the king
with a greate knife to have stabbed him. It fell out that at the instant
as he pressed to have donne the execution, the king espying in the
chamber Monsieur de Montigny the gouvernor of Bloys (with whom
he is accustomed to be pleasant) newelie arryved went towardes him
and made him a lowe sallutacion, at the which tyme the fellowe
having presented his blowe and thincking to have stricken him in
the brest or bellye the happynes was that by the occasion of his said
stooping he received it on the uppermost lipp of the right side of the
face and the hurte onlie that he hath a litle cutt downe the lipp and
pearced into the toothe without other inconvennience wourthie the
speaking.... The king uppon receiving of the blowe uttred dyvers
tymes, and perticulerlie to the Mareshall of Retz when he came in (to
whom it was well addressed) that he did owe that obligation to those
that had ben mainteyners, and intercessors for the Jesuittes.*[451]

PORTRAIT OF ROBERT DEVEREUX, EARL OF ESSEX

Several English portraits also provide us with a window on the past as
they contain depictions of events in France. One portrait of Essex held
by the National Portrait Gallery, London (NPG 6241),[452] may be linked
directly to his campaign in France. The painting by Nicholas Hilliard is
quite small (only 24.8 x 20.3cm).

A closer examination of the background is necessary. The large
encampment with artillery, earthworks and a gabion in the background
of the portrait suggest their presence at a siege. There are three pieces of
artillery and a gunner depicted in fortified positions. A sapper's tool used
for digging trenches is perhaps also visible. Mounted horsemen are present

in the background on the left as well as pikemen behind the encampment. The evidence leads us to either Gournay-en-Bray or Rouen during his campaign in France, that is to say, 1591. It could be asked why Essex would choose Rouen as it was ultimately a failure. There are two possibilities: either the portrait was painted during the siege or he saw Rouen as something to remember. In another well-known engraving by Thomas Cockson, the siege of Rouen does appear next to his moment of glory at Cadiz.[453]

There are also other clues which direct us to the year 1591. Interestingly, many of the portraits of Essex may be dated by the length of his beard. In our portrait, the beard is fairly new. If we look at other dated portraits it may be seen that in 1588 he had a moustache and the beginnings of a beard. In 1590 he had only a moustache and by around 1595 his beard was fully grown. He was as bearded as ever upon his return from Cadiz. Comparisons may also be made with other paintings such as those at Balliol College, Oxford, the portrait by Marcus Gheeraerts from around 1597 at the National Portrait Gallery and that at Trinity College, Cambridge, also by Gheeraerts. To these we may add Cockson's engraving of 1601.

Finally, we have one other item linking this portrait to the campaign in France. Essex is also wearing a white sash (perhaps bearing fleurs-de-lys) on his right arm as well as a white crest in his helmet and his horse. White was the colour adopted by Henri IV. La Popelinière states that white was already being used as a distinguishing colour in battle in 1569.

THE LITERARY LEGACY

While the civil wars may have caused great destruction in France, in England they provided inspiration for artists and writers alike, contributing to the country's cultural blossoming. Byrd, Marlowe and Shakespeare each produced works linked directly to the wars. It must be remembered that two of Shakespeare's plays, *Henry IV* and *Henry V*, were written during English campaigns in France.

> *Cry, 'Courage! – to the field!' and thou hast talk'd*
> *Of sallies, and retires; of trenches, tents,*
> *Of palisadoes, frontiers, parapets;*
> *Of basilisks, of cannon, culverin;*
>
> *Of prisoners' ransom, and of soldiers slain…*[454]
>
> *Once more unto the breach, dear friends, once more;*
> *Or close the wall up with our English dead!*[455]

These lines were written around 1597 and 1599 respectively with the English successes of Crozon and Amiens fresh in Shakespeare's mind.

The events of the religious troubles quickly entered English popular culture. For example, the plight of the Huguenots was performed in English theatres with *Massacre at Paris* by Christopher Marlowe. In this play, Henri III thinks to inform Queen Elizabeth of events shortly before dying:

> *Agent for England, send thy mistress word*
> *What this detested Jacobin hath done.*
> *Tell her, for all this, that I hope to live;*
> *Which if I do, the papal monarch goes*
> *To wreck, and [th'] antichristian kingdom falls:*
> *These bloody hands shall tear his triple crown,*
> *And fire accursed Rome about his ears;*
> *I'll fire his crazed buildings, and enforce*
> *The papal towers to kiss the lowly earth. –*
> *Navarre, give me thy hand I here do swear*
> *To ruinate that wicked Church of Rome,*
> *That hatcheth up such bloody practices;*
> *And here protest eternal love to thee,*
> *And to the Queen of England specially,*
> *Whom God hath bless'd for hating papistry…*
> *…I die, Navarre; come bear me to my sepulchre.*
> *Salute the Queen of England in my name,*
> *And tell her, Henry dies her faithful friend.*[456]

This play may have been discontinued following French protests.

Unfortunately, texts from other plays have been lost. Thomas Dekker and Michael Drayton wrote a play called simply *I, II, & III The Civil Wars of France*. This was performed by the Admiral's Men at the Rose Theatre in 1598. The year after, they performed *The First Introduction of the Civil Wars of France*.

Interest in the wars continued in the reign of James I. George Chapman wrote *The Conspiracy and Tragedy of Charles Duke of Byron* (London, 1608). This was based on the fate of Charles Gontaut, duc de Biron.

The death of one English soldier, Sir William Sackville, drew the attention of John Ross who wrote the poem *Th'authors teares upon the death of his honorable Friende Sir William Sackvile Knight of the order de la colade in France sonne to the right honorable the Lord of Buckhurst Anno Domini. 1592.*

> *As they, so was our English knight of breath bereft*
> *In forrein partes, too worthie for his end:*
> *And of soe brave a man is nothing left*
> *But that his vertues may his life commend*
> *Of whome all those that love the Christian king*
> *While Fraunce is Fraunce sad elegies will sing…*
>
> *This (for yt was the censure of a king*
> *Whose long experience taught him judge aright)*
> *I thought not much impertinent to bring*
> *As for the warrant of our English knight*
> *And (that which may perhapps seeme straunge to tell)*
>
> *The french both hie and low, all lov'd him well.*[457]

The English reaction to French refugees was mixed. Sir Thomas Leighton was particularly worried about the large number of refugees arriving in the Channel Islands, being convinced that they would cause food shortages. On 12 April, Easter Monday 1563, Sir John White, the mayor of London, attended a service at St Mary's Church. The congregation showed its generosity in giving £45 to French refugees. A fresh wave of refugees began to arrive in England in the wake of the massacres in Paris and Rouen. Certain Englishmen, meanwhile, doubted their motives:

> *The French now come to Rye in multitudes with bagg and baggage, there desiring to have leav to com over into England to save themselves and we hear be doutful whether thei com in Trojans horse or els of pure necessitie. God for his mercys sak so provid for his elect that if thei come indeed for consciens they may be here releived, or els if it be not contre his glory that it wold please him to deliver this poore England from treason.*[458]

The following extracts from a hymn reflect public opinion.[459] One particular concern, shown in the second verse, was inflation.

> *God doth blesse this realme for the*
> *receyving of straungers being persecuted*
> *for the gospell, although some do repine therat*

It is not as some deeme,
which by their carping seme
Pore straungers to invay,
as all the matter laye –
That they be here to make thinges deare
and banishe wealth away...

Thou shalt not be the worse,
o england, if thou nourse
Theise exiles come of late
(What so theise papistes prate?),
Who, to retaine their christ, are faine
to chose this banisht state...

Two Frenchmen, Claudius Hollyband (alias Claude de Sainliens) and Peter Erondell, taught in London. They wrote an early phrase-book entitled *The French Schoole Maister* (London, 1573).[460] This was followed by *The French Garden* in 1605. They are particularly useful today in helping to establish the pronunciation of French words in the sixteenth century. *The French Schoole Maister*, for example, teaches its students that the letter 's' is silent in words such as *chasteau*. De Sainliens included a bilingual passage in his school textbook, with the English printed opposite the French.

What newes in France?	*Que dit-on de nouveau en France?*
Truelie nothing good. How so?	*Certes rien de bon Comment cela?*
The civil warre is there so enflamed,	*La guerre civile y est tellement enflammée*
that the father is against the sonne, and	*que le pere est contre le filz, &*
the sonne against the father and are so	*le fils contre le pere & sont tellement*
madde, that they drawe their swordes against their proper bowels,	*forcenez, qu'ilz desgainent leurs espées contre leurs propres entrailles.*
God preserve us from civill warres, for it is an evell fleale: is it true that I have hearde saye?	*Dieu nous preserve de la guerre civile, car c'est un mauvais fleau est-il vray ce que j'ay ouï dire?*
What Syr? That they have doone	*Quoy Monsieur? Qu'on a fait*

such a great murther in Paris?	*un si grand meutre à Paris?*
That I knowe not: when came	*Cela ne sçay-je pas: quand vindrent*
the newes?	*les nouvelles?*
Yesternight by a post.	*Au soir par un poste.*
O immortall God, how men bee	*O Dieu immortel, que le homes sont*
unconstant: well, one must have	*inconstan bien, il faut avoir*
patience: wee shall have peace	*patience: nous aurons la paix*
when it will please God...	*quand il plaira à Dieu...*

Elizabeth reveals her own personal thoughts in one of her prayers to thank God:

> *Thy most holy benediction, from the which I know peace to have come, accompanied with many good things, which until now, to Thy honor and the comforting of Thy Church, I have enjoyed while my nearest neighbors have felt the evils of bloody war and the poor, persecuted children have found an assured dwelling with rest.*[461]

CONCLUSION

There were both immediate and long-term consequences of English intervention in the French Wars of Religion. In the debate 'Why did the Wars of Religion last so long?', English intervention must be considered as a prime factor. Without Elizabeth's aid, it could be argued that Huguenot resistance would soon have collapsed under Royalist pressure. For this reason, intervention succeeded in helping to maintain Protestantism in France. During the first war, the English occupation of Le Havre deflected the strength of the royal army. Then, in 1573, English relief ensured the continued resistance of La Rochelle. This in turn led to the Edict of Boulogne in July and the granting of freedom of worship.

Around 30,000 Englishmen landed in France between 1562 and 1597 to participate in the wars. The main strength of the English army was not in the number of men but the ability to intervene in numerous theatres of war (sometimes simultaneously) thanks to the vessels of the Royal Navy.

Occasionally, the simple presence of English forces on the field of battle was enough to gain a decisive victory. This was shown at the siege of Aumale. Here the French allies threatened to unleash *les Angloys* on anyone who refused to surrender. The English presence in France also added the element of 'friendly competition' first with the Huguenot and then the Royalist forces. De Thou describes such an instance at the siege of Crozon: 'there was between the French and the English a praiseworthy rivalry as to who could distinguish themselves the most'.[462] Both armies would have benefited, each wanting to prove their martial ability and courage in front of their ally, and thus also preventing acts of cowardice.

Military intervention in France was, in general, different in character from that in the Netherlands. While the English regiments pursued a defensive war in the Netherlands, in France they were constantly on the offensive. In the Netherlands, the English troops were usually placed in garrison to defend Dutch towns. Two important exceptions were the battles of Tournhout on 24 January 1597 and Nieuport on 2 July 1600 under Horace and Francis Vere. In France the English army participated in very few large-scale open battles in significant numbers. In France, English soldiers were often constantly on the march, laying siege to numerous towns. In the Netherlands, they aided a friendly local population. In Ireland they fought against rebels who in turn received Spanish support, such as at the siege of Kinsale in 1601. In France, they often found themselves facing the hostile local peasantry. This was particularly the case in Brittany where the population was largely Catholic.

THE PRICE OF INTERVENTION

The total cost of English intervention in France between 1562 and 1598 is difficult to establish. The loss of provisions alone at Le Havre was estimated to have cost 100,000 *écus* (£33,333 6s 4d). Naval costs must also be considered with those of the army. The construction of new ships, the repair of masts and rigging as well as losses must also be included in the equation. During just three years, from 1587 to 1590, £217,370 19s 7d was spent supporting Henri (including loans and pay for the army). Given that subsequent campaigns cost more than £300,000 and adding the subsidies to the German princes together with naval costs, there was probably little change from a million pounds.

The non-payment of debts to Elizabeth had one effect. The queen herself was left looking to borrow money in 1600. One suggested solution was for her to borrow 300,000 crowns from Venice, which could be repaid over a period of five or six years.

The temporary unification of Huguenot and Royalist forces to drive the English from Le Havre had one unforeseen though significant consequence in terms of religion. *Meslez les loups et les brebis ensemble* ('mixing the wolves and the sheep together') was how Claude Haton described the situation.[463] At the same moment that the Catholic Royalist army was winning Le Havre, it was losing its men to the new religion. Haton continues:

> *All the soldiers and men of war of the King's camp were all Catholics before the said confusion [&] were for the most part made Huguenots. [They] … did nothing in the fields and cantonments but attempt to draw these Catholic soldiers to their religion.… [They] sang their songs of David … and went to their sermons where they were introduced to their pretended religion. And by these means the number of Huguenots in France grew by half more than it was.*[464]

Religion provided the right, excuse and the power behind English intervention. There were, however, some nuances; the picture was not entirely black and white. The Lutherans did not regard the wars in France as being strictly religious. Some German Protestants thought that the Huguenots were worse than the Catholics. For men such as these, English money was far more enticing than pleas to save a religion. Sir Nicholas Throckmorton also remarked that many of the Englishmen who had laid down their lives at the siege of Le Havre were in fact Catholic. This is perhaps not surprising as 600 men were drawn from the county of Norfolk, one of the last refuges of Catholicism in the country.

The defeat of English forces during the first war temporised Elizabeth's foreign policy for more than twenty years. For some, the loss of Le Havre was accepted as being the will of God. William Cecil considered that the surrender of Le Havre was the right choice to make given that God himself had created this 'denne of poyzon': 'the rendryng of Newhaven, which, seing it pleased Almighty God to visit with such incurable infection, being as it semeth a denne of poyzon, it was well bargained to depart it'.[465] The war had been continued at sea, mainly by the English privateers. Their actions against the Spanish made peace more desirable for Elizabeth.[466] One of the consequences had been an embargo on cloth and English cloth and wool at Antwerp. This in turn led to the search for new markets.

The French capture of Le Havre forced the English to strengthen their positions in the Channel Islands. Consequently, a military colony was established on the Isle of Sark in 1565 under Helier de Carteret, the first *seigneur*. The isle was divided into forty parcels, each with a soldier and his family. Each soldier had his own part of the coast to guard. These forty parcels still exist today.

What is remarkable is the transition in relations between England and France. Though the deep-rooted natural rivalry lasted for generations, it took only a number of years to create a tenable alliance. These two allies were a *couple mal assorti*. The new alliance was disturbed by the sporadic massacres of Protestants and by English claims on Calais. The transformation of English foreign policy under Elizabeth was recognised by Burghley when he wrote, 'The state of the world is marvellously changed when we true Englishmen have cause for our own quietness to wish good success to a French King and a king of Scots.'[467] Elizabeth summed up her thoughts on *rapprochement* when she commented: *Que l'amitié des François pouvoit valoir quelque chose, mais non leur voisinage* ('That the friendship of the French may be worth something but not their proximity').[468]

The importance of continuing English support was demonstrated in 1569 following the major Huguenot defeat at Moncontour. This support convinced the Huguenots that the fight was not yet lost. According to Henri de La Popelinière, Henry Champernowne 'with his English cornet he went there, but upon his arrival at Niort, and having seen the long trail of men fleeing the sadness of this day, they joined the mass of escapers'.[469] This contingent was small, but this type of support ensured that the Huguenot army did not melt away after the battle. They gave Coligny a force which was still intact to use to help regroup his army.

The real proof of the success of Elizabeth's foreign policy is the simple fact that England, despite numerous crises, avoided being invaded by a major force during this period. The 'hidden hand' of English diplomacy helped to preserve Elizabeth. France was effectively neutralised. The years of work of Sir Nicholas Throckmorton in France were ultimately not in vain. The siege of Le Havre exhausted not only the finances of Charles IX but also his army. It would take thirty years, however, to break the power of the house of Guise. Intervention prevented the unification of France and Spain in an alliance against England. English intervention and the continuation of the wars in France ended French designs in both Scotland and the Low Countries.

The year 1589 is the pivotal year of English intervention in France. It is the year in which Philip II was drawn to aid the *Ligue* more actively in France. Philip, like Elizabeth, hoped to see the civil wars continue to neutralise a potential aggressor. It was now that the war between France and Spain began in real terms. As Geoffrey Parker has previously shown, the decisive moment was when Henri de Navarre was recognised as the king of France. Philip wrote to warn the duke of Parma:

> *My principal aim is to secure the well-being of the Faith, and to see that in France Catholicism survives and heresy is excluded.... If, in order to ensure this exclusion and to aid the Catholics so that they prevail, you see that it is necessary for my troops to enter France openly.... The affairs of France create obligations that we cannot fail to fulfil because of their extreme importance; and since we must not undertake too many things at once, because of the risk that they will all fail (and because my treasury will not allow it), it seems that we must do something about the war in the Netherlands, reducing it to a defensive footing.[470]*

The following of such a strategy and the diverting of the main thrust away from England were crucial. Philip's action was the key to English success. It presented Elizabeth with the chance to go on the offensive and maintain the advantage following the defeat of the Armada. Attack, taking the fight to the enemy, was her best form of defence.

Philip's new strategy is apparent in the accounts of the army of the Spanish Netherlands. Their projects in France absorbed three quarters of the money received between August 1590 and May 1591. On 11 January 1590, Philip promised 18,500 men to support the *Ligue*. The diverting of Spanish forces away from the Netherlands made the position of the Anglo-Dutch garrisons more secure, but English intervention in France became more necessary. For some *Ligueurs*, however, such as this unknown man, English intervention justified the alliance with Spain: 'I know well that you oppose us that we have made a league with Spain [but] you have done with the English heretic to exterminate our religion…. We have done so with Catholic Spain to defend it.'[471]

THE IMPACT OF THE *REITER*

A decisive element in the wars was Elizabeth's willingness to pay German *Reiter* to invade France from the east: the Count of Oldenburg in 1562, the powerful army of Wolfgang of Bavaria, Duke of Zweibrücken, in 1569, Johann Casimir (four times between 1575 and 1587), Baron Fabian von Dohna in 1587 and then Christian I, prince of Anhalt, between 1589 and 1593. The *Reiter* posed a constant threat which the Catholics and later the *Ligue* could never ignore. The German armies were well placed to strike at the heart of the Guise lands in Lorraine such as Joinville and Nancy. The Germans devastated the country, not only when invading France but also on their return home. In 1568, following the peace of Longjumeau (23 March), the *Reiter* 'retook the route that they took via Bourgogne pillaging all that they found from good houses of the villages and towns where they stayed and took back so much booty from France that their horses and harnesses could not take everything back to their country'.[472]

Bourgogne suffered once more the following year when the Duke of Zweibrücken sacked the town of Beaune. The presence of *Reiter* in the Protestant army allowed Coligny to take the offensive following the defeat at Moncontour on 3 October 1569. The *Reiter* maintained the pressure on the Guises in 1575, though their army was defeated on 10 October at Dormans on the Marne between Château-Thierry and Épernay.

The campaign led by Casimir in 1575–76 was won without giving battle. The payments that he imposed (by the edict of Beaulieu) further exacerbated the state of the royal finances. The campaign of 1587 is another example. Chaumont, Joinville and Nancy were all threatened. Though the expedition finally ended with defeats at Vimory (26 October) and Auneau (24 November), Elizabeth's money was not wasted. The invasion succeeded in attracting Catholic forces away from other regions. Two Royalist armies were thus distracted, leaving only one to face Henri at Coutras. The equality in forces facilitated Henri's first victory. According to Michel de La Huguerye, as many as 1,300 horse were sent to Nancy by Parma.

The scenario was repeated in 1590 before the battle of Ivry. Mayenne's army was seriously weakened when part of his force left to fight in the east. The invasions succeeded in emptying Catholic coffers, affecting their fighting ability in future campaigns. The sacking of Lorraine by the *Reiter* and *Landsknechte* was equal to any victory in open battle. They left an indelible imprint on the psyche of the population. By 1589, the duc de Guise was seeking to extricate Lorraine from the war. He accepted proposals from Casimir for a confederation of the Rhine. Later, Lorraine was once again threatened by fresh levies made by the German princes. Michel de La Huguerye was sent to negotiate with them. From this moment, Lorraine would be on the defensive. The physical evidence of this is apparent, for example, in the great bastion added to the fortifications at Chaumont (1592–94).

According to Sir John Norris, the reputation of the Germans also played a significant part. Their presence in the king's army in the 1590s served to attract French gentlemen who would otherwise have stayed at home. Similarly, many Catholics chose to remain neutral. The employment of the German mercenaries by Elizabeth also prevented their use by the enemy.

Elizabeth's aggressive policies were equalled and aided by the passivity of the Holy Roman Emperor, Maximilian II. He did not forbid his own subjects from aiding the Huguenots, hoping to avoid trouble at home. This passivity had in many ways been earned by Elizabeth. The prospect of marriage between her and the emperor's brother, Archduke Charles, had helped matters. When the likelihood of marriage disappeared, Elizabeth sent her diplomats to invest Maximilian with the Order of the Garter.

By the mid-1590s, the German princes had become less obliging in sending aid, faced with fresh Ottoman threats from the east. 1593 saw the battle of Sisak and the beginning of the Fifteen Year War against the Ottomans. This threat coincided with a reduction in English funding. By this time, the war with Spain was consuming any surplus. Meanwhile, the Dutch were beginning to take a more active role. Having been mainly on the defensive in the 1570s and 1580s, they were free to take the offensive once the Spanish turned their main efforts to France.

INTERVENTION AND HENRI IV

The importance of English forces in Normandy in 1589 had been recognised by Richard Wernham. He held that they formed the core of Henri's army. The men, however, did not fight for 'this ungrateful nation' [473] but for their own queen and country. Though there were deserters, they could generally be trusted to remain on the field of battle and they did not refuse to fight for lack of pay. Thanks, in part, to English support, Henri could lengthen his campaigning season. Whereas many men of the indigenous population sought to return home at the beginning of August (for the harvest), the English could be held in the field. According to Sir William Cecil, Lord Burghley, all the soldiers from Normandy and most from Brittany had either disbanded or returned home by August 1591. The same happened a year later when Morgan Colman commented, 'In France on all sides they seem to be asleep, and will not wake, till the harvest and vintage be ended.' Colman continues, 'when having provided to fill the belly, the insatiable humour of dissention will be doing'.[474]

English aid influenced Henri's strategy to extremes, allowing the luxury of choice. By using the English as a holding force he would be free to operate in other theatres of war at will. The recruitment of foreigners to fight in a civil war was a risk but the degeneration of the French fleet and artillery, two pillars of monarchy, made English aid desirable. In the last phase of the wars, English aid became essential to Henri IV's fragile position. English forces proved vital to the very survival of his throne. As John Nolan comments, 'It can be argued that Norreys's long holding action in Brittany significantly altered the strategic balance in the Anglo-Spanish War, and may have prevented the temporary detachment of that province from the French Crown.'[475]

On Henri, must we give judgement or verdict? According to Lord Burghley, he was 'the most ingratefull King that lyveth'.[476] This he said even before Vervins. The opinion of the soldier Sir Thomas Coningsby was hardly better. He found that he lacked ability at the siege of Rouen. His own servants said that he was *le meilleur prince, mais le plus mauvais ministre* ('the best prince, but the worst minister').[477] Henri was a great military leader but he was handicapped by the political and financial situation of his country. The lack of support that he provided in Normandy and Brittany was not purely the consequence of a lack of means but also a product of his own will. He could leave the English to operate here quasi-independently with limited support, while retaining the mass of his army ready to fight in set-piece battles elsewhere. By forcing decisive battles, he could avoid the need for keeping the French and Swiss in the field for long. He could thus allow them to return home (so also making economies), knowing that the English were still available.

Henri has been described as a second-rate strategist. He was criticised by his contemporaries as well as recent historians, but he was also governed by politics. One reason why the town of Noyon was invested was because the family of Gabrielle d'Estrées, Henri's mistress, had interests there. Similarly, Sir Roger Williams was forced to relinquish St-Valery-en-Caux, as Henri feared alienating his own subjects. As Sir Thomas Lake told Sir Philip Sidney, 'The cunning of Princes is great, and cannot be discerned by every countenance.'[478] Ultimately, Henri's strategy was successful. He achieved the essential, preserving the integrity of his kingdom when faced by his enemies, but also by his own allies. He found the peace at Vervins that his country desired. Faced with bankruptcy, the favourable terms offered by the Spanish proved irresistible.

Henri found the right formula on the field of battle. If he had one gift, it was knowing where to fight. Coutras, Arques, Ivry and Amiens: on all four occasions his army occupied a chosen field of battle strongly defended by either fortifications or natural obstacles. In the same battles, Henri allowed the enemy horse to attack him first. His tactics appear to have influenced, either directly or indirectly, Field Marshal Erwin Rommel during the Second World War. Where possible, Henri avoided pursuing sieges of large towns to the end. By seeking open battle (where half of the men engaged were foreigners) he could avoid damaging and therefore alienating his own inheritance.

Though France was too large to defend, it was, equally, too large to conquer. Despite English aid and despite success in the field, Henri was still obliged to buy back much of his kingdom. His abjuration of 1593 (that is, his conversion to Catholicism) opened the way to peace. Towns such as Chartres in 1591 declared that they would not submit until the king was 'a Catholic, crowned and sacred at Rheims'.[479] Benjamin Aubéry du Maurier was sent to Elizabeth in 1592 to calm rumours of his conversion. Elizabeth likewise sent Sir Thomas Wilkes in an effort to dissuade him, but he arrived too late to make an impression. Elizabeth's vexation was clearly shown in her famous letter to Henri in July 1593. In this, she referred to the biblical story of Isaac's sons, Esau and Jacob. Esau sold his inheritance to Jacob for a 'mess of pottage'.[480] Elizabeth had hoped to gain from Henri's capture of Rouen. She was particularly angry at Essex for not having concentrated on the city itself. Henri decided, quite simply, against taking Rouen by force. He sanctioned efforts against the fort on Ste-Catherine instead of the town itself. On numerous occasions he found opportunities to withdraw his forces (and himself) to fight elsewhere. He was probably as relieved as the Rouennais at the arrival of Parma with his relief force. Besieging a town was a costly business. If we take the price of powder at 1s per pound, the simple action of firing a single cannon shot cost more than £2 (20 *livres*) and a culverin at least £1. At the siege of Le Mans in 1590, for example, twenty-one pieces fired a costly 800 shots against the town. Set-piece battles, requiring fewer shots and using lighter pieces (requiring less gunpowder), were less expensive than a costly siege. Here, therefore, Henri could find further justification for his strategy.

The only meeting between Elizabeth and Henri was a fictional one in Voltaire's *Henriade*. One opportunity was missed when Elizabeth arrived in Portsmouth on 26 August 1591. She was displeased by Henri's non-arrival after five days of waiting. He was, after all, busy campaigning for his kingdom. Noyon had just surrendered, with English help, on 19 August. A second chance was also missed when Henri was at Calais in 1601. 'I had promised myself this happiness and contentment … of kissing and embracing you in two arms as being your very loyal sister and faithful ally.'[481] Henri wrote to Béthune following Elizabeth's death in 1603:

> *My friend, I have been advised of the death of my good sister the Queen of England who loved me so cordially. To whom I owed so much. How her virtues were great and admirable … the loss to me and all good Frenchmen is inestimable … as she was … so generous and just that she was my double.*[482]

THE IMPACT ON THE ECONOMY

The impact of the French wars on England's economy was not negligible. The amount of material aid given (and sold) to France produced an Elizabethan 'industrial revolution'. The wars generated a demand for gunpowder, leading to an increase in the extraction of alum. The demand for cannonballs led to an increase in the mining of graphite. Greater numbers of cannon led to an increase in copper extraction and iron production. The production of more iron in turn led to the expansion of coal mining and more trees being felled for charcoal. More uniforms increased the demand for wool. All of these increased the flow of capital, and, in short, fostered the development of mining, metallurgy and textiles – the same key factors that would drive the industrial revolution two centuries later. The mechanisation of production that we associate with the eighteenth century had already begun in Elizabethan England. English and French armies, for example, required growing numbers of socks. It was perhaps in an effort to keep up with demand from the English and French armies that Reverend William Lee invented the first knitting machine: he came up with the stocking frame in 1589. Lee's patron was Sir Henry Carey, Lord Hunsdon, former ambassador to France. Lee established a factory at Rouen with his brother and nine workers. French refugees introduced to England new techniques in the dyeing and finishing of cloths. This helped English exports to France of woven and finished cloths to increase. Many Huguenot refugees returned to France in early 1574. Others chose to stay in England; for example, some of those from Normandy and Lorraine established a partnership (with Jean Carré from Arras) in the Weald in 1567 for the production of glass.

Several individuals and families profited directly from the wars. Sir Henry Sidney (ambassador in France in 1562) was a partner in the foundry at Robertsbridge in Sussex. Robert, son of Thomas Sackville, Lord Buckhurst, was granted the monopoly to transport new pieces of artillery. Buckhurst was ambassador to France in 1571. The end of English intervention in France coincided with, and contributed to, the demise in prosperity of the port of Rye, which had been so important during the wars.

The civil wars, on the other hand, held back economic growth in France and French colonisation overseas. The growth of the French merchant fleet was in turn impeded. The Earl of Warwick prevented two Huguenot expeditions leaving from Le Havre: seven ships were to have set sail for North America while another was to have sailed to Brazil, where the French colony had previously been lost in 1560. Such hindrances would not have helped any attempts at recolonisation. The political climate led to Frenchmen (that is, Huguenots) helping the English in their own projects in the New World. Huguenot sailors such as Jean Ribaut played their part – he received a pension from the English Crown in recognition of his services. Trade with Brazil continued and the Huguenots may well have invited Englishmen to join them, which perhaps explains the presence of Brazilian Indians on the 1569 monument to Edmund Harman at Burford Church in Oxfordshire. Thomas Stukeley had a project to replace French colonists in Florida with Englishmen in 1565. The garrison of Fort Caroline in Florida was offered safe passage by Sir John Hawkins. Not having the authority to use force, he left them one of his ships, the *Tiger* (50 tonnes). Guillaume Le Testu from Le Havre joined Sir Francis Drake in 1573 to attack Panama. Le Testu was an accomplished cartographer and brought his own knowledge of America to the voyage. In 1556, he had dedicated his illuminated manuscript, *Cosmographie universelle*, to *amiral* Coligny. This atlas comprised fifty-six maps. The author of the so-called *Drake Manuscript*,[483] a journal of Drake's circumnavigation of the world (1577–80), was also a Frenchman. Sir Humphrey Gilbert was granted the right to establish an English colony in Virginia in 1578. The founding of Virginia (named after Elizabeth) was another method of countering French (and Spanish) expansion in America.

THE RETURNING MEN

Was William Shakespeare thinking of English soldiers recently returned from France when he wrote the following?

> *Why, 'tis a gull, a fool, a rogue; that now and then goes to the wars, to grace himself, at his return to London, under the form of a soldier. And such fellows are perfect in great commanders' names: and they will learn you by rote, where services were done; – at such and such a sconce, at such a breach, at such a convoy; who came off bravely, who was shot, who disgraced, what terms the enemy stood on; and this they con perfectly in the phrase of war, which they trick up with new-tuned oaths: and what a beard of the general's cut, and a horrid suit of the camp, will do among foaming bottles, and ale-washed wits, is wonderful to be thought on! But you must learn to know such slanders of the age, or else you may be marvellously mistook.*[484]

Shakespeare's *Henry V* was written around 1599, so the recent siege of Amiens (1597) made his portrayal even more relevant. Between 1589 and 1597, more than 4,000 men were recruited in London. It is certain that a good number, if not all, of them would have told their tales of adventure on their return in their local inns such as the George and the White Hart in Southwark. Did not Shakespeare think that these 'rogues' could have been telling the truth? Did he believe that the great scenes of history were acted out only in the distant past?

Just as Elizabeth gave reasons for occupying Le Havre, she also explained the return of her army. A royal proclamation was issued on 1 August 1563:

> *because the town where they were in garrison is left by composition*
> *to the French King, as it was always so intended upon reasonable*
> *conditions: it is to be known that there wanted no truth, courage,*
> *nor manhood in any one of the said garrison, from the highest*
> *to the lowest, who were fully (yea rather, as it were, obstinately)*
> *determined with one full assent to have abidden the whole force of*
> *France and their helpers to the uttermost of their lives.*[485]

Former employers were also pushed to take men back. The experience earned by the soldiers in France was of particular importance to the Crown. The men could be used to train and advise others. Each county maintained a list of 'martial men' detailing the soldiers' experience. In a list dating from the crisis of 1588, we find, for example, the names of veterans who had served at Le Havre, twenty-five years before. Were these men now regarded as being the backbone of an English army set to resist an invading force?

The Earl of Warwick was rewarded with the lordship of Ruthin in Wales. He retained his office of Master of the Ordnance and went on to serve during the Rising of the North in 1569. The wound he incurred at Le Havre troubled him in old age. His splendid tomb may be seen in Beauchamp Chapel at the Church of St Mary at Warwick. Edward, Lord Clinton, also served again with Warwick during the revolt. Captain Thomas Leighton, one of the hostages in 1563, was sent on diplomatic missions to France. He participated in the second siege of Rouen. The engineer Sir Richard Lee continued his work at Berwick, being consulted as late as 1573 on the art of fortification. His colleague, Giovanni Portinari, was recalled to serve at Berwick in 1564. He was joined here by Jacopo Contio and William Pelham in the same year. Pelham accompanied Cobham and Walsingham to the Low Countries in 1578 and later became Lord Justice of Ireland. Some other English soldiers would go on to use their experience in the war in the Netherlands and in Ireland. Several officers who had served at Le Havre left for Dublin in December 1565. Sir John Norris, following a short stay in London, rejoined his men in Ireland. Ireland was also the destination for Captain Henry Docwra, veteran of the siege of Rouen. Four bands under Sir Arthur Savage, Sir John Brooke, Sir Arthur Chichester and Sir Jarret Harvey were sent from Picardy to reinforce the garrison of Ostend in December. Following a *séjour* at St-Valery the other men were transported to serve in Ireland. They would embark at Dieppe for Waterford. Sir Henry Power was instructed not to reveal the destination to the men. Sir Robert Drury, another veteran of the siege of Rouen, fought at the battle of Nieuport on 2 July 1600. The Anglo-Dutch victory against a Spanish army at Nieuport was the crowning moment of military success. Charles Blount, Lord Mountjoy, who had served under Norris in Brittany, became an important commander in Ireland. It was Mountjoy who took the surrender of Don Juan del Águila at Kinsale in 1602. His success was partly due to the advice of Arthur Chichester, veteran of the siege of Amiens. Chichester became Lord Deputy of Ireland and governor of Carrickfergus. Another of the veterans that would go on to serve in Ireland was Captain Samuel Bagnall.

The reward for Willoughby came in the form of a diamond ring (now untraced) given by Henri IV. The rigours of the campaign, however, probably also contributed to his decline in health. Willoughby was appointed as the governor of Berwick-upon-Tweed by the end of February 1598, arriving at his post on 28 April. He died there in 1601 and was buried at St James's Church, Spilsby, Lincolnshire. Sir Ferdinando Gorges, who had been wounded at the siege of Rouen in 1591, became a key figure in the colonisation of North America. The veteran of the siege of Amiens, Thomas Dudley (son of Roger Dudley, killed at the battle of Ivry in France in 1590), was elected vice-governor of the state of Massachusetts in October 1629. The diplomat Sir Thomas Bodley, having retired from public life in 1597, began the re-establishment of a library at the University of Oxford the following year.[486] Sir Roger Williams was honoured by being buried at St Paul's Cathedral following his death in London on 12 December 1595, as was Sir Thomas Baskerville. Unfortunately, the tombs were destroyed in the great fire of 1666, but a copy of Baskerville's epitaph may be found at the church of St Leonard, Sunningwell, in Berkshire.

Sir Henry Unton and Sir Francis Walsingham both died in debt. Most of their debts had been accumulated in France. On his death, Unton left debts of £23,000. The Normandy expedition of 1590 cost the Earl of Essex more than £14,000. He was finally executed in 1601 following his attempted *coup d'état.* During the Picardy campaign of 1596–97, the treasurer Sir Thomas Sherley was questioned over his accounting. An audit found that he owed the Crown £23,000, an enormous amount for the period. It is therefore not surprising that he found himself in the Fleet prison in London. His home at Wiston, West Sussex, built in 1573, was sequestrated by the Crown in 1602. This was in contrast to Peter Houghton, veteran of the campaign in the Gironde. Upon his death in 1596, he had grown wealthy enough to bequeath £600 to four London hospitals.

Both merchants and soldiers received compensation for their part in the wars. John Awger received compensation of £50 two years after the loss of his barque in 1562. Marguerite de Valois, the Queen of Navarre (1553–1615), offered a ship in compensation for the loss incurred near La Rochelle in 1569. The merchants John Kelly and Richard Trenhall from Dartmouth petitioned for the loss of their 140-tonne ship the *Crescent* and their cargo of salt in 1593. Kelly also petitioned regarding merchandise taken from his ship the *Siren* (100 tonnes). In return for his services, the wounded Captain Edmund Power was given the lease of Crown land with a value of £40 for thirty-one years. Captain William Ashenden, who had been taken prisoner near Laval during the Brittany campaign in 1593, now petitioned the queen. He was willing to pay £40 a year for 6d on every *seame* of grain (8 bushels) exported from the country in consideration of his service, imprisonment and wounds.

An Act of Parliament of 1563 is significant, as the collection of money for relief of the poor now became obligatory. The Poor Laws were in part aimed at men returning home from France. Sick men returning from Le Havre in 1563 were lodged and treated at Portchester Castle in Hampshire. Some of the men were still there in September. The return of so many sick men was a danger recognised by the authorities:

> *The Queen's Majesty, considering the return of no small numbers of her faithful subjects having truly and valiantly served at Newhaven and being many of the same sick or touched with infection of such sickness as reigned there, hath thought meet, because the same numbers shall return to sundry places of her realm being clear from such contagious sickness, to will and require her said captains and soldiers, and every of them, to have charitable and neighbourly regard to the preservation of their neighbours from infection, and to forbear for some season to be conversant with any more than of mere necessity they ought.*[487]

On the return of the same soldiers, Elizabeth reminded people that it was their Christian duty to help the sick and poor:

> *for otherwise they may feel the sharp hand of God.... Her true, good, and valiant subjects, having thus served and now returning to their habitations, shall find at this time (as they have well merited) favour, help, and charitable succour, according to their estates; and hereafter honour, love, and praise of their country whilst they live.*[488]

There were other factors that attracted intervention by the Crown. The confiscation of land from the Catholic Church during the Reformation led to there being fewer places to treat wounded soldiers. Nevertheless, Sir Thomas Sherley announced to captains in 1593 that sick soldiers would never be refused entry to hospitals. Private benefactors played an important role at a local level. Sir Robert Dudley established a hospital at Warwick in 1571.[489] Its charter set up a corporation with a Master and twelve residents (Brethren). Elderly and wounded soldiers could live in the hospital with their wives. The cost of running this came from land with an annual revenue of £200.

Sick and wounded soldiers returning from France could expect the payment of conduct money. Willoughby's men, for example, received 10s at the port of Rye in 1589. The following year, the Mayor of Rye wrote to Walsingham requesting £55 11s 3d to treat his men:

> *The diseased soldiers … rested upon the town's charge eight days in most miserable sort, full of infirmities in their bodies, wonderfully sick and weak, some wounded, some their toes and feet rotting off and lame, the skin and flesh of their feet torn away with continual marching, all of them without money, without apparel to cover their nakedness, all of them full of vermin, which (no doubt) would have devoured them in very short time if we had not given them most speedy supply. Whereby we were constrained to wash their bodies in sweet waters, to take from them all their clothes and strip them into new apparel, both shirts, petticoats, jerkins, breeches and hose, made of purpose for them. Then we appointed them several houses for their diet, and keepers to watch and attend them, and also surgeons to cure their wounds and rottenness; by this means we have saved some forty-eight of them, which will be able to do*

*Her Majesty good service.… And this has been to the town of Rye so
great a burden as we are not able to bear. And that now happeneth
amongst us is much to our grief (God of His mercy stay in His good
time), for the persons in whose houses they were lodged and dieted,
and the women that did attend and watch them are for the most
part fallen very sick, and every day there dieth four or five of them
with the infection which they had from the soldiers. We therefor
humbly pray that the burden of this great charge, performed from
charity and duty to God and Her Majesty, may not lie upon us,
which charge, as appears by the book herewith sent, amounts to the
sum of £55 11s 3d; besides the charge of the soldiers that remain in
Rye, which will be above 50s every day.*[490]

The system of relief for wounded soldiers and sailors continued to
develop throughout the period. The traditional sources of revenue proved
insufficient for the growing number of men. Sir Thomas Coningsby joined
a commission in March 1593 on this issue. The commission proposed
an early form of income tax. It was proposed that those in wealthier
professions should make annual payments. Innkeepers and wine
merchants should pay 4s, ale-house keepers, cooks, carriers of corn,
grain, butter and cheese and cattleherds should pay 2s. A month later, an
order was made in the House of Lords regarding wounded men returning
from France. Archbishops, marquises, earls and viscounts were to pay
40s, bishops 30s and barons 20s.

Those who had lost their livelihood through the wars could also claim
relief. John Wilkins, a sailor from Harwich in Essex, had his ship and
merchandise with a value of £200 taken by the French during the first
war. He was granted the right to collect alms for both himself and his
family across six counties. There were some, however, who sought to
take advantage of this 'social security':

*there are divers persons pretending to have served in the late wars
and service as soldiers that remain within and about the cities of
London and Westminster, whereof some are maimed, others have
received hurts or wounds, or have other infirmity whereof they are
not as yet perfectly cured; and some amongst these have neither
been maimed nor hurt nor yet served at all in the wars, but take
that cloak and colour to be the more pitied, and do live about the
city by begging and in disorderly manner.*[491]

Those who had been wounded could at least expect medical treatment that was becoming more scientific. Thomas Gale, perhaps directly inspired by the work of Ambrose Paré, wrote a work entitled *An Excellent Treatise of wounds made with Gonneshot...*, published in London in 1563. Ambrose Dudley would no doubt have been very interested in this book. Medical links with the wars do not end here. Two surgeons, John Banester and William Clowes, both served at Le Havre during the siege. John Banester later became known for his *Antidotarie* of 1589. Clowes produced his own work, *A prooved Practise for all young Chirurgians concerning Burnings with Gunpowder, and Woundes made with Gunshot, Sword, Halbard, Pike, Launce, or such other.* Since it was published in 1591, it is probable that Clowes also knew of the work of Paré. Joseph Du Chesne's work on the same subject was translated into English in 1590. It is probable that the siege of Le Havre led Ambroise Paré to conduct his own research on the causes of the plague. His work appeared in 1568 under the title *Traicté de la peste, de la petite vérolle et rougeolle.* William Clowes is also known for his work on syphilis, *A Short and Profitable Treatise* (1579). It was his colleague from Le Havre, Banester, who wrote the epilogue of this book.

THE HISTORY OF THE FUTURE

Elizabeth's policy of paying subsidies to allied combatants was followed, not without success, by successive British governments. The wars against Louis XIV, Louis XV and Napoléon I were largely fought on the back of British subsidies.

Peace was established between England and Spain following the death of Elizabeth in 1603, despite the efforts of Henri IV. This time, he was keen to see England carry on the fight. Sir Robert Cecil participated in the conference held at Somerset House in London in 1604.[492] The new king of England, James I (and VI of Scotland), told Béthune, 'How can you ask me to live at war in order that you may live in peace?'[493] The Protestant alliance also brought dividends. The marriage of Elizabeth Stuart, daughter of James I, to the Elector Palatine Frederick V in 1613 provided the House of Hanover to succeed to the throne in due course.

The expulsion of the English from Le Havre in 1563 was celebrated with an annual procession on 27 July until the French Revolution. The memory of the 'bosom serpent', however, has lived on in Joinville where the town's ties with Mary, Queen of Scots are frequently celebrated.

The fact that Henri IV was the last French king to receive the Order of the Garter until Louis XVIII in 1814 was a reflection of how Anglo-French relations degenerated and how the two countries once more became rivals. On Elizabeth's death, the possibility of French intervention in England reappeared. Henri hoped, perhaps, to intervene in a rising against James and place a candidate of his choice on the throne. Whatever his thoughts, this would have been impossible without outside help, as the French fleet was still too weak. Henri's conniving is implied in a letter written by Villeroy to Béthune following James's peaceful succession, 'draw our pin from the game as gently as we can'.[494]

Whether Henri had previously given the Earl of Essex words of encouragement in his rebellion in 1599 would be pure conjecture. The fact that Sir Henry Neville, resident ambassador to France, became involved with Essex would certainly have made this possible. Neville was imprisoned in the Tower and received a heavy fine of £5,000.

If Henri had escaped assassination as he did the payment of his debts, he would have maintained the internal peace of his country. With the death of the two principal actors, Elizabeth and Henri, we see the appearance of the 'second cast' trying to perform the same play. This time, however, there would be a different ending. James I had lost interest in intervention in France by November 1612. French Royalist forces succeeded in finally capturing La Rochelle in 1628, after having beaten off the English relieving force under George Villiers, Duke of Buckingham, followed by Lord William Fielding and the Earl of Lindsay. Previously, Buckingham had sought the contract to provide Louis XIII with the ships for the siege. It is possible that in doing this the English had hoped to prevent the renaissance of the French navy. The reorganisation of the navy by Cardinal de Richelieu in 1626 and 1627 resulted in the French Crown's supremacy at sea over the Huguenots.

The failure of English intervention in the second generation of religious wars in France was a factor in the collapse of the Huguenots as a political force. Meanwhile, the cost of this operation led to a crisis between Charles I and Parliament. The French also succeeded in obtaining their English marriage. One of the daughters of Henri IV, Henriette-Marie (1609–1669), married Charles in 1625. Her being Catholic (thanks to her father) did not help Charles's position, contributing to the tumults of which the outcome was civil war in England. Henrietta and Charles solicited French support. Though the French army was occupied with its campaign in the Rhine, the French clergy made a contribution of £40,000. Arms were also sent. Charles, meanwhile, preferred to manufacture arms himself at Bristol, given the poor quality of imports. It is probable that Charles was looking for inspiration from Henri IV when, at Oxford, he set about reading an English translation of Henrico Davila's book *The Historie of the Civill Warres of France* (1648). One veteran of the French campaigns, Sir Ferdinando Gorges, survived long enough to participate in this war.

Meanwhile, Europe had fallen into a new conflict, the Thirty Years War from 1618 to 1648. English volunteers assisted in efforts against Ambrosio Spínola. The Spaniards once more managed to penetrate deep into France's interior. This time they reached Corbie, less than 15 kilometres from Amiens. Louis XIII led the relief of the town in 1636. The Danish king, Christian IV, also participated in this war from 1625 to 1629. It was the English, once again, who undertook to provide a subsidy, this time for 300,000 florins per month. Such Elizabethan-type policies were undermined by Charles I, who allowed Spanish soldiers en route for the Netherlands to land in England.

The quest to re-establish an English bridgehead in Europe was achieved by Oliver Cromwell, a hundred years after the loss of Calais. England received Dunkirk following the Anglo-French victory over the Spanish at the battle of the Dunes in 1658. The English occupants remained for only four years before the sale of the town to France by a newly restored monarchy.

With the arrival of Louis XIV, the script had been almost completely rewritten. In a twist of fate, James, Duke of York (the future James II), sought refuge in France. He was obliged to sell the Grand Sancy diamond to Cardinal Mazarin, who in turn bequeathed it to Louis. Louis abandoned the policy of religious toleration with the revocation of the Edict of Nantes by the Edict of Fontainebleau in 1685. *Maréchal* Villars was ordered to put down a Protestant uprising in the Cévennes. London once again became a refuge for Huguenots. Previously, Louis attempted to buy an alliance with England against the Dutch. By the secret treaty of Dover (1 June 1670), Charles II accepted the French subsidies in return for his support and conversion to the Catholic faith. Charles took the money, signed a separate peace with the Dutch and remained Anglican (at least in public). Elizabeth and Henri IV would have been proud.

POSTSCRIPT

Anglo-French rivalry remained the norm throughout the eighteenth and much of the nineteenth century. Elizabeth would have been particularly proud of one of her guns, a demi-culverin, cast by Henry Pitt in 1590 and now in the collection of the Royal Artillery. This was still ready to fight the French in the War of the Spanish Succession (1701–14), the Seven Years War (1756–63) and, possibly, beyond.

The English claim to the French throne was finally abandoned by George III in 1800. Intervention by Louis XVI in the American colonies had ultimately led to the French Revolution. There now simply was no French throne to claim. The fleur-de-lys was removed from the British royal coat of arms in 1801.

The old foes met once again during the French Revolutionary Wars (1792–1802) and then the Napoleonic Wars (1803–15). Once again, the English leather and wool trade profited from supplying French armies. With the defeat of Napoléon I in 1815 and the restoration of the monarchy, the immediate threat from France was removed. Indeed, France once again became an ally during the Crimean War (1853–56). Ties between the two countries deepened, even after the abdication of Napoléon III. He chose to live out his exile at Camden Place, Chislehurst, in Kent. His son, Louis-Napoléon, died in British service in the Zulu War in 1879.

France increasingly became popular as a tourist destination for the English. This was something worth defending. Queen Victoria visited France and, in particular, the Côte d'Azur frequently. Nice became her destination of choice in the winter, when she stayed at the Hôtel Excelsior Régina Palace. The Promenade des Anglais is a reminder today of this close relationship. Imperial rivalry came to a head at Fashoda in 1898 but the *rapprochement* with France was confirmed by the *Entente Cordiale* (1905) and put to the test during the First World War (1914–18).

Sir Winston Churchill's proposal for a Franco-British Union on 16 June 1940 was certainly not without historic precedent. Just as at Vervins in 1598, however, France (now the Third Republic) signed a separate peace with the enemy in 1940. It could be said that the spectre of the Guises returned to haunt Churchill. His relationship with General Charles de Gaulle is comparable to that of Elizabeth and Henri. De Gaulle refused to use France's gold reserves to help pay for the war. The cross of Lorraine probably was the hardest cross Churchill had to bear.

APPENDIX I

Passport issued in the name of Charles IX
for Sir Nicholas Throckmorton, 5 January 1562

[*The Manuscripts of Sir Archibald Edmonstone of Duntreath* in H.M.C. *Report on Manuscripts in Various Collections* (Hereford, 1909) Vol. V. p.93]

The passport is addressed to officers of the French crown. It delivers safe passage for the ambassador, Sir Nicholas Throckmorton, en route to visit Catherine de' Medici. It expressly requests that assistance is given with board and lodging at 'reasonable cost'.

De par le Roy.

A tous noz lieutenants generaulx, gouvermeures, baillyz, seneschaulx, prevosts, cappitaines, chefs et conducteurs de nos gens de guerre tant de cheval que de pied, cappitaines, aussi maires, consols, et eschevins de villes, villaiges, bourgs et bourgades et à tous nos justiciers, officiers et subgects ausquels ces presentes seront monstrees, salut. L'Ambassadeur de notre treschere et tresamee seur, la Royne d'Angleterre, resident pres de notre personne nous a faict dire quil delibere partir bien tost du lieu ou il est pour aller trouver notre treshonoree dame et mere la Royne la part ou elle sera affin de luy faire entendre aucunes choses de la part de notre seur, et pourceque nous desirons quil fait son voyage avec la seurete et liberte qui est deue au lieu qu'il tient aupres de nous, nous vous mandons, commandons et expressement enjoignons, que par les villes et lieux ou il passera vous luy faictes faire tout le meillieur et plus gratieux traictement que faire se pourra, l'accommodes et faictes accommoder de logeis vivres et toutes choses qui luy seront necessaires, en payant raisonnablement, et ne luy mesfaictes ou mesdictes ne souffres estre mesfaict ou mesdict ne a ses gens et serviteurs ne au passaige de ses mullets train et bagaige faict mits ou donne aucun trouble destourbier ny empeschement, et ou aucun luy seroyt faict faictes incontinant le tout reparer et remettre au premier estat et deu, et ny faictes faulte sur tant que craigntes nous desobeyr et desplaire et dencourir notre indignation. Car tel est nostre plaisir. Donne a Paris le ve jour de Janvier, 1562.

[*signed*]
Charles Bourdin

APPENDIX II

Proclamation of Elizabeth I, 27 September 1562

[Hector de LA FERRIÈRE (ed.), *Le XVIe Siècle et les Valois...* (Paris, 1879), pp.76–77; see also Louise-Félicité GUINEMENT DE KERALIO, *Histoire d'Élisabeth, Reine d'Angleterre tirée des écrits originaux anglois, d'actes, titres, lettres & autres pièces manuscrites qui n'ont pas encore paru* (Paris, 1788), Vol.V, pp.158–61]

In this proclamation, Elizabeth sets out her reasons for English intervention in France in 1562. She states that the aim is to defend the rights of the people of Normandy against the house of Guise. Elizabeth also confirms that her quarrel is not with the French king, Charles IX, 'who … because of his young age is unable to prevent his subjects from ruining and destroying one another…'

Elizabeth par la grace de Dieu royne d'Angleterre, de France de Irlande, defenderesse de la foy chrestienne, à tout tant Anglois que François, qui ces presentes lettres verront ou oyront, salut. Comme depuis peu de temps en ça plusieurs lamentables doleances et plainctes nous ayant esté faictes par une grande multitude des subjectz de nostre bon frere le roy trés-chrestien habitans en Normandye, dont il appert manifestement qu'ilz se trouvent en grandes et pitoyables extremités à raison des cruelles persecutions dont l'on use et qu'on adressera contre eulx, par voye d'une grande force de gens de guerre louée et amassée en la duchye de Normandye par le duc d'Aumale[1] et ses adherans de la maison de Guyse, pour les ruiner et sacager et les constraindre de delaisser la pure religion, les persecuter en leurs corps et biens comme desjà ilz ont faict en plusieurs endroictz et lieux; considerant aussi (comme piteusement ilz remonstrent) que le roy leur souverain et la royne sa mere ne peuvent presentement les secourir et defendre en leur obeyssance à raison que la dicte maison

de Guyse et leurs adherans se sont emparez de la superiorité du gouvernement en tout affaires d'Estat et militaires au dict royaulme, ne voulant permettre aux dictz peuples de vivre selon les edictz du dict pays en la liberté de leurs consciences envers Dieu et le roy leur souverain; sur ce leur souvenant comment puis nagueres nous aydasmes à delivrer le peuple et subjectz de la royne d'Escosse, estant lors en la mesme misere et adversité par la semblable persecution d'icelle maison de Guyse, du danger, destruction et ruyne, les conservant par tel moyen à l'obeyssance de leur royne de la quelle presentement elle jouyt. Ilz nous ont requis avecques toute humilité et pitoyable lamentations à grossses larmes comme le prince qui est en bonne amityé avecques le roy leur souverain et proche voysin au dit pays; et pour l'amour que nous portons et debvons au dict roy en ce sien jeune aage et fascheux temps, et pour le regard que comme princes chrestiens, debvons avoir à la conservation du sang des chrestiens et de tant plus tost estant les plus prochains à nostre royaulme, de vouloir solliciter de moyenner quelque fin de heureuse yssue de ces cruelles et sanguinolentes persecutions, et cependant de faire transporter vers eux quelques bon nombres de noz subgectz soubz la conduicte de quelques fideles, asseurées, discretes personnes et d'honneur, pour la conservation d'aucunes de leurs villes maritimes et autres adjacentes, et peuples d'icelles ensemble pour sauver leurs vies et libertés de ruyne, submission et totalle desolation. Ce consideré (bien que pensasmes nous deporter du tout, de nous y entremesler) avons esté mue de solliciter premierement par tous bons moyen dont nous sommes peu adviser, que ces persecutions faictes par la maison de Guyse cessassent. Et les ayant trouvez à ce peu inclinans, et entendant aussi pour vray que le dict peuple de Normandye, principalement les habitans de Rouen, Dieppe, de Havre de Grace sont en danger evident d'estre en brief du tout destruictz par force, si à tempz ilz ne sont secouruz de quelque ayde, et que l'occasion de leur persecution n'est pour autre chose, sinon qu'ilz cherchent conserver leur consciences libres au faict et publié au moys de janvier dernier: nous, avecques bonnes et sinceres intentions envers le roy nostre bon frere (lequel nous sçavons que, à raison de son jeune aage, ne peult conteniret empescher ses subjectz de se ruyner et destruire les uns les aultres), avons ordonné et commandé d'ayder et deffendre icelles villes, et toutes autres qu'ilz pourront, de confusion et desolation, et conserver toutz les subjectz du dict roy es dictz lieux, de quelque qualité qu'ilz soyent, en leurs vies, libertés, biens et possessions, contre ceulx qui par violence les vouldront envahir en leurs demeurances. Et pour ample declaration de ce que dessus, avons faict mettre en escript ceste nostre intension, laquelle estant scellée de notre scel, avons baillée à nostre lieutenant pour estre par luy ou par ses commiz monstrée et manifestée à tous subgectz du dict seigneur roy qui ont requis ou requerront nostre ayde, faveur et secours. Auxquelz nous promettons en parolles de prince chrestien que n'entendons, ne voulons souffrir que aucun de nos subgectz, armé ou sans armes, nuyse ou offense aucune personne dedans icelles villes qui requerront nostre ayde; ains à leur possible les soustiendront et maintiendront en leurs habitations, vies, libertés, biens et possessions. Et quant à nous, cependant, nous ne oublirons de leur solliciter et procurer tout bon moyen de repos, paix, libertés et delivrance de la violance de la dicte maison de Guyse ou d'aucuns adherans d'icelle. Donné à nostre maison de Hampton court, le 27ᵉ jour de septembre l'an 1562, et de nostre reigne le quatriesme.

APPENDIX III

Lettres patentes du Roy par lesquelles est permis de porter vivres au camp (May 1563) [TNA SP 70/56]

Proclamation issued by Charles IX declaring all victuals (including wine, meat, wheat and oats) carried to the besieging forces at Le Havre duty- & toll-free (May 1563)

LETTRES PATENTES DU ROY par lesquelles est permis de porter vivres au camp & armie, qui est de present es environs du Havre de grace, pour en expulser les Anglois.

Charles par la grace de Dieu Roy de France, au Prevost de Paris ou son Lieutenant, salut. Nous vous mandons que par tous les lieux & endroictz de vostre ressort ou on a accoustumé de faire criz & proclamations, vous faictes crier & proclamer à son de trompe & cry public, que nostre vouloir & intention est, que tous Marchands & autres, de quelque qualité qu'ilz soyent, qui vouldront faire mener & conduyre pain, vin, chairs, bledz, avoines, & toutes autres sortes de vivres au camp & armée que nous avons de present en Normandie, es environs du Havre de grace, pour en expulser les Anglois, soyent tenuz quittes, francs & exempts de payement de tous droictz & subsides, péages & passages qu'ilz pourroyent debvoir à cause desdictz vivres, en quelque lieu que ce soit. En baillant bonne & suffisante caution aux lieux ou ilz en debvront faire l'acquit, de rapporter certification des Commissaires generaulx de vivres de nostre armée comme ilz auront faict mener & conduyre entierement en icelle armée lesdictz vivres, pour lesquelz ilz auront baillé lesdictes cautions, & desquelz droictz nous avons desapresent comme pour lors acquitté & affranchy, acquittons, affranchissons lesdictz Marchands: aux charges & conditions dessusdictes. De ce faire vous avons donné & donnons pouvoir: car tel est nostre plaisir.

Donné à sainct Germain en Laye, le septiesme jour de Mai, l'an de grace ce mil cinq cens soixante trois, & de nostre regne le troisiesme.

Signé par le Roy en son consell
BOURDIN,

Et séellé sur simple queue, de cire jaulne, du grand séel dudict Seigneur

Levés & publiées à son de trompe & cry public de par le Roy & monsieur le Prevost de Paris ou son Lieutenant Civil, es lieux & places accoustumées à faire criz & publications, par moy Pierre Gaudin Sergent à verge au Chastellet, Prevosté de Paris, commis de Paris Chrestien Crieur juré du Roy nostre sire, es ville, Prevosté & Viconté de Paris, accompaigné de Bertrand & Pierre Braconnier, & autres Trompetes en ceste ville de Paris. Le Lundy dixiesme jour de May, mil cinq cens soixante trois.
P. GAUDIN

APPENDIX IV

The Articles of Surrender signed by Ambrose Dudley, Earl of Warwick, at Le Havre, 28 July 1563

[Bibliothèque Nationale de France, MS français 3243 ff.12r–13r]

Que led. Conte de Warwick remectra la ville du Havre de Grace entre les mains dud. Seigneur connestable aveques toute l'artillerye, munitions de guerre aptenant au Roy et a ses subjectz qui y sont.

Qu'il laissera les navires qui sont en lad. Ville appartenant tant au Roy que a ses subjectz avec tout leur esquipaige et generallement toutes les marchandises et autres choses qui appartiennent au Roy et a sesd. Subjectz qui y sont.

Et pour seurette de ce que dessus que led. Conte mectre pntement la grosse tour du Havre entre les mains dud. Seigneur connestable sans que les soldatz qui seront miz dedans la tour puiyssent entrer dedans la ville et que monsieur le conte de Warwick fera garder les portes du couste de la ville jusques a__ sera commandé par mond. Sr le connestable sans arborer enseigne sur lad. Tour le tout suyvant ceste cappitullation et aussi que led. Seigneur conte baillera.

f.12v

Quatre oustaiges telz que led. Seigneur connestable nommera pareillement que dedans demain matin heure de huict heures led. Sr. conte fera rettyrer les soldatz qui sont dedans le fort pour le consigner incontinant entre les mains dud. Seigneur connestable ou ceulx qu'il remectra pour le recepvoir dedans lesd. Huict heures demain matin.

Que tous prisonyers qui ont este prins devant led. Havre seront delivres tant d'un couste quc d'autrc sans paycr aucunc rancon.

Et que monseigneur le connestable de son couste permectra aud. Sr. conte de Warwick et a tous ceulx qui sont en garnison aud. Havre den partir avecques tout ce qui appartient a la Royne d'Angleterre et a ses subjectz.

Que pour le transport tant aud. Sr conte que deslogement des gens de guerre et autres choses susd. Led. Seigneur connestable a accord six jours entiers a commencer demain devant lesquelz ilz pourront librement et franchement desloger & emporter toutes lesd. Choses et la ou les ventz et mauvays temps empescheroys led.

f.13r

Transport pouvoir estre faict dedans ce terme en ce cas led. Seigneur connestable luy accordera temps et delay raisonable pour ce faire.

Led. Seigneur connestable a semblablement permis que tous les navires et vaysseaux angloys et autres qui sont ou seront ordonnez pour led. Transport entreront et sortiront dans le havre franchement et seurement sans leur donner aucun arrest ou empeschement soyt en ce camp ny ailleures.

Lesd. Quatre oustaiges don't mention est faicte seront messieurs Ollivyer Maners frere de mons. Le conte de Routheland, les cappitaines Horsey, Pallen et Lelton en tesmoing de quoy et pour servir de promesse lesd. Srs. Ont signe les pus articles faict le vingt et huictiesme jour de Juillet l'an mil v c soixante et troys.

[*signed*]
Warwyck

Trans.:

First: That the said Earl of Warwick places the town of Havre de Grace into the hands of the Lord Constable [Anne de Montmorency] with all the artillery, munitions of war belonging to the King and his subjects.

That he leaves the ships that are in the said Town belonging to both the King and his subjects with their crews and generally all the merchandise and other items that belong to the King and his said Subjects.

And for the guarantee based on the aforesaid that the said Earl places the great tower of Havre into the hands of the said Lord Constable so that the soldiers that will be placed inside cannot enter the town and that monsieur the Earl of Warwick will guard the gates on the side of the town until he will be commanded by my Lord Constable without keeping a flag on the said Tower following this surrender and also that the said Lord will give four hostages which the said Lord Constable will name. Likewise by eight o'clock tomorrow morning, the said Earl shall withdraw his soldiers that are in the fort so that it may be handed to the said Lord Constable … by eight o'clock tomorrow morning.

That all the prisoners that were taken before the said Havre shall be released by each side without paying any ransom.

And that monsieur the Constable allows the sieur Earl of Warwick and all those that are in garrison at the said Havre to leave with all that belongs to the Queen of England and to her subjects.

That for the transport for the Lord Earl that removal of the men of war and other items the said Lord Constable has accorded six whole days starting tomorrow in which he may freely leave and take all the said items.… Where the winds and bad weather prevent the said transportation being made within the term … the said Lord Constable will accord time and reasonable delay.…

The said Lord Constable has similarly allowed that all the English ships and vessels and others that are or will be ordered for the said transport will enter and leave the harbour freely and safely without being stopped or hindered in this camp or elsewhere.

The said Four hostages of whom mention is made will be messieurs Ollivyer Maners [Oliver Manners] brother of monsieur the Earl of Rutland [Henry Manners, 2nd Earl of Rutland], the captains [Edward] Horsey, Pallen [William Pelham] and Lelton [Thomas Leighton] … to serve as guarantees the said seigneurs have signed the articles made the twenty-eighth day of July the year one thousand six hundred sixty and three.

[*signed*]
Warwyck

APPENDIX V

Mémoire fourni par l'ambassadeur de France des frais faits par la Reine d'Angleterre pour la guerre de France

('Memorandum provided by the French ambassador on the expenses made by the Queen of England for the war in France') British Library Egerton MS 742

[Hector de LA FERRIÈRE, *La Normandie à l'Étranger* (Paris, 1873), pp.187–89]

This document details the costs incurred during the first campaign in Normandy, 1562–63. It includes, for example, the costs of the Earl of Warwick and for the shipping of men. Other costs include losses, pay and the building of fortifications.

La depesche du mois d'octobre pour six mille hommes de pied environ envoiés au Havre de Grace et pour l'estat du comte de Warwick, gouverneur de l'armée, et pour l'estat du mareschal trésorier controleur pour les frais de la mer, pour faire passer les soldatz se monte en tout à la somme de 32,480 escus.

Item la dépense du mois de novembre pour le Havre de Grace, comprins la dépense faite pour environ 400 hommes à Dieppe et 300 hommes de pied à Rouen avec l'estat du gouverneur des fortifications faites au Havre se monte en tout à la somme de 31,750 escus.

Item la dépense du mois de novembre comprins la perte de deux cens porcs et quatre vingts bœufs et quarante mullets portant du pain ou biscuit perduz par fortune de mer avec les frais de la fortification se monte à la somme de 32,000 escus.

Item la despense du mois de janvier comprins les fortifications et bois portez de ce pays au Havre pour faire ung mont se monte en tout à la somme de 31, 560 escus.

Item la despense du mois de febvrier comprins les frais des fortifications du mont se monte en tout à la somme de 31,400 escus.

Item la despense du mois de mars comprins les frais pour envoier mille hommes de pied à M. l'Admiral et estat de Throckmorton pour son voiaige se monte à la somme de 32,633 ½ escus.

La somme à quoi se monte la despense de six mois pour le Havre 191,823 escus ⅓.

Item l'estat du comte de Warwick se monte par mois 700 escus à VII l. sterl. par jour.

L'estat du mareschal trésorier controleur et ung conseiller adjoint au gouverneur se monte par mois 320 escus.

L'extrordinaire qui se fait au Havre, tant pour les fortifications et despenses des navires qui portent le bois pour faire les fortifications, non comprins les munitions, se monte par mois l'ung portant l'aultre 4,500 escus.

Les gaiges de chascun soldat, l'ung portant l'aultre, revient, pour chascun V escus par moys; les gaiges de capitaines 33 escus ⅓ par moys; les gaiges des capitaines 33 escus ⅓ par moys, l'homme de cheval n'a que quatre gros[2] et demy par jour qui sont sept escus et demy par moys, et leur capitaine 40 escus par moys, son lieutenant 20 escus par moys.

Depuis six mois, de février 1561 (1562) au mois de mars 1562 (1563) avant Pasques, les despenses ont été faictes pour le faict de la guerre de France, réunies aux despens de la royne, tant pour l'argent déboursé à lAmiral et fraiz faitz par Throckmorton durant ces praticques en France et les despenses du Havre, sans les armes, pouldres et bouletz comprins, tout le mois de mars, la somme de 455,156 escuz.

Item, l'argent délivré pour Gresham en Allemaigne, pour la première solde des Allemans, au moys de juin 1563 133,333 escus.

L'argent délivré par Throckmorton, ce mois de mars à monsieur l'admiral à Caen 50,000 escus.

Item l'intérest que la Royne a payé à Anvers pour ung an pour l'argent qu'elle a tiré pour les guerres 30,000 escus.

Item pour les frais que Throckmorton a faitz en France depuis le commencement des troubles jusqu'à son retour 30,000 escus.

APPENDIX VI

Prise du Havre: Approche Toy, Jeune Roy Debonnaire[3]
Guillaume Costeley, *Musique…* (Paris, 1570)

[in: Henry EXPERT (ed.), *Les Maîtres Musiciens de la Renaissance Française* (Paris, 1904), pp.50–66]

As the title suggests, the song written by Guillaume Costeley celebrates the French capture of Le Havre by Charles IX and Anne de Montmorency. It includes the 'sounds' of war in the form of 'walls and ramparts cast down', with drums beating, fifes piping, trumpets blowing and cannons thundering.

Approche toy, approche toy, jeune roy
debonnaire
Du fier Angloys pour le prendre à
mercy,
Et s'il ne veut, pour à coup le deffaire,
Laisse marcher le fort Mommorency,
Ne sçay il pas s'il n'est trop endurcy,
Qu'injustement en ton havre il repose
Si donc il veut, tenir contre cecy
C'est à bon droit qu'à ruine on l'expose.

Ren toy, Angloys, ren toy, ren toy,
Le roy te vient semondre,
Car entrer veult là dedens,
Sans sejout.
Tu ne veux donc que bravades
respondre
Or voirras tu tes murs et rempars fondre
Avant qu'il soit la longueur de ce jour.
Chaque tabour Frappe à son tour,
Fiffres, sifflez, Cornetz, enflez,
Sonnez, clerons, sonnez, clerons,
Tonnez, canons, tonnez, canons…
Entron, soldatz, Les murs sont bas,
La tour est esbranlée.
Prenons ces loupz, tuon les tous…
Ilz sont à nous, ilz sont à nous,
Leur gloire est escoulée…

A mort, à mort, traistres, à mort.
De rien ne vous sert votre effort,
Vous vous fiez en vos murailles,
Et nous au grand-Dieu des batailles,
Lequel en faveur de sa loy
Donne victoyre, à notre Roy…

Helas, Seigneurs, ayez compasion
De l'innocent en son affliction,
Ne meurtrissez le Françoys Catholicque,
Pour le forfait du rebelle et inicque,
Car tresloyaux avons tousjours esté…

Voycy le Roy, des Roys le magnificque,
Canticque donc en soit à Dieu chanté…

Loué soit Dieu, notre Roy souhaitté
Vient entre nous pour les siens
recongnoistre,
Arriere donc, arriere, le Prince seducteur,
Car cestuy là n'est point, le vray Pasteur
Qui veut ceans entrer par la fenestre…

APPENDIX VII

Proclamation de la paix faicte entre les Roy de France Treschrestien
Charles IX de ce nom, & Elizabet Roine d'Angleterre (Paris, 1564)

Proclamation of peace published in Paris, 23 April 1564

The proclamation re-establishes the peace with the right to communicate, trade and pass freely between the two countries.

DE PAR LE ROY

On faict assavoir à tous, Que bonne, ferme, sincere, stable & perpetuelle paix, amitié & reconciliation est faicte & accordee Entre treshault, tresexcellent et trespuissant Prince Charles par la grace de Dieu Roy de France Treschrestien, nostre souverain Seigneur: Et treshaulte, tresexcellente & trespuissante Princesse Elizabet, par la mesme grace de Dieu Roine d'Angleterre, leurs vassaulx, subjects & serviteurs, en tous leurs Royaumes, pays, terres & seigneuries de leurs obeissances. Et est ladicte paix generalle & communicative entre eulx et leursdicts subjects, Pour aller, venir & sejourner, retourner, conserver, marchander, communiquer & negotier les uns avec les autres, és pays les uns des autres librement & seurement, Par mer, par terre, & eaues doulces, tant deçà que delà la mer: Et tout ainsi qu'il est accoustumé faire en temps de bonne, sincere & amiable paix, telle qu'il a pleu à Dieu par sa bonté envoyer & donner ausdicts Prince & Princesse, & à leurs peuples & subjects.

Defendant & prohibant tresexpresseement ledict Seigneur Roy a tous ses subjects, de quelque estat, qualité & condition qu'ils soyent, Quils ne ayent à entreprendre, attenter, ne innover aucune chose au contraire: Sur peine d'estre punis comme infracteurs de paix & perturbateurs du bien & repos public.

Faict à Troyes, l'unzieme jour d'Avril, l'an mil cinq cens soixante quatre, apres Pasques.

CHARLES
Et au dessoubs, BOURDIN

Leve & publiee à son de trompe & cry public en ceste ville de Paris par les Rois d'armes & Heraults de sa Majesté ses pays de Champaigne & Bourgongne, le Dimanche vingttroisieme jour d'Avril, mil cinq cens soixante quatre.

Signé
CHAMPAIGNE BOURGONGNE

Auquel jour, par le commandement dudict Seigneur furent aussi faicts grands feux de joye par ladicte ville & faulxbourgs d'icelle, & plusieurs autres solennitez en tel cas requises & accoustumees.

APPENDIX VIII

Letter from Elizabeth I to Peregrine Bertie, Lord Willoughby, 6 December 1589

[MARCUS, MUELLER & ROSE (eds), *Elizabeth I: Collected Works* (Chicago, 2000), pp.360–61]

Right trusty and well beloved, we greet you well. Albeit your abode and of our troops in that realm hath been longer than was first required and by us meant; whereof, as it seemeth, your yielding to divers services there hath been partly a cause, contrary to our expectation, to the king's purpose at the first declared, and to your own writing also hither, whose advertisements moved us to give order for certain ships of ours to be sent for the safe conducting of you and our subjects with you; yet now perceiving the great contentment and satisfaction the king, our good brother, hath received by your good service, and of our companies under your charge, whereby also such as heretofore might have conceived an opinion either of our weakness or of the decay and want of courage or other defects of our English nation may see themselves much deceived, in that the contrary hath now well appeared in that country by so small a troop as is with you, to the great honor and reputation of us and of our nation, and to the disappointing and (as we hope) the daunting of our enemies.

We have, upon request of our said good brother that king, declared by his ambassador here, accorded unto them, and hereby we signify unto you, that we are pleased you shall continue your abode there with the numbers under you for this month longer, hoping the king will then be content to dismiss you with liberty and his good favor to return into this our realm, in case he shall not be able to keep them in pay and satisfy them for any longer time; and that in the meantime he will be careful for the well using of you and them, so as ye may neither want pay nor suffer otherwise too many wants. And for that it is our no small comfort to perceive the forward endeavors and valor, both of yourself and of those under you, we are pleased not only to let you understand the same by these our own letters, with our thankful acceptation to yourself in particular; but also we will and require you to signify so much, both to the whole company of our soldiers there, and to such captains and gentlemen particularly as you shall think most worthy thereof, who we trust we show the continuance of their valiant and willing minds, rather more than less, knowing the same shall be an increase of our comfort, and of the honor of the whole realm and nation, and to their own more reputation.

You shall also say unto the king that although we have cause, in respect of the wants which we heard our men endured sundry ways there, to be unwilling that they should remain there any longer time, yet when we understood that he hoped to do himself the more good by the use of them than otherwise he might look for, wanting them, we were – we know not how – overcome and enchanted by the king to yield thereunto. Given under our signet at Richmond, the sixth day of December, 1589, in the thirty-second year of our reign.

APPENDIX IX

Challenge issued by Sir Henry Unton to the duc de Guise

[Thomas RYMER (ed.) *Foedera* (London, 1727), Vol.XVI, p.118]

The English ambassador, Sir Henry Unton, challenges the duc de Guise to a duel on either horse or foot in defence of the honour of the Queen. This was actually Unton's third challenge. He accused Guise of 'playing deaf and dumb'.

Au Duc de Guise
D'Autant que dernierement, au logis de Monsieur du Mayne, & en public, vous mesdites impudemment, indiscretement & temerairement de ma Souverayne, la Personne de la quelle je represente en ce Pais, pour maintenir pour la langue l'espee son Honneur, qui n'a jamais este mis en question entre les Gens de bien & de vertu, je vous dis que vous avez meschamment menty en mesdisant da ma Soverayne & mentirez tousjours quand vous taxerez son Honneur, encores que pour sa Personne, qui est l'une des plus vertueuses & accomplies Princesses qui soit au Monde. Ille ne puisse estre tachee par la bouche d'un tel Traistre & Perfidi a son Roy & a sa Patrie, comme vous estes; & sur ce je vous defie de vostre Personne a la mienne avec telles Armees que vous voudrez choisir, soit a Pied ou a Cheval; & ne debuez penser qu'il y ait inegalite de personnes entre nous, estant yssu d'aussy grande & noble Race

& Maison; que vous massignant ung lieu indifferent, & me donnant certain Jour, je vous soustiendray les propos & le deuuenty que je vous donnes que ne debuex aucunement endurer; sy avez tant soit peu de Couraige si vous ne vous feray tenir par tout pour le plus Mesdisant Poltron & le plus Couerd qui soit en France.

J'attends vostre Responce.

Monsieur de Guyse encores que vous ayez ja receu de moy deux semblables Cartelz que cestuicy par deux des vostres mesmes; toutesfois par ce que vous avez faict le Sourd & le Muet, je le vous r'envoye encores maintenant pour la Troisiesme fois, a fin que j'en puisse avoir quelque Responce, autremlent je vous advise que je le feray publier par tout.

Henry Unton. Ambassadeur de la Serenissime Royne d'Angleterre prez le Roy Treschrestien.

APPENDIX X

Letter from Elizabeth I to Henri IV, July 1593

[H.M.C. *Calendar of the Manuscripts of the Marquis of Salisbury* (London, 1892), Vol.IV, p.343, cited by John BLACK, *Elizabeth and Henry IV...* (Oxford, 1914), pp.65–66. Other versions, see also: Leah MARCUS and Janel MUELLER (eds), *Elizabeth I: Autograph Compositions and Foreign Language Originals* (Chicago, 2003), pp.165–66]

Elizabeth rebukes Henri IV after he had abjured in July 1593. She refers to this as being an *acte si inique*. This comes across as being a slightly stronger word than the English 'iniquitous'. Elizabeth wanted to remonstrate the full meaning of *inique* as 'unjust, unrighteous, naughtie, wicked' and 'impious' as defined in Randle Cotgrave's dictionary of 1611.[4]

Ah! que doleurs, oh! quels regrets, oh! que gemissementz je sentois en mon ame per le son de telles nouvelles que Morlains m'a compté! Mon Dieu est il possible que mondain respect aulcun deut effacer le terreur que la crainte divine nous menace? pouvons nous par raison mesme attendre bonne sequele d'acte si inique? Celuy qui vous ayt maintes annees conservé par sa main, pouvez vous imaginer qu'il vous permettat aller seul au plus grand besoign? Ah! c'est dangereux de mal faire pour en faire du bien! Encore j'espere que plus saine inspiration vous adviendra. Cependant, je ne cesseray de vous mettre au premier reng de mes devotions à ce que les mains d'Esau ne gastent la benediction de Jacob. Et ou me promettes toute amitie et fidelité, je confesse l'avoir cherement merité, et ne m'en peuteray pourveu que ne changies du pere; aultrement vous seray je que soeur bastarde, au moins non de par le pere? car j'aimeray mieulx tousjours le naturel que l'adopt, comme Dieu le mieulx cognoist, qui vous guide au droict chemin du meilleur sentir.

Votre tres asseuree soeur si ce soit à la vielle mode; avec la nouvelle je n'ay que faire.

E.R.
[Endorsed 'M. of her majesty's letter to the French king. Julii 1593']

APPENDIX XI

Instructions to Sir Thomas Baskerville, 1596

[John DASENT (ed.), *Acts of the Privy Council* (London, 1902), Vol.XXVI, pp.244–47]

Instruccions given to Sir Thomas Baskevile, knight, appointed to have the principall charge of 2,000 Englishe souldiers sent into Fraunce to the ayde of the Frenche Kinge in manner followinge:

First, you shall have a particular charge as collonell of 1,000 of the sayde nomber with the wages ordinarye of tenn shillinges by the daye, and in augmentacion thirtie shillinges more in respect you shall have the superior charge of the whole two thousand. And 1,000 of the two thousand shalbe under the rule of Sir Arthur Savage as a particular collonell of them, and yet the sayd Sir Arthur and the nombers of his regiment shalbe at the comaundement of you, Sir Thomas Baskervile, when you shall have cause to require their service.

Item, you, the sayde Sir Thomas Baskervile, shall understand that her Majestie hath assented to give to the Frenche Kinge the ayde of these 2,000 men to joyne and serve with the like nombers of French souldiers, sufficiently armed, in the townes of Bulloyn [Boulogne] and Muttrell [Montreuil-sur-Mer] and no other where, except when the Kinge shalbe persoballie in Picardy, then you, the sayde collonell, with her Majesty's soldiers shall serve the Kinge where he shall comaund them in Picardye.

Item, it is further covenaunted that the sayde 2,000 men shall enter into wages from the tyme they shall arrive in Fraunce at the porte of St. Valerye's in Picardye, beinge appoynted for the same, unto the tyme of their retourne, which shalbe at the farthest

at the ende of six monethes, and in that tyme they shall everye moneth make their musters and give their oathes to the King's Commissioners faithfully to serve the French King, savinge all fidelitye and allegeaunce due to her Majestie. And their wages shalbe payd by a pay-master appoynted by her Majestie according to the number as they shalbe duelie mustered, and according to a schedule of the severall wages and allowaunces signed by her Majesty's Counsell and delivered to the paye-master, all which paymentes shalbe made by her Majesty's officers.

Item, the sayde soldiers shalbe for their defaultes to be committed against the orders of their collonelles and against their owne discipline corrected by the Cheif Collonell or by suche other principall officers as shalbe authorized to governe their companies, and if any other offences shalbe comitted against the King's orders generall, then the offendours to be ordered by the King's armye, so as the collonelles and captaines of the English men be called thearto for assistance of the King's officers in their judgementes.

Item, the sayde Sir Thomas Baskervile shall take suche care as belongeth to a Captain Generall and Governour of the sayde forces as they may be preserved in all good estate, to be provided of victuall, lodginge and other furniture whereby they may be contynued without daunger, and spetiallie you are to have greate care how to avoyde the repaire or lodginge of the soldiers in anye howses infected with the Plague. And if it shall happen so that you shalbe required to serve in places where you shall know the Plague to raine, you shall if you be directed by the King or his officers of his armye to carrie your forces to suche places of infeccion in all dutifull manner protest against the same, and shall utterly refuse to put her Majesty's people in suche evident daunger, affirminge that her Majestie hath sent you and her people, being her naturall subjectes, to ayde and assist the Kinge against the force of his and her Majesty's common enemyes, but not to endaunger their lives wilfullye by infeccion of the Plague without thereby offending of th'enemy, who rather would take pleasure thereof to see her Majesty's people destroyed by mortallitye then by anye martiall accion.

You shall also have care that neither you nor her Majesty's people servinge under you be drawn to hazard your selves farther then you shall see the Frenche readie to accompanye you, neither shall you put the people in any manifest hazard where they may be farr over matched with the enemy, nor yet shall permitt or directe the people to adaventure by waye of assault where the places assaultable are not likelye to be without daunger of life and expence of bloud recovered.

You shall uppon any occacion given you wherein you shall thincke your self and her Majesty's people hardlye used by the Frenche advertize the same to her Majesty's Ambassadour leiger by your letters or message, who shall therein deale with the King and his Councell to procure your redresse of any thing whereof you shall have cause to complaine.

Moreover, you shall use the best meanes you maye that the whole forces of the two thousande men maye serve joynctlie togither or that they be not severred farr a sonder, but that you may be readie to helpe your selves and withstande any daunger by your joynt concurrencie togither as naturall Englishmen borne one to defende the other ought to be.

You shall also, considering you are in a straunge countrie, give charge to all the captaines and officers of the bandes severelye to keepe their people in good order without suffring them to quarrell with the Frenche or to spoyle any howses or the persons of the Frenche, or otherwise to comitt any outrage against the Frenche by takinge from them anye of their goodes or victualles without the goodwill or satisfaccion of the owners by payment for the same, and spetiallie you shall see that none of her Majesty's subjectes do enter disordredly into any church or religious howses or anye wise to use anye violence to any the monumentes of the sayd churches, religious howses or religious persons. But you shall take care and charge for bothe your regimentes that there be usuall prayers made (as neere as may be) everye daye according to the use of this realme of England, not doubting but therein you will accordinge to your duties praye for our Soveraigne Ladie the Queen's Majestie.

And where by her Majesty's comission given to you under the Great Seale of England for the government and ordering of these people comitted to your charge, amonge other thonges it is conteyned that you shall have power to punishe offendours according to the orders and lawes of martiall discipline accustomed in anye of her Majesty's armyes and forces which have served in other places, you shall understand that for your better direccion therein we have by her Majesty's comaundement conceaved and set downe by writinge in certaine heades suche orders as were established for the ordering of the armye late sent into Spayne, and have subscribed the same with our handes to be delivered unto you, to be observed and folowed in the governement of these her Majesty's people now committed unto you, to which orders you shall understand that clause of her Majesty's comission to have reference. And to the ende all the souldiers and officers under your charge may take knowledge of the sayde orders and of the discipline they are to live under and guide themselves [by] thereafter, you shall immediately uppon your landinge in Fraunce at some daye of muster or otherwise publishe the sayde orders by waye of proclamacion in suche manner as they may be enformed thereof.

APPENDIX XII

Certaine Prayers set foorth by Authoritie, to be used for the prosperous success of her Majesties Forces and Navy (London, 1597), pp.11–13

The prayers of the day are an important source that show the role of religion in both the army and navy. In particular, there was a belief that 'If God be on our syde, who can be agaynst us?' (*The Holie Bible* [*The Bishops' Bible*], 1572 Romans 8:31)

O Eternall God in power most mighty, in strength most glorious, without whom the horse & Chariot is in vaine prepared against ye day of battell: vouchsafe (wee beseech thee) from thy high throne of Majestie, to heare and receive the heartie & humble prayers, which on bended knees, we ye people of thy pasture and sheepe of thy hands, doe in an unfayned acknowledgement of thy might and our owne weakenesse, powre out before thee on the behalfe of our gratious Soveraigne, and on the behalfe of her Armies, her Nobles, her Valiants, and men of warre: who by thee inspired have put their lives in their hands, and at this time doe oppose themselves, against the malice and violence of such, as beare a mortall hate at thy Sion, and doe dayly conspire and rise up against it, even against the church, thine Annointed, and the people of this her Land. Arise then (O Lord) and stand up we pray thee, to helpe and defend them: be thou their Captaine to goe in and out before them, and to lead them in this journey: teache their fingers to fight, and their hands to make battaile. The Generall and Chieftaines blesse with the spirite of wisdome, counsell, and direction: the Souldiers with mindes ready to performe and execute. Gird them all with strength, and powre out upon them the spirite of courage: give them in the day of battell, heartes like the hearts of Lions, invincible and fearlesse against evill, but terrible to such as come out against them. Where the enemie doteth rage, and danger approche, be thou (O Lord) a rocke of salvation, and a tower of defence unto them. Breake the enemies weapons: As smoke vanisheth, so let their enemies be scattered, and such as hate them, flie before them. Thou seest (O Lord) the malice of our adversaries howe for thy Name which is called on over us, and for the trueth of thy Gospell wherein we rejoyce; they beare a tyrannous hate against us, continually vering and troubling us, that faine would live in peace. Styrre up therefore (O Lord) thy strength, and avenge our just quarrell: turne the sword of our enemie upon his owne head, and cause his delight in warre to become his owne destruction: As thou hast dealt with him heretofore, so now scatter his Forces, and spoile his mighty Ships, in which he trusteth. So shall we the people of thine inheritance, give praise unto thy Name, and for thy great mercy give thankes unto thee in the great Congregation: yea, the World shall know, and the Nations shall understand to the praise of thy glory, that thou alone defendest them that trust in thee, and givest victorie unto Princes. Heare us (Olord our strength) in these our prayers for Jesus Christ his sake. Amen.

APPENDIX XIII

La Proposition faicte par Monsr. l'Ambassadr. D'Angleterre a Messrs du Conseil du Roy le dernier du May 1599

This account of the negotiations between the ambassador Sir Henry Neville and Henri's council reflects the focus of late Elizabethan diplomacy. It shows concerns over Ireland, the continued threat of Spain and the issue over the repayment of Henri's debts. The council gave assurances that they would prevent Frenchmen shipping wheat and other grains to supply Spanish ships preparing for war.

('Suggestions made by the Lord Ambassador of England to the Lords of the King's Council 31 May 1599')

[Bibliothèque de l'Institut de France, Godefroy MS 512 ff.114r–115r]

f.114r

La roine ayant a faire la guerre en Irlande a ses rebelles qui cognoissans la grandeur de leur faulte, et estans soustenus par les supports du roy d'Espagne se pourront opiniastrer a la defense, et par consequent faire trainer ceste guerre en longueur qui ne peut estre que de despence incroyable a la dicte Dame roine, pour estre ce pais la, desnué de victuailles et toutes choses necessaires pour faire vivre une armee, et pour estre la dicte Dame aussi contrai[n]te d'y entretenir perpetuellement outre l'armee de terre, une flotte de vaisseau non seulement pour empescher le secours que leur pourroit estre envoye d'ailleurs, mais aussi pour y apporter des vivres et autres choses requises, et ayant outre ce, la dicte dame occasion de se munir, et fortifier en son royaume, contre les desseins et preparatifs du dict roy qui sont notoires a tout le monde, qui ne peut estre qu'evcq une charge et despence extreme,

elle s'est neantmoins resolüe comme princesse genereuse qui a tout jours eu devant les yeulx l'honneur, et la conservation de son estat, de se roidir alencontre de toutes les difficutes qui se sont presentees en cest affaire, et de s'evertuer courageusement a la defense; ayant delibere d'y emploier tout ce que dieu luy à donne des moyens et amis. Et encores que par la loy d'amitie et de raison, elle peust justement, et a bon droict semondre ses amis et allies, et singulierement le roy son bon frere, de luy rendre les mesmes offices et effects d'amitie qu'il a tiré d'elle en son besoin, si est ce qu'elle s'est contentee de ne luy faire autre instance pour l'heure, sinon, qu'il luy plaise de l'accomoder de quelques sommes de deniers qu'elle l'accomoder de quelques sommes de deniers qu'elle luy à preste, ou bien employé pour son secours et service durant les troubles de son royaume. Ce qu'estant si juste, et raisonnable, et la moindre de toutes les faveurs qu'elle peut attendre du roy son bon frere et allie, elle espere qu'il prendra l'affaire a cueur, et advisera promptement et serieusement aux moyens de luy en donner contentement et satisfaction. Et encore que le roy ne faisant que sortir des troubles, et n'ayant f.114v

que bien peu gouste des effects de la paix,
puisse pretendre qu'il n'a pas encor le
moyen de luy donner entiere satisfaction:
toutesfois la royne à ceste ferme opinion,
et asseurance de sa bonne volonte qu'il
aura esgard a l'estat present de ses affaires,
et ne se servira pas des ces excuses en son
endroict estant toutsjours plus raisonnable
que le dict seigneur roy s'efforce encores
qu'avecq quelque difficulte, et par moyens
extraordinaires de rendre a la dte dame
cest argent, dont elle l'a accomode, que par
faulte de ce qu'elle soit contrainte d'endurer
des difficultes et extremites, qu'il luy faudra
pour en recouvrer par autre moyen. Et
ayant ladte Dame roine receu promesse
du roy par son ambassadeur resident
aupres d'elle, qu'en temps suspect, quand
le roy d'espagne feroit des preparatifs de
guerre par mer, il donneroit ordre que ses
subjects ne portassent du bled ou autre
grain en espaigne, dont ce roy la se pourroit
servir pour l'avittuaillement de sa flotte:
et ayant ladte Dame fort fraischement eu
advertissement des grands preparatifs qui
se font a present de ce coste la, et que pour
estre prests de faire voile ilz n'attendent que
le bled qui leur doibt estre fourni de France,
elle prie pourtant le roy son bon frere d'y
donner tel ordre, que sera conforme a sa
dicte promesse, et a la vraie perfaicte amitie
qu'elle s'est toutsjours promise de luy.

    Et comme la dte. Dame sur l'asseurance
aussi de la bonne volonte et amitie du roy,
et a l'instance de son ambassadeur, a este
contente d'ottroyer libre passage en Espagne
a touts navires francois, et à faict defendre sur

griefves peines a ses subjects, de les arrester,
rechercher, ou autrement incommoder
sur quelq. pretexte que se soit, le tout,
sur la promesse du roy faicte par son dt.
ambassadr. qu'il ne permettroit pas, que ses
subjects en abusassent au prejudice de la dte.
Dame, ou en prestant les noms faussement
aux biens et marchandises de ses ennemis ou
en leur fournissant par voie de marchandise,
ou autrement, des armes, munitions

f.115r

et autres materiaux de guerre par mer
ou par terre la dte Dame pourtant
cognoissa[nce] bien l'importance de cest
affaire a la conservation de son estat, a
trouve bon, de prier le roy son bon frere
d'y promptement pourvoir, en telle sorte
qu'il luy semblera propre pour le bien de
ses affaires: et mesme qu'il luy plaise de luy
faire entendre par quel moyen il à delibere
d'y pourvoir, a fin que comme ils sont
d'accord de la matiere, et substance, ilz se
puissent aussi accorder de la forme et du
moyen d'y parvenir.

    Ladte Dame estant aussi advertie,
qu'un sien subject nommé Collesford qui
à autresfois demeure a Anvers, et s'est
totalement emploie aux pratiques et menees
pernicieuses contra son estat, s'est venu,
depuis nagueires, rendre a Calais, pour avecq
plus de commodite vacquer a la poursuitte
de ses mauvais desseings, à trouvé bon,
de faire instance au roy, selon les anciens
traictes de perpetuelle alliance entre ces deux
courronnes, de donner commandemen[t]
qu'il vuide promptement de la dte ville de
Calais et autres places de son obeisance.

APPENDIX XIV

Memoire des sommes de deniers que la Royne d'Angleterre a prestees ou desboursees pour le Roy tres Chrestien

('Memorandum of sums of *deniers* [money] that the Queen of England had lent to or disbursed for the very Christian King [Henri IV]') [Bibliothèque Nationale de France, MS français 15980, f.5]

The French document sets out the costs incurred and amounts lent by Elizabeth I to aid first Henri III then Henri IV between 1587 and 1596 [/7]. The amounts are set out in both pounds sterling and French *écus*.

1587	Desboursé par les mains du seigr Horace Pallavicini pour la levee de l'armee Allemande conduicte par le Baron d'Aunau, pour laquelle somme Il ya obligation des ambassadeurs du Roy dattee a Francfort	Livraz sterling 30468 scudoz francie 101560
1589 *Septembris*	Preste sur l'obligation de Messrs Beauvoir, Bichy, Buzenvale	Livraz sterling 22350 scudoz francie 71165 20 sol
1589	Desboursé pour la lissence et transport des soldatz envoyez au secours du Roy soubz la conduicte du baron Willoughby	Livraz sterling 6000[5] scudoz francie 10000
1590	Presté pour la levee de l'armee Allemande soubz la conduicte du prince d'Anhalt sur l'obligation de Monsr. le viconte de Turenne a ceste __ duc de Buillon	Livraz sterling 10000 scudoz francie 33333 20 s
1590 *25 Sepbre*	Presté sur l'obligation de Monsr. de Beauvoir	Livraz sterling 10000 scudoz francie 33333 20 s
1590 *29 Novembris*	Presté sur l'obligation de Messrs de Beauvoir et d'Incarville[6] par le Maire de Londres	Livraz sterling 2100 scudoz francie 7000
1592	Presté sur l'obligation de Messrs deBeauvoir et de Fresnes[7]	Livraz sterling 15750 scudoz francie 52500
f.5v		
1591	Desboursé pour la despense de l'armee soubz la conduicte de Monsr le Conte d'Essex en Normandye oultre les rabatz	Livraz sterling 60192 22 s scudoz francie 200640

1591–1594	Desboursé pour la despense des soldatz employez en Bretaigne depuis le moys d'avril 1591 jusques au moys de fevr. anno 1594 oultre les rabatz	Livraz sterling 190350 10 7508 scudoz francie 634501 46s
1594	Desboursé pour la despense des Navires employez par le commandement du Roy a Brest	Livraz sterling 14173 scudoz fran. 47243 20s
1596	Desboursé pour la despensé des 2000 soldatz en Picardye pour quatorze moys oultre les rabatz	Livraz sterling 40351 46s scudoz fran. 134505

Summa Livraz sterling   401734 16s 6d
<u>scudoz francie</u>   <u>1339116 20s</u>

NOTES TO APPENDICES

1 Claude de Lorraine, duc d'Aumale (1526–1573).

2 *groat* = 4d.

3 Violins which may have played this very music may be seen today at the Ashmolean Museum, Oxford (e.g. WA1939.20). These were among the thirty-eight violins produced by Andrea Amati de Cremona in Italy between 1564 and 1574 for Charles IX.

4 *A Dictionarie of the French and English Tongues* (London, 1611).

5 According to William Camden, Elizabeth spent 20,000 [*couronnes*?] on Willoughby's army. *Annals, or, the historie of… Elizabeth…* (London, 1635), p.390.

6 Charles de Saldaigne, seigneur d'Incarville (*fl.* 1589–1596).

7 Philippe Canaye, siegneur de Fresnes.

SOURCES

In 1972, John Evans wrote, 'If we did not have state documents, mainly those in the Public Record Office [The National Archives] and the British Museum [British Library], we would have trouble proving Elizabeth despatched a single soldier to France in response to Henry IV's desperate pleas.'[495] There is some truth in this, though there are numerous sources elsewhere. Here is an introduction to the most important sources.

Elizabethan England and Europe: Forty Unprinted Letters from Elizabeth I to Protestant Powers (1982) by Erkki Kouri contains an introduction to the sources of foreign policy (pp.3–11).

In my research, I have concentrated in the first instance on the years of direct intervention: from 1562 to 1563, from 1589 to 1594 and from 1596 to 1597; and secondly on the years of indirect intervention from 1568 to 1577 and 1587.

The scale of intervention is apparent from the abundance of documents in the State Papers of the National Archives (formerly the Public Record Office) at Kew[496] as well as the papers of Lord Salisbury at Hatfield House. The sieges of Le Havre and Rouen and the correspondence of the ambassadors occupy and dominate swathes of archives of Elizabeth's reign.

At the National Archives, on the first part of the reign, the State Papers Foreign (from November 1558 to June 1577) contain manuscripts concerning France. (The month of October 1562, for example, occupies the series SP 70/42 and SP 70/43.) From 1 July 1577 until December 1598 the State Papers France are spread across SP 78/1 to SP 78/42. Each series occupies a calendar period. For the manuscripts covering the first war, for example, a series may contain between twelve days (February 1563) and one month (August 1563) of documents. It is interesting to note that the series covering the periods in peacetime contain up to two months of documents; thus there are only three series, 70/73, 70/74 and 70/75, that cover the period from July to December 1564. There are, meanwhile, certain lacunae. Unfortunately, the register of the *Acts of the Privy Council* for the period from 23 January to 10 August 1563 is missing.[497] It must be remembered, though, that these archives remained principally the domain of the two Cecils: William and his son, Robert. Their 'foreign policies' are therefore better represented than those of the Earl of Essex.

The manuscripts of the British Library are classed differently. Their classification by collection is simply an accident of history. The archives here are an agglomeration of donations from private collections. Manuscripts on the siege of Le Havre, for example, may be found dispersed across different collections such as the Cotton Augustus, Egerton, the Additional MSS and especially Additional MS 35831. Several documents of the Egerton MSS may be found in the work, already cited, by Hector de La Ferrière, *La Normandie à l'Étranger*. Among Cotton MS Galba (E VI) a journal of Willoughby's expedition of 1589 may be found.

Other manuscript collections include those of Rawlinson in the Bodleian Library, Oxford. The Quarter Books (MS A200) of Benjamin Gonson, the Treasurer of the navy, are an important source and give an idea of the character of the Royal Navy during the wars. These accounts detail the construction and maintenance of ships in the naval dockyards of Deptford, Gillingham and Portsmouth during the first part of the reign. They show the scale of activity along the south coast of England during the first expedition to Normandy. They also provide us with the names and wages of both the sailors and shipwrights alike.

In France, it is the Bibliothèque Nationale that possesses most manuscripts relevant to the subject. On the siege of Le Havre, for example, MSS français 15878 and 3243 may be cited. Visits to the libraries of the Institut de France, the Arsenal and the Assemblée Nationale in Paris were all worthwhile. A number of manuscripts of the Godefroy collection (MS 257) of the Institut de France refer to the Normandy campaign of 1563. The Bibliothèque de l'Arsenal possesses a real jewel in the form of MS 2307. This book, *Statuts de L'Ordre de la Jarretière*, was presented to Henri IV by Elizabeth in 1596. The Assemblée Nationale possesses copies of the letters of the French ambassador in England, Christophe de Harlay (MS 285). Finally, the archive of the Ministère des Affaires Étrangères in Paris provides rare details concerning the treaty of Magdeburg (Correspondance Politique Vol. 22 f.373).

The publication of papers had begun by the seventeenth century. The most important guides and sources for the papers of state from 1562 to 1588 are the *Calendars of State Papers, Foreign Series*, published between 1897 and 1950 (these also include documents from the British Library). For the years 1589 to 1596, the guide appears in another format, *List and Analysis of State Papers, Foreign*. This guide describes only the documents of the National Archives. These seven volumes were edited between 1964 and 1999 by Richard Wernham, but the work was interrupted by his death in 1999.

The volumes VII to XXVIII of the *Acts of the Privy Council*, edited between 1893 and 1904 by John Dasent, are also an important mine of information.

These guides are complemented by older editions of published letters. Many documents relative to this study are included in volumes XV and XVI of *Foedera, conventiones litterae et cujuscunque generis, acta publica, inter reges Angliae et alios quosvis imperatores, reges, pontifices, principes vel communitates*. Volume XV covers the period from 1544 to 1586 and volume XVI from 1587 to 1616. Published in London between 1704 and 1735, the first fifteen volumes were edited by Thomas Rymer. Rymer had been appointed as historiographer to Charles II in 1692. Following his death his work was taken up by Robert Sanderson. Volume XVI of *Foedera* contains many useful sources, although, as with many selections of documents, there are gaps. This volume does not contain, for example, any document on the siege of Amiens. A useful abridged version of *Foedera* was translated into French by Paul Rapin de Thoyras, *Extrait des Actes de Rymer* (Amsterdam, 1728), in a single volume.

An important number of documents relative to the siege of Le Havre were edited by Patrick Forbes in his *A Full View of the Public Transactions in the reign of Queen Elizabeth...* (London, 1740–41), 2 vols.

Another useful source includes the speeches given to Parliament: Simonds d'Ewes, *A Compleat Journal of the Votes, Speeches & Debates ... House of Lords ... & Commons ... Queen Elizabeth* (1682, 1693, new edn Shannon, 1973). This work is completed by the three volumes edited by Terence Hartley, *Proceedings in the Parliaments of Elizabeth* (Leicester, 1981–95). In volume III, for example, is the speech given by Lord Burghley during the eighth Parliament (19 February to 10 April 1593) on the Spanish menace in France.[498]

The other collection of 'State Papers', which is in fact private, is that of the two Cecils: William, Lord Burghley, and his son Robert, Earl of Salisbury. These manuscripts, which are to be found at Hatfield House, were edited by the Historic Manuscripts Commission. The first eight volumes as well as volume XXIII of *Calendar of the Manuscripts of the Most Honourable the Marquis of Salisbury...* cover the period concerned.

A number of letters of Lord Burghley were edited in two volumes by Samuel Haynes, William Murdin and William Bowyer, *A Collection of State papers relating to affairs in the reign of queen Elizabeth from the year 1571 to 1596. Transcribed from original papers and other authentic memorials never before published, left by William Cecil Lord Burghley and reposited in the library at Hatfield House* (London, 1740–59).

A large number of manuscripts from the British Library and private collections are to be found dispersed across anthologies of letters. The two volumes of *Memoirs of the Reign of Queen Elizabeth...* (London, 1754) edited by Thomas Birch are indispensable; they contain letters of Robert Devereux, Earl of Essex. *Cabala sive scrinia sacra...* (London, 1691) contains numerous letters written by Sir William Cecil to the ambassador in Paris, Sir Henry Norris. Several letters of Norris are also printed in *Miscellaneous State Papers* edited by Philip Yorke, Earl of Hardwicke (1720–90) in two volumes (London, 1778). (This work is also known as the *Hardwicke State Papers.*)

A great number of letters of Sir Nicholas Throckmorton, the champion of early Elizabethan foreign policy, appear in the two volumes of *Queen Elizabeth and Her Times...* (London, 1838), edited by Thomas Wright (also indispensable).

Collections of letters of three other important ambassadors (Sir Thomas Edmondes, Sir Henry Unton and Sir Francis Walsingham) have also been published. Those of Walsingham were edited by Dudley Digges (1582/83–1639) in the *Complete Ambassador* as early as 1655. This was translated into French and published in Amsterdam in 1700 under the title of *Mémoires et Instructions pour les Ambassadeurs. The Correspondence of Sir Henry Unton* (London, 1847, edited by Joseph Stevenson) and *The Edmondes Papers* (London, 1913, edited by Geoffrey Butler) have also been of immense value to this study.

The agents of the Crown, the 'spies', are also an important source, notably Ottywell Smith and William Lilly.

Annals of the Reformation... by John Strype (1643–1737) also deserves attention for the primary sources, including documents of the British Library. I used the second edition of London, 1735 (three volumes). The principal sources used by Strype were the archives of manuscripts of Sir William Hickes, great-grandson of Sir Michael Hickes, secretary to Sir William Cecil.

Correspondence between Sir Robert Cecil and Sir Henry Neville in the first volume of *Memorials of Affairs of State in the reigns of Queen Elizabeth and King James I* (London, 1725), edited by Edmund Sawyer, sheds light on the period post-Vervins (i.e. from 1598).

English soldiers themselves have also left their own eyewitness accounts. Sir Thomas Coningsby and Robert Carey have left us several pages on the siege of Rouen in 1591. Those of the latter were edited by F. Mares, *The Memoirs of Robert Carey* (Oxford, 1972).[499] More soldiers have given us their accounts of the siege of Amiens in 1597. We find, for example, the nuanced letters of Sir Arthur Savage and Captains Arthur Chichester, John Phillips and Henry Power. These letters complement those of the ambassador Sir Anthony Mildmay and William Lilly.

The perspective of the *Reiter* (German mercenary soldiers) serving the Protestant cause in France is provided by Michel de La Huguerye (*fl*.1545–1606). His *Mémoires inédits 1570–1602* (Paris, 1877–80) (in three volumes), edited by Alphonse de Ruble, and *Ephéméride de l'Expédition des Allemands en France...1587* (Paris, 1892) are both copious *recueils*. Interestingly, La Huguerye saw service on both sides. Some *Reiter* also served in the French army during the first war. One of the most prominent was the Rhinegrave (Rheingraf Johann-Philipp, Wild und von Salm, 1520–1566/67). Many of his letters were edited by David Potter in *Les Allemands et les armées françaises au XVI Siècle. Jean-Philippe Rhingrave, chef de lansquenets Étude suivie de sa correspondance en France, 1548–1566* in the journal *Francia.*[500]

The indispensable source on intervention in Brittany from 1591 to 1594 is Emmanuel van Meteren (1535–1612). His *A true discourse historicall of the ... civil wars ... with the memorable services of our ... English ... soldiers especially under Sir John Norice ... from the yeere 1577 until the yeere 1589, and afterwards in Portugall, France, Britaine and Ireland until the yeere 1598*, translated by Churchyard and Robinson (London 1602, new edn Amsterdam & New York, 1968), describes the campaigns of Sir John Norris.

There is also an abundant mass of published documents to be found in France. One eighteenth-century *recueil* is *Histoire d'Elisabeth Reine d'Angleterre*

Tirée des Originaux Anglois, d'Actes, Titre, Lettres & Autres Pièces Manuscrites Qui n'ont pas encore paru (Paris, 1786–88) in five volumes. This work by Louise-Félicité Guinement de Keralio is quite rare in England and, consequently, rarely cited. The works already cited by La Ferrière and Kermaingant also include important texts from English archives translated into French.

The correspondence of two of the principal actors in this history, Catherine de' Medici and Henri IV, were published in the nineteenth century. *Lettres de Catherine de Médicis* (Paris, 1885) was edited by Hector de la Ferrière in ten volumes. The first five volumes of *Lettres Missives d'Henri IV* (Paris, 1843–76), edited by Jules Berger de Xivry and Joseph Gaudet, were relevant to this study.

In his memoirs touching on the first war, Michel de Castelnau, sieur de la Mauvissière (1520–1592), is informative. His memoirs (written to instruct his son) cover until 1569. He therefore does not include details of his embassy to England between 1575 and 1585. Meanwhile, Castelnau's accounts are important due to their impartiality, a rare gift for the epoch.

Other accounts have been left by another French ambassador, André Hurault de Maisse (d.1607). His journal was translated and published in English in London in 1931, *De Maisse a journal of all that was accomplished by Monsieur de Maisse Ambassador in England from King Henri IV to Queen Elizabeth Anno Domini 1597*. There are several other memoirs. Those covering the first war include *Mémoires de Claude Haton* (a curate who lived in Provins in Champagne between around 1535 and 1605) and *Mémoires de Condé* (London, 1743). The latter of these is actually a compilation. The minister of finance to Henri IV, Maximilien de Béthune (later duc de Sully), has left us his own particular points of view. Although his memoirs, entitled *Oeconomies Royales,*[501] were probably written as instruments of propaganda, they contain useful information on the sieges of Rouen and Amiens. The memoirs of François de La Noue (1531–1591) are a disappointment. Even though he fought side by side with the English, he rarely mentions them at all. This is in some ways not surprising as La Noue perhaps sought to distance himself to avoid charges of treason.

Events surrounding the treaty of Vervins are well represented in the letters of the diplomats Pomponne de Bellièvre (1529–1607) and Nicolas Brulart de Sillery (1544–1624) published in *Lettres, mémoires et negociations de messieurs de Bellievre et de Silleri contenant un journal concernant la Negociation de la Paix Traitée à Vervins l'an 1598...* (The Hague, 1725). An English perspective is given in *An historical view of the negotiations between the courts of England, France and Brussels, from the year 1592 to 1617...* (London, 1749), edited by Thomas Birch. There is also a copious account of the negotiations among the manuscripts of Lord Salisbury at Hatfield House.

A collection of French manuscripts may also be found in Russia at the Saltykov-Shchedrin Public Library (Rossiiskaya Natsional'naya Biblioteka) in St Petersburg. The manuscripts come from the abbaye de St-Germain-des-Prés in Paris and were acquired by Pierre Doubrovsky in 1792. Doubrovsky had served as secretary at the Russian embassy in Paris from 1777. His collection came into the possession of the Public Library in 1805.[502] 127 letters written between January 1561 and December 1563 were edited by Aleksandra Lublinskaya. *Documents pour servir à l'histoire des guerres civiles en France (1561–63)* was published in Moscow in 1962.

The chroniclers and historians of the sixteenth and seventeenth centuries provide us with a richness of material. The English historians would have been aided in their task by an Order of Council dated 7 July 1568. By this order, the holders of ancient and historic documents were required to open their archives to all authorised people.[503] It is perhaps for this reason that *The Chronicles of England...* (London, 1577) in two volumes[504] by Raphael Holinshed has such a resonance. Holinshed is the source *par excellence* on the siege of Le Havre. He provides us with a detailed (and apparently precise) narrative of the siege. The only regret is that his work ends in 1577. The chronicler who 'had a special eye on the truth of things' died in 1580.

One historian who traverses the reign of Elizabeth is William Camden (1551–1623). He was himself a witness to the events of these years. At the age of twelve, he had been lucky to escape the ravages of the plague while living in London in 1563. His work was originally published in Latin, *Annales rerum anglicarum et hibernicarum regnante Elizabetha* (London, 1615), followed by the augmented edition of Leyde in 1625. It is the 1635 edition, translated into English by Robert Norton, that I have used for this study, *Annals, or, the historie of the most renowned and victorious princesse Elizabeth, late Queen of England.*

Fragmenta Regalia[505] by Sir Robert Naunton (1563–1635) is the work of a diplomat sent to France in 1596 and 1597. He describes the people at the court of Elizabeth, including the generals Peregrine Bertie, Lord Willoughby, Sir John Norris and Robert Devereux, Earl of Essex.

There are three French chronicler-historians who stand out from the rest: Henri Lancelot Voisin de La Popelinière

(1541–1608), Théodore-Agrippa d'Aubigné (1552–1630) and Jacques-Auguste de Thou (1553–1617). The work by Jacques-Auguste de Thou is one of the most useful. His *Historiarum sui temporis* appeared in 1620. Volumes IV and XI to XIII of the French edition, *Histoire Universelle depuis 1543 jusqu'à 1607*, contain the most relevant information. Having been president of the *Parlement* in Paris and *Maître de la bibliothèque du roi* (1593), De Thou was clearly writing from a position of authority. Furthermore, Catherine de Thou was the mother of Christophe de Harlay, ambassador to England in 1594. It is apparent that De Thou used English sources in his research. We know that he was in contact with William Camden and traces of the influence of Raphael Holinshed are to be found in his work.

La Popelinière is an important commentator on the wars, thanks to his geographic position. It is from the Huguenot stronghold of La Rochelle that he describes English intervention between 1568 and 1573 in *La Vraye et entière histoire des troubles et choses mémorables avenues, tant en France qu'en Flandres et pays circonvoisins, depuis 1562...* (La Rochelle, 1573). Similarly, d'Aubigné, witness of the repression of the conspiracy of Amboise, served in the wars and was present at the siege of Rouen in 1591. François de Belle-Forest (1530–1583) may also be cited as *historiographe du roi*. Belle-Forest writes on the first phase of English intervention in his *L'Histoire des Neuf Roys Charles de France* (Paris, 1568). To this list we may add an Italian, Henrico Caterino Davila (1576–1631), who also participated in the wars as a combatant. In particular, he saw service at the siege of Amiens. His *Historia delle guerre civili di Francia...* of 1630 appeared in French in 1657.

The sources of other countries are also interesting. The correspondence of the Venetian ambassador Marc'Antonio Barbaro (1518–1595) is contained in volume VII of *Calendar of State Papers and manuscripts relating to English affairs in the archives and collections of Venice and in other libraries of Northern Italy* (London, 1890), edited by George Bentinck and Rawdon Brown. The bank of the Fuggers of Augsburg produced their own news bulletins. A number of these bulletins were edited by Victor von Klarwill in *The Fugger Newsletters 1568–1605* (London, 1924–26) in two volumes.

Other authors mention the English in passing. For example, Pierre-Victor Palma-Cayet (*c.*1525–1610) rarely talks about them but he does provide us with a detailed description of the entry into Compiègne made by the Earl of Essex in 1591. The French surgeon Ambroise Paré is another example. Present at the siege of Le Havre in 1563, he gives his own unique eyewitness account in *Apologie, et traicté contenant les voyages faicts en divers lieux.*[506]

The sources do not end here. We find reference to the English through music, poems, maps, drawings, paintings and contemporary engravings. The portraits of the military commanders also sometimes provide views of the wars in France. In the background of two portraits of Robert Devereux, Earl of Essex (including one at the National Portrait Gallery[507]), there are scenes of the siege of Rouen. The siege of Crozon in Brittany appears in an engraving of Sir Martin Frobisher by Robert Boissard. This was published in the book by Henry Holland, *Baziliologia, A Booke of Kings* (London, 1618).[508]

The largest collections of maps are at the British Library (most form part of the Cotton Augustus MSS) and at the National Archives. There are several maps that remain virtually unknown in France. The map of the Gironde showing the siege of Blaye in 1593 (Cotton MS Augustus I.ii.80) at the British Library and the plan of the siege of Chartres (The National Archives SP 78/24 f.75) are two examples. Some interesting maps are to be found at Hatfield House, such as one depicting the English occupation of Le Havre (CPM II/45). Even in France itself there are little-known maps. The English woodcut showing the battle of Arques in 1589 (Bibliothèque Nationale de France, GeDD 627, pl.78) is one such example. Other interesting views of Amiens, Crozon, Gournay-en-Bray and Rouen are also reproduced in this study.

Not content with studying these plans from a distance, I visited the sites directly. Seeing the battlefields and fortresses helped me to acquire a better understanding. Much of Le Havre has either been modified with the expansion of the port or destroyed during the Second World War. The Tour François I was demolished in 1861 but French photographers provide clear depictions of the entrance to the port (see, for example, the work of Jean-Victor Macaire-Warnod held by the Archives municipales in Le Havre). Remains of the Spanish fortress at Roscanvel (Crozon) are still visible and this is well worth a visit. Other sites have

weathered time better, such as the castles of Tancarville, Goué (La Dorée), Montjean and the fortress of Blaye. At Amiens, there are remains of the fortifications that pre-date the work of Jean Errard de Bar-le-Duc. Aerial photographs taken by Roger Agache during the 1960s reveal the elaborate system of earthworks constructed during the siege. Some remains of the headquarters of Henri IV at *La Madelayne* outside Amiens have also survived. Though now much (and recently) altered, it may be viewed from what is today known as rue Franklin Roosevelt.

The discovery of a wreck off the Isle of Alderney in 1977 has added a new and intriguing dimension to the study of the subject. On the history surrounding this wreck, the work by David Loades may be consulted, *The Channel Islands and Tudor policy: The context of the Alderney wreck*.[509] The interim archaeological report was edited by Mensun Bound and Jason Monaghan: *A Ship Cast Away About Alderney: Investigations of an Elizabethan Shipwreck* (Alderney, 2001). This also includes a number of essays on the finds. The wreck is still being researched and we may anticipate further interesting finds. Let us hope too that the *Greyhound*, which sank off Camber near Rye during the Le Havre campaign, will also be located.

LEARNING THE LANGUAGE

For many in the ruling classes, learning foreign languages was important. Sir Philip Sidney, for example, is known to have solicited Elizabeth and was given permission on 25 May 1572 to leave England for two years with three valets and four horses to learn foreign languages. Elizabeth herself is known to have understood several languages, French of course among them. She had a French tutor named John Belmain, a Huguenot who had taught Edward VI. Understanding both foreign allies and enemies alike could be vital in the army. Henry Barrett in his *A briefe booke unto private captaynes* (1562) wrote that the drums and fifes should be 'ingenious of sondery languages',[510] that is to say, should know several languages because it was one of their functions to parley with the enemy.

Even though Latin was still used in letters to Germanic and Scandinavian countries, French had become the accepted language of discourse between England and France by 1560. Sir William Cecil wrote, 'their ministers speak in their own tongue, and we in theirs'.[511] The English were therefore at a disadvantage. Sir Thomas Smith gave the reason, stating that Latin was ill-suited to the modern world. It was on the Latin version of the treaty of Blois, however, that they placed their seals and signatures. The French ambassador, Paul de Foix, was charged with translating the articles of the treaty so that Charles IX could understand. The complete transformation took time. During the first war, Elizabeth suggested that Smith should learn to speak Latin because his French was not very good. Another ambassador, Sir Anthony Mildmay,

maintained that he had not seen France for twenty-one years and that he knew neither the language nor the country well enough. The Earl of Shrewsbury also had problems with French, so that the son of the governor of Dieppe, La Fontaine, had to be employed as an interpreter. Other ambassadors were better prepared. Sir Amias Paulet was fluent, being from predominantly French-speaking Jersey. Sir Henry Unton had spent some time in the French Midi and his mother, Lady Anne Seymour (the future Countess of Warwick), had had a French tutor, Nicolas Denisot, during her youth.

Sir Robert Cecil employed a secretary to write his letters in French. A 'Secretary for the French Tongue' was also employed at court, an office held for life. Thomas Edmondes succeeded Charles Yetsweirt in 1596. His salary was fixed at £16 13s 4d per year.

At the moment when French was becoming the *lingua franca*, few Frenchmen spoke English. One exception was Gabriel de Montgomery. His third daughter, Roberte, married Gawine, son of the English admiral Sir Arthur Champernowne. Even if 'secret' letters fell into the hands of the French, they would certainly have lost time in attempting to translate them. The French would have been aided in their task by the *Grammaire anglaise et francaise pour facilement et promptement apprendre la langue anglaise et francaise*, published in Rouen fairly late, in 1595.

The first published French–English dictionary appeared only in 1593. This did not prevent the translation of works by French authors into English. *Instruction sur le faict de la guerre* by Guillaume Du Bellay was translated by Paul Ive and published under the title *Instructions for the warres...* in 1589. *Discours Politiques & Militaires* by François de La Noue was available in English by 1587 (*The Politicke and Militarie Discourses of the Lord de La Noue*), translated by E. Aggas.

Useful sources include: *A Dictionary French and English* by Claude Desainliens (London, 1593); Edmond Huguet, *Dictionnaire de la langue française du XVIe siècle* (1925–67); John Evans (ed.), *The Works of Sir Roger Williams* (Oxford, 1972, pp.248–59); *The Oxford English Dictionary* (1989), 20 vols; *The Visual Dictionary of*

Military Uniforms (London, 1992), French translation by Paul Leynaud, *Les habits de l'histoire* (Paris, 1992); *Marine d'Hier et d'Aujourd'hui* (Paris, 1991), translated by Jean Randier.

Thanks to the intervention in France, many Englishmen became adept at speaking French. Some, such as John Stubbe, were able to differentiate between dialects. As he wrote to Michael Hicks in 1590, 'I have used up all my French, even that which is the best and from the region of Orléans, so that all I have left is a little bit of French from Normandy and Picardy, which is too uncultured and wholly unworthy of being read by you, sir.'[512]

A NOTE ON TIME

The Gregorian calendar was adopted by France in 1582 (at the same time as Spain). France had already adopted 1 January as New Year's Day (in 1564). England retained the Julian calendar until 1752, together with 25 March as New Year's Day. This *décalage* is evident in the sources. Pope Gregory XIV decreed that 5 October 1582 should become 15 October. There is therefore a difference of ten days between England and France. Other countries followed: the Catholic German states, Holland, the Spanish Netherlands and Switzerland (1583), the Protestant German states, the Netherlands and Denmark (1700). 1 January was adopted in the following order: the German states (1544), the Spanish Netherlands (1556), Denmark and Sweden (1559), the Netherlands (1583) and Scotland (1600). Certain Englishmen used the Gregorian calendar in France, writing 'ns' (new style). Others, including the ambassador Sir Thomas Smith, wrote 'by English Account', 'English style' or 'os' (old style). Meanwhile, most Englishmen did not give any precision.

A NOTE ON CURRENCY

Approximate French currency equivalents:

couronne:	6 shillings
écu d'or soleil (3 *livres*):	6 shillings
livre (*sol-denier*) (20 *sols*):	2 shillings
livre tournois (*franc*):	2 shillings

Other French denominations:

écu blanc (*argent*)	(15 *sols*)
demi-écu	
quart-écu	(15 *sols*)
teston	(14 *sols*)
douzain	(1 *sol*)
sol	(12 *deniers*)

NOTES

ABBREVIATIONS

Ancaster MSS *Report on the Manuscripts of the Earl of Ancaster preserved at Grimsthorpe*

APC John DASENT (ed.), *Acts of the Privy Council*

BNF Bibliothèque Nationale de France

CSPD Mary EVERETT GREEN (ed.), *Calendar of State Papers Domestic*

CSPF *Calendar of State Papers Foreign Series*

Joseph STEVENSON (ed.), Vols I–VII (London, 1863–70)

Allan CROSBY (ed.), Vols VIII–XI (London, 1871–80)

Sophie LOMAS (ed.), Vols XVIII–XXI, part i (London, 1914–27)

HMC Historic Manuscripts Commission

L &A Richard WERNHAM (ed.), *List and Analysis of State Papers Foreign*

ODNB *Oxford Dictionary of National Biography*

QEHT Thomas WRIGHT (ed.), *Queen Elizabeth and Her Times*

Salisbury MSS *Calendar of the Manuscripts of the Most Honourable the Marquis of Salisbury … preserved at Hatfield House*

TNA The National Archives

Trans. Translated from the original French

1   Other useful chronologies may be found in: John SALMON (ed.), *The French Wars of Religion…* (Boston, 1967), pp.xiii–xx; *Henri IV et la reconstruction du royaume*, exhibition catalogue (Paris, 1989), pp.427–30; Denis CROUZET, *Les Guerriers de Dieu* (Seyssel, 1990), I, pp.23–41; Michel VERGÉ-FRANCESCHI, *Chronique Maritime de la France d'Ancien Régime* (Paris, 1998); Arlette JOUANNA *et al.*, *Histoire et Dictionnaire des Guerres de Religion* (Paris, 1998), pp.1383–1403; Jean BARBIER-MUELLER, *La Parole et les Armes: Chronique des Guerres de religion en France 1562–1598* (Paris, 2006), pp.249–65.

2   *On a Tudor Parade Ground: The Captain's Handbook of Henry Barrett 1562* (London, 1978), p.1.

3   Cited in Michael GRAVES, *Burghley: William Cecil, Lord Burghley* (London, 1998), p.203.

4   Alfred ROWSE, *The Expansion of Elizabethan England* (London, 1957), pp.356–57.

5   Albert POLLARD, *The Political History of England…* (London, 1923), VI, p.248.

6   Lawrence STONE, *An Elizabethan: Sir Horatio Palavicino* (Oxford, 1956), p.174, cited in Simon ADAMS, *The Protestant cause: religious alliance with the west European Calvinist communities as a political issue in England, 1585–1630*, University of Oxford PhD (1973), p.125.

7   Henri ZUBER in *Henri IV et la reconstruction du royaume* (Paris, 1989), p.105 (exhibition catalogue: Château de Pau & Archives Nationales, Paris 1989–90). Trans.: *cet expédition s'achève sur un disastre, tandis qu'une autre armée envoyée en Bretagne (1591–1592) se fait exterminer par les Ligueurs.*

8   George HARRISON (ed.), *De Maisse A Journal… 1597* (London, 1931), p.109, cited in Paul JORGENSEN, 'Moral Guidance and Religious Encouragement for the Elizabethan Soldier', *Huntington Library Quarterly* (1949), XIII, p.244.

9   William CAMDEN, *Annals, or, the historie of the most renowned and victorious princesse Elizabeth, late Queen of England…* (London, 1635), p.400.

10   *Henriade*, p.5. Trans.: *Je sais qu'entre eux et nous une immortelle haine/Nous permet rarement de marcher réunis.*

11   Charles BEEM (ed.), *The Foreign Relations of Elizabeth I* (New York, 2011), pp.77–100.

12   (1997) XL, pp.1–21. 'Newhaven' was the English name given to Le Havre. It was also the name given to Ambleteuse in

Picardy during the English occupation of
1549.

13 Elizabeth's motto, *SEMPER EADEM*
('Always the same').

14 All monetary equivalents given
throughout are those current in the
sixteenth century.

15 An event recaptured in the painting *The
Field of Cloth of Gold*, Royal Collection
No.23. Reproduced in Christopher LLOYD
and Simon THURLEY, *Henry VIII: Images
of a Tudor King* (London, 1995), pp.62–
63.

16 British Library, Additional MS 5498 f.8.

17 See the plan of the siege: British Library,
Cotton MS Augustus I.i.49.

18 BNF, MS français 3117 ff.42-44. Trans.:
*La Majesté du roy d'Angleterre se voyt
qu'il n'a pas d'argent, et les tailles
qu'il a imposées sur tout son royaulme
dernièrement tant spirituel que temporel,
le peuple ne le veult pas payer, en disant
que le conseil deppend en aultre usaige
que pour le service du roy, de sorte qu'il
y deffauld argent. La Majesté … doibt
grande somme d'argent à ceulx de la ville
d'Anvers qu'il a prise à intérest, et on dict
que le roy doibt aux marchans deux cens
mil livres esterlins.*

19 *Vice-amiral* Bouillé to the governor
of Brittany, cited in Charles de LA
RONCIÈRE, *Histoire de la Marine
Française* (1923), Vol.IV, p.31. Trans.:
*Le monde est si changé, la crainte et
l'obéissance si faillie, la division et
partialité si grande que s'il ne plaist au
roy y pourveoir, la place de Saint-Malo se
perdra et passera aux Anglais.*

20 Alphonse de RUBLE, *Le Traité de Cateau-
Cambrésis* (Paris, 1889), p.149, who cites
his letter of 20 March 1560. Trans.: *Ils ont
grande peur que les Anglois débarquent
troupes en Bretagne ou Normandie, où ils
seroient bien reçus des habitants.*

21 British Library, Additional MS 35831
(Hardwicke Papers), f.34, Sir Nicholas
Throckmorton to Cecil, 26 May 1562.

22 Thomas RYMER (ed.), *Foedera,
conventiones litterae et cujuscunque*

*generis, acta publica, inter reges Angliae
et alios quosvis imperatores, reges,
pontifices, principes vel communitates*
(1727), Vol.XVI, p.138, Sir William Cecil to
Sir Henry Unton. The traditional opinion
is that Cecil visited the Continent only
once, the Low Countries in 1554.

23 Paul HUGHES and James LARKIN (eds),
Tudor Royal Proclamations (1969), Vol.II,
p.206 (24 September 1562); Louise-Félicité
GUINEMENT DE KERALIO, *Histoire
d'Élisabeth, Reine d'Angleterre tirée des
écrits originaux anglois, d'actes, titres,
lettres & autres pièces manuscrites qui
n'ont pas encore paru* (Paris, 1788), Vol.V,
pp.155–57.

24 Trans.: *delivrance de la violance de la
dicte maison de Guyse.* See Appendix II
for the proclamation in full.

25 TNA SP 70/42 f.46, Charles IX to Elizabeth
I, October 1562. Trans.: *nous avons sceu
de verité qu'il se retrouve aujourdhuy an
Angleterre grand nombre de noz subjectz
declarez sedicieux & Rebelles par arrest
de notre court de parlement a Paris.*

26 *QEHT* (1838), Vol.I, p.135 (1 August 1563).

27 Hector de LA FERRIÈRE (ed.), *Lettres de
Catherine de Médicis* (Paris, 1885), Vol.
II, p.122 note. A treaty had been signed
on 23 September 1563 to keep the
peace along the frontiers of England and
Scotland.

28 Victor GRAHAM, 'The 1564 Entry of
Charles IX into Troyes', *Bibliothèque
d'Humanisme et Renaissance* (1986),
XLVIII, i, p.114. Trans.: *monté sur quatre
boules, avec quelques engins qui le
faisoient tourner de tous costez sans
aucuns chevaulx.*

29 Alexandre TEULET (ed.), *Supplément à
la Correspondance diplomatique de …
La Mothe Fénelon* (Paris, 1840), Vol.VII,
p.301. Trans.: *Dieu, de sa grâce, avoit
séparés et bornés de la mer pour un
grand bien ces deux royaulmes.*

30 BNF, MS nouvelles acquisitions françaises
5127 f.89, Elizabeth I to Charles IX, 29
December 1564. Trans.: *amitié qui nous
semble davoir ja prins si bonne racine en*

vre cueur, qu'elle ne se pourra aiseement esbranler ny diminuer sur la quelle esperance entendons et aussi avons desja commencé de planter en nre cueur la mesme plante de vraye amite envers vous, si que nous esperons que avec l'ayde de dieu ces deux plantes seront de longue durée, et produiront telz fruictz … Noz Royaumes païs et peuple en recepuront aussi grand proufit.

31 Laurent BOURQUIN (ed.), *Mémoires de Claude Haton* (Paris, 2003), Vol. II, pp.277–78. Trans.: *Ilz huguenotz taschoient à tirer d'elle secours d'hommes anglois, mais oncques ung se volut metre sus mer pour eux, se resouvenans bien de la pauvre recompense qu'ilz avoient eu d'eux aux premiers troubles … avec tout domage de leurs biens et vies.*

32 *Cabala, sive scrinia sacra: Mysteries of State and Government...* (1691), p.144, Sir William Cecil to Sir Henry Norris, n.d.

33 François de Noailles to the duc d'Anjou, 16 August 1571. LA RONCIÈRE, *op. cit.*, Vol.IV, pp.121–22, who cites BNF, Dupuy MS 658, f.123. Trans.: *Il y a, derrière l'Angleterre, un Pérou. C'est le royaume d'Irlande, l'un des meilleurs païs du monde. Et je veux estre dégradé de noblesse, si le sieur de Strossy et le capitaine Gourges, avec sept ou huit mil arquebusiers françois, huit cens ou mil chevaulx et six pièces d'artillerie, ne font toute la réduction de ce royaume en moins d'un an: lequel, bien réglé et mesnagé, en moins de vingt ans après sa réduction, sera de plus grand revenu que celui d'Angleterre.*

34 CAMDEN, *Annals…*, p.394, who cites Elizabeth. See also Guillaume du VAIR, *Les oeuvres du Sr. du Vair garde des seaux de France* (Rouen, 1619), p.34, *Le jour que la France sera conquise par l'Espagnol, sera la veille de la ruine du Royaume d'Angleterre.*

35 Albert OSBORN, *Sir Philip Sidney en France* (Paris, 1932), p.11, who cites BNF, MS français 5134, f.162 v.

36 Trans.: *Pourquoi votre souveraine n'épouserait-elle pas le roi très chrétien? Il a plus d'inclination à l'Evangile qu'on ne pense, et l'union des deux couronnes serait un coup écrasant pour le papisme,* cited in Henri duc d'AUMALE, *Histoire des Princes de Condé* (Paris 1863), Vol.I, p.236.

37 *Cabala, op. cit.*, p.338. See also COLLINS (ed.), *Letters and Memorials of State* (1746), Vol.II, p.290.

38 CAMDEN, *Annals…*, p.235.

39 Leah MARCUS, Janel MUELLER and Mary ROSE (eds), *Elizabeth I Collected Works* (Chicago, 2000), pp. 302–03.

40 *QEHT* (1838), Vol.II, p.152, Elizabeth I to Sir Edward Stafford, n.d.

41 *L & A* (2000), Vol. VII, p.195.

42 *QEHT* (1838), Vol.I, p.181, Sir William Cecil to Sir Thomas Smith, 15 December 1564.

43 *QEHT* (1838), Vol.I, p.438, Bishop of London to Lord Burghley, 5 September 1572.

44 *QEHT* (1838), Vol.I, p.459, Sir Thomas Smith to Lord Burghley, 12 February 1573.

45 Jean NAGEREL, *Description du Pays et Duché de Normandie...* (Rouen, 1573). Trans.: *La Royne d'Angleterre... s'efforçoit de mettre le souffre au feu, nourrir nos lamentables querelles et rejetter le peuple de l'obéissance de son prince, et par le sentier de ses predecesseurs, venir pour s'agrandir de nos ruines.*

46 GUINEMENT DE KERALIO, *op. cit.* (1788), Vol.V, p.367, who cites British Library, Harleian MS CLVIII, f.349, Castelnau to Henri III, 14 February 1584. Trans.: *s'ils se mectent ensemble, principallement par la mer sur la deffencive, & pour le regard de l'offencive, si leur ligue peut aller en avant avec les protestans de la Germanie, & les huguenots de vostre royaulme, ils auront des hommes & de l'argent pour allumer le feu & faire la guerre partout, afin de s'en exempter chez eux.*

47 *QEHT* (1838), Vol.II, p.192, W. Parry to Lord Burghley, 4 March 1582.

48 Cited in Charles WILSON, *Queen Elizabeth and the Revolt of the*

Netherlands (London, 1970), p.125. As Richard Wernham remarked, English policy in the Netherlands was influenced by French actions.

49   *QEHT* (1838), Vol.II, pp.346–47, Sir Francis Walsingham to Lord Burghley, 12 September 1587.

50   Simonds D'EWES, *The Journals of All the Parliaments during the Reign of Queen Elizabeth* (1682, new edn Shannon, 1973), p.457.

51   *Certaine Prayers set fourth by Authoritie, to be used for the prosperous successe of her Majesties Forces and Navy* (London, 1597), p.8.

52   Michel NOSTRADAMUS, *Les Propheties de M. Michel Nostradamus* (Lyons, 1557). Trans.: *Lyon & Coq; non trop confederez/ En lieu de peur, l'un l'autre s'aidera.*

53   RYMER, *Foedera, op. cit.*, Vol.XVI, p.26, cited in John BLACK, *Elizabeth and Henry IV: Being a short study in Anglo-French relations, 1589–1603...* (Oxford, 1914), p.14.

54   p.71, cited by Myriam YARDINI, 'Antagonismes Nationaux…', *Revue d'Histoire Moderne et Contemporaine* (1966), XIII, p.281. Trans.: *Davantage, les Anglois et Allemands sont par nous soudoyez et payez, se meslent de nos affaires aussi avant et aussi peu qu'il nous plaist, n'ont autre retraicte en ce Royaume, que les quartiers que les Mareschaux de Camp leur donnent en nos armées: en un mot nous nous servons d'eux, non eux de nous.*

55   *L & A* (2000), Vol.VII, p.196, instructions to Gilbert Talbot, Earl of Shrewsbury, September 1596.

56   Victor VON KLARWILL (ed.), *The Fugger News-letters* (London, 1924), p.203, 'News from Venice', 6 December 1596.

57   BNF, MS français 15878, f.21r., the Rhinegrave to Catherine de' Medici, 6 June 1563. Trans.: *Madame cest a tous les jours et je ne voy point que rien sadvance pour mes secours ny gens ny equippage, mesmement les Francois comme je vous ay mande sen vont nont point dargent*

pour vivre sont malcontente les miens de mesme se mescontantent de vivre ainsy demprunct ce qui maffoiblit tous les jours et noz voisins se renforcissent.

58   Aleksandra LUBLINSKAYA, *Documents pour servir à l'histoire des guerres civiles en France* (1561–65), (1962), p.264; David POTTER, 'Les Allemands et les armées françaises au XVI Siècle. Jean-Philippe Rhingrave, chef de lansquenets Étude suivie de sa correspondance en France, 1548–1566', *Francia* (1995), XXI, ii, p.51. Trans.: *toutes choses sont cheres, que le soldat ne peult vivre de l'air, et ordonner pour nostre payement. Car là où la fain est, et necessité; il advient desordre. Le dommaige tumbera pour le service du roy et de vous, madame*, the Rhinegrave to Catherine de' Medici, 3 June 1563.

59   François de LA NOUE, *Mémoires*, cited in Jean de PABLO, 'L'Armée Huguenote entre 1562 et 1573', *Archiv für Reformationsgeschichte* (1957), Vol.XLVIII, pp.199–200. Trans.: *ils ne parlaient que de retourner chez eux quand les choses ne tournaient pas à leur fantasie.*

60   RYMER (ed.), *Foedera, op. cit.*, Vol.XVI, p.132, to Elizabeth I, 1591.

61   Antoine VARILLAS, *Histoire de Charles IX* (Paris, 1683), Vol.II, p.259. Trans.: *Les Anglois à la verité estoient si bien montez, que les chevaux de leurs Ecuyers ne cedoient ny pour la taille, ny pour la vigueur à ceux des Hommes-d'Armes Francois.*

62   Cited in John BLACK, *Elizabeth and Henry IV...* (1914), p.51.

63   H.M.C. *Salisbury MSS* (1899), Vol.VII, p.39, William Lilly to the Earl of Essex, 25 January 1597.

64   *Ibid.* p.38.

65   Robert DALLINGTON, *The View of Fraunce* (London, 1604, new edn 1936), n.p.

66   H.M.C. *Salisbury MSS* (1894), Vol.V, p.21, de Sancy to the Earl of Essex, 13/23 November 1594. Trans.: *Il y a long temps que j'ai proposé d'employer des Anglois au lieu de Suisses, tant pour la*

commodité que nous avons de remplir les compagnies, que pour ce qu'ils se laissent employer en toutes occasions, ce que ne font pas les Suisses.

67   H.M.C. *Salisbury MSS* (1889), Vol.III, p.113, Castelnau to Archibald Douglas, 24 October/3 November 1585. Trans.: *la Reine et déesse de la mer.*

68   Jean PASSERAT, *Chant d'Allegresse pour l'entree de … Prince Charles IX … en sa ville de Troie* (Troyes, 1564), f.3v. Trans.: *Puisse CHARLES un jour, l'aïant conquis en guerre,/A son frere donner le sceptre d'Angleterre./O dieus ô quelle joïe aura sur ses vieus ans/Quand la Mere verra tous deus Rois ses enfans?*

69   BNF Cinq Cents, Colbert MS 35, f.226v, cited in LA RONCIÈRE, *op. cit.*, Vol.IV, p.248. Trans.: *Vos vaisseaux? Mais vous vendez la peau de l'ours. Je sais bien que le roi n'en a pas.*

70   Rawdon BROWN and George BENTINCK (eds), *Calendar of State Papers…Venice* (London, 1890), Vol.VII, p.487.

71   *QEHT* (1838), Vol.I, p.125, Sir William Cecil to Sir Thomas Smith, 27 February 1563.

72   *CSPF* (1874), Vol.IX.

73   *L & A* (London, 1964), Vol. I, p.413, Sir Horatio Palavicino to Elizabeth I, 4 May 1590.

74   *Vous savez que l'argent est le principal nerf de la guerre*, cited in Hector de LA FERRIÈRE, *La Normandie à l'étranger* (1873), p.68, and Léon MARLET, *Le Comte de Montgomery* (Paris, 1890), p.24.

75   The authority is Frederick DIETZ, *English Public Finance, 1558–1641* (1932).

76   Trans.: *en l'absence du Roi, les fantassins, n'étant point soldés, se sont répandus dans les villages et ont abandonné leurs postes et tous leurs devoirs*, Charles de Zerotin (a Bohemian gentleman in the Royalist army), cited in LEON VAN DER ESSEN, *Alexandre Farnese…*, Vol.V, p.348.

77   *Cabala, op. cit.*, p.336, Sir Philip Sidney to Elizabeth I, n.d.

78   Trans.: *en estant allé d'aujourd huy desja v canonniers et les aultres officiers ne voulent servir sans argent*, Bernard BARBICHE and David BUISSERET (eds), *Oeconomies Royales de Sully* (Paris, 1970–88), Vol.II, p.1597.

79   Trans.: *si nos soldats n'ont de l'argent il ne s'assujettiront jamais aux tranchée et jeray très mal servy.*

80   Trans.: *furent faicts de grands larcins par les soldats mesmes sur les finances de S[a].M[ajesté]*. Claude CHASTILLON, *La Retraicte d'Albert Cardinal d'Austriche* (1597, single sheet with engraving). The fact that there were two simultaneous fires shows that this was not an accident.

81   'Journal of the Siege of Rouen, 1591' in *Camden Miscellany*, Vol.I (1847), p.51.

82   There were other more creative ways of increasing revenue. A lottery was held in London in 1569 to finance the renovation of the port (the first lottery had been in 1566).

83   DIETZ, *op.cit.*, p.17 (note).

84   Cited in Richard OUTHWAITE, 'Royal borrowing in the reign of Elizabeth I: the aftermath of Antwerp', *The English Historical Review* (1971), LXXXVI, p.255.

85   For a note on French money see David POTTER, *The French Wars of Religion Selected Documents* (1997), p.xiv. For a comparison of English money with that of Europe see Erkki KOURI, *England and the attempts to form a Protestant Alliance…* (Helsinki, 1981), p.200.

86   Trans.: *ung grand collier où y a douze grands diamans, celluy du millieu en poincte, les onze en table, dont l'ung pend, au bout du dict collier, avec trois grosses perles en poire et douze couplets de cordelliere d'or, garnie chascune cordelliere de huit perles, dont y a default de trois perles sur le tout; plus une bague à pendre d'ung gros ruby Ballai et une grosse perle en poire qui pend au bout*, LA FERRIÈRE (ed.), *Le XVIe Siècle et les Valois…* (1879), p.245.

87   Trans.: *Item, le roy fut tenu de payer les reistres et estrangers, tant Allemans que Anglois, de l'argent que ledit sieur prince et ceux de la cause estoient tenus de leur*

payer, et de les renvoyer en leurs pays avec vivres pour eux et leurs chevaux. BOURQUIN (ed.), *op. cit.*, p.394.

88 Trans.: *le roy s'obligera seymesme, et ses heirs, le plus seurement que faire se poura, que le dict roy accordera a sa majestie, ses heirs et successeurs, par un escript autentiquement sele du grand seau de Fraunce, avant la descente en Normandie de ses dictes troupes, que sa majestie et ses commis recevront et cueilleront tout le profitt de touts sortes des tailles, taxes, coustumes, et droicts, qui porront rensir du dedans et des invirons de la ville de Roan et du Havre de Grace, par le noms des impositions, et domaine forraine, et des gabelles des sels, et par le nom des quatriesmes des vins, ou alcunes aulteres choses, ou d'aultres impositions, appelles les nouvelles impositions, pour l'entree des merchandises*, RYMER (ed.), *Foedera, op. cit.*, Vol.XVI, pp.102, 125–26; STEVENSON (ed.), *Correspondence of Sir Henry Unton* (1847), p.9.

89 Trans.: *Item, fault entendre que sa Majestie et ses commis commenceront a recevoir les dict comodites dans la dict ville de Rouen, ou Havre de Grace tout aussy tost que l'une ou l'autre sera reduict en l'obeissance du roy*, RYMER (ed.), *ibid.*; STEVENSON (ed.), *ibid.*

90 Cited by KERVYN DE LETTENHOVE, *Les Huguenots et les Gueux* (Bruges, 1883–85), Vol.IV (1884), p.359. Trans.: *au delà du Rhin ... c'est là que se sème le grain dont on fait le pain; mais le levain se trouve en Angleterre.*

91 Jean DUMONT (ed.), *Corps Universel Diplomatique* (The Hague, 1728), Vol.V, pt I, pp.211–15, the treaty of Blois: *Item. Est acordé, convenu, & conclu, que à celui des deux Confederez, que quelque Prince, Potentat, Communauté, ou autre quelconque auroit assailli par voie de fait hostilement, l'autre Confederé vendra à prix raisonnable, si sa commodité le porte, ou permettra être venduës & transportées hors son Roiaume, des Harquebuses, Morions, Corselets, Poudre*

à Canon, Boulets, Soulfre, Salpétre, & autres semblables choses, qui servent pour repousser les Ennemis.

92 For an interesting insight into the complicated system of measures used in the lead industry see Michael GILL and William HARVEY, 'Weights and Measures used in the Lead Industry', *British Mining* (1998), LXI, pp.129–40.

93 Culverins weighed around 4,500 lbs.

94 William BOURNE, *The Arte of Shooting in Great Ordnaunce* (1578, 1587), ii, p.74. The figures given by William Harrison writing on the defence of England differ slightly: cannon 44 lbs, culverin 18 lbs, falcon 5 lbs. See Albert POLLARD, *Tudor Tracts* (London, 1903), p.399.

95 Trans.: *jusques à six mil habitz composez de chausses et mandilles pour noz gens de guerre*, letter of 26 November 1597, cited in Pierre LAFFLEUR DE KERMAINGANT, *Mission de Jean de Thumery Sieur de Boissise (1598–1602)* (Paris, 1886), p.3.

96 1 ell (French *aune*) = 45 inches.

97 *APC* (1899) Vol.XVIII, p.133 (22 September).

98 See, for example, *CSPD* (1867), Vol.III, pp.385, 393.

99 *Ibid.*, p.491.

100 Paul HUGHES and James LARKIN (eds), *Tudor Royal Proclamations* (New Haven, 1969), Vol.III, p.78 (Proclamation of 14 April 1591).

101 *QEHT* (1838), Vol.I, p.426 (Sir Francis Walsingham to Lord Burghley, 25 July 1572). This letter does not appear in Dudley DIGGES (ed.), *Mémoires et Instructions pour les Ambassadeurs* (Amsterdam, 1700).

102 Philip YORKE (ed.), *Miscellaneous State Papers/Hardwicke Papers* (1778), Vol. I, p.215 (Sir Edward Stafford to Elizabeth I, 26 December 1583).

103 Geoffrey BUTLER (ed.), *The Edmondes Papers* (1913), p.210 (Lord Burghley to Sir Thomas Edmondes, 23 January 1595).

104 Henri, duc de Guise (1549–1588), leader of the *Ligue* 1576–88. Assassinated on the orders of Henri III at Blois.

105 Charles de Lorraine, duc de Mayenne (1554–1611), leader of the *Ligue* 1588–95.

106 H.M.C. *Salisbury MSS* (1892), Vol.IV.

107 Edmund SAWYER (ed.), *Memorials of Affairs of State in the reigns of Queen Elizabeth and King James I* (London, 1725, 1972), p.97 (Sir Robert Cecil to Sir Henry Neville, 1599).

108 Emmanuel College, Cambridge, ECP 19, unknown artist (see p. 93).

109 STEVENSON (ed.), *op. cit.*, p.14.

110 For the original of this map see BNF Res. Ge B 8814.

111 British Library, Additional MS 62540. The map is quite small: 21.2 x 30.9 cm. Its size, as well as the three vertical folds, indicate that it was a 'portable' map.

112 British Library Cotton MS Augustus I.ii.62.

113 British Library Cotton MS Augustus I.i.14.

114 See for example, TNA SP 70/42. f.200, map in pen and ink of around 1562 showing parts of Normandy and Picardy. Rouen is in the centre.

115 British Library, Augustus I.ii.58 (see pp. 96–97).

116 RYMER (ed.), *Foedera, op. cit.*, Vol. XVI p.124 (24 September 1591).

117 Hakluyt was the author of *Principal Navigations, Voyages and Discoveries of the English Nation* (London, 1589), revised (1598–1600) in 3 vols.

118 Trans.: *Elle ne fut pas guerrière; mais elle sçût si bien former des Guerrièrs*, Pierre-Joseph d'ORLEANS, *Histoire des Revolutions d'Angleterre* (Paris, 1693), Vol. II, p.459; cited in DIGGES (ed.), *op. cit.*, pp.571–72.

119 Guise had taken Calais in 1558.

120 *Hommes Illustres et Grands Capitaines François* in *Oeuvres Complètes* (Paris, 1842), p.559.

121 See Appendix XI.

122 *CSPD* (1869), Vol. IV, p.435 (Elizabeth I to Sir Arthur Savage, 8 June 1597).

123 Christopher HAIGH, *Elizabeth I* (London, 1988), p.138.

124 Thomas Howard, 3rd Duke of Norfolk (1473–1554).

125 John HAYWARD, *Annals of the First Four Years of the Reign of Queen Elizabeth* (London, 1840), p.100.

126 HOLINSHED, *The Chronicles of England...* (1577, new edn 1807), Vol.IV, p.223.

127 TNA SP70/49 f.87r. (Earl of Warwick to Lord Robert Dudley, 23 January 1563).

128 This letter leads us to another portrait, that of Sir Robert Dudley, attributed to Steven van der Meulen, at Waddesdon Manor (Rothschild Collection). Warwick refers to him sending Dudley 'ye best settere in all France'.

129 The Ashmolean Museum, Oxford, possesses a portrait of Clinton dating from 1562 (WA1845.4).

130 Anne DUFFIN, 'Clinton, Edward Fiennes de, first earl of Lincoln (1512–1585)', *ODNB* (2008–).

131 Reginald MARSDEN (ed.), *Select Pleas in the Court of Admiralty...* (London, 1897), p.128.

132 Several portraits exist including that at Drummond Castle, Tayside, attributed to Hieronymus Custodis; Grimsthorpe Castle, Lincolnshire, artist unknown.

133 Sir Roger Williams to the Privy Council, 17 April 1591, cited in John EVANS (ed.), *The Works of Sir Roger Williams* (1590, new edn 1972), p.xliv.

134 *L & A* (1964), Vol.I, p.252.

135 EVANS (ed.), *op. cit.* (1590, new edn 1972), p.41.

136 *Sir John Norreys and the Elizabethan Military World* (1997), p.241.

137 'Journal of the Siege of Rouen, 1591' in *Camden Miscellany*, Vol.I (1847), p.44.

138 Pierre PALMA-CAYET, *Chronologie Novenaire* (Paris, 1838), p.299; Christopher LLOYD, *The Rouen Campaign* (1973), p.110. Trans.: *Quand à la personne dudit comte d'Essex et de ceux de sa suitte, il ne se pouvoit rien voir de plus magnifique, car, entrant dans Compiegne, il avoit devant luy six pages montez sur de grands chevaux, habillez de velours orangé tout en broderie d'or, et luy avoit une casaque de velours orangé toute couverte de pierreries; la selle, la bride, et le reste du harnois de son cheval accommodé de mesme; son habit et la parure de son cheval valoient seuls plus*

de soixante mil escus: il avoit douze grands estaffiers, et six trompettes qui sonnoient devant luy.

139 John CLAPHAM (Conyers READ, ed.), *Elizabeth of England* (Philadelphia, 1951), p.94.

140 STEVENSON (ed.), *op. cit.*, p.3 (instructions to Sir Henry Unton).

141 A number of portraits of Norris have survived. The best of these remains relatively unknown, in a private collection (see p. 106). The doublet worn by Norris is similar, if not identical, to that worn by Sir Francis Vere in a portrait currently on loan to the National Portrait Gallery, London. There is an inferior copy of this portrait at Knole House in Kent. Reproduced in Garrett MATTINGLY, *The Defeat of the Spanish Armada* (London, 1960), facing p.304. An engraving of around 1630 was also made after this portrait, which shows his wound received during his campaigning in the Low Countries. *QEHT* (1838), Vol. II, p.156 (Christopher Hoddesdon to ? 15 October, 1581). To this list we must also add the statue of Norris to be found in Westminster Abbey. Reproduced in Alfred ROWSE, *The England of Elizabeth* (London, 1953), facing p.64.

142 See the table on pp. 24–25.

143 These obligations were confirmed by the statute of 1558.

144 Charles CRUICKSHANK, *Elizabeth's Army* (1966), Appendix 3, p.291; *APC* (1902), Vol.XXVI, p.194 (23 September 1596).

145 There is one absence, the Irish soldiers known as the *Kern*, who had served in previous campaigns in France. See Dean WHITE, 'Henry VIII's Irish Kern in France and Scotland, 1544–1545', *Irish Sword* (1958,) III, pp.213–25.

146 The real drain on the English army was Ireland: 38,992 men were sent there.

147 The protests were aimed against the new *Book of Common Prayer*. Exeter was besieged for six weeks.

148 British Library Cotton MS Augustus I.ii.90 (see p. 164).

149 *L & A* (1964), Vol.I, p.331. Though the exchange of orders among sovereigns was acceptable, Elizabeth was less keen on seeing her own subjects being rewarded by others. Anthony Sherley was made a knight of the order of St-Michel by Henri IV during Sir Robert Sidney's special embassy of 1593. The English authorities were concerned about the oath that Sherley had sworn to Henri. He was consequently sent to the Fleet prison in London – the law of precedent did not help him. Whereas Burgh had been honoured by a Protestant king, Sherley was knighted by a Catholic. Sherley gained his release and was allowed to retain his title, though he did have to return the regalia. The same destiny awaited Sir Nicholas Clifford. He wore an order presented by Henri at court. Elizabeth, discontented that he had not sought her permission, told him, 'My dogs wear my collars!' Before giving the Order of St George to François de Montmorency in 1572, she first asked permission from the French king.

150 Cleveland Museum of Art, USA, 1926.554.

151 Roger ASCHAM, *Toxophilus* (London, 1545, new edn Manchester, 1985), p.5.

152 Given that there are 24 arrows in a sheaf.

153 *Toxophilus, op. cit.*, p.89.

154 John STOW, *A Survey of London* (London, 1599), p.77.

155 See the engraving of Robert Devereux by Thomas Cockson, in Penry WILLIAMS, *The Later Tudors* (Oxford, 1995), plate 6; Roy STRONG, *Gloriana* (London, 2003), p.33.

156 Trans.: *les Anglois … nous vindrent sur minuit donner une escalade, mais ils sentent si dru les pepins de grenade … plouvoir dessus leur dos. Discours Veritable de ce qui s'est fait et passé durant le siege de Rouën* (Paris, 1592), p.10.

157 HUGHES and LARKIN (eds), *Tudor Royal Proclamations* (1969), Vol.II, pp.74, 191, 282, 462.

158 The drums themselves could be quite large. The famous 'Drake's drum' at Buckland Abbey near Plymouth, made of ash, has a diameter of 24 inches and a depth of 21 inches.

159 H. OAKES-JONES, 'The old march of the English Army', *Journal of the Society for Army Historical Research* (1927), VI, pp.7–8; Maurice BYRNE, 'The English March and Early Drum Notation', *The Galpin Society Journal* (1997), L, pp.43–80.

160 William BYRD (Hilda ANDREWS, ed.), *My Lady Nevells Book* (London, 1926): 'The Marche before the Battell', 'The Marche of Footemen', 'The March of Horsmen', 'The Irish Marche' and 'The Marche to the Fighte'. This music was recently interpreted on a virginal muselar by Davitt Moroney.

161 A number of Italians had worked in England since the reign of Henry VIII.

162 See pp. 244–45.

163 HOLINSHED, *op. cit.*, Vol.IV, p.208.

164 KNIGHTON (ed.), *CSPD* (London, 1998), p.209 (10 February 1555–56).

165 RYMER (ed.), *Foedera, op. cit.*, Vol.XVI, p.138 (Sir William Cecil to Sir Henry Unton, 1 December 1591).

166 Roger ASCHAM, *The Scholemaster* (London, 1570, new edn 1932), p.64.

167 John HALE (ed.), *On a Tudor Parade Ground: The Captain's Handbook of Henry Barrett 1562* (London, 1978), p.27.

168 H.M.C. *Salisbury MSS* (1895), Vol.VI, p.523 (Sir John Aldrich to the Earl of Essex, 13 December 1596).

169 Estimates of tonnage varied, because of varying methods of calculation as well as changes to the ships themselves. In one list, the *Aid* appears as a ship of 180 tonnes.

170 The Ashmolean Museum, Oxford (WA1845.4)

171 See Patrick FORBES (ed.), *A Full View of the Public Transactions...* (1740–41), p.104.

172 H.M.C. *Salisbury MSS* (1899, Vol.VII, p.250.

173 Rye harbour has changed considerably due to silting. For an interpretation of its harbour in the sixteenth century see Graham MAYHEW, *Tudor Rye* (Falmer, 1987), p.263. For charts of Rye and the coast see British Library Cotton MS

Augustus I.ii.6; The National Archives (TNA), MPF 3; 'John Prowze', map of Rye Harbour, 1572/1595? The National Archives (TNA), MPF 1/212; Philip Symondson, chart of Rye, Romney & Walland Marshes, 1594 (Rye).

174 Francis MARES (ed.), *The Memoirs of Robert Carey* (1972), p.12.

175 Charles CRUICKSHANK, *The organisation and administration of the Elizabethan foreign military expeditions 1585–1603*, Oxford PhD (1940), Abstract, p.11.

176 See: HOLINSHED, *op. cit.*, Vol.IV, p.210.

177 Emmanuel VAN METEREN, *A True Discourse Historicall...* (1602, new edn 1968), pp.119–20.

178 Lord Willoughby to Sir Francis Walsingham, 14 November 1589; see Georgina BERTIE, *Five Generations of a Loyal House* (1845), p.278.

179 BIRCH, *Memoirs…* (1754), Vol.I, p.88 (Captain Francis Goad to Bacon, October 1592).

180 RYMER (ed.), *Foedera, op. cit.*, Vol.XVI, p.115 (Lord Burghley, 18 August 1591).

181 GUINEMENT DE KERALIO, *op. cit.* (1788), Vol.V, p.458 (Elizabeth I to Henri IV, 27 July 1591). Trans.: *j'…ose promettre que nos sujets y sont de si bonne disposition, & ont les cœurs si vaillants, qu'ils vous feront services qui vous ruineront beaucoup d'ennemis … je vous demande ces deux requestes: la première, que leur vie est sans vous soyent si à cœur que rien ne soit omis pour leur regard; ains qu'ils soyent chéris comme qui servent non comme mercénaires, mais franchement de bonne affection; aussi qu'ils ne portent le faix de trop violents hazards.*

182 British Library, Stowe MS 166 (Edmondes Papers, Vol.I), f.64 (23 September 1593).

183 BUTLER (ed.), *op. cit.*, p.186.

184 COLLINS (ed.), *Letters and Memorials of State* (1746), Vol.I, p.344 (22 August 1595).

185 British Library, Stowe MS 166 (Edmondes Papers), Vol.I, f.299 (Sir Robert Cecil to Sir Thomas Edmondes, 31 March 1596).

186 Trans.: *il vaut mieux, pour le service du Roi, que le duc de Lorraine prenne la*

place par force, que si le Roi l'engageoit à un prince étranger, quel qu'il fût, parce que le Roi est obligé de conserver, autant qu'il est en lui, la monarchie en son entire; qui leur faisoit pareille demande. Gabriel-Henri GAILLARD (ed.), 'Négociation de Mrs. de Bouillon et de Sancy, En Angleterre, en 1596 pour une ligue offensive & defensive contre l'Espagne', in *Notices et Extraits des Manuscrits de la Bibliothèque du Roi* (1789), Vol.II, p.121.

187   GAILLARD (ed.), *ibid.*, pp.121–22. Trans.: *si les Espagnols le prenoient, nous espérions le reprendre sur eux, & si nous le lui avions quitté, nous ne saurions par quel moyen le lui redemander; & quand nous le voudrions, nous l'offenserions, & au lieu d'un ennemi, nous en aurions deux.*

188   Trans.: *être mordu par un lion que par une lionne.* GAILLARD (ed.), *ibid.*, p.119. Another version given by Agostino Nani was that Henri 'wished to free himself first from the lion's paws, and then he could easily protect himself from the cat's claws'. Cited in Phyllis HANDOVER, *The Second Cecil...* (London, 1959), p.172.

189   Trans.: *où il vivoit à l'Alemande en attendant son payement.* François Eudes dit de MÉZERAY, *Abrégé chronologique ou extraict de l'histoire de France* (Paris, 1668), Vol.III, p.1119.

190   Guillaume VALDORY, *Relation du Siége de Rouen en 1591* (Rouen, 1592, new edn Rouen, 1871), pp.4v–5r.

191   See pp. 175–76.

192   Jean PASSERAT, *Chant d'Allegresse pour l'entree de Tres-Chrestien ... Charles IX ... en sa ville de Troïe* (Paris, 1564).

193   *CSPF* (1867), Vol V, p.288 (The Governors of Rouen to Sir William Cecil, 8 September 1562); LA FERRIÈRE, *La Normandie à l'Étranger* (Paris, 1873), pp.13–14. Trans.: *laquelle nous préservera, s'il lui plaist, nous estans ces subjectz naturelz comme avons esté aultre foys.*

194   Trans.: *pour la gloire de Dieu et la délivrance de la minorité du roi.*

      Alphonse de RUBLE, *Le Traité de Cateau-Cambrésis* (1889), p.169, who cites BNF MS français 15877, f.189.

195   BOURQUIN (ed.), *op. cit.*, p.343. Trans.: *Dudit mont Sainte Katherine on descouvre et veoit-on par toute les rues dudit Rouen.*

196   John COLLIER (ed.), *Old ballads, from early printed copies* (London, 1840), pp. 42–45.

197   François de LA NOUE, *Discours Politiques et Militaires* (Basle, 1587, new edn Geneva, 1967), Discours XXVI p.650. Trans.: *Mais par la resistance que fit le fort de saincte Catherine, qui defendoit la montagne, ils cognurent qu'il y auroit de l'affaire à chasser les pigeons de ce colombier. Il y avoit dedans avec le Conte de Montgommery sept ou huit cens soldats des vieilles bandes, & enseignes Angloises, commandees par le Seigneur Kilgré qui firent tous merveilleux devoir.*

198   TNA SP70/42 f.5. This may have been translated by Ambrose Dudley, Earl of Warwick, October 1562: *A Renard dormant il ne tumbe rien en la gorge.* Warwick and the editor, Joseph Stevenson, translate *armes* in the French text as 'armour'. *CSPF* (1869), Vol.VI, p.332.

199   Born in 1157, Richard died at the siege of the castle of Châlus in 1199.

200   As at Leith in 1560, the sight of Englishmen fighting side by side with Scotsmen was something of a novelty. Union between the two countries would not be established until 1603. It could be claimed that the 'British' Army already existed. The Welsh had long been integrated into it; the Irish also served alongside Englishmen in Ireland and fought at the siege of Boulogne in 1544. See the Cowdray engraving. Later, in 1594, both English and Scots took part in the siege of Groningen in the Netherlands. British Library, Cotton MS Augustus I.ii.93.

201   *Il y fut tué un Cappitaine Anglois estimé en matiere de Sappe, qui fut extremement regretté.* Agrippa D'AUBIGNÉ, *Histoire Universelle* (new edn 1982), Vol.II, p.145.

202 HOLINSHED, *op. cit.*, Vol.IV, p.209. See also *QEHT* (1838), Vol.I, p.119, note.

203 Claude-Bernard PETIOT (ed.), *Mémoires de Castelnau* (Paris, 1823), p.482. Trans.: *que l'on ne pouvait abandonner sans mettre le pays à la mercy des Anglois.*

204 BRANTÔME (Jean BUCHON, ed.), *Oeuvres Complètes...* (Paris, 1842), Vol.I, p.696.

205 Bibliothèque de l'Institut de France, Godefroy MS 257, f.197v (Brissac to Catherine de' Medici, 18 June 1563).

206 Jean NAGEREL, *Description du Pays et Duché de Normandie...* (Rouen, 1573). Trans.: *.imprenable pour estre en lieu maresquageux, non commandé de montaignes, autant bien remparé que ville qui soit.*

207 TNA S.P. 70/42, printed in Patrick FORBES (ed.), *A Full View of the Public Transactions...* (1741), p.104.

208 TNA SP 70/49 f.27v.

209 *Ibid.*

210 *Ibid.*

211 *Ibid.*

212 A seventeenth-century plan of Le Havre shows the names later given to the bastions of Fort Warwick: Bastions Royal, Richelieu, St-Jean and de la Reine. BNF (Cartes & Plans), Ge.D. 2208.

213 *Mémoires de Vieilleville* (Paris, 1866), p.349. Trans.: *car les Anglois, se fyants en ceste profondeur de mer, avoient negligé de remparer ceste muraille, qui estoit très foible.*

214 *CSPF* (1869), Vol.VI, p.48 (Harry King to Sir Thomas Chaloner, 16 January 1563).

215 HOLINSHED, *op. cit.*, Vol.IV, p.214.

216 LA FERRIÈRE (ed.), *Lettres de Catherine de Médicis* (1885), Vol.II, p.26 (27 April 1563). Trans.: *de sorte que nous en puissions avoir de trente à quarante bons pour faire une furieuse bapterie.*

217 Musée National de la Renaissance (EC17); Musée du Louvre (OA 694 6).

218 LA FERRIÈRE (ed.), *op. cit.* (1885), Vol. II, p.65 (note). Trans.: *Si nous laissons l'entreprise du Havre, sommes en danger de perdre le royaume, car la perte du Havre emporte la perte de la Normandie.*

219 LA FERRIÈRE (ed.), *ibid.*, p.54 (10/15 June, 1563). Trans.: *considérant voz petites forces, et qu'ilz sont aussi fortz dedans la ville comme vous estes dehors et qu'il leur seroit aysé, ayant moyen d'estre renforcez par la mer, d'entreprendre quelque chose sur le peu d'hommes que vous avez, cela me faict vous prier et presser bien fort de ne venir point à ces grosses escarmouches, mays tenir ung peu bride jusqu'à ce que les Suisses que je vous envoye.*

220 *Discours au vray de la reduction du Havre de Grace en l'obeissance du Roy* (Paris, 1563), p.9.

221 LA FERRIÈRE (ed.), *La Normandie à l'Étranger* (1873), p.167; *Lettres de Catherine de Médicis* (1885), Vol.II, p.69 (13 July 1563).

222 BNF, MS français 10193, f.339v. Trans.: *Ilz sont souvent escarmouches, auxquelles les Anglois ont toutzjours eu du meilleur jusques a maintenant, car ilz ne sortent point moings de deux ou trois mil hommes et endommaigent grandement les François de leur artillerie.*

223 LUBLINSKAYA (ed.), *op. cit.*, p.246 (Richelieu to Catherine de' Medici, 27 May 1563). Trans.: *ilz ont perdu beaucoup de gens ... et entre aultres ont perdu ung de leurs cappitaines de quevallerye (nous avons prins son cheval qui est fort bien dore).*

224 LA FERRIÈRE, *La Normandie à l'Étranger* (1873), p.156.

225 British Library, Cotton MS Augustus I.ii.78a.

226 *CSPF* (1869), Vol.VI, p.455 (Elizabeth I to the Earl of Warwick, 16 July 1563).

227 Ambroise PARÉ, *Les Œuvres d'Ambroise Paré* (Paris, 1585, new edn Bièvres, 1969), Vol.III, p.1237. Trans.: *Lors qu'on faisoit les approches pour asseoir l'artillerie, les Anglois qui estoyent dedans, tuerent quelques-uns de nos soldats, & plusieyrs pionniers qui gabionnoyent, lesquels, lors qu'on voyoit estre tant blessez qu'il n'y avoit nulle esperance de guarison, leurs compagnons les despouilloyent, & les mettoyent encore vivans dedans les gabions, qui leur servoyent d'autant de remplage.*

228 *Mémoires de Vieilleville* (Paris, 1866), p.351.

229 François DE LA TREILLE, *Discours des villes, chasteaux, et forteresses batues, assaillies & prises, par la force de l'Artillerie durant les regnes des treschrestiens Roys Henry second, & Charles IX* (Paris, 1563).

230 George BENTINCK and Rawdon BROWN (eds), *Calendar of State Papers... Venice...* (1890), Vol.VII, p.364 (Marc'Antonio Barbaro to the Signory, 29 July 1563).

231 Ambroise PARÉ, 'Apologie, et traicté contenant les voyages faicts en divers lieux', in *op. cit.*, Vol.III, pp.1237–38. Trans.: *Les Anglois voyans qu'ils ne pourroyent soustenir un assaut, parce qu'ils estoyent fort attaints de maladies, & principalement de la peste, ils se rendirent bagues sauves. Le Roy leur feit bailler des vaisseaux pour s'en retourner en Angleterre, bien joyeux d'estre hors de ce lieu infecté de peste.*

232 De THOU, *Histoire Universelle...* (1734), Vol.IV, p.542. Trans.: *selon l'usage des Anglois, on présenta à ceux de nos François, qui s'étoient avancés jusqu'aux retranchements des ennemis, des brocs d'argent pleins de vin, & l'on but abondamment à la santé les uns des autres.*

233 PARÉ, 'Apologie', *op. cit.*, Vol.III, p.1238. Trans.: *lesquels n'avoyent nulle peur de la peste & furent bien joyeux d'y entrer, esperans y faire bonne chere.* Paré ends his account of his experience at Le Havre, *Mon petit Maistre, si vous y eussiez esté, vous eussiez faict comme eux* ('My dear Master, if you had been there you would have done the same'.)

234 Printed in *Mémoires de Condé* (London & Paris, 1743), Vol.V, p.4 (BNF MS français, 3243, f.39). Trans.: *Les ditz soldatz ont depuys ladicte réduction, non obstant ladicte peste, ravy & pillé tous les meubles qui restoient par la fuyte des ditz Angloys; & non contens de ce, destruisent journellement & bruslent le maryen, boys & fenestres des dictes maisons; voire en la présence des Bourgois mesmes qui ne les peuvent empescher.*

235 Bibliothèque de l'Institut de France, Godefroy MS 257, f.195r. Trans.: *A juste raison pourra le Roy Treschrestien pour ce coup cy s'attribuer et dire de soy mesme ces motz et parolles de Jules Caesar: Veni, Vidi, Vici. Et votre Majesté celles du prophete Isaye: Honorem Meum Alteri Non Dabo, dont tous les amys de ceste couronne et les affectionnez serviteurs de voz Majestez se doibvent resjouyr: et moy plus que tous les aultres, pour estre ministre de qui je le suis* (1 August 1563).

236 pp.111–12.

237 Henri de LA POPELINIÈRE, *La Vraye et Entiere Histoire des Troubles...* (La Rochelle, 1573), p.335v. Trans.: *Le Baron de Garde ... choisit l'Anglois lequel il tasche d'environner de tous costez par ses galleres, qui le salvent de telles & telles cannonades, qu'elles le percent à jour. L'Anglois se met à la voile ... & quant ayant rangé toutes ses pieces d'un costé, les descharge en mesme temps sur une des galleres. Puis les affustant sur l'autre bande, retourne court, & avec traits caillous, & harquebuzades qu'il faisoit pleuvoir du haut des hunes, cependant il recharge sur celle qui le poursuyvoit de plus pres, de laquelle il rompt les rames, bancs & tout ce qui se presenta au devant. Mais il ne fut plustost hors de ceste presse qu'il veit les quatres autres qui le venoyent derechef saluer, tellement qu'apres la save ils ramoyent à toutes forces pour l'aborder & enclorre, le sommant de se rendre. A quoy l'Anglois ne respondoit qu'à coups d'artillerie, de harquebuze.*

238 The cost of maintaining two ships for two months in 1592 was £298 5s. *CSPD* (1867), Vol.III, p.243.

239 Houghton was also responsible for collecting customs duties in London. He was named Sheriff in London in 1593.

240 British Library, Cotton MS Augustus I.ii.80. Attributed to Jacques de Goyon, comte de Matignon.

241 BNF Cinq Cents, Colbert MS 31, ff.557r–558r.

242 The French expedition to the Isle of Wight gives an idea of galley tactics. See Martin Du BELLAY, *Les Mémoires de Mess. Martin Du Bellay Seigneur de Langey* (Paris, 1572), pp.340r–345v. Blaise de Monluc refuses to comment upon the French fleet during this period: 'our deeds are better on land than on water, where I know not that our nation has ever won any great battles' (*nostre fait est plus propre sur la terre que sur l'eau, où je ne sçay pas que nostre nation ait jamais gagné de grandes batailles*). *Commentaires* (new edn, Paris, 1964), p.179.

243 See Claude de SAINLIENS, *A Dictionarie French and English* (London, 1593).

244 Tom GLASGOW, in 'List of Ships in the Royal Navy from 1539–1588', *The Mariner's Mirror* (1970), Vol.LVI, No.1, p.304, suggests that this could be a vessel dating from 1538.

245 Reproduced in Charles ONIONS (ed.), *Shakespeare's England: An Account of the Life & Manners of his Age* (Oxford, 1962), p.147.

246 For Willoughby's journal see British Library, Additional MS 4155, ff.57–67.

247 BNF (Cartes & Plans), Ge.DD.627, pl.78 (see pp. 240–41). For a modern plan of the battle see Robert KNECHT, *The French Civil Wars* (2000), p.244 (error at foot of page).

248 Cited by LA RONCIÈRE, *op. cit.*, Vol.IV, p.221. Trans.: *vestuss comme les figures de l'antiquité, avec jacques de maille et casques de fer, couverts de drap noir comme bonnet de presbtre.*

249 Staatliche Museen, Berlin (Kupferstichkabinett).

250 CAMDEN, *Annals…*, p.387.

251 BERTIE, *op. cit.*, p.271. Trans.: *Madame, que jy aye esté sy veurtueusement servy de vos troupes, et avec tant de preuves de sage conduite et valeur du Baron de Willeby, dignement secondée aussy de tous les autres jantyshommes vos sigets* (Henri IV to Elizabeth I, *c.*5 November 1589). Note the spelling of the word *sigets* here – probably a reference to Henri's accent from the south-west of France.

252 CAMDEN, *Annals…*, p.398.

253 RYMER (ed.), *Foedera, op. cit.*, Vol. XVI, p.98. Trans.: *le Sire Roger Wylemes montra sa Valleur, par le bon devoir qu'yl y feyt avec sa trouppe, de sorte que la Vyctoyre ce peut propremant dyre entre vostre byen* (Henri IV to Elizabeth I, 3 June 1591).

254 RYMER (ed.), *Foedera, op. cit.*, Vol.XVI, p.118 (Elizabeth I to Sir Henry Unton, 22 August 1591).

255 Guillaume VALDORY, *Relation du Siége de Rouen en 1591* (Rouen, 1592, new edn Rouen, 1871), pp.4v–5r.

256 Rachael POOLE, 'A Journal of the Siege of Rouen in 1591', *The English Historical Review* (1902), Vol.XVII, p.530.

257 British Library Cotton MS Augustus I.ii.90 (see p. 164).

258 TNA SP 9/200 46 (MPF 153). See pp. 166–67.

259 Walter DEVEREUX, *Lives and Letters of the Devereux, Earls of Essex* (London, 1853), Vol.I, p.245 (3 October 1591).

260 F.H. MARES (ed.), *The Memoirs of Robert Carey* (1972), p.15.

261 BNF (Estampes), Collection Lallemant de Betz, Vx 23 f.14 rés.

262 See note 256.

263 British Library, Cotton MS Augustus I.ii.91 (see p. 168).

264 'Journal of the Siege of Rouen, 1591' in *Camden Miscellany*, Vol.I (1847), pp.43–44.

265 BARBICHE and BUISSERET (eds), *op. cit.*, Vol.I, p.283. Trans.: *fort foible en de certains endroicts, et par censequent fort facile a prendre.*

266 British Library, Cotton MS Augustus I.ii.89. The fortifications were improved in 1595 with stone from the demolished church. A decree was made in 1597 for the demolition of the fort.

267 *L & A* (1980), Vol.III, p.225 (Sir Henry Unton to Lord Burghley, 3 December 1591).

268 *Coq a l'asne fort* (Paris, 1592), extract.

269 BARBICHE and BUISSERET (eds), *op. cit.*, Vol.I, p.286. Trans.: *apres un combat de deux heures durant, ou l'on dit que les*

Anglois firent des merveilles, ilz en furent enfin chassez, laissant plus de cinquante des leurs morts ou pris et la trenchee perdue pour le Roy.

270 BARBICHE and BUISSERET (eds), *ibid.*, p.287. Trans.: *la noblesse d'Angleterre, qui avoit insisté d'avoir la pointe, et fustes sy vaillamment assistez par les mousquetaires, picquiers et hallebardiers anglois, que, les ennemis estonnez d'un tant impeteux assaut faict en tant de divers endroicts, qu'ilz quitterent tout et fillerent vers le fort... et furent les tranchees regangnees en demie heure. Dans lesquelles les Anglois se logerent sy fortement, et se tindrent tousjours depuis sy bien sur leurs armes, qu'il fut non seullement impossible aux ennemis de les desloger, mais aussy empescher qu'ilz ne s'advançassent vers les contre-escarpes de leurs ravelins.*

271 H.M.C. *Salisbury MSS* (1892), Vol.IV, p.212 (extract from a song dated 22 June 1592).

272 Cited in Auguste POIRSON, *Histoire du Règne de Henri IV* (Paris, 1856), p.120.

273 BARBICHE and BUISSERET (eds), *op. cit.*, p.283. Cited in POIRSON, *op. cit.*, Vol.I, p.120. Trans.: *.il faisoit toutes choses par despit et ne vouloit nullement que sa ville se prist.*

274 Louis LEGER, 'Le Siége de Rouen par Henri IV d'après les documents tchèques', *Revue Historique* (1878), VII, p.72.

275 H.M.C. *Salisbury* MSS (1892), Vol.IV, p.196. Trans.: *je nay moyan dampescher quils ne ce remetent, sur ce que je ne puys sans layde de la Reyne, madame ma bonne soeur, à laquelle sur cete ocasyon, jescrys ancores meyntenant pour le nouveau cecours dont je lay suplyee, donnant charge au Sieur de Beauvoyr, mon ambassadeur.*

276 Wemyss was the governor of St-Valery-sur-Somme until the capture of the town by Aumale on 28 October 1592.

277 Sir Roger Williams to Lord Burghley, 2 August 1592, cited in EVANS (ed.), *op. cit.*, p lxvi.

278 Trans.: *Si les Maritimes soyent perdus, comment garderez vous le* [*r*]*estre,*

do[*u*] *vient toute vostre ayde?* RYMER (ed.), *Foedera, op. cit.*, Vol. XVI, p.116 (Elizabeth I to Henri IV, August 1591).

279 Henri HAUSER, *François de La Noue* (Paris, 1892, new edn Geneva, 1970), pp.269–70. La Noue was highly regarded in England. His *Discours Politiques & Militaires* appeared in English in 1587 under the title *The Politicke and Militarie Discourses of the Lord de La Noue.*

280 De THOU, *op. cit.*, Vol.XI, p.520.

281 For a manuscript version see BNF MS français 5045 ff.368r–369r, *Discours de la défaitte des princes de Conti et de Dombes au siège de Craon en Bretagne, Mai 1592.*

282 According to De Thou, Wingfield had a force of 700 men. *Op. cit.*, p.527.

283 Urbain de Montmorency-Laval, seigneur de Boisdauphin (1557–1629). Made *maréchal de France* in 1597; he was governor of Anjou 1604–19.

284 *L & A* (1984), Vol.IV, p.255. De Thou mentions 200 *Ligueurs* dead in one encounter. La Guerche is perhaps the site as, according to Camden, they suffered heavy losses here. De THOU, *op. cit.*, Vol. XII, p.57; CAMDEN, *Annals...*, p.420.

285 Gaston DE CARNÉ (ed.), *Correspondance du Duc de Mercœur & des Ligueurs Bretons avec l'Espagne* (Rennes, 1899), Vol.2, p.33 (Archivo General de Simancas MS K1591).

286 See TNA SP 9/200 48 (MPF1/151).

287 BUTLER (ed.), *op. cit.*, p.192 (Burghley to Sir Thomas Edmondes, 27 November 1594).

288 Jean MOREAU, *Les Guerres de la Ligue en Bretagne* (new edn, Quimper, 1960), p.204. Trans.: *ceux qui tomboient entre les mains des François étoient humainement retenus prisonniers; mais les Anglois, ennemis jurés des Espagnols, ne pardonnoient pas à un seul, et, qui pis est, s'ils en voyaient quelques-uns prisonniers des François, ils se ruoient dessus et les tuoient entre leurs bras.*

289 BUTLER (ed.), *op. cit.*, p.186 (Sir John Norris to Sir Thomas Edmondes, 12 November 1594).

290 H.M.C. *Salisbury MSS* (1895), Vol.VI, p.85 (letter dated 16 March 1596). Trans.: *j'ay esté assuré par deux pataches … venants d'Espaigne, qu'il sy faisoit de grands preparatifs, tant de levee de gens de guerre que armée navalle, pour rebastir leur fort de Craodon et ung autre sur l'autre poincte du goulet à l'opposite, se deliberants par ung mesme tenir ceste place asiegée.… Vous pouvez juger que la perte de ceste place, tombante entre les mains de l'Espaignol, est non moings de consequence à l'estat du royaume d'Angleterre qu'à celuy de la France.*

291 *Ibid.* (1895), Vol.VI, pp.54–55 (Villeroy, 25 January 1596). Trans.: *Je ne vous puis dire combien toute la France est offencee des froideurs d'Angleterre, et sur cela nous sommes pressez de touttes parts d'entendre a quelque accord.*

292 H.M.C. *Salisbury MSS* (1894), Vol.V, p.300 (Ottywell Smith to the Earl of Essex, 2 August 1595) and p.301 (Governor of Dieppe to the Earl of Essex, 12 August 1595). Trans.: *A quoy je vous supplie tres humblement, selon votre bonté accoustumée et pour l'affection que je vous ay tousjours recongneue porter au bien advancement de cet estat, de me vouloir ayderde votre autorité et faveur envers la dite Reine pour obtenir ma requeste, et que je puisse bientost avoir les dits gens de guerre.*

293 BNF, MS français 4014, f.164v. Trans.: *tesmoigner par toutes sortes decisions le contentement que nous retirons de leur venue.*

294 H.M.C. *Salisbury MSS* (1899), Vol.VII, p.39.

295 *Ibid.*, p.45 (letter to Sir Robert Cecil dated 29 January 1597).

296 H.M.C. *Salisbury MSS* (1895), Vol.VI, p.66 (Captain Wilton to the Earl of Essex, 2 March 1597).

297 H.M.C. *Salisbury MSS* (1899), Vol.VII, p.30 (letter dated 20 January 1597).

298 *APC* (1902), XXVI, p.244. See Appendix XI.

299 *Discours Touchant la Prise Admirable de la Grande et Puissante Ville d'Amiens …*
par les Espagnols… (Antwerp, 1597). Trans.: *les uns estoyent a l'eglise & la plus part des cytoyens dormoyent encore à la Francoyse, comme on dict communement.*

300 H.M.C. *Salisbury MSS* (1899), Vol.VII, p.127. Trans.: *La perte d'Amyens a renversé tous mes desayns. Je faysays estat d'assayllyr mon annemy et commancer des le moys d'Avryl, mes il faut que je cherche la defancyve.* Note that the accent of the south-west of France re-appears once more: *defancyve.*

301 Albéric de CALONNE, *Histoire de la Ville d'Amiens* (Amiens, 1900), p.188, citing BNF, MS français 3464. Trans.: *Je suis trop faible pour résister à la puissance de l'ennemy fortifié en la puissance qu'il a acquis.*

302 H.M.C. *Salisbury MSS* (1899), Vol.VII, p.176 (Henri IV to Elizabeth I, 6 May 1597). Trans.: *Ma chute attirera la votre, car notre ennemi est insatiable.*

303 BIRCH, *Memoirs…* (1754), Vol.II, p. 323.

304 Pierre MATTHIEU, *Histoire des derniers troubles de France…* (1600), V, p.69. Trans.: *Ce siege doit estre tenu pour un des plus grans et remarquables de nostre temps … principalement avec un incroyable et indicible travail au remuement de terres, si que ny leur grand nombre d'artillerie, ny la profondeur de leurs fossez, ny la force de la place n'ont peu empescher ny garder qu'on ne se soit logé pied à pied jusqe sur leur repart et ravelin.*

305 *CSPD* (1869), Vol.IV, p.405 (letter of 2 May 1597).

306 The photographs are reproduced in 'Aerial Reconnaissance in Picardy', *Antiquity* (1964), XXXVIII, pp. 113–19; 'Images du siège d'Amiens, 1597', *Terre Picarde* (1985), IX, pp. 32–40; 'La Poliorcétique revue d'avion. Le cas du siège d'Amiens par Henri IV, 1597', *Revue d'Archéologie moderne et d'archéologie générale* (1986), IV, pp. 15–32.

307 British Library, Cotton MS Augustus I.ii.86 (81 x 58 cm) (see pp. 188–89). Reproduced in David BUISSERET, *Henry*

IV (London, 1984), plate 10. For the key of the plan see TNA SP 78/40 f.78 r.

308   As does the painting by Peter Paul Rubens, *Henri IV de France au siège d'Amiens* (Göteborgs Konstmuseum). This painting had been commissioned by Marie de' Medici and was one of a series of twenty-four to hang in the Palais de Luxembourg in Paris. The series was never completed.

309   François Eudes dit de MÉZERAY, *Abrégé Chronologique ou Extraict de l'Histoire de France* (Paris, 1668), Vol.III, p.1317.

310   British Library, Cotton MS Augustus I.ii.86; TNA SP 78/40 f.78r.

311   Henrico DAVILA, *Les Guerres Civiles de France…* (Amsterdam, 1757), Vol.II, Bk XV, p.101. Trans.: *le regiment des Suisses & celui des Anglois se portoient avec plus d'activité que tous les autres; car à l'exception des regimens de Picardie & de Navarre, l'Infanterie Françoise étoit toute composée de nouvelles levées, qui n'étoient point à la fatigue des travaux, ni à camper en plein air.*

312   De THOU, *op. cit.*, Vol.XIII, p.115. Trans.: *Nous aurions succombé sous le grand nombre, si un régiment Anglois ne fût pas accouru à notre secours.*

313   TNA SP 78/40 f.14 (Sir Arthur Savage [to Sir Robert Cecil], 9 July 1597), cited in BUISSERET, *op. cit.*, p.66.

314   Agrippa d'AUBIGNÉ, *Histoire Universelle* (new edn Geneva, 1981–), Vol.IX, p.124.

315   Robert DALLINGTON, *The View of Fraunce* (London, 1604, new edn 1936), n.p.

316   Bibliothèque de l'Institut de France, MS Godefroy, 512 f.113r. Trans.: *que la Reine laisse les compagnies Angloises qui sont tres necessaires au siege et qu'il luy plaise les renforcer.*

317   Jean de SERRES, *Inventaire général de l'Histoire de France* (Paris, 1597), p.854. Trans.: *j'attens la continuation de la batterie de l'ennemy par trois costez. Les discours humains sont faillis, nostre esperance est en Dieu, & en la pressee venuë de V[otre] A[ltesse] pour donner bataille.*

318   TNA SP 78/40 f.74v.

319   DAVILA, *Les Guerres Civiles de France…* (1757), Vol.III, p.112. Trans.: *les François & les Anglois monterent à l'assaut de deux côtés, & se rendirent maîtres du ravelin. Mais la fatigue & point du jour, le Capitaine Durando les y attaqua avec vigueur, & les en delogea, tandis qu'on lançoit de dessus les remparts, quantité de feux d'artifice, & que les Mousquetaires du Capitaine Ollana faisoient en flanc un feu terrible.*

320   Bibliothèque Municipale d'Amiens, MS 2110. Trans.: *sans battre le tambour ny sonner les trompettes.*

321   Jules BERGER DE XIVREY (ed.), *Lettres Missives de Henri IV* (1848), Vol.IV, pp.847–48 (Henri IV to Elizabeth I, 19 September 1597). Trans.: *Madame, Dieu et le bonheur de vos anmes dont j'ay esté assisté m'ont rendu ma ville d'Amiens.… j'envoye au bon la Fontaine pour vous presenter, avec le discours veritable du succés de l'entreprinse faicte par le cardinal Albert pour la secourir, pour lequel je m'asseure que vous jugerés comme moy que, s'il est venu en soldat, il s'en est retourné en prestre. Ce fut le quinziesme qu'il arriva, et n'attendit le seize pour s'en retourner.… je desirerois fort qu'il voulust revenir pour decider en un coup toutes vos querelles et les miennes. Madame, comme vos prosperitez seront tousjours les miennes, je vous prie aussy estre contente que je me resjouisse avec vous de ceste victoire, au fruict de laquelle vous aurés tousjours telle part que Vostre plus humble frere et serviteur, HENRY.*

322   British Library, 9200.aa.5 in-8o.

323   George HARRISON (ed.), *De Maisse a Journal… 1597* (1931), p.121. For the articles of surrender see BNF MS français 4744 f.74, *Redition de la ville d'Amiens à sa Majesté le 25 Septembre 1597* (Lyons, 1597), pp.8–13. The capture of Amiens was reproduced by Ambroise Dubois in the Galerie d'Ulysse at Fontainebleau. Sylvie BÉGUIN, Jean GUILLAUME and Alain ROY, *La Galerie d'Ulysse à Fontainebleau* (Paris, 1985), p.105.

324 British Library Additional MSS 21117 f.26r., reproduced in BUISSERET, *op. cit.* (Paris, 2002), p.76.

325 TNA SP 70/42 f.25v (October 1562).

326 H.M.C. *Ancaster MSS* (Dublin, 1907), pp.289–91.

327 Michael OPPENHEIM, *A History of the Administration of the Royal Navy...* (London, 1896, 1988), p.125 (note 7).

328 Jules BERGER DE XIVREY (ed.), *Recueil des Lettres Missives de Henri IV* (1846), Vol. III, p.118 (Henri IV to Lord Willoughby, 14 January 1590).Trans.: *Monsr de Vileby, J'ay entendu du sr de Beuvron, qu'il y a quelques soldats anglois logez en sa maison de Beuvron, où ils ont faict plusieurs degastz et insolences: dont je suis malcontent, d'autant que le dict sr de Beuvron est l'un de mes speciaulx serviteurs, lequel me sert à present en mon armée avec sa compaignie de gens d'armes; qui me faict vous prier de donner ordre que les dicts soldats anglois deslogent incontinent de la maison et paroisses du dict sr de Beuvron, et qu'ils luy rendent et restituent les bestiaulx et autres commoditez qu'ils luy ont prins. Vous ferés en cela chose qui me sera trés agreable: et n'estant la presente à aultre effect, je prie Dieu, Monsr de Vileby, qu'il vous ayt en sa saincte garde. Du camp devant Lisieux, le xiiiie janvier, 1590. HENRY.*

329 BIRCH, *Memoirs...* (1754), Vol.II, p.2.

330 John DASENT (ed.), *Acts of the Privy Council* (London, 1902), Vol.XXVI, pp.244–47. See also Appendix XI.

331 This prayer was written for services on Sundays, Wednesdays and Fridays throughout the kingdom. STRYPE, *Annals of the Reformation...* (1735), Vol.I, p.283.

332 Thomas STERNHOLD, John HOPKINS and William WHITTINGHAM, *The Whole Book of Psalmes...* (London, 1578).

333 *CSPF* (London, 1867), Vol.V, p.408 (Sir Nicholas Throckmorton to Sir William Cecil, 30 October 1562), in Patrick FORBES, *A Full View of the Public Transactions...* (1741), Vol.II, p.156. Throckmorton did not yet know that Rouen had fallen.

334 p.16. See Appendix XII.

335 See Appendix XI.

336 'Brief discours des choses plus mémorables advenues en la Ville de Rouen, durant le Siege...' (Rouen, 1592), in *Mémoires de la Ligue, contenant les évenemens les plus remarquables depuis 1576, jusqu'à la Paix accordé entre le Roi de France & le Roi d'Espagne, en 1598* (Amsterdam, 1758), Vol.V, p.103. Trans.: *où furent commises des impiétés horribles, y aïant été par les Hérétiques le très Saint Sacrement de l'Autel foulé aux pieds, l'Extrême-Onction, & Lavoirs Baptismaux réduits en pure prophanation par les Anglois.*

337 RYMER (ed.), *Foedera, op. cit.,* Vol.XVI, p.103; STEVENSON (ed.), *op. cit.,* p.1.

338 *APC* (1893), Vol.VII, p.139 (to the Earl of Warwick, 10 August 1563).

339 TNA SP 78/40 f.38v.

340 *L & A* (1984), Vol.IV, p.214.

341 *L & A* (1969), Vol.II, p.335 (George Yate to William Meredith, Dieppe, 28 April/3 May 1591).

342 *L & A* (1964), Vol.I, p.330 (Henri IV to Beauvoir la Nocle & de Fresnes), [17]/27 December 1589.

343 *APC* (1902), Vol.XXVI, pp.216–17; TNA SP 70/42, 70/49; *L & A* (2000), Vol.VII, p.192; LA FERRIÈRE, *La Normandie à l'Étranger* (Paris, 1873), p.188, citing British Library, Egerton MS 742.

344 *APC* (1901), Vol.XXIV, p.420.

345 *APC* (1902), Vol.XXVI, pp.216–17; *L & A* (2000), Vol.VII, p.192.

346 Much of the information in this table can be found in TNA.

347 De THOU, *op. cit.,* Vol.XI, p.483. Trans.: *l'eau de la Seine qui couloit dans le voisinage, étant troublée par la marée n'étoit pas bonne à boire, & causoit des incommodités.*

348 1 tun (barrel) = 216 gallons: *c.*982 litres. *CSPF* (1867), Vol.V, p.338.

349 A quart = 1.14 litres; 2 quarts = 2.27 litres (4 pints).

350 *APC* (1899), Vol.XVIII, p.119.

351 'Journal of the Siege of Rouen, 1591' in *Camden Miscellany*, Vol.I (1847), p.14.

352 BRANTÔME, *Les Vies des Grands Capitaines Estrangers du Siècle dernier* in *Oeuvres Complètes* (Paris, 1842), p.88.

353 BUTLER (ed.), *op. cit.*, p.261; BIRCH, *Memoirs…* (1754), Vol.I, p.275.

354 H.M.C. *Salisbury MSS* (1895), Vol.VI, p.193 (letter to Sir Robert Cecil, 22 May 1596).

355 H.M.C. *Salisbury MSS* (1892), Vol.IV, p.31 (copy of a letter dated 8 May 1590). Trans.: *tout est ruyn ici à l'entour. C'est pourquoi il y a du desordre en ceste armee, chacun estant aussi empesché, ou plus, à la queste des vivres qu'à la conqueste des ennemis.*

356 *L & A* (1984), Vol.IV, p.212.

357 *CSPD* (1867), Vol.III, p.192.

358 Marquis François d'O (1535–1594), minister of finance under Henri IV.

359 'Journal of the Siege of Rouen, 1591' in *Camden Miscellany*, Vol.I (1847), p.30.

360 *Ibid.*, p.53.

361 Gaston de CARNÉ (ed.), *Correspondance du Duc de Mercœur…* (Rennes, 1899), Vol. 2, p.69 (citing Archivo General de Simancas MS K1598).

362 'Journal of the Siege of Rouen', *op. cit.*, p.54.

363 *Ibid.*, p.60.

364 A number of English women crossed the Channel. In the Huguenot army, if any soldiers were found with women in camp, they were forced to marry them.

365 William SHAKESPEARE, *Richard II*, Act II, Scene i.

366 Pierre de RONSARD, *Discours des Misères de ce Temps* (new edn Paris, 1979), p.138, lines 665–68.

367 H.M.C. *Salisbury MSS* (1892), Vol. IV, pp.404–05 (letter of October 1593, Elizabeth I to Henri IV). Trans.: *Mons. mon frere. L'appeller de nos troupes, apres tant de morts, [e]stropies, blessées et ruinés, ne vous semblera estrange…?*

368 CAMDEN, *Annals…*, p.480.

369 *L & A* (1993), Vol.V, p.310 (d'Aumont to Elizabeth, [18]/28 November 1594).

370 John BARROW, *Memoirs of the Naval Worthies of Queen Elizabeth's Reign: of their gallant deeds, daring adventures, and services, in the infant state of the British Navy* (London, 1845), citing British Library, Cotton MS Caligula.

371 David STEWART, 'The English Army Surgeon in the Sixteenth Century', *Journal of the Royal Army Medical Corps* (1947), LXXXVIII, p.240.

372 *APC* (1901), Vol.XXIV, p.154.

373 LA FERRIÈRE, *La Normandie à l'Étranger* (1873), p.149; POTTER, 'Les Allemands…', *Francia* (1995), XXI, ii, p.49 (the Earl of Warwick to the Rhinegrave, 31 May 1563). Trans.: *Et quant aux prisonniers qui sont ycy, si vous plaist donner ordre à deux de vos gentilzhommes de se trouver demayn en quelque endroict entre cy et vostre camp, deux des miens l'encontreront pour deviser ensemble à l'eure que vous assigneres, sur quoy je ne doubte point que nous n'en serons bien tost d'accord.*

374 POTTER, *ibid.*, p.50 (Hugh Paulet to the Rhinegrave, 31 May 1563). Trans.: *Monsieur, j'ay receu vostre lettre et quant à ce qu'il vous plaist que je vous trouve demain, parce que je ne veulx faire aulcun empeschement en vostre camp, si vous plaist je vous trouveray à Vytenval sur le dix heures de matin. Me recommandant de bien bon cœur à vostre bonne grace.*

375 Richard HAKLUYT, *The Principall Navigations Voiages & Discoveries of the English Nation* (London, 1589, new edn Cambridge, 1965), Vol.I, p.142.

376 Ribaut was released on the request of Charles.

377 POTTER, *op. cit.* (1995), XXI, ii, p.55 (the Earl of Warwick to the Rhinegrave, 17 July 1563). Trans.: *Monsieur, vous m'aves plusieurs fois escript pour faire bonne guerre, lequel j'ay tousjours accomply, mais je treuve que vous faictes aultrement car, aultre jour au dernier escarmouche, après que voz gens avoient prins quelques cinq ou six de miens, les ayans amenés cinquante ou soixante pas, les ont tué en la veue de cinq ou six de mes cappitaines, chose trop cruelle. Si l'on vous render la pareille, pour avoir ainsy commence, ne me blasmes point.*

378 H.M.C. *Salisbury MSS* (1895), Vol.VI, p.193.

379 *QEHT* (1838), Vol.I, p.306 (Sir Henry Norris to Sir William Cecil, 9 February 1568).

380 Piero Strozzi (1510–1558) (pseud. Sciarra Fiorentino), *Maréchal* of France; Leone Strozzi (1515–1554) commanded the French fleet sent to Scotland in 1547 in support of Mary, Queen of Scots.

381 John NICHOLS (ed.), *The Progresses and Public Processions of Queen Elizabeth…* (London, 1823), Vol.III, p.86.

382 Henry Percy, 9th Earl of Northumberland (1564–1632).

383 H.M.C. *Salisbury MSS* (1895), Vol.VI, p.260 (letter to Sir Robert Cecil, 13 July 1596).

384 BIRCH, *Memoirs…* (1754), Vol.I, p.300 (1595).

385 DIGGES (ed.), *op. cit.* (1655), p.21 (Sir Francis Walsingham to Sir William Cecil, 2 January 1571).

386 Simonds D'EWES (ed.), *The Journals of All the Parliaments during the Reign of Queen Elizabeth…* (London, 1682, new edn Shannon, 1973), p.406. Walsingham announced the displeasure of Henri III: *QEHT* (1838), Vol.II, p.335 (Sir Francis Walsingham to Robert Dudley, Earl of Leicester, 3 April 1587).

387 BRANTÔME, 'Hommes Illustres et Grands Capitaines François' in Jean BUCHON (ed.), *Oeuvres Complètes de Pierre de Bourdeille…* (Paris, 1842), p.401. Trans.: *M. de la Garde en fit un si superbe appareil de ses galleres et aprests d'ornement, qu'on dit qu'il luy cousta plus de vingt mille escus: entre autres, le plus beau fut que tous les forçats de sa realle eurent chascun un habillement de velours cramoisy, à la matelotte … la pouppe et la chambre de pouppe toute tapissée et parée de mesme velours, avecques une broderie d'or et d'argent large d'un grand pied, avecques pour devise une palme en broderie d'or et d'argent, soufflée et agitée de tous vents…. Les licts, couverts, orillers, bancs de chambre et de pouppe de mesmes; les estandards flambans, banderolles moictié*

de mesmes et moictié de damas, tous frangés d'or et d'argent. Bref, c'estoit un chose très-magnifique à veoir.

388 Simon GOULART, *Mémoires de l'estat de France sous Charles neufiesme* (Middelburg, 1577), Vol.II, p.468. Trans.: *les exces & magnificences de tous les ambassadeurs precedens, y eut une insolence de faire porter par navires, non seulement tous utensiles de cuisine de toutes sortes, jusques aux landiers & lardoires, tout le linge, tapisserie & autres meubles de chambre, mais aussi tout ce qui luy fut servi pour son boire, manger & agencement, il le fit porter de France en Angleterre.*

389 BOURQUIN (ed.), *op. cit.*, Vol.I, p. 462. Trans.: *beaucoup de meubles comme linge, tapisserie, vessaille, utancilles de cuysinne comme chiennetz de feu … chaufferettes de cuyvre et ayrain, estain de toute sorte et espece.*

390 For the passport issued to Sir Nicholas Throckmorton dated 5 January 1562 see Appendix I.

391 (Throckmorton to Elizabeth I, 23 July, 1562). See POTTER (ed.), *op. cit.* (1997), p.50.

392 TNA SP 70/42 f.86.

393 Jean HOTMAN, *A Casket full of rich jewels…* (London, 1609), p.51. Trans.: *Je suis sous le sauvegarde des droits des nations, et sous le protection du Roi, à qui vous êtes que des sujets et serviteurs.*

394 See DOREZ, 'Sonnets d'Angleterre et de Flandre' in *Bulletin du Bibliophile*, cited in Georges ASCOLI, *La Grande-Bretagne devant l'opinion française…* (Paris, 1927), p.115. Trans.: *Lors un nuage epais de reitres allemands/Pleuvait a gros bouillons pour noyer notre terre;/ Mais moi, loin des malheurs, j'habitais l'Angleterre,/Ennemi de discord et de ses remuements.*

395 H.M.C. *Salisbury MSS* (1895), Vol.VI, p.112 (William Paule to the Earl of Essex, 21 March 1596).

396 H.M.C. *Salisbury MSS* (1895), Vol.VI, p.102 (Sir Henry Unton to Lord Burghley, 17 March 1596). See also H.M.C. *Salisbury*

MSS (1895), Vol.VI, p.99 (Montmartin to the Earl of Essex, 25 March 1596).

397 National Portrait Gallery, London, NPG 710. For a description see Roy STRONG, 'Sir Henry Unton and his Portrait', *Archaeologia* (1965), XCIX, p.65.

398 Bibliothèque de l'Assemblée Nationale, MS 285 f.8r (Christophe de Harlay to Villeroy, 29 January 1602).

399 Of all the ambassadors whom Elizabeth received, it was perhaps Villeroy that she liked least. George HARRISON (ed.), *De Maisse A Journal... 1597* (London, 1931), pp.28, 72. Villeroy was vexed when, in 1567, Elizabeth refused him an audience. See *QEHT* (1838), Vol.I, p.251 (Sir Nicholas Throckmorton to Sir William Cecil, 2 July 1567).

400 *Lettres, mémoires et negociations de messieurs de Bellievre et de Silleri contenant un journal concernant la Negociation de la Paix Traitée à Vervins l'an 1598...* (The Hague, 1725), p.170. Trans.: *Je croi qu'il ne me dit pas sa charge, du moins le secret d'icelle, car il le reserve à sa Majesté, comme il est bien raisonnable Toutesfois il voulut que je creusse par son langage qu'il avoit l'esprit plus pacifique que guerrier; Disant que sa Souveraine étoit pour son sexe, pour son âge & de son natural, plus encline au repos qu'aux armes.*

401 Service Historique de la Défense, Vincennes MS 1/9, p.297 (Henri IV to de Bellièvre and de Sillery, 9 April 1598), in *Lettres… de Bellièvre et de Silleri* (1725), p.208. Trans.: *je ne doubte point qu'ilz ne soient tres marris que Calais me soit rendu.*

402 *Lettres, mémoires et negociations de messieurs de Bellievre et de Silleri...* (1725), p.52 (12 February 1598). Trans.: *si nous nous arrêtons aux Conseils de la Reine d'Angleterre & Etats, nous aurons dix ans de guerre, & jamais de Paix.*

403 Service Historique de la Défense, Vincennes, MS 1/9, p.297, Henri to de Bellièvre & de Sillery, 9 April 1598. See also *Lettres, mémoires et negociations de messieurs de Bellievre et de Silleri* (1725), p.207. Trans.: *En quoie puis dire que les Anglois les ont plustost fortiffiés que desmeus; Combien quilz m'ayent tenus et a plusieurs de mes serviteurs des langages tout contraires a cela.... ilz … ont pour but de nous faire nager ou noyer dans la mer de leur incertitude et irresolution naturelle et artificielle pour continuer a triompher de noz calamitez et miseres.*

404 *Lettres … de Bellièvre et de Silleri* (1725), p.224 (Bellièvre and Sillery to Villeroy, 13 April 1598). Trans.: *car à ce que nous comprenons, il desiroit fort pour divers respects que nous conclussions ce Traité sans elle.*

405 LAFFLEUR DE KERMAINGANT, *op. cit.*, Pièces Justicatives, pp.6–7 (Henri IV to Elizabeth I, 24 April 1598). Trans.: *Madame ma bonne seur les choses estans en tels termes, je vous prye de trouver bon que je poursuyve ce chemin, que la necessité de mon Estat et l'incertitude des volontés de mes confederés et voisins m'ont forcé de prendre, ayant promis à vostre dict ambassadeur d'en differer la finale resolution.*

406 Cited in Phyllis HANDOVER, *The Second Cecil…* (London, 1959), p.176.

407 CAMDEN, *Annals…*, p.487.

408 BIRCH, *Memoirs…* (1754), Vol.II, p.281 (16 February 1597).

409 H.M.C. *Savile Foljambe MSS* (1897), p.70 (Elizabeth I to Sir Francis Vere, 25 July 1599).

410 LAFFLEUR DE KERMAINGANT, *op. cit.*, p.vi. Trans.: *nous pouvons affirmer qu'une chose seule l'a absorbé, l'Espagne, toujours l'Espagne, et la crainte de voir Elizabeth et son conseil céder à leur très vif désir de faire la paix.*

411 Simonds D'EWES, *The Journals of All the Parliaments during the Reign of Queen Elizabeth* (London, 1682, new edn Shannon, 1973), p.599.

412 Bibliothèque de l'Assemblée Nationale, MS 285, f.5v. (letter dated 29 January 1602). Trans.: *donner des raisons pour luy faire connoistre qu'elle a plustost gagné que perdu en cette paix.*

413 BARBICHE and BUISSERET (eds), *op. cit.*, Vol.II, p.243. Trans.: *j'en auray d'autant plus de moyen de… secourir d'argent, soubz pretexte de payements de debtes.*

414 Cited in Lucien-Anatole PRÉVOST-PARADOL, *Elisabeth et Henri IV 1595–1598* (Paris, 1863), p.147 (footnote). Trans.: *nous ne payons pas jamais et nous ne souvenons de ce que nous empruntons, cela s'appelle Vidasmer ou faire le Vidasme.*

415 RYMER (ed.), *Foedera, op. cit.*, Vol.XVI, p.25 (letter from Beauvoir La Nocle and de Fresnes, [17]/27 September 1589). Trans.: *le dict Secours soit aux Depens de celuy qui sera tenu le donner.*

416 CAMDEN, *Annals…*, p.411.

417 Claude DE SAINLIENS, *The French Schoole-Maister* (London, 1573), pp.192–93.

418 Cited in Claude-Bernard PETIOT (ed.), *Mémoires de Castelnau* (Paris, 1823), p.210. Trans.: *L'Hospital insistoit tousjours qu'il ne la falloit forcer, et que c'estoit une mauvaise conqueste que de conquerir sur soy-mesme par armes.*

419 Edmund SAWYER (ed.), *Memorials of Affairs of State … of Sir Ralph Winwood* (London, 1725, new edn New York, 1972), Vol.I, p.38 (Sir Henry Neville to Villeroy, 6 June, 1599). Trans.: *Mais presupposant (ce que je ne puis pourtant accorder) que le Roy n'a pas le moien pour le present, de luy donner contentement en argent contant; Comment vous excuserez vous du contract de l'an 1591? par lequel le Roy s'est obligé de consigner entre les mains de la Royne, pour le remboursement de plusieurs sommes y specifiees, les Gabelles du Sel, & autres impositions provenantes dans les Villes de Roüen & Havre de Grace. Vous deviez pour le moins luy avoir offert cela, qui est tousjours en la puissance du Roy.*

420 *Ibid.*, Vol.I, p.91 (Sir Robert Cecil to Sir Henry Neville, 17 August 1599).

421 *Ibid.,* Vol.I, p.87.

422 Emmanuel LE ROY LADURIE and MORINEAU, *Histoire Économique et Sociale de la France*, Vol. 2 (Paris, 1977), pp.700–01. Trans.: *la volaille ecclésiastique a été plumée … modérément.*

423 SAWYER (ed.), *op. cit.*, Vol.I, p.308 (Elizabeth I to Henri IV, January 1601).

424 Cited by Alfred ROWSE, *Ralegh and the Throckmortons* (London, 1962), p.222.

425 Bibliothèque de l'Assemblée Nationale, MS 285 (Vol.I), f.12 r. Trans.: *Monsieur, Jay offert a la Royne les cent cinquante mil livres, elle s'est un peu mise en colere mais beaucoup plus modestement … que je n'aurois esperé sur un tel suis. Je vous suplie de tenir la main que cet argent soit porté auplutost a Dieppe affin que je puisse remettre le Roy en meilleur Credit qu'il rest envers cette princesse.*

426 SAWYER (ed.), *op. cit.*, Vol.I, p.413 (Ralph Winwood to Sir Robert Cecil, 25 May 1602).

427 'Journal of the Siege of Rouen, 1591' in *Camden Miscellany* (1847), Vol.I, p.39.

428 Misattributed to Petrus Ramus.

429 'Journal of the Siege of Rouen, 1591' in *Camden Miscellany* (1847), Vol.I, pp.17–18.

430 Sir Thomas Smith to Sir William Cecil, 4 February 1563. See POTTER (ed.), *op. cit.* (1997), p.63.

431 *L & A* (1980), Vol.III, p.264 (Sir Edmund Yorke to Lord Burghley, 23 April 1592); Mark Charles FISSEL, *English Warfare, 1511–1642* (2001), p.165.

432 'Journal of the Siege of Rouen, 1591' in *Camden Miscellany* (1847), Vol.I, p.40.

433 Gabrielle d'Estrées. H.M.C. *Salisbury MSS* (1895), Vol.VI, p.66 (letter to the Earl of Essex, 2 March 1596).

434 H.M.C. *Salisbury MSS* (1895), Vol.VI, p.522 (letter to the Earl of Essex, 13 December 1596).

435 'Journal of the Siege of Rouen, 1591' in *Camden Miscellany* (1847), Vol.I, p.40.

436 *Ibid.*, p.45.

437 TNA MPF 1/313, reproduced in Anne LOMBARD-JOURDAN, 'La bataille de St-Denis…', *Paris et Ile-de-France* (1978), XXIX, p.23; Anne LOMBARD-JOURDAN et al (eds), *Commentaires sur la Guerre Civile de France…* (Paris, 2005), p.17.

438 Report by Norris (SP 70/106). See POTTER (ed.), *op. cit.* (1997), p.113.

439 H.M.C. *Ancaster MSS* (1907), pp.2–3.

440 *QEHT* (1838), Vol.I, p.479.

441 BNF (Cartes & Plans), GeDD 627, pl.78 (see pp. 240–41).

442 British Library, Cotton MS Augustus I.ii.88, reproduced in *Archaeologia* (1832), XXIV, p.298, plate LI.

443 See p. 160.

444 H.M.C. *Salisbury MSS* (1892), Vol.IV, pp.20–21 (anonymous English account of around March 1590).

445 For a plan of the battle of Ivry see Charles OMAN, *The Art of War in the XVIth Century* (London, 1937), p.501.

446 TNA SP 78/24 f.75 (see pp. 244–45).

447 Agrippa d'AUBIGNÉ, *Histoire Universelle* (Geneva, 1994), VIII, pp.197–99.

448 De THOU, *op. cit.*, XI, pp.346–47, 352–53.

449 BNF (Estampes), Collection Hennin No.1113. Pen and ink drawing reproduced in *Le Traité de Vervins* (Paris, 2000). Painting reproduced in Janine GARRISON, *Henri IV le roi de la paix* (Paris, 2000), p.88.

450 De THOU, *op. cit.*, p.353. Trans.: *On appliqua contre les murs une machine de l'invention de Châtillon, avec un pont pour foudroyer ceux qui combattoient sur le rampart.*

451 BUTLER (ed.), *op. cit.*, pp.197–98. On the attempt see Jean-Pierre BABELON, *Henri IV* (Paris, 1982), pp.603–07.

452 See p. 105.

453 Reproduced in Penry WILLIAMS, *The Later Tudors* (Oxford, 1995), plate 6; Roy STRONG, *Gloriana* (London, 2003), p.33.

454 William SHAKESPEARE, *Henry IV* Part I, Act II, Scene iii (Dame Percy to Hotspur).

455 William SHAKESPEARE, *Henry V* Act III, Scene I (Henry V).

456 M. RIDLEY (ed.), *Marlowe's Plays and Poems* (London, 1967), pp. 295–329.

457 Richard HARDIN (ed.), *Poems on Events of the Day 1582–1607* (New York, 1991).

458 H.M.C. *Ancaster MSS* (1907), p.3.

459 British Library, Sloane MS 1896, ff.56v–58, in Hyder ROLLINS (ed.), *Old English Ballads 1553–1625* (Cambridge, 1920), p.180.

460 Reprinted 1582, 1972.

461 MARCUS, MUELLER and ROSE (eds), *op.cit.*, p. 314.

462 See *Histoire Universelle...* (London [Paris], 1734), Vol. XII, p.312. Trans.: *il y avoit entre les François & les Anglois une louable émulation à qui se distingueroit le plus.*

463 BOURQUIN (ed.), *op. cit.*, Vol.I, p.434.

464 *Ibid.* Trans.: *Car tous les soldatz et gens de guerre du camp du roy estoient tous catholiques avant ladite meslée, lesquelz pour la plus grand part furent faictz huguenotz ne faisoient aultre chose par les champs et ès logis que tascher à attirer iceux soldatz catholicques à leur religion; devant lesquelz, mesdisoient des prebstres de l'eglise catholicque et de ses sacremens, des sainctz et de leur puissance, faisoient leurs prieres, chantoient leurs chansons de David, se disoient-ilz, et alloient à leurs presches ou les introduisoient pour leur apprendre leur pretendue religion. Et par ce moyen s'acrut le nombre des huguenotz en France, la moytié plus grand qu'il n'estoit.*

465 *QEHT* (1838), Vol I, p.136 (Sir William Cecil to Sir Thomas Smith, 4 August 1563). Perhaps Cecil was influenced by the Bishop of London, who had written to him only three days before, talking of the hand of God at Le Havre. See *ibid.*, p.135.

466 The Spanish claimed reparations of 2 million ducats from the English for their actions at sea.

467 Cited by Simon ADAMS, *The Protestant cause: religious alliance with the west European Calvinist communities as a political issue in England, 1585–1630*, University of Oxford PhD (1973), p.119; Mark GREENGRASS, *Henri IV et Elisabeth: les dettes d'une amitié* in *Henri IV: Le Roi et le reconstruction du royaume* (Paris, 1989), p.367 (note).

468 Only published in the French version of DIGGES (ed.), *Memoires et Instructions pour les Ambassadeurs...* (1700), p.622.

469 LA POPELINIÈRE, *op. cit.*, p.284v. Trans.: *avec sa Cornette d'Anglois, y alloit: mais arrivé qu'il fut à Niort, & ayant veu par la longue suite des fuyars le malheur de ceste journee, se joignit à la masse des reschappez.*

470 Cited by PARKER, *op. cit.* (Philip II to the duke of Parma, 7 September 1589).

471 *Remonstrance à la noblesse catholique de France qui tient le party du roy de Navarre* (Paris, 1590), cited by Henri HAUSER, *Sources de l'Histoire de France* (Paris, 1915), Vol.IV, p.141. Trans.: *Je sçay bien que vous nous opposerez que nous avons faict ligue avec l'Espagne [mais] vous l'avez avec l'Anglois hérétique pour exterminer nostre religion, et nous l'avons faicte avec l'Espagne catholique pour la deffendre.*

472 BOURQUIN (ed.), *op. cit.*, Vol.II, p.231. Trans.: *reprindrent le chemin qu'ilz avoient tenu par la Bourgogne en pillant tout ce qu'ilz trouvoient de bon ès maisons des villages et bourgs où ilz logoient, et renmenerent tant de butin de la France que leurs chevaux et harnois ne purent enmener le tout en leurs pays.*

473 H.M.C. *Salisbury MSS* (1895), Vol.VI, p.523 (Sir John Aldrich to the Earl of Essex, 13 December 1596).

474 BIRCH, *Memoirs…* (1754), Vol.I, p.86 (Morgan Colman to Anthony Bacon, 8 September 1592).

475 John S. NOLAN, *Sir John Norreys and the Elizabethan Military World* (1997), p.243.

476 *QEHT* (1838), Vol.II, p.456 (Lord Burghley to Sir Robert Cecil, 26 January 1596).

477 BIRCH, *Memoirs…* (1754), Vol.I, p.350 (Ersfield to the Earl of Essex, 21 December 1595).

478 BIRCH, *An Historical View...* (1749), p.44.

479 *L & A* (1969), Vol. II, p.263.

480 See Appendix X.

481 Jean-Pierre BABELON, *Henri IV* (Paris, 1982), p.888. Trans.: *Je m'étais promis ce bonheur et contentement que de vous baiser et embrasser des deux bras, comme étant votre très loyale sœur et fidèle alliée.*

482 Cited by Michel DUCHEIN, 'Élisabeth Ière et l'Édit de Nantes', in Mari-José LACAVA and Robert GUICHARNAUD, *L'Édit de Nantes: Sûreté et éducation* (Montauban, 1999). Trans.: *Mon ami, j'ai eu avis de la mort de ma bonne sœur la reine d'Angleterre, qui m'aimait si cordialement, à laquelle j'avais tant d'obligation. Comme ses vertus étaient grandes et admirables, aussi est inestimable la perte que moi et tous les bons Français … car elle était … tant généreuse et judicieuse qu'elle m'était un second moi-même.*

483 Pierpont Morgan Library, New York, MS 3900.

484 William SHAKESPEARE, *Henry V*, Act 3 Scene vi (Captain Gower to Fluellen).

485 Paul HUGHES and James LARKIN (eds), *Tudor Royal Proclamations* (New Haven, 1969), Vol.II, p.230.

486 The Bodleian replaced the library established by Humphrey, Duke of Gloucester.

487 HUGHES and LARKIN (eds), *op. cit.*, Vol. II, p.229.

488 *Ibid.*

489 This hospital survives today, housing veterans just as in the sixteenth century.

490 David STEWART, 'Disposal of the Sick and Wounded of the English Army during the Sixteenth Century', *Journal of the Royal Army Medical Corps* (1948), XC, p.34 (the Mayor of Rye to Sir Francis Walsingham, 5 February 1590).

491 HUGHES and LARKIN (eds), *op. cit.*, Vol.III, p.105 (Privy Council ordering examination of vagrant soldiers, 28 February 1592).

492 See National Portrait Gallery, London, NPG 665.

493 BROWN, Horatio (ed.), *Calendar of State Papers Venice 1603–1607* (London, 1897), Vol.X, p.55 (Giovanni Carlo Scaramelli to the Doge and Senate, 26 June 1603), cited by David BUISSERET, *Henry IV* (London, 1984), p.120.

494 BOSSY, *Elizabethan Catholicism, the link with France*, University of Cambridge PhD (1960), p.332, who cites BNF MS français 3487 f.145 (14 July 1603). Trans.: *tirer nostre espingle du jeu le plus doucement que nous pourrons.*

495 EVANS (ed.), *op. cit.*, p.xxxix.

496 The National Archives embody the Public Record Office, Historic Manuscripts Commission, Office of Public Sector Information and Her Majesty's Stationery Office.

497 *APC* (1893), Vol.VII, p.137.

498 pp.24–26.

499 Compare with the eyewitness accounts by the Bohemian Charles de Žerotin: Louis LEGER, 'Le Siège de Rouen par Henri IV d'après des documents tchèques', *Revue historique* (May–August 1878), VII, pp.66–77.

500 (1993) XX, ii, pp. 1–20; (1994) XXI, ii, pp. 1–61.

501 BARBICHE and BUISSERET (eds), *op. cit.*, 2 vols.

502 LUBLINSKAYA, *op. cit.*, p.11.

503 British Library, Additional MS 35831 f.279.

504 Republished in London 1807–08 in six volumes by Henry Ellis.

505 *Travels in England and Fragmenta Regalia* (Boston, n.d.), pp.51–95.

506 In *Les Œuvres d'Ambroise Paré* (Paris, 1585, new edn Bièvres, 1969), Vol.III.

507 NPG 6241 (see p. 105).

508 One copy of the portrait is held by the National Maritime Museum, Greenwich (PAD 4572).

509 *Alderney Society Bulletin* (1997), XXXII, pp.52–62.

510 John HALE (ed.), *On a Tudor Parade Ground: The Captain's Handbook of Henry Barrett 1562* (London, 1978), p.40.

511 *Cabala, op. cit.*, p.157 (Sir William Cecil to Sir Henry Norris, 26 October 1566).

512 Lloyd BERRY (ed.), *John Stubbs's Gaping Gulf…* (Charlottesville, 1968), p.143. Trans.: *J'ai depense et consume toute ma franchise meme toute celle que fut la plus bonne et d'Orleanne, ainsi que ne restait a moi qu'une pauvre demeurant de francaise Normandaise ou Picarde trop barbare et tout indigne d'etre lu par vous Monsieur.*

RECOMMENDED READING

See also the Introduction and Sources

BLACK, John: *Elizabeth and Henry IV* (Oxford, 1914)

BONNEY, Richard: *The King's Debts. Finance and Politics in France 1589–1661* (Oxford, 1981)

BOUND, Mensun, and MONAGHAN, Jason: *A Ship Cast Away About Alderney: Investigations of an Elizabethan Shipwreck,* Alderney Maritime Trust, Guernsey (2001)

BOYNTON, Lindsay: *The Elizabethan Militia* (London, 1967)

BUISSERET, David: *Henry IV* (London, 1982)

CHILDS, David: *Tudor Seapower: The Foundation of Greatness* (2009)

COX, Angela: *Sir Henry Unton: Elizabethan Gentleman* (Cambridge, 1982)

CRUICKSHANK, Charles: *Elizabeth's Army* (Oxford, 1966)

DIETZ, Frederick: *English Public Finance, 1558–1641* (New York, 1932)

DORAN, Susan: *Elizabeth I and Religion, 1558–1603* (London, 1994)

— *England and Europe 1485–1603* (Harlow, 1996)

— *Monarchy and Matrimony: The Courtships of Elizabeth I* (London, 1996)

— *England and Europe in the Sixteenth Century* (Basingstoke, 1999)

DORAN, Susan, and RICHARDSON, Glen (eds): *Tudor England And Its Neighbours* (Basingstoke, 2005)

FISSEL, Mark: *English Warfare, 1511–1642* (London, 2001)

GEHRING, David: *Anglo-German Relations and the Protestant Cause: Elizabethan Foreign Policy and Pan-Protestantism* (London, 2013)

GRAVES, Michael: *Burghley* (London, 1998)

HAIGH, Christopher: *Elizabeth I* (London, 1988)

HAMMER, Paul: *Elizabeth's Wars: War, Government and Society in Tudor England, 1544–1604* (Basingstoke, 2003)

HOLT, Mack: *The French Wars of Religion, 1562–1629* (Cambridge, 1995)

JONES, Norman: *Governing by Virtue: Lord Burghley & the Management of Elizabethan England* (Oxford, 2015)

JOUANNA, Arlette, *et al.: Histoire et Dictionnaire des Guerres de Religion* (Paris, 1998)

KNECHT, Robert: *The French Wars of Religion* (London, 1989)

— *Catherine de' Medici* (London, 1998)

— *The French Civil Wars* (London, 2000)

— *The French Religious Wars 1562–1598* (Oxford, 2002)

KONSTAM, Angus: *Tudor Warships*, Vol. II (Oxford, 2008)

KOURI, Erkki: 'England and the attempts to form a Protestant Alliance in the late 1560s', *Annales Academiae Scientiarum Fennicae* (1981), Ser. B, CCX, p.79

LABOURDETTE, Jean-François, POUSSOU, Jean-Pierre, and VIGNAL, Marie-Catherine (eds), *Le Traité de Vervins* (Paris, 2000)

LEE, Maurice: *James I and Henri IV: an essay in English Foreign Policy 1603–1610* (London, 1970)

LLOYD, Howell: *The Rouen Campaign 1590–92* (Oxford, 1973)

LOADES, David: *The Tudor Navy* (Aldershot, 1991)

— *The Cecils: Privilege and Power Behind the Throne* (Kew, 2007)

— *The Making of the Elizabethan Navy, 1540–1590: From the Solent to the Armada* (Woodbridge, 2009)

DE MAISSE, Hurault, HARRISON, George, and JONES, R. (eds): *A Journal of all that was accomplished by Monsieur de Maisse ambassador in England from King Henri*

IV to Queen Elizabeth Anno Domini 1597 (London, 1931)

BARBIER-MUELLER, Jean: *La Parole et les Armes: Chronique des Guerres de religion en France 1562–1598* (Paris, 2006)

NOLAN, John: *Sir John Norreys and the Elizabethan military world* (Exeter, 1997)

OMAN, Charles: *History of the Art of War in the Sixteenth Century* (London, 1937)

PARKER, Geoffrey: *The Grand Strategy of Philip II* (London, 1998)

PARMELEE, Lisa: *Good newes from Fraunce: French anti-league propaganda in late Elizabethan England* (Rochester, 1996)

POTTER, David (ed.): *The French Wars of Religion: Selected Documents* (London, 1997)

SAUNDERS, Andrew: *Fortress Britain* (Liphook, 1989)

SHIMIZU, Junko: *Conflict of Loyalties. Politics and Religion in the career of Gaspard de Coligny Admiral of France 1519–1572* (Geneva, 1970)

SIMONIN, Michel: *Charles IX* (Paris, 1995)

TEESDALE, Edmund: *Gunfounding in the Weald in the Sixteenth Century* (London, 1991)

SCOTT-THOMPSON, Gladys: *Lords Lieutenants in the Sixteenth Century* (London, 1923)

WEBB, Henry: *Elizabethan Military Science: The Books and the Practice* (Madison, 1965)

WERNHAM, Richard: *Before the Armada: the Growth of English Foreign Policy, 1485–1588* (Oxford, 1966)

— *The Making of Elizabethan Foreign Policy, 1558–1603* (Berkeley, 1980)

— *After the Armada: Elizabethan England and the struggle for Western Europe 1588–1595* (Oxford, 1984)

— *The Return of the Armadas* (Oxford, 1994)

WOOD, James: *The Army of the King: Warfare, Soldiers and Society during the Wars of Religion in France, 1562–1576* (Cambridge, 1996)

INDEX

Published in 2019 by
Unicorn, an imprint of Unicorn Publishing Group LLP
5 Newburgh Street
London
W1F 7RG

www.unicornpublishing.org

Text © William Heap
Images © see individual captions

ISBN 978-1-912690-49-7

10 9 8 7 6 5 4 3 2 1

Designed by Isobel Gillan
Printed in China for Latitude Press Ltd